AFRICAN AMERICAN HERITAGE HYMNAL

GIA PUBLICATIONS, INC.
CHICAGO

Cover art by William Dorsey. Cover design by Yolanda Duran.
Music engraving by Philip Roberts and Jeffry Mickus.
Book design and layout by Jeffry Mickus.

G-5400

ISBN 1-57999-091-6
ISBN 1-57999-124-6 Trade Edition
ISBN 1-57999-122-X Deluxe Binding

19 20

PREFACE

In 1987, GIA Publications made its first effort to publish for the African American church community through the publication of *Lead Me, Guide Me,* a hymnal intended primarily for African American Catholics. Prompted in part by the success of that edition, the Rev. Dr. Delores Carpenter, pastor of the Michigan Park Christian Church in Washington, DC, speaking on behalf of an informal group of pastors and musicians, approached GIA in 1992 with the idea of creating a similar edition for all African American Christian congregations. GIA's interest was immediate and enthusiastic. Dr. Carpenter, along with her musical colleague, the Rev. Nolan Williams, Jr., assembled an outstanding committee of pastors and musicians, and on January 17, 1993, the first meeting was held in Washington.

Almost eight years to the day of that first meeting, the *African American Heritage Hymnal,* a history-making publication, went to press. During those eight years the publisher had the privilege of meeting and working with an incredible group of biblical scholars, theologians, pastors and musicians of the highest caliber, each possessing an extraordinary degree of dedication to the worship of the church. It has been a wonderful and inspiring journey.

We especially wish to recognize several GIA staff members: project coordinator Jeffry Mickus, proofreaders/editorial assistants Clarence Reiels and Victoria Krstansky, and copyright permissions coordinator, Laura Cacciottolo.

May the words and melodies printed on these pages continually issue forth from the mouths of the people of God as they give him the glory and praise that is due.

Edward J. Harris
    Publisher
Robert J. Batastini
    Executive Editor

COMMITTEE

Rev. Dr. Delores Carpenter, General Editor
Rev. Nolan E. Williams, Jr., Music Editor

EDITORIAL COMMITTEE

Dr. James Abbington
Ms. Jane Carpenter
Mrs. Charlene Moore Cooper
Mr. L. Stanley Davis
Rev. Dr. Valerie Eley
Ms. Valeria Foster
Dr. Robert T. Fryson (dec.)

Mrs. Betty Gadling
Mrs. Teresa Gilmore
Mr. Joseph Joubert
Rev. Dr. Raymond Kelly, Jr.
Mr. Stephen Key
Rev. Dr. William McClain
Rev. Dr. Otis Moss

Bishop Alfred Owens
Mr. Walter Owens
Mr. Jeffrey Radford
Mrs. Evelyn Simpson-Curenton
Rev. Dr. J. Alfred Smith
Mr. Louis Sikes (dec.)
Rev. Dr. Wyatt Tee Walker

ADVISORY COMMITTEE

Dr. Willis L. Barnett
Mrs. Beverly Benjamin
Dr. Timothy Tee Boddie
Dr. Roland Carter

Dr. Melva Costen
Rev. James Demus, III
Rev. Robert Dickerson (dec.)
Mr. Arthur McClenton

Bishop Kenneth Moales
Dr. Don Lee White
Rev. Dr. Jeremiah Wright

ACKNOWLEDGMENTS

To ensure a broad cross-section of litany and Scripture selections, material was solicited from numerous persons. The general editor developed the final versions from these multiple submissions, which were then reviewed by members of the editorial committee. Others assisted in a clerical or administrative capacity. We hereby acknowledge and thank the following individuals. They are associated with Howard University School of Divinity, Michigan Park Christian Church, and the Editorial Committee.

Alex Achonwa, Fay Acker, David Akins, Icie Akoto, Lester Allen, Harlan Bailey, Kip Banks, Wyndell Banks, Joyce Barton, Louise Battle, Cassandra Bedeau, Earl E. Blackwell, Nathaniel Bouknight, Belinda Boyer, Barbara Breland, Brian Brown, Cedric Brown, Homer Brown, Kenneth Brown II, Kenneth Brown, Sr., Victor Brown, William Bryant, Stanley Bryd, Bert Carter, George Carter, William Chatman, DeeDee Chavers, Carlyle Church, Countess Clark, Jason Clark, Philip Cole, Charmayne Cook, Carlson Cox, Josephine Crawford, Barbara Crosby, Warren Crudup, Jr., Henri Mae Davis, L. Stanley Davis, Marjani Deli, Kevin Donaldson, Elaine Dorsey, Sallie Douglas, Angela Driver, Valerie Eley, Trenace Fayton, Angeloyd Fenrick, Tonya Fields, Velma Fleming, Valeria Foster, Mary Fowler, Carmen Francis, Don Franklin, Wilda Gafrey, Sondra Gaines, Robert Gibson, Joseph Gilmore, Jr., Margo Gilmore, Teresa Gilmore, Etoria Goggins, Beverly Goines, Dave Goss, Anita Gould, Lillie Gray, Rena Griffin, Jonathan Hancock, Clifton Hardy, Sheila Harvey, Randolph Haynes, Wanda Henry, Glynis Herns, Vanessa Hill, Carolyn Hodge, Elizabeth Hodge, Charlene Hogan, Alison Hyder, Monica Jackson, Deborah Jackson-Myers, Ruby James, Kevin Jefferson, Loretta Johnson, Mary Johnson, Ben Jones, Blanche C. Jones, Joe Jones, Kenneth Jones, Thelma Jones, Reniece Kabando, Raymond Kelly, Jr., Theriot King, Cheryl A. Kirk-Duggan, Frank Lance, Annie Lanier, Marcus Leathers, Nancy Lee, Carmen Lottimore, Kathy Letto, James Lewis, Walt Lictenberger, Flai Livingston, Deborah Logan, Atlantis Long, Patricia Long, Antoine Love, Muriel Lucas, Willie Lynch, Angelique Mason, Denise Mason, Darryl Matthews, Mary Mazyck, Joan McCarley, William McClain, William McCoy, James McMillian, Maenell Means, Yvonne Mercer-Staten, James Miles, Gloria Miller, Alberta Mitchell, Kenneth Moales, Jim Moody, Parnell Moody, Charlene Moore-Cooper, Lawerence Morganfield, Marlene Morris, Kenute Myrie, Pramedai Naraine, Robert Nash, Mary Newton, Michelle Nickodemus, Kevin Norton, Gloria Nurse, Gail Oliver, Jacob Oliver, Jr., Uzoma Opaigbeogu, Alfred Owens, Maurice Parker, Oliver Phillips, Robert Pitts, Kathleen Price, Andral Raphael, Thomas Renegar, Sharon Roberts, Vince Robertson, Westley Robinson, Leroy Rust, Denise Ryles-McKoy, Corrine Sampson, James Shand, Georgia Shanks, Louis Sikes, Evelyn Simpson-Curenton, Angela Sims, Barbara Skinner, Alfred Smith, Marion Smith, Mitzi Smith, Beverly Sonnier, Marlene Sumes, Mattie Tabron, Kimberly Taylor, Deborah Threats, Alfray Thomas, Randy Thomas, Ruby Thomas, Tiffany Towberman, Teresa Tribble, Susie Tucker, Francine Vinson, Wyatt T. Walker, John Walton, Rinaldo Washington, Matthew Watley, Louis Wells, Jr., Dorothy Whitley, Sarah Whye, Vanessa Wiliford, Barbara Williams, Nolan Williams, Jr., Percy Williams, George Wilson, Jane Wilson, Lavalla Wilson, Wayne Wilson, Louise Winfield, Yolanda Winkler, Linda Witherspoon, Jamila Woods, Curtise Woodward, Daniel Wright, Madelyn Yates, Margaret Young

INTRODUCTION

The *African American Heritage Hymnal* is probably the most important addition to Protestant hymnody within the past century. It promises to have an impact similar to Dr. Isaac Watts's collections of hymns introduced in America in the early eighteenth century, which revolutionized hymn singing in American Protestantism. It is a compilation of the very best in Protestant hymnody, but its greatest significance is that it is inclusive of the hymnody of the African American religious tradition. No collection of hymns has been as broad and as inclusive as this hymnal.

The majority Protestant community in the United States has not paid very much serious attention to the exercise of faith and practice in African American life. The telling impact of gospel music in the religious life of the nation and of the world is a sign that America is probably poorer culturally and spiritually for ignoring the musical tradition of African American Christians. Over the last two decades, the gospel tradition of Black music has been universally embraced as an authentic American art form. It has become one of our primary cultural exports to the world. The *African American Heritage Hymnal* holds promise of strengthening that conclusion.

The moving spirit in the development of the *African American Heritage Hymnal* is the Reverend Dr. Delores Carpenter, Senior Pastor of the Michigan Park Christian Church in the nation's capital. Dr. Carpenter and her former pastoral assistant, the Reverend Nolan E. Williams, Jr., a musician of concert competency, gathered an impressive array of pastor/theologians, musicologists, cultural historians, and practitioners in the field of church music into a committed and aggressive working committee. That working group, with full candor, examined the tradition of music in the worship experience of African American Christians with a view of producing a distillation of that which was best and most authentic and noting the impact of the Protestant hymn-form on Black worship styles, North, South, East, and West. All of the regional nuances of musical tradition have been carefully considered, and there has been no short shrift of the use and impact of Euro-American authored compositions. Notably, composers in the African American religious community are included after years of being ignored by main-line hymnal committees. There are also the compositions of the collective worshiping community in black life, those hymns of the antebellum slaves and the prayer and praise hymns of the post-Reconstruction era, which have no individual authors. They are the product of community assent on the things of the God in whom they trusted.

It is the breadth and sweep of this *African American Heritage Hymnal* that commends it to worshiping Christians. It is all-inclusive of the American religious experience, but it has the imprimatur of Africa in its spirit and vitality. The Black community in America has, since the turn of the century, made broad use of Euro-American authored hymns, but our use and singing was distinctly different from the musical notation in the hymnal. This is another feature of the *African American Heritage Hymnal* in that the musical notations follow very closely the style of performance when African Americans are at worship. There are field Spirituals, jubilee Spirituals, the sorrow-song Spirituals—all representative of the baseline music art-form on which all American-born music depends. There are lined (meter) hymns, musically notated to demonstrate the unique imprint of African American Christians on the meter music born in Europe. Of special value is the inclusion of the prayer and praise hymns, which remain at-risk because so few of this genre have ever been musically notated other than in the hearts and memories of believers. A large number of Euro-American authored hymns are included on the basis of use in African American church circles. Surveys across the country produced the digest of these hymn selections, and they are musically notated as mentioned above. The *African American Heritage Hymnal* probably boasts in number and breadth more authentic gospel compositions than any hymnal available in the English-speaking world. There are compositions of the "Godfather of Gospel," Thomas A. Dorsey, as well as Andraé Crouch, Dr. Margaret Douroux, and Dr. Robert Fryson. Of course, there are the standards of Lucie Campbell, James Cleveland, and Sally and Roberta Martin. Our global vision has induced us to include praise songs from Ghana, South Africa, and the Caribbean in the language of the country of origin! The *African American Heritage Hymnal* will be difficult to match because of its inclusiveness and its great breadth of musical forms found in African American worship services.

In addition to the great and broad body of musical pieces in this hymnal, there is also the feature of the Litanies, based on the Black Church Year, which provides an outline for "52 Sundays of Worshipful Celebration" with companion responsive readings. Special celebratory litanies are included for special days such as Mother's and Men's Day, Martin Luther King Sunday, Elders' Day, etc. The hymnal begins with 104 Scripture readings from the Old and New Testaments. These texts have sustained and lifted the souls of black folk and they are the fountain from which much of black sacred music is drawn. These worship tools greatly enhance the usefulness of the *African American Heritage Hymnal*.

Wyatt Tee Walker
Senior Pastor
Canaan Baptist Church of Christ
New York

ESSAYS

The Ecumenical Nature of African American Church Music

Under the leadership of the Reverend Dr. Delores Carpenter and the Reverend Nolan Williams, Jr., the African American Heritage Hymnal Committee is made up of ministers and musicians who are committed to preserving and promoting the best congregational music of our ecumenical African American Christian tradition. This tradition is rooted in the richness of our historical past, but it is also dynamic and evolutionary with the continuing creativity of God-inspired persons. This essay will provide the reader with a brief, descriptive portrayal of the religious musical heritage of the seven denominations that comprise the African American ecumenical tradition.

The seven major historic black denominations are the African Methodist Episcopal (A.M.E.) Church; the African Methodist Episcopal Zion (A.M.E.Z.) Church; the Christian Methodist Episcopal (C.M.E.) Church; the National Baptist Convention, U.S.A., Incorporated (N.B.C.); the National Baptist Convention of America, Unincorporated (N.B.C.A.); the Progressive National Baptist Convention (P.N.B.C.); and the Church of God in Christ (C.O.G.I.C.). These formal denominational bodies came into being after the Free African Society of 1787. It is a commonly accepted view among scholars of the black church that more than 80 percent of all black Christians are in these denominations.

C. Eric Lincoln and Lawrence H. Mamiya, in their monumental classic, *The Black Church in the African American Experience,* describe with detail and preciseness the history of these churches. They write with clarity about the spirituality, theology, and music of the black church, even tracing black musical eloquence back to African origins, retentions, and cultural transmissions. They inform us that "a study of black singing . . . is in essence a study of how black people 'Africanized' Christianity in America as they sought to find meaning in the turn of events that made them involuntary residents in a strange and hostile land."[1] Therefore, the genesis of African American church music predates the founding of the denominational structures of African Americans. This music was ecumenical as a norm for our slave mothers and fathers, since it emerged from the common ground of their sufferings, sorrows, and search for survival and liberation in a land that was new, strange, and hostile.

The late Dr. J. M. Ellison, former chancellor of Virginia Union University in Richmond, Virginia, spoke of the ecumenical nature of African American faith and praxis in exclaiming, "They sang through the crisis." With the exception of the Church of God in Christ, which was incorporated as a denomination in 1897 by founding bishop Charles Harrison Mason, black Methodists and Baptists adopted their denominational identity from white Christians who evangelized them. But the ecumenical nature of black worship, which had its own cultural distinctiveness in the song, sermon, and shout, emanated from merging both the surviving Africanisms of the old world with the creative adaptation of the Bible of the new world into a new synthesis for liberation. Dr. Gardner C. Taylor, in writing the foreword for scholarly Wyatt Tee Walker's *Somebody's Calling My Name: Black Sacred Music and Social Change,* undergirds my thesis: "the slaves and their children gave to Christian faith a modern glossolalia" where the masters said the Bible declared one thing and the slaves heard something far different about what the Bible declared.[2] The slave masters spoke of God's ordained slavery. The slaves sang of "Go down Moses, tell Pharaoh to let my people go."

The ecumenical nature of African American church music, according to the late Professor Wendell Whalum of Morehouse College of Atlanta, Georgia, had an oral tradition origin. This tradition, which manifested itself in the spirituals, has been under attack by those who question its authenticity. Dr. Whalum says that critics of the spirituals call the literature primitive or naive. He encourages the reader to study the scholarly response to the critics by Harold Courlander: "If Negro religious imagery is truly 'naive,' then the burden of responsibility must be borne by the Bible, out of which the imagery is primarily extracted.[3] Those who would research in greater depth the ecumenical nature of spirituals would do well to investigate the following works:

Dena J. Epstein, *Slave Music in the United States Before 1860: A Survey of Sources in Notes of the Music Library Association*. Washington, D.C.: Howard University Press, 1963, pp. 195–212, 377–80.

James Weldon Johnson and J. Rosamond Johnson, *The Books of American Negro Spirituals*. New York: Viking Press, 1942, pp. 21–23.

Miles Mark Fisher, *Negro Slave Songs in the United States*. Ithaca, New York: Cornell University Press, 1953, p. 25.

R. Nathaniel Dett, *Listen to the Lambs*. New York: G. Schirmer, Inc., 1914.

Dr. Whalum stressed giving a comprehensive treatment to the ecumenical nature of African American spirituals because "the spiritual became the musical basis for all later church music."[4]

After the black ecumenical development of spirituals sung by the congregation, the new evolutionary development in African American Christian music was choral singing, which took place at Bethel A.M.E. Church of Philadelphia between 1841 and 1842. Although Bishop Richard Allen (1760–1831) wrote hymns, and was not successful in eradicating the emotional singing of spirituals and folk songs, Bishop Daniel Payne (1811–1893) of the A.M.E. church promoted hymn singing, especially the hymns of Dr. Isaac Watts, an English minister and physician. Before 1875, black Methodists and Baptists endorsed the hymns of Dr. Watts, but it was the black Baptist influence that "blackened" the style of singing Watts's hymns. A Baptist deacon would give out two lines of the hymn at a time and the congregation would repeat the hymns with a cappella harmonizing. The preacher even to this day keeps the tradition alive by leading a metrical hymn or spiritual before preaching. Sometimes the preacher in any of the seven black church denominations will lead a metrical hymn, spiritual, or gospel during the sermon or at its conclusion.

In 1914, R. Nathaniel Dett introduced anthems to the black church. In 1916, Harry T. Burleigh published spirituals for a solo voice. Sociological changes such as black migration from the Egypt land of the South to the promised land of the North, the soulful creativity of the Church of God in Christ, and a host of Pentecostal and holiness churches gave rise to gospel music around 1930. Pearl Williams Jones describes this new development in saying the music at hand was an idiom with which they were all familiar and that it could be created spontaneously. The preacher, the song leader, and congregation all shared equally in these creative moments.[5] Thomas A. Dorsey, Dr. C. A. Tindley, Lucie Campbell, Sallie Martin, Roberta Martin, Doris Akers, Theodore Frye, Lillian Bowes, Kenneth Morris, and many others weathered the storms to make this new music acceptable in the black church ecumenical family. I am deeply indebted to Wyatt Tee Walker for his commentary on gospel music. He divided gospel music into two distinct historical periods. They are 1930 to 1960, and the period of 1960 to the present. Within each of the periods, distinct eras exist.

In the period of The Historic Gospel, there is the *pre*-gospel era between 1905 and 1925 that produced classics such as "Some Day" and "He'll Understand and Say, Well Done." During the Dorsey era of 1930 to 1945, the National Convention of Gospel Choirs and Choruses was organized. This first black gospel music convention was ecumenical in nature. During this era Mahalia Jackson was introduced to America. Gospel's golden era between 1945 and 1960 was the time when black-oriented radio stations reached the masses with gospel music and a few gospel singers appeared in nightclubs. Well-remembered "Lead Me, Guide Me" and "Holding My Savior's Hand" mark the productivity of the Golden Era of gospel.

The period of Modern Gospel from 1960 to the present has produced for us gospel singers who later became celebrities in the secular world of entertainment. Many well-known secular vocalists have "gotten their start" in the black church. Among them are Aretha Franklin, Roberta Flack, Donny Hathaway, the late Sam Cooke, and the late Nat "King" Cole. Persons like James Cleveland and Edwin Hawkins have enjoyed celebrity status without crossing over into the field of secular music. Nonetheless, the danger is that the singing of gospel music for the glory and honor of God can be subverted into singing simply for religious entertainment or for the values of religious aesthetics.

During the period from 1960 to the present, gospel choirs have appeared on college campuses. Members of many of these choirs are atheistic, agnostic, Jewish, or otherwise non-Christian in their faith posture. They have chosen to sing about God, Jesus, the Holy Spirit, and the providence of God, not for the sake of worship, praise, and adoration of God, but for the motivation of satisfying their own emotional needs or for the embracing of aesthetic appreciation for a musical-cultural art form. The intentionality of African American musicians in the black church ecumenical family has always been to creatively express, with the community engaged in worship, the deepest feelings of love for and dependence on the God who has come to us in Jesus Christ.

May the love of God, the grace of the Lord Jesus Christ, and the sweet communion of the Holy Spirit be ever present as you utilize the resources of this hymnal. May you come to know more about the richness and diversity of the ecumenical nature of African American church music as you attend national black Christian ecumenical gatherings such as the annual Hampton University Ministers and Choir Directors Institute, which occurs the first week in June. May the future creators in the ecumenical tradition of African American church music be touched with the creative inspiration of their predecessors so that coming generations will say of them:

O black and unknown bards of long ago,
How came you to touch the sacred fire?
How, in your darkness, did you come to know
The power and beauty of the minstrel's lyre?
Who from midst [her] bonds lifted [her] eyes?
Who from out the still watch, lone and long,
Feeling the ancient faith of prophets rise
Within [her] dark, kept soul, burst into song?

—James Weldon Johnson

J. Alfred Smith, Sr.
Senior Pastor
Allen Temple Baptist Church
Oakland, California

Professor of Preaching and Christian Ministries
The American Baptist Seminary of the West
Berkeley, California

---

1. C. Eric Lincoln and Lawrence H. Mamiya, *The Black Church in the African American Experience* (Durham and London: Duke University Press, 1990), 348.

2. Wyatt Tee Walker, *Somebody's Calling My Name: Black Sacred Music and Social Change* (Valley Forge, Penn.: Judson Press, 1979), 12.

3. Harold Courlander, *Negro Folk Music,* U.S.A. (New York: Columbia University Press, 1963), 39.

4. Wendell Whalum, "Black Hymnody," in *Black Church Life Styles,* ed. Emanuel L. McCall (Nashville: Broadman Press, 1986), 85.

5. Wendell Phillips Whalum, "Black Hymnody," *Review and Expositor* 7, no. 3 (Summer 1973): 353, quoted from Pearl Williams Jones, *Afro-American Gospel Music (1930–1970)* (Howard University College of Fine Arts Project in African Music, Washington, D.C., n.d.).

African American Music and the Freedom Movement

In much of American and Western history individuals for generations have been led to believe that the African humanity housed in the bowels of slave ships was a mass of ignorance, illiteracy, superstition, and madness. It was the work of a slave culture to transport all the intrinsic and extrinsic wickedness of the slave trade, the slave masters, and the slave mistresses throughout the western world through contrived myths that would seek to partially exonerate the oppressors and miseducate the victims. This was partially successful. However, there are two quotes, often used by Dr. Martin Luther King, Jr., from William Cullen Bryant and Thomas Carlyle—"Truth, crushed to earth, shall rise again" and "No lie can live forever"—that demonstrate how the myths of the slave masters were exposed and vetoed. There is a European proverb that says: "Lies have short legs." Eventually, truth will overtake falsehood. It might take an hour or two, or even a century or two. Therefore, there was in the slave culture an inherent contradiction that would eventually contribute to its downfall. But the walls of tyranny do not fall gently.

The greatest judgments against slavery were deposited in the belly of the slave ships, in the "harmony and melody" of millions of God's prophetic, poetic, history making, and civilization bearing children. W. E. B. DuBois says our ancestors, our foremothers and forefathers, maintained a "harmony and melody in an ill-harmonizing and unmelodious land." Henry Mitchell says it's "difficult to kill culture."

The Africans, the makers of the first musical instruments, the creators of science, the parents of medicine, art, architecture, agriculture, and the first exponents of monotheism, could not be totally crushed in a 400-year triangular slave trade. Neither could their music be exterminated in a 244-year American holocaust (chattel slavery).

There was a philosophy of freedom, a theology of liberation, a song of protest that would not surrender to the slave master's rawhide and the hangman's noose. Through our "weary years" and along our "stony road," the silenced drum keeps beating and marching souls keep traveling triumphantly.

We took the apocalyptic literature of the biblical tradition and sent it marching across cotton fields, cane fields, corn fields, and plantations. The message was strange to the slave master because he thought, at times, he was being entertained when he was in reality being judged, "weighed in the balances" of truth and found guilty. We can hear the sounds, the songs and the protest! "Wade in the water, children," "Everybody talking 'bout Heaven ain't going there," "God's gonna move this wicked race and raise up a nation that will obey," "Satan, your kingdom must come down," "Steal away," "Swing low, sweet chariot" [Freedom's Chariot], "Didn't my Lord deliver Daniel," "Follow the drinking gourd" [Escape to Freedom].

The African-American generation of the 1950s and 1960s, beginning in 1955, took the songs and hymns of our ancestors into our marches, jail cells, and mass meetings and fashioned the faith of a movement that reintroduced the African drum, chant, and music in an undisguised and transforming symphony of protest and revolution.

I remember being arrested and taken to a crowded jail in Atlanta and hearing a welcome song echoing from another section of the jail, "Ain't gonna let nobody turn me 'round." I remember another occasion when the jailer called the Reverend A. D. King and myself aside for a private conversation. At first, we were a little suspicious. But when he began to tell us how he did not want his "soul to be lost," we knew that the spirituality of our movement was akin to that of Paul, Silas, and John. The jailer was carrying side arms with the authority to kill. We were armed with righteousness and the power to heal. The music of the movement did not create this power but communicated it and motivated the messengers, teachers, and leaders.

In a mass meeting where voter registration was the focus, a Dorothy Cotton could take the song "Have you got good religion? Certainly, Lord" and translate it into "Are you registered to vote? Certainly, Lord" and "Will you help somebody else? Certainly, Lord." Voting took on the dimension of spiritual social action and sacred commitment. Those who do not understand the music of our movement will often declare war on their own culture—African culture. Those who do not understand African theology will often declare war on the God of liberation.

A few years ago, I sat down with our minister of music, the late Barbara Collier, to discuss the morning hymn for the following Sunday. The choir would do three selections, but the three selections would be three arrangements of the same hymn, "Guide Me, O Thou Great Jehovah"—the congregational hymn, the anthem, and the common meter hymn. Ms. Collier artistically and spiritually weaved this into our worship experience in such a way that we had education, edification, and liberation in our worship and praise. This was the mission of the music of the civil rights movement. However, when a few souls with good intentions, but a delinquent sense of history and culture, announced, "We are not going to sing anymore," they broke the ancestral linkage and silenced the African drum. In the name of rebellion they obeyed the edict of the slave master. To give up the music of the movement is to adopt the habits of the oppressor. The music of the movement is the language of liberation. This language must be intentionally and methodically taught from generation to generation. A civil rights movement without music loses its "Africanness" and takes on an "iceman" characteristic. Dr. Howard Thurman, Dr. Wyatt Tee Walker, Dr. Jeremiah Wright (my Doctor of Ministry classmate), and many others have written classic and enduring publications on this subject from a theological perspective.

I have dreamed for many years of an African hymn book to stand beside an African Bible and an African history book. This must be the heart, the core curriculum, for our children and their children's children. This hymn book is a necessary installment on our continuing spiritual liberation. The unconditional love of Jesus Christ must be translated in sermons, songs, service, revolutionary action, and practice.

A few days ago in a conversation with Robert D. Nesbitt, Sr., deacon and lifelong member of Dexter Avenue Baptist Church, Montgomery, Alabama, who was a close friend and confidant to both Dr. Vernon Johns and Dr. Martin Luther King, Jr., I was reminded of the fact that five churches were bombed in Montgomery on the same night during the course of the Montgomery Movement. It is important for this generation of young people to know that these churches were not bombed by white racists, KKK, because they were preaching a "white" theology. They were bombed because they were the centers of a liberation, protest, and a revolutionary theology. The music heard in these churches and in the weekly mass meetings was the music of protest and hope, justice and love, righteous revolution, and non-violent confrontation. It is instructive to note that during this period in the black community the crime rate went down in a way that was phenomenal. The echoes of these freedom songs can still be heard:

> Oh Freedom, Oh Freedom
> Oh Freedom over me,
> And before I'd be a slave
> I'll be buried in my grave,
> And go home to my God and be free.

These songs became the drum beat and melody for tens of thousands as we marched singing:

> I woke up this morning with my mind stayed on Freedom,
> I woke up this morning with my mind stayed on Freedom.
> Hallelu, Hallelu, Hallelujah!

When the Klan, police, sheriffs, governors, and courts said, "You will not march," our sermons and songs said:

> I'm gonna do what the Spirit says do,
> I'm gonna do what the Spirit says do,
> What the Spirit says do,
> I'm gonna do, O Lord, I gonna do what the Spirit says do.

> I'm gonna march when the Spirit says march. . . .
> I'm gonna vote when the Spirit says vote. . . .
> I'm gonna live like the Spirit says live. . . .

Those who did not understand African theology and African spirituality sought to silence this drum beat and jail the song leaders, like the prophetic James Bevel and the gifted vocalist Bernice Johnson Reagan. Each generation must sing its song, but if we are to sing with power and purpose, we must know the songs of our ancestors and embrace the spirit of their songs. It is incomprehensible to think of Dr. King as the leader of a songless movement. African and African American theology has never been and never will be a songless theology.

Rev. Otis Moss, Jr., D.Min.
Pastor
Olivet Institutional Baptist Church
Cleveland, Ohio

CONTENTS

1. ANOINTING

Old Testament: Isa. 61:1-3; Ps. 23:5-6, 20:6; 1 Chr. 16:19-22; 2 Sam. 22:51

New Testament: Acts 10:36-38; 2 Cor. 1:20-22; 1 Jn. 2:27-28; Heb. 1:8-9

The spirit of the Lord GOD is upon me, because the LORD has anointed me;

He has sent me to bring good news to the oppressed, to bind up the brokenhearted,

To proclaim liberty to the captives, and release to the prisoners;

To proclaim the year of the LORD's favor, and the day of vengeance of our God;

To comfort all who mourn; to provide for those who mourn in Zion—

To give them a garland instead of ashes, the oil of gladness instead of mourning,

The mantle of praise instead of a faint spirit.

You anoint my head with oil; my cup overflows.

Surely goodness and mercy shall follow me all the days of my life,

And I shall dwell in the house of the Lord my whole life long.

Now I know that the Lord will help his anointed; he will answer him from his holy heaven with mighty victories by his right hand.

When they were few in number, of little account, and strangers in the land, wandering from nation to nation, from one kingdom to another people,

He allowed no one to oppress them; he rebuked kings on their account, saying, "Do not touch my anointed ones; do my prophets no harm."

He is a tower of salvation for his king, and shows steadfast love to his anointed, to David and his descendants forever.

You know the message he sent to the people of Israel, preaching peace by Jesus Christ— he is Lord of all. That message spread throughout Judea, beginning in Galilee after the baptism that John announced:

How God anointed Jesus of Nazareth with the Holy Spirit and with power;

How he went about doing good and healing all who were oppressed by the devil, for God was with him.

For in him every one of God's promises is a "Yes." For this reason it is through him that we say the "Amen," to the glory of God.

But it is God who establishes us with you in Christ and has anointed us, by putting his seal on us and giving us his Spirit in our hearts as a first installment.

As for you, the anointing that you received from him abides in you, and so you do not need anyone to teach you.

But as his anointing teaches you about all things, and is true and is not a lie, and just as it has taught you, abide in him.

And now, little children, abide in him, so that when he is revealed we may have confidence and not be put to shame before him at his coming.

But of the Son he says, "Your throne, O God, is forever and ever, and the righteous scepter is the scepter of your kingdom.

You have loved righteousness and hated wickedness; therefore God, your God, has anointed you with the oil of gladness beyond your companions."

2. BLESSINGS

Old Testament: Deut. 30:15-20; Mal. 3:10; Gen. 12:2-3

New Testament: Eph. 1:3-6; 2 Cor. 9:7-8; Rom. 15:25-26; 1 Pet. 3:8-9

See, I have set before you today life and prosperity, death and adversity.

If you obey the commandments of the LORD your God that I am commanding you today, by loving the LORD your God, walking in his ways, and observing his commandments, decrees, and ordinances, then you shall live and become numerous,

And the LORD your God will bless you in the land that you are entering to possess. But if your heart turns away and you do not hear, but are led astray to bow down to other gods and serve them,

I declare to you today that you shall perish; you shall not live long in the land that you are crossing the Jordan to enter and possess.

I call heaven and earth to witness against you today that I have set before you life and death, blessings and curses.

Choose life so that you and your descendants may live, loving the LORD your God, obeying him, and holding fast to him; for that means life to you and length of days,

So that you may live in the land that the LORD swore to give to your ancestors, to Abraham, to Isaac, and to Jacob.

Bring the full tithe into the storehouse, so that there may be food in my house, and thus put me to the test, says the LORD of hosts; see if I will not open the windows of heaven for you and pour down for you an overflowing blessing.

"I will make of you a great nation, and I will bless you, and make your name great, so that you will be a blessing.

I will bless those who bless you, and the one who curses you I will curse; and in you all the families of the earth shall be blessed."

Blessed be the God and Father of our Lord Jesus Christ, who has blessed us in Christ with every spiritual blessing in the heavenly places,

Just as he chose us in Christ before the foundation of the world to be holy and blameless before him in love.

He destined us for adoption as his children through Jesus Christ, according to the good pleasure of his will, to the praise of his glorious grace that he freely bestowed on us in the Beloved.

Each of you must give as you have made up your mind, not reluctantly or under compulsion, for God loves a cheerful giver.

And God is able to provide you with every blessing in abundance, so that by always having enough of everything, you may share abundantly in every good work.

At present, I am going to Jerusalem in a ministry to the saints; for Macedonia and Achaia have been pleased to share their resources with the poor among the saints at Jerusalem.

Finally, all of you, have unity of spirit, sympathy, love for one another, a tender heart, and a humble mind.

Do not repay evil for evil or abuse for abuse; but, on the contrary, repay with a blessing. It is for this that you were called—that you might inherit a blessing.

3. CHILDREN

Old Testament: Deut. 6:4-9; Prov. 20:11, 22:6;
Eccl. 12:1; Ps. 78:5-8; Isa. 11:6

New Testament: Lk. 2:41-43, 46-49, 52; Mk. 10:13-
15

Hear, O Israel: The LORD is our God, the LORD alone.

You shall love the Lord your God with all your heart, and with all your soul, and with all your might. Keep these words that I am commanding you today in your heart.

Recite them to your children and talk about them when you are at home and when you are away, when you lie down and when you rise.

Bind them as a sign on your hand, fix them as an emblem on your forehead, and write them on the doorposts of your house and on your gates.

Even children make themselves known by their acts, by whether what they do is pure and right. Train children in the right way, and when old, they will not stray.

Remember your creator in the days of your youth, before the days of trouble come, and the years draw near when you will say, "I have no pleasure in them."

He established a decree in Jacob, and appointed a law in Israel, which he commanded our ancestors to teach to their children;

That the next generation might know them, the children yet unborn, and rise up and tell them to their children,

So that they should set their hope in God, and not forget the works of God, but keep his commandments; and that they should not be like their ancestors, a stubborn and rebellious generation.

The wolf shall live with the lamb, the leopard shall lie down with the kid, the calf and the lion and the fatling together, and a little child shall lead them.

Now every year his parents went to Jerusalem for the festival of the Passover. And when he was twelve years old, they went up as usual for the festival.

When the festival was ended and they started to return, the boy Jesus stayed behind in Jerusalem... After three days they found him in the temple, sitting among the teachers, listening to them and asking them questions. And all who heard him were amazed at his understanding and his answers.

When his parents saw him they were astonished; and his mother said to him, "...Look, your father and I have been searching for you in great anxiety." He said to them,

"Why were you searching for me? Did you not know that I must be in my Father's house?" And Jesus increased in wisdom and in years, and in divine and human favor.

People were bringing little children to him in order that he might touch them; and the disciples spoke sternly to them. But when Jesus saw this, he was indignant and said to them,

"Let the little children come to me; do not stop them; for it is to such as these that the kingdom of God belongs. Truly I tell you, whoever does not receive the kingdom of God as a little child will never enter it."

4. THE CHURCH

Old Testament: Ps. 15, 27:4-6; 1 Kgs. 7:51—8:1; 2 Chr. 5:1-2, 6:20

New Testament: 1 Cor. 12:12-14, 20, 26-27; Eph. 4:4-6; 1 Cor. 3:10-11; Eph. 2:19-22

O LORD, who may abide in your tent? Who may dwell on your holy hill?

Those who walk blamelessly, and do what is right, and speak the truth from their heart; who do not slander with their tongue, and do no evil to their friends,

Nor take up a reproach against their neighbors; in whose eyes the wicked are despised, but who honor those who fear the LORD; who stand by their oath even to their hurt;

Who do not lend money at interest, and do not take a bribe against the innocent. Those who do these things shall never be moved.

One thing I asked of the LORD, that will I seek after: to live in the house of the LORD all the days of my life, to behold the beauty of the LORD, and to inquire in his temple.

For he will hide me in his shelter in the day of trouble; he will conceal me under the cover of his tent; he will set me high on a rock.

Now my head is lifted up above my enemies all around me, and I will offer in his tent sacrifices with shouts of joy; I will sing and make melody to the LORD.

Thus all the work that Solomon did for the house of the Lord was finished. Solomon brought in the things that his father David had dedicated, and stored the silver, the gold, and all the vessels in the treasuries of the house of the LORD.

Then Solomon assembled the elders of Israel and all the heads of the tribes, the leaders of the ancestral houses of the people of Israel, in Jerusalem, to bring up the ark of the covenant of the LORD out of the city of David, which is Zion.

May your eyes be open day and night toward this house, the place where you promised to set your name, and may you heed the prayer that your servant prays toward this place.

For just as the body is one and has many members, and all the members of the body, though many, are one body, so it is with Christ.

For in the one Spirit we were all baptized into one body—Jews or Greeks, slaves or free—and we were all made to drink of one Spirit. Indeed, the body does not consist of one member but of many.

As it is, there are many members, yet one body. If one member suffers, all suffer together with it; if one member is honored, all rejoice together with it.

Now you are the body of Christ and individually members of it.

There is one body and one Spirit, just as you were called to the one hope of your calling, one Lord, one faith, one baptism, one God and Father of all, who is above all and through all and in all.

According to the grace of God given to me, like a skilled master builder I laid a foundation, and someone else is building on it. Each builder must choose with care how to build on it. For no one can lay any foundation other than the one that has been laid; that foundation is Jesus Christ.

So then you are no longer strangers and aliens, but you are citizens with the saints and also members of the household of God, built upon the foundation of the apostles and prophets, with Christ Jesus himself as the cornerstone.

In him the whole structure is joined together and grows into a holy temple in the Lord; in whom you also are built together spiritually into a dwelling place for God.

5. COMFORT

Old Testament: Eccl. 4:1; Isa. 40:1-2; Ps. 119:50, 52, 76-77; Isa. 51:3, 66:10, 13-14, 51:16

New Testament: Mt. 2:17-18, 5:4; Phil. 2:1-5; Rev. 7:16-17; 2 Thess. 2:16-17; 2 Cor. 1:3-4

Again I saw all the oppressions that are practiced under the sun. Look, the tears of the oppressed—with no one to comfort them! On the side of their oppressors there was power—with no one to comfort them

Comfort, O comfort my people, says your God. Speak tenderly to Jerusalem, and cry to her that she has served her term, that her penalty is paid, that she has received from the LORD's hand double for all her sins.

This is my comfort in my distress, that your promise gives me life. When I think of your ordinances from of old, I take comfort, O LORD.

Let your steadfast love become my comfort according to your promise to your servant. Let your mercy come to me, that I may live; for your law is my delight.

For the LORD will comfort Zion; he will comfort all her waste places, and will make her wilderness like Eden, her desert like the garden of the LORD; joy and gladness will be found in her, thanksgiving and the voice of song.

Rejoice with Jerusalem, and be glad for her, all you who love her; rejoice with her in joy, all you who mourn over her... As a mother comforts her child, so I will comfort you; you shall be comforted in Jerusalem.

You shall see, and your heart shall rejoice; your bodies shall flourish like the grass; and it shall be known that the hand of the LORD is with his servants, and his indignation is against his enemies.

I have put my words in your mouth, and hidden you in the shadow of my hand, stretching out the heavens and laying the foundations of the earth, and saying to Zion, "You are my people."

Then was fulfilled what had been spoken through the prophet Jeremiah: "A voice was heard in Ramah, wailing and loud lamentation, Rachel weeping for her children; she refused to be consoled, because they are no more."

Blessed are those who mourn, for they will be comforted.

If then there is any encouragement in Christ, any consolation from love, any sharing in the Spirit, any compassion and sympathy, make my joy complete:

Be of the same mind, having the same love, being in full accord and of one mind.

Do nothing from selfish ambition or conceit, but in humility regard others as better than yourselves. Let each of you look not to your own interests, but to the interests of others. Let the same mind be in you that was in Christ Jesus.

They will hunger no more, and thirst no more; the sun will not strike them, nor any scorching heat; for the Lamb at the center of the throne will be their shepherd,

And he will guide them to springs of the water of life, and God will wipe away every tear from their eyes."

Now may our Lord Jesus Christ himself and God our Father, who loved us and through grace gave us eternal comfort and good hope, comfort your hearts and strengthen them in every good work and word.

Blessed be the God and Father of our Lord Jesus Christ, the Father of mercies and the God of all consolation, who consoles us in all our affliction,

So that we may be able to console those who are in any affliction with the consolation with which we ourselves are consoled by God.

6. COMMITMENT

Old Testament: Ruth 1:6, 16-17, 22; 1 Kings 18:20-21, 38-39; Ps. 37:3-6

New Testament:: Jn. 17:4-6; Rom. 12:1-2; Col. 4:2; Eph. 6:10-13; 2 Tim. 4:7-8

Then she started to return with her daughters-in-law from the country of Moab, for she had heard in the country of Moab that the LORD had considered his people and given them food.

But Ruth said, "Do not press me to leave you or to turn back from following you! Where you go, I will go; where you lodge, I will lodge; your people shall be my people, and your God my God.

Where you die, I will die—there will I be buried. May the LORD do thus and so to me, and more as well, if even death parts me from you!"

So Naomi returned together with Ruth the Moabite, her daughter-in-law, who came back with her from the country of Moab. They came to Bethlehem at the beginning of the barley harvest.

So Ahab sent to all the Israelites, and assembled the prophets at Mount Carmel. Elijah then came near to all the people, and said, "How long will you go limping with two different opinions? If the LORD is God, follow him; but if Baal, then follow him." The people did not answer him a word.

Then the fire of the LORD fell and consumed the burnt offering, the wood, the stones, and the dust, and even licked up the water that was in the trench. When all the people saw it, they fell on their faces and said, "The LORD indeed is God; the LORD indeed is God."

Trust in the LORD, and do good; so you will live in the land, and enjoy security. Take delight in the LORD, and he will give you the desires of your heart.

Commit your way to the LORD; trust in him, and he will act. He will make your vindication shine like the light and the justice of your cause like the noonday.

I glorified you on earth by finishing the work that you gave me to do. So now, Father, glorify me in your own presence with the glory that I had in your presence before the world existed.

"I have made your name known to those whom you gave me from the world. They were yours, and you gave them to me, and they have kept your word.

I appeal to you therefore, brothers and sisters, by the mercies of God, to present your bodies as a living sacrifice, holy and acceptable to God, which is your spiritual worship.

Do not be conformed to this world, but be transformed by the renewing of your minds, so that you may discern what is the will of God—what is good and acceptable and perfect.

Devote yourselves to prayer, keeping alert in it with thanksgiving.

Finally, be strong in the Lord and in the strength of his power.

Put on the whole armor of God, so that you may be able to stand against the wiles of the devil.

For our struggle is not against enemies of blood and flesh, but against the rulers, against the authorities, against the cosmic powers of this present darkness, against the spiritual forces of evil in the heavenly places.

Therefore take up the whole armor of God, so that you may be able to withstand on that evil day, and having done everything, to stand firm. I have fought the good fight, I have finished the race, I have kept the faith.

From now on there is reserved for me the crown of righteousness, which the Lord, the righteous judge, will give me on that day, and not only to me but also to all who have longed for his appearing.

7. COVENANT

Old Testament: Gen. 9:8, 11, 17:1-2; Ex. 19:5-6; Ps. 105:7-11; Jer. 31:33-34

New Testament: Lk. 1:67-75; 2 Cor. 1:20; Mt. 26:27-28; Heb. 13:20-21

Then God said to Noah and to his sons with him, "I establish my covenant with you, that never again shall all flesh be cut off by the waters of a flood, and never again shall there be a flood to destroy the earth."

When Abram was ninety-nine years old, the Lord appeared to Abram, and said to him, "I am God Almighty; walk before me, and be blameless. And I will make my covenant between me and you, and will make you exceedingly numerous."

Now therefore, if you obey my voice and keep my covenant, you shall be my treasured possession out of all the peoples. Indeed, the whole earth is mine, but you shall be for me a priestly kingdom and a holy nation.

He is the LORD our God; his judgments are in all the earth. He is mindful of his covenant forever, of the word that he commanded, for a thousand generations, the covenant that he made with Abraham, his sworn promise to Isaac,

Which he confirmed to Jacob as a statute, to Israel as an everlasting covenant, saying, "To you I will give the land of Canaan as your portion for an inheritance."

But this is the covenant that I will make with the house of Israel after those days, says the LORD: I will put my law within them, and I will write it on their hearts; and I will be their God, and they shall be my people.

No longer shall they teach one another, or say to each other, "Know the LORD," for they shall all know me, from the least of them to the greatest, says the LORD;

For I will forgive their iniquity, and remember their sin no more.

Then his father Zechariah was filled with the Holy Spirit and spoke this prophecy: "Blessed be the Lord God of Israel, for he has looked favorably on his people and redeemed them.

He has raised up a mighty savior for us in the house of his servant David, as he spoke through the mouth of his holy prophets from of old,

That we would be saved from our enemies and from the hand of all who hate us. Thus he has shown the mercy promised to our ancestors, and has remembered his holy covenant, the oath that he swore to our ancestor Abraham,

To grant us that we, being rescued from the hands of our enemies, might serve him without fear, in holiness and righteousness before him all our days.

For in him every one of God's promises is a "Yes." For this reason it is through him that we say the "Amen," to the glory of God.

Then he took a cup, and after giving thanks he gave it to them, saying, "Drink from it, all of you; for this is my blood of the covenant, which is poured out for many for the forgiveness of sins.

Now may the God of peace, who brought back from the dead our Lord Jesus, the great shepherd of the sheep, by the blood of the eternal covenant make you complete in everything good

So that you may do his will, working among us that which is pleasing in his sight, through Jesus Christ, to whom be the glory forever and ever. Amen.

8. THE CROSS

Old Testament: Isa. 50:6-7, 53:3-5, 7; Jer. 31:34; Zech. 9:11

I gave my back to those who struck me, and my cheeks to those who pulled out the beard; I did not hide my face from insult and spitting.

The Lord GOD helps me; therefore I have not been disgraced; therefore I have set my face like flint, and I know that I shall not be put to shame.

He was despised and rejected by others; a man of suffering and acquainted with infirmity; and as one from whom others hide their faces he was despised, and we held him of no account.

Surely he has borne our infirmities and carried our diseases; yet we accounted him stricken, struck down by God, and afflicted.

But he was wounded for our transgressions, crushed for our iniquities; upon him was the punishment that made us whole, and by his bruises we are healed.

He was oppressed, and he was afflicted, yet he did not open his mouth; like a lamb that is led to the slaughter, and like a sheep that before its shearers is silent, so he did not open his mouth.

I will forgive their iniquity, and remember their sin no more.

As for you also, because of the blood of my covenant with you, I will set your prisoners free from the waterless pit.

New Testament: Lk. 23:33-34, 42-46; Jn. 19:26-30; Mt. 27:46, 54

When they came to the place that is called The Skull, they crucified Jesus there with the criminals, one on his right and one on his left.

Then Jesus said, "Father, forgive them; for they do not know what they are doing." And they cast lots to divide his clothing.

Then [the criminal] said, "Jesus, remember me when you come into your kingdom." He replied, "Truly I tell you, today you will be with me in Paradise."

It was now about noon, and darkness came over the whole land until three in the afternoon, while the sun's light failed; and the curtain of the temple was torn in two.

Then Jesus, crying with a loud voice, said, "Father, into your hands I commend my spirit." Having said this, he breathed his last.

When Jesus saw his mother and the disciple whom he loved standing beside her, he said to his mother, "Woman, here is your son." Then he said to the disciple, "Here is your mother." And from that hour the disciple took her into his own home.

After this, when Jesus knew that all was now finished, he said (in order to fulfill the scripture), "I am thirsty." A jar full of sour wine was standing there. So they put a sponge full of the wine on a branch of hyssop and held it to his mouth.

When Jesus had received the wine, he said, "It is finished." Then he bowed his head and gave up his spirit.

And about three o'clock Jesus cried with a loud voice, "Eli, Eli, lema sabachthani?" that is, "My God, my God, why have you forsaken me?"

Now when the centurion and those with him, who were keeping watch over Jesus, saw the earthquake and what took place, they were terrified and said, "Truly this man was God's Son!"

9. DISCIPLESHIP

Old Testament: Ex. 20:3-5, 7-8, 12-17; 1 Kings 19:19, 21

New Testament: Mk. 6:7-13, 10:28-30; Lk. 14:26-27; Jn. 13:34-35

You shall have no other gods before me. You shall not make for yourself an idol, whether in the form of anything that is in heaven above, or that is on the earth beneath, or that is in the water under the earth.

You shall not bow down to them or worship them; for I the LORD your God am a jealous God.

You shall not make wrongful use of the name of the LORD your God, for the LORD will not acquit anyone who misuses his name.

Remember the sabbath day, and keep it holy. Honor your father and your mother, so that your days may be long in the land that the LORD your God is giving you.

You shall not murder. You shall not commit adultery. You shall not steal. You shall not bear false witness against your neighbor.

You shall not covet your neighbor's house; you shall not covet your neighbor's wife, or male or female slave, or ox, or donkey, or anything that belongs to your neighbor.

So he set out from there, and found Elisha son of Shaphat, who was plowing. There were twelve yoke of oxen ahead of him, and he was with the twelfth. Elijah passed by him and threw his mantle over him.

Then he set out and followed Elijah, and became his servant.

He called the twelve and began to send them out two by two, and gave them authority over the unclean spirits.

He ordered them to take nothing for their journey except a staff; no bread, no bag, no money in their belts; but to wear sandals and not to put on two tunics.

He said to them, "Wherever you enter a house, stay there until you leave the place. If any place will not welcome you and they refuse to hear you, as you leave, shake off the dust that is on your feet as a testimony against them."

So they went out and proclaimed that all should repent. They cast out many demons, and anointed with oil many who were sick and cured them.

Peter began to say to him, "Look, we have left everything and followed you." Jesus said, "Truly I tell you, there is no one who has left house or brothers or sisters or mother or father or children or fields,

For my sake and for the sake of the good news, who will not receive a hundredfold now in this age—houses, brothers and sisters, mothers and children, and fields with persecutions—and in the age to come eternal life.

Whoever comes to me and does not hate father and mother, wife and children, brothers and sisters, yes, and even life itself, cannot be my disciple. Whoever does not carry the cross and follow me cannot be my disciple.

I give you a new commandment, that you love one another. Just as I have loved you, you also should love one another. By this everyone will know that you are my disciples, if you have love for one another."

10. FAITHFULNESS

Old Testament: Ps. 36:5-6, 40:10, 89:1-2, 5-8; Lam. 3:22-23

New Testament: 1 Cor. 10:13, 1:9; 2 Thess. 3:1-3; 2 Tim. 2:11-13; 1 Jn. 1:8-9; Heb. 10:23; Rev. 2:10

Your steadfast love, O LORD, extends to the heavens, your faithfulness to the clouds.

Your righteousness is like the mighty mountains, your judgments are like the great deep; you save humans and animals alike, O LORD.

I have not hidden your saving help within my heart, I have spoken of your faithfulness and your salvation; I have not concealed your steadfast love and your faithfulness from the great congregation.

I will sing of your steadfast love, O LORD, forever; with my mouth I will proclaim your faithfulness to all generations. I declare that your steadfast love is established forever;

Your faithfulness is as firm as the heavens. Let the heavens praise your wonders, O LORD, your faithfulness in the assembly of the holy ones. For who in the skies can be compared to the LORD?

Who among the heavenly beings is like the LORD, a God feared in the council of the holy ones, great and awesome above all that are around him?

O LORD God of hosts, who is as mighty as you, O LORD? Your faithfulness surrounds you.

The steadfast love of the LORD never ceases, his mercies never come to an end; they are new every morning; great is your faithfulness.

No testing has overtaken you that is not common to everyone. God is faithful, and he will not let you be tested beyond your strength, but with the testing he will also provide the way out so that you may be able to endure it.

God is faithful; by him you were called into the fellowship of his Son, Jesus Christ our Lord.

Finally, brothers and sisters, pray for us, so that the word of the Lord may spread rapidly and be glorified everywhere, just as it is among you, and that we may be rescued from wicked and evil people; for not all have faith.

But the Lord is faithful; he will strengthen you and guard you from the evil one.

The saying is sure: If we have died with him, we will also live with him; if we endure, we will also reign with him; if we deny him, he will also deny us;

If we are faithless, he remains faithful—for he cannot deny himself.

If we say that we have no sin, we deceive ourselves, and the truth is not in us.

If we confess our sins, he who is faithful and just will forgive us our sins and cleanse us from all unrighteousness.

Let us hold fast to the confession of our hope without wavering, for he who has promised is faithful.

Be faithful until death, and I will give you the crown of life.

11. FAMILY

Old Testament: Deut. 6:4-7; Prov. 23:12-13, 15, 22:6; Isa. 54:4-8

New Testament: Mk. 3:31-35; Lk. 11:11-13; Jn. 19:26-27; Col. 3:14-15, 18-21

Hear, O Israel: The LORD is our God, the LORD alone. You shall love the LORD your God with all your heart, and with all your soul, and with all your might.

Keep these words that I am commanding you today in your heart.

Recite them to your children and talk about them when you are at home and when you are away, when you lie down and when you rise.

Apply your mind to instruction and your ear to words of knowledge. Do not withhold discipline from your children.

My child, if your heart is wise, my heart too will be glad.

Train children in the right way, and when old, they will not stray.

Do not fear, for you will not be ashamed; do not be discouraged, for you will not suffer disgrace;

For you will forget the shame of your youth, and the disgrace of your widowhood you will remember no more.

For your Maker is your husband, the LORD of hosts is his name; the Holy One of Israel is your Redeemer, the God of the whole earth he is called.

For the LORD has called you like a wife forsaken and grieved in spirit, like the wife of a man's youth when she is cast off, says your God.

For a brief moment I abandoned you, but with great compassion I will gather you.

In overflowing wrath for a moment I hid my face from you, but with everlasting love I will have compassion on you, says the LORD, your Redeemer.

Then his mother and his brothers came; and standing outside, they sent to him and called him. A crowd was sitting around him; and they said to him, "Your mother and your brothers and sisters are outside, asking for you."

And he replied, "Who are my mother and my brothers?"

And looking at those who sat around him, he said, "Here are my mother and my brothers! Whoever does the will of God is my brother and sister and mother."

Is there anyone among you who, if your child asks for a fish, will give a snake instead of a fish? Or if the child asks for an egg, will give a scorpion?

If you then, who are evil, know how to give good gifts to your children, how much more will the heavenly Father give the Holy Spirit to those who ask him!

When Jesus saw his mother and the disciple whom he loved standing beside her, he said to his mother, "Woman, here is your son."

Then he said to the disciple, "Here is your mother." And from that hour the disciple took her into his own home.

Above all, clothe yourselves with love, which binds everything together in perfect harmony. And let the peace of Christ rule in your hearts, to which indeed you were called in the one body. And be thankful.

Wives, be subject to your husbands, as is fitting in the Lord. Husbands, love your wives and never treat them harshly.

Children, obey your parents in everything, for this is your acceptable duty in the Lord. Fathers, do not provoke your children, or they may lose heart.

12. FORGIVENESS

Old Testament: Gen. 45:4-7, 11; Ps. 103:2-3; 2 Chr. 6:21; Neh. 9:17

New Testament: Mt. 5:3-12; Col. 3:12-13; Mt. 26:27-28

Then Joseph said to his brothers, "Come closer to me." And they came closer. He said, "I am your brother, Joseph, whom you sold into Egypt.

And now do not be distressed, or angry with yourselves, because you sold me here; for God sent me before you to preserve life.

For the famine has been in the land these two years; and there are five more years in which there will be neither plowing nor harvest.

God sent me before you to preserve for you a remnant on earth, and to keep alive for you many survivors.

I will provide for you there—since there are five more years of famine to come—so that you and your household, and all that you have, will not come to poverty.'

Bless the LORD, O my soul, and do not forget all his benefits—who forgives all your iniquity, who heals all your diseases.

And hear the plea of your servant and of your people Israel, when they pray toward this place; may you hear from heaven your dwelling place; hear and forgive.

They refused to obey, and were not mindful of the wonders that you performed among them;

But they stiffened their necks and determined to return to their slavery in Egypt.

But you are a God ready to forgive, gracious and merciful, slow to anger and abounding in steadfast love, and you did not forsake them.

Blessed are the poor in spirit, for theirs is the kingdom of heaven. Blessed are those who mourn, for they will be comforted.

Blessed are the meek, for they will inherit the earth. Blessed are those who hunger and thirst for righteousness, for they will be filled.

Blessed are the merciful, for they will receive mercy. Blessed are the pure in heart, for they will see God.

Blessed are the peacemakers, for they will be called children of God. Blessed are those who are persecuted for righteousness' sake, for theirs is the kingdom of heaven.

Blessed are you when people revile you and persecute you and utter all kinds of evil against you falsely on my account.

Rejoice and be glad, for your reward is great in heaven, for in the same way they persecuted the prophets who were before you.

As God's chosen ones, holy and beloved, clothe yourselves with compassion, kindness, humility, meekness, and patience.

Bear with one another and, if anyone has a complaint against another, forgive each other; just as the Lord has forgiven you, so you also must forgive.

Then he took a cup, and after giving thanks he gave it to them, saying, "Drink from it, all of you;

For this is my blood of the covenant, which is poured out for many for the forgiveness of sins."

13. THE COMING OF THE LORD

Old Testament: Isa. 13:9; Am. 5:18; Mal. 4:1-3;
Zeph. 1:17-18; Dan. 12:1-2

See, the day of the LORD comes, cruel, with wrath and fierce anger, to make the earth a desolation, and to destroy its sinners from it.

Alas for you who desire the day of the LORD! Why do you want the day of the LORD? It is darkness, not light.

See, the day is coming, burning like an oven, when all the arrogant and all evildoers will be stubble; the day that comes shall burn them up, says the LORD of hosts, so that it will leave them neither root nor branch.

But for you who revere my name the sun of righteousness shall rise, with healing in its wings. You shall go out leaping like calves from the stall.

And you shall tread down the wicked, for they will be ashes under the soles of your feet, on the day when I act, says the LORD of hosts.

I will bring such distress upon people that they shall walk like the blind; because they have sinned against the LORD,

Their blood shall be poured out like dust, and their flesh like dung. Neither their silver nor their gold will be able to save them on the day of the LORD's wrath; in the fire of his passion the whole earth shall be consumed;

For a full, a terrible end he will make of all the inhabitants of the earth.

There shall be a time of anguish, such as has never occurred since nations first came into existence. But at that time your people shall be delivered, everyone who is found written in the book.

Many of those who sleep in the dust of the earth shall awake, some to everlasting life, and some to shame and everlasting contempt.

New Testament: Heb. 13:14; 2 Cor. 5:10; 1 Cor.
15:51-52, 54-55; 1 Thess. 4:16-17; 2 Thess. 2:3-4;
Rev. 22:20

For here we have no lasting city, but we are looking for the city that is to come.

For all of us must appear before the judgment seat of Christ, so that each may receive recompense for what has been done in the body, whether good or evil.

Listen, I will tell you a mystery! We will not all die, but we will all be changed, in a moment, in the twinkling of an eye, at the last trumpet.

For the trumpet will sound, and the dead will be raised imperishable, and we will be changed.

When this perishable body puts on imperishability, and this mortal body puts on immortality, then the saying that is written will be fulfilled: "Death has been swallowed up in victory." "Where, O death, is your victory? Where, O death, is your sting?"

For the Lord himself, with a cry of command, with the archangel's call and with the sound of God's trumpet, will descend from heaven, and the dead in Christ will rise first.

Then we who are alive, who are left, will be caught up in the clouds together with them to meet the Lord in the air; and so we will be with the Lord forever.

Let no one deceive you in any way; for that day will not come unless the rebellion comes first and the lawless one is revealed, the one destined for destruction.

He opposes and exalts himself above every so-called god or object of worship, so that he takes his seat in the temple of God, declaring himself to be God.

The one who testifies to these things says, "Surely I am coming soon." Amen. Come, Lord Jesus!

14. FRUIT OF THE HOLY SPIRIT

Old Testament: Ps. 143:10; Isa. 32:14-15, 42:1, 44:3-4, 61:1; Ezek. 36:25-27

New Testament: Gal. 5:16-23, 24-26, 6:7-10

Teach me to do your will, for you are my God. Let your good spirit lead me on a level path.

For the palace will be forsaken, the populous city deserted; the hill and the watchtower will become dens forever, the joy of wild asses, a pasture for flocks;

Until a spirit from on high is poured out on us, and the wilderness becomes a fruitful field, and the fruitful field is deemed a forest.

Here is my servant, whom I uphold, my chosen, in whom my soul delights; I have put my spirit upon him; he will bring forth justice to the nations.

For I will pour water on the thirsty land, and streams on the dry ground; I will pour my spirit upon your descendants, and my blessing on your offspring.

They shall spring up like a green tamarisk, like willows by flowing streams.

The spirit of the Lord GOD is upon me, because the LORD has anointed me; he has sent me to bring good news to the oppressed, to bind up the brokenhearted, to proclaim liberty to the captives, and release to the prisoners.

I will sprinkle clean water upon you, and you shall be clean from all your uncleannesses, and from all your idols I will cleanse you.

A new heart I will give you, and a new spirit I will put within you; And I will remove from your body the heart of stone and give you a heart of flesh.

I will put my spirit within you, and make you follow my statutes and be careful to observe my ordinances.

Live by the Spirit, I say, and do not gratify the desires of the flesh. For what the flesh desires is opposed to the Spirit, and what the Spirit desires is opposed to the flesh;

For these are opposed to each other, to prevent you from doing what you want. But if you are led by the Spirit, you are not subject to the law.

Now the works of the flesh are obvious: fornication, impurity, licentiousness, idolatry, sorcery, enmities, strife, jealousy, anger, quarrels, dissensions, factions, envy, drunkenness, carousing, and things like these.

I am warning you, as I warned you before: those who do such things will not inherit the kingdom of God.

By contrast, the fruit of the Spirit is love, joy, peace, patience, kindness, generosity, faithfulness, gentleness, and self-control.

And those who belong to Christ Jesus have crucified the flesh with its passions and desires.

If we live by the Spirit, let us also be guided by the Spirit. Let us not become conceited, competing against one another, envying one another.

Do not be deceived; God is not mocked, for you reap whatever you sow. If you sow to your own flesh, you will reap corruption from the flesh;

But if you sow to the Spirit, you will reap eternal life from the Spirit. So let us not grow weary in doing what is right, for we will reap at harvest time, if we do not give up.

So then, whenever we have an opportunity, let us work for the good of all, and especially for those of the family of faith.

15. GIFTS OF THE HOLY SPIRIT

Old Testament: Ex. 35:30-33, 35; Isa. 11:1-3; Ezek. 37:1, 3, 7, 10

New Testament: 1 Cor. 12:4-10; Rom. 12:6-8; 1 Cor. 12:28; Eph. 4:11-13

Moses said to the Israelites: See, the LORD has called by name Bezalel son of Uri son of Hur, of the tribe of Judah;

He has filled him with divine spirit, with skill, intelligence, and knowledge in every kind of craft,

To devise artistic designs, to work in gold, silver, and bronze, in cutting stones for setting, and in carving wood, in every kind of craft. He has filled them with skill to do every kind of work done by an artisan or by a designer

Or by an embroiderer in blue, purple, and crimson yarns, and in fine linen, or by a weaver—by any sort of artisan or skilled designer.

A shoot shall come out from the stump of Jesse, and a branch shall grow out of his roots. The spirit of the LORD shall rest on him, the spirit of wisdom and understanding, the spirit of counsel and might, the spirit of knowledge and the fear of the LORD.

His delight shall be in the fear of the LORD.

The hand of the LORD came upon me, and he brought me out by the spirit of the LORD and set me down in the middle of a valley; it was full of bones.

He said to me, "Mortal, can these bones live?" I answered, "O Lord GOD, you know."

So I prophesied as I had been commanded; and as I prophesied, suddenly there was a noise, a rattling, and the bones came together, bone to its bone.

I prophesied as he commanded me, and the breath came into them, and they lived, and stood on their feet, a vast multitude.

Now there are varieties of gifts, but the same Spirit; and there are varieties of services, but the same Lord; and there are varieties of activities, but it is the same God who activates all of them in everyone.

To each is given the manifestation of the Spirit for the common good.

To one is given through the Spirit the utterance of wisdom, and to another the utterance of knowledge according to the same Spirit, to another faith by the same Spirit, to another gifts of healing by the one Spirit,

To another the working of miracles, to another prophecy, to another the discernment of spirits, to another various kinds of tongues, to another the interpretation of tongues.

We have gifts that differ according to the grace given to us: prophecy, in proportion to faith; ministry, in ministering; the teacher, in teaching; the exhorter, in exhortation;

The giver, in generosity; the leader, in diligence; the compassionate, in cheerfulness.

And God has appointed in the church first apostles, second prophets, third teachers;

Then deeds of power, then gifts of healing, forms of assistance, forms of leadership, various kinds of tongues.

The gifts he gave were that some would be apostles, some prophets, some evangelists, some pastors and teachers, to equip the saints for the work of ministry, for building up the body of Christ,

Until all of us come to the unity of the faith and of the knowledge of the Son of God, to maturity, to the measure of the full stature of Christ.

16. GLORY

Old Testament: Ps. 24:9-10, 96:3, 8-9; Hag. 2:9; Isa. 60:1; Ps. 64:10, 57:5; Isa. 42:8; Ps. 72:19

New Testament: Lk. 2:9-11, 14; Jn. 1:14; 2 Cor. 3:18, Rom. 2:7; Jn. 7:18; 1 Cor. 10:31; Mt. 25:31; Rev. 19:1, 7

Lift up your heads, O gates! and be lifted up, O ancient doors! that the King of glory may come in.

Who is this King of glory? The LORD of hosts, he is the King of glory.

Declare his glory among the nations, his marvelous works among all the peoples.

Ascribe to the LORD the glory due his name; bring an offering, and come into his courts.

Worship the LORD in holy splendor; tremble before him, all the earth.

The latter splendor of this house shall be greater than the former, says the LORD of hosts; and in this place I will give prosperity, says the LORD of hosts.

Arise, shine; for your light has come,

And the glory of the LORD has risen upon you.

Let the righteous rejoice in the LORD and take refuge in him. Let all the upright in heart glory.

Be exalted, O God, above the heavens. Let your glory be over all the earth.

I am the LORD, that is my name; my glory I give to no other, nor my praise to idols.

Blessed be his glorious name forever; may his glory fill the whole earth.

Then an angel of the Lord stood before them, and the glory of the Lord shone around them, and they were terrified.

But the angel said to them, "Do not be afraid; for see-I am bringing you good news of great joy for all the people:

To you is born this day in the city of David a Savior, who is the Messiah, the Lord.

Glory to God in the highest heaven, and on earth peace among those whom he favors!

And the Word became flesh and lived among us, and we have seen his glory, the glory as of a father's only son, full of grace and truth.

And all of us, with unveiled faces, seeing the glory of the Lord as though reflected in a mirror,

Are being transformed into the same image from one degree of glory to another; for this comes from the Lord, the Spirit.

To those who by patiently doing good seek for glory and honor and immortality, he will give eternal life.

Those who speak on their own seek their own glory; but the one who seeks the glory of him who sent him is true, and there is nothing false in him.

So, whether you eat or drink, or whatever you do, do everything for the glory of God.

When the Son of Man comes in his glory, and all the angels with him, then he will sit on the throne of his glory.

Hallelujah! Salvation and glory and power to our God. Let us rejoice and exult and give him the glory.

17. GOOD SHEPHERD

Old Testament: Ps. 23; Jer. 23:1-2; Ps. 80:1; Ezek. 34:11, 15-16

New Testament: Jn. 10:11-16; Lk. 15:3-6; Acts 20:28; 1 Pet. 5:4

The LORD is my shepherd, I shall not want. He makes me lie down in green pastures;

He leads me beside still waters; he restores my soul. He leads me in right paths for his name's sake.

Even though I walk through the darkest valley, I fear no evil; for you are with me; your rod and your staff—they comfort me.

You prepare a table before me in the presence of my enemies; you anoint my head with oil; my cup overflows.

Surely goodness and mercy shall follow me all the days of my life, and I shall dwell in the house of the LORD my whole life long.

Woe to the shepherds who destroy and scatter the sheep of my pasture! says the LORD. Therefore thus says the LORD, the God of Israel, concerning the shepherds who shepherd my people:

It is you who have scattered my flock, and have driven them away, and you have not attended to them. So I will attend to you for your evil doings, says the LORD.

Give ear, O Shepherd of Israel, you who lead Joseph like a flock! For thus says the Lord God: I myself will search for my sheep, and will seek them out.

I myself will be the shepherd of my sheep, and I will make them lie down, says the Lord GOD. I will seek the lost, and I will bring back the strayed,

And I will bind up the injured, and I will strengthen the weak, but the fat and the strong I will destroy. I will feed them with justice.

I am the good shepherd. The good shepherd lays down his life for the sheep. The hired hand, who is not the shepherd and does not own the sheep, sees the wolf coming and leaves the sheep and runs away—and the wolf snatches them and scatters them.

The hired hand runs away because a hired hand does not care for the sheep. I am the good shepherd. I know my own and my own know me,

Just as the Father knows me and I know the Father. And I lay down my life for the sheep. I have other sheep that do not belong to this fold.

I must bring them also, and they will listen to my voice. So there will be one flock, one shepherd.

So he told them this parable: "Which one of you, having a hundred sheep and losing one of them, does not leave the ninety-nine in the wilderness and go after the one that is lost until he finds it?

When he has found it, he lays it on his shoulders and rejoices. And when he comes home, he calls together his friends and neighbors, saying to them, Rejoice with me, for I have found my sheep that was lost.

Keep watch over yourselves and over all the flock, of which the Holy Spirit has made you overseers, to shepherd the church of God that he obtained with the blood of his own Son.

And when the chief shepherd appears, you will win the crown of glory that never fades away.

18. GOODNESS OF GOD

Old Testament: Ps. 106:1, 34:8, 73:1, 37:3, 84:11; Neh. 9:20; Deut. 6:18; Ps. 143:10; 1 Chr. 16:34

New Testament: 3 Jn. 11; 1 Tim. 4:4; Lk. 11:10-13; 2 Cor. 9:8; Lk. 6:38; 2 Pet. 3:9; Rom. 12:2; Phil. 2:13

Praise the LORD! O give thanks to the LORD, for he is good; for his steadfast love endures forever.

O taste and see that the LORD is good; happy are those who take refuge in him.

Truly God is good to the upright, to those who are pure in heart.

Trust in the LORD, and do good; so you will live in the land, and enjoy security.

For the LORD God is a sun and shield; he bestows favor and honor. No good thing does the LORD withhold from those who walk uprightly.

You gave your good spirit to instruct them, and did not withhold your manna from their mouths, and gave them water for their thirst.

Do what is right and good in the sight of the LORD, so that it may go well with you,

And so that you may go in and occupy the good land that the LORD swore to your ancestors to give you.

Teach me to do your will, for you are my God. Let your good spirit lead me on a level path.

O give thanks to the LORD, for he is good; for his steadfast love endures forever.

Beloved, do not imitate what is evil but imitate what is good. Whoever does good is from God; whoever does evil has not seen God.

For everything created by God is good, and nothing is to be rejected, provided it is received with thanksgiving.

For everyone who asks receives, and everyone who searches finds, and for everyone who knocks, the door will be opened.

Is there anyone among you who, if your child asks for a fish, will give a snake instead of a fish? Or if the child asks for an egg, will give a scorpion?

If you then, who are evil, know how to give good gifts to your children, how much more will the heavenly Father give the Holy Spirit to those who ask him!

And God is able to provide you with every blessing in abundance, so that by always having enough of everything, you may share abundantly in every good work.

Give, and it will be given to you. A good measure, pressed down, shaken together, running over, will be put into your lap; for the measure you give will be the measure you get back.

The Lord is not slow about his promise, as some think of slowness, but is patient with you, not wanting any to perish, but all to come to repentance.

Do not be conformed to this world, but be transformed by the renewing of your minds, so that you may discern what is the will of God—what is good and acceptable and perfect.

For it is God who is at work in you, enabling you both to will and to work for his good pleasure.

19. THE POOR

Old Testament: Ex. 20:1-3, 22:21-23, 25-27; Isa. 3:15; Ps. 72:2, 12-13; Prov. 14:21, 17:5, 19:17

New Testament: Jas. 2:1-7; Lk. 14:1, 12-14

Then God spoke all these words: I am the LORD your God, who brought you out of the land of Egypt, out of the house of slavery; you shall have no other gods before me.

You shall not wrong or oppress a resident alien, for you were aliens in the land of Egypt. You shall not abuse any widow or orphan.

If you do abuse them, when they cry out to me, I will surely heed their cry.

If you lend money to my people, to the poor among you, you shall not deal with them as a creditor; you shall not exact interest from them.

If you take your neighbor's cloak in pawn, you shall restore it before the sun goes down; for it may be your neighbor's only clothing to use as cover; in what else shall that person sleep?

And if your neighbor cries out to me, I will listen, for I am compassionate.

What do you mean by crushing my people, by grinding the face of the poor? says the Lord GOD of hosts.

May he judge your people with right-eousness, and your poor with justice.

For he delivers the needy when they call, the poor and those who have no helper. He has pity on the weak and the needy, and saves the lives of the needy.

Those who despise their neighbors are sinners, but happy are those who are kind to the poor.

Those who mock the poor insult their Maker; those who are glad at calamity will not go unpunished.

Whoever is kind to the poor lends to the LORD, and will be repaid in full.

My brothers and sisters, do you with your acts of favoritism really believe in our glorious Lord Jesus Christ?

For if a person with gold rings and in fine clothes comes into your assembly,

And if a poor person in dirty clothes also comes in, and if you take notice of the one wearing the fine clothes and say, "Have a seat here, please," while to the one who is poor you say, "Stand there," or, "Sit at my feet,"

Have you not made distinctions among yourselves, and become judges with evil thoughts?

Listen, my beloved brothers and sisters. Has not God chosen the poor in the world to be rich in faith and to be heirs of the kingdom that he has promised to those who love him?

But you have dishonored the poor. Is it not the rich who oppress you?

Is it not they who drag you into court? Is it not they who blaspheme the excellent name that was invoked over you?

On one occasion when Jesus was going to the house of a leader of the Pharisees to eat a meal on the sabbath, they were watching him closely.

He said also to the one who had invited him, "When you give a luncheon or a dinner, do not invite your friends or your brothers or your relatives or rich neighbors, in case they may invite you in return, and you would be repaid.

But when you give a banquet, invite the poor, the crippled, the lame, and the blind. And you will be blessed."

20. GRACE

Old Testament: Gen. 6:5-8; Jer. 31:2-3, 23:4; Isa. 10:20-21, 27

New Testament: Jn. 1:1-2, 14, 16-17; Eph. 3:5-8; Rom. 3:23-25, 8:1

The LORD saw that the wickedness of humankind was great in the earth, and that every inclination of the thoughts of their hearts was only evil continually.

And the LORD was sorry that he had made humankind on the earth, and it grieved him to his heart.

So the LORD said, "I will blot out from the earth the human beings I have created—people together with animals and creeping things and birds of the air, for I am sorry that I have made them." But Noah found favor in the sight of the LORD.

Thus says the LORD: The people who survived the sword found grace in the wilderness;

When Israel sought for rest, the LORD appeared to him from far away.

I have loved you with an everlasting love; therefore I have continued my faithfulness to you.

I will raise up shepherds over them who will shepherd them, and they shall not fear any longer, or be dismayed, nor shall any be missing, says the LORD.

On that day the remnant of Israel and the survivors of the house of Jacob will no more lean on the one who struck them,

But will lean on the LORD, the Holy One of Israel, in truth. A remnant will return, the remnant of Jacob, to the mighty God.

On that day his burden will be removed from your shoulder, and his yoke will be destroyed from your neck.

In the beginning was the Word, and the Word was with God, and the Word was God. He was in the beginning with God.

And the Word became flesh and lived among us, and we have seen his glory, the glory as of a father's only son, full of grace and truth.

From his fullness we have all received, grace upon grace. The law indeed was given through Moses; grace and truth came through Jesus Christ.

In former generations this mystery was not made known to humankind, as it has now been revealed to his holy apostles and prophets by the Spirit:

That is, the Gentiles have become fellow heirs, members of the same body, and sharers in the promise in Christ Jesus through the gospel.

Of this gospel I have become a servant according to the gift of God's grace that was given me by the working of his power.

Although I am the very least of all the saints, this grace was given to me to bring to the Gentiles the news of the boundless riches of Christ.

Since all have sinned and fall short of the glory of God; they are now justified by his grace as a gift, through the redemption that is in Christ Jesus,

Whom God put forward as a sacrifice of atonement by his blood, effective through faith. He did this to show his righteousness, because in his divine forbearance he had passed over the sins previously committed.

There is therefore now no condemnation for those who are in Christ Jesus.

21. CHRISTIAN MATURITY

Old Testament: Ps. 1:1-3, 92:12-15, 144:12; Job 17:9, Isa. 40:28-29

New Testament: Lk. 2:51-52; Col. 1:9-10, 2:6-7, 9-10; 2 Tim. 3:14-17; Eph. 4:12-13

Happy are those who do not follow the advice of the wicked, or take the path that sinners tread, or sit in the seat of scoffers; but their delight is in the law of the LORD, and on his law they meditate day and night.

Then he went down with them and came to Nazareth, and was obedient to them. His mother treasured all these things in her heart. And Jesus increased in wisdom and in years, and in divine and human favor.

They are like trees planted by streams of water, which yield their fruit in its season, and their leaves do not wither. In all that they do, they prosper.

For this reason, since the day we heard it, we have not ceased praying for you and asking that you may be filled with the knowledge of God's will in all spiritual wisdom and understanding,

The righteous flourish like the palm tree, and grow like a cedar in Lebanon. They are planted in the house of the LORD; they flourish in the courts of our God.

So that you may lead lives worthy of the Lord, fully pleasing to him, as you bear fruit in every good work and as you grow in the knowledge of God.

In old age they still produce fruit; they are always green and full of sap, showing that the LORD is upright; he is my rock, and there is no unrighteousness in him.

As you therefore have received Christ Jesus the Lord, continue to live your lives in him, rooted and built up in him and established in the faith, just as you were taught, abounding in thanksgiving.

May our sons in their youth be like plants full grown, our daughters like corner pillars, cut for the building of a palace.

For in him the whole fullness of deity dwells bodily, and you have come to fullness in him, who is the head of every ruler and authority.

The righteous hold to their way, and they that have clean hands grow stronger and stronger.

But as for you, continue in what you have learned and firmly believed, knowing from whom you learned it, and how from childhood you have known the sacred writings that are able to instruct you for salvation through faith in Christ Jesus.

Have you not known? Have you not heard? The LORD is the everlasting God, the Creator of the ends of the earth.

All scripture is inspired by God and is useful for teaching, for reproof, for correction, and for training in righteousness, so that everyone who belongs to God may be proficient, equipped for every good work.

He does not faint or grow weary; his understanding is unsearchable. He gives power to the faint, and strengthens the powerless.

To equip the saints for the work of ministry, for building up the body of Christ, until all of us come to the unity of the faith and of the knowledge of the Son of God, to maturity, to the measure of the full stature of Christ.

22. HEALING

Old Testament: Ex. 15:26; Jer. 17:14; Ex. 23:24-25; Ps. 103:2-4; Jer. 8:22; Ps. 41:1-3

He said, "If you will listen carefully to the voice of the LORD your God, and do what is right in his sight, and give heed to his commandments and keep all his statutes, I will not bring upon you any of the diseases that I brought upon the Egyptians; for I am the LORD who heals you."

Heal me, O LORD, and I shall be healed; save me, and I shall be saved; for you are my praise.

You shall not bow down to their gods, or worship them, or follow their practices, but you shall utterly demolish them and break their pillars in pieces.

You shall worship the LORD your God, and I will bless your bread and your water; and I will take sickness away from among you.

Bless the LORD, O my soul, and do not forget all his benefits—who forgives all your iniquity, who heals all your diseases,

Who redeems your life from the Pit, who crowns you with steadfast love and mercy.

Is there no balm in Gilead? Is there no physician there? Why then has the health of my poor people not been restored?

Happy are those who consider the poor; the LORD delivers them in the day of trouble.

The LORD protects them and keeps them alive; they are called happy in the land. You do not give them up to the will of their enemies.

The LORD sustains them on their sickbed; in their illness you heal all their infirmities.

New Testament: 3 Jn. 2; Mt. 9:35; Mk. 5:25-29; Mt. 14:35-36; Acts 3:4-7; Jas. 5:14-16

Beloved, I pray that all may go well with you and that you may be in good health, just as it is well with your soul.

Then Jesus went about all the cities and villages, teaching in their synagogues, and proclaiming the good news of the kingdom, and curing every disease and every sickness.

Now there was a woman who had been suffering from hemorrhages for twelve years. She had endured much under many physicians, and had spent all that she had; and she was no better, but rather grew worse.

She had heard about Jesus, and came up behind him in the crowd and touched his cloak, for she said,

"if I but touch his clothes, I will be made well." Immediately her hemorrhage stopped; and she felt in her body that she was healed of her disease.

After the people of that place recognized him, they sent word throughout the region and brought all who were sick to him, and begged him that they might touch even the fringe of his cloak; and all who touched it were healed.

Peter looked intently at him, as did John, and said, "Look at us." And he fixed his attention on them, expecting to receive something from them. But Peter said, "I have no silver or gold, but what I have I give you; in the name of Jesus Christ of Nazareth, stand up and walk."

And he took him by the right hand and raised him up; and immediately his feet and ankles were made strong.

Are any among you sick? They should call for the elders of the church and have them pray over them, anointing them with oil in the name of the Lord.

The prayer of faith will save the sick, and the Lord will raise them up; and anyone who has committed sins will be forgiven. Therefore confess your sins to one another, and pray for one another, so that you may be healed. The prayer of the righteous is powerful and effective.

23. THE HOLY SPIRIT

Old Testament: Num. 11:24-29; 1 Kings 18:36, 38; Joel 2:28

New Testament: Lk. 1:12-13, 15; Acts 2:38, 10:44-47, 19:1-2, 4-6

So Moses went out and told the people the words of the LORD; and he gathered seventy elders of the people, and placed them all around the tent.

Then the LORD came down in the cloud and spoke to him, and took some of the spirit that was on him and put it on the seventy elders; and when the spirit rested upon them, they prophesied.

Two men remained in the camp, one named Eldad, and the other named Medad, and the spirit rested on them; they were among those registered, but they had not gone out to the tent, and so they prophesied in the camp.

And a young man ran and told Moses, "Eldad and Medad are prophesying in the camp." And Joshua son of Nun, the assistant of Moses, one of his chosen men, said, "My lord Moses, stop them!"

But Moses said to him, "Are you jealous for my sake? Would that all the LORD's people were prophets, and that the LORD would put his spirit on them!"

At the time of the offering of the oblation, the prophet Elijah came near and said, "O LORD, God of Abraham, Isaac, and Israel,

Let it be known this day that you are God in Israel, that I am your servant, and that I have done all these things at your bidding."

Then the fire of the LORD fell and consumed the burnt offering, the wood, the stones, and the dust, and even licked up the water that was in the trench.

Then afterward I will pour out my spirit on all flesh; your sons and your daughters shall prophesy,

Your old men shall dream dreams, and your young men shall see visions.

When Zechariah saw him, he was terrified; and fear overwhelmed him. But the angel said to him, "Do not be afraid, Zechariah, for your prayer has been heard. Your wife Elizabeth will bear you a son, and you will name him John.

For he will be great in the sight of the Lord. He must never drink wine or strong drink; even before his birth he will be filled with the Holy Spirit."

Peter said to them, "Repent, and be baptized every one of you in the name of Jesus Christ so that your sins may be forgiven; and you will receive the gift of the Holy Spirit."

While Peter was still speaking, the Holy Spirit fell upon all who heard the word.

The circumcised believers who had come with Peter were astounded that the gift of the Holy Spirit had been poured out even on the Gentiles,

For they heard them speaking in tongues and extolling God.

Then Peter said, "Can anyone withhold the water for baptizing these people who have received the Holy Spirit just as we have?"

Paul came to Ephesus, where he found some disciples. He said to them, "Did you receive the Holy Spirit when you became believers?"

They replied, "No, we have not even heard that there is a Holy Spirit." Paul said, "John baptized with the baptism of repentance, telling the people to believe in the one who was to come after him, that is, in Jesus."

On hearing this, they were baptized in the name of the Lord Jesus. When Paul had laid his hands on them, the Holy Spirit came upon them, and they spoke in tongues and prophesied.

24. HOPE

Old Testament: Ps. 71:4-6, 146:5-9; Lam. 3:19-24

New Testament: 1 Pet. 1:3; Heb. 6:11-12, 19-20; Col. 1:26-27; Eph. 1:17-19; Rom. 15:13

Rescue me, O my God, from the hand of the wicked, from the grasp of the unjust and cruel.

For you, O Lord, are my hope, my trust, O LORD, from my youth. Upon you I have leaned from my birth;

It was you who took me from my mother's womb. My praise is continually of you.

Happy are those whose help is the God of Jacob, whose hope is in the LORD their God, who made heaven and earth, the sea, and all that is in them; who keeps faith forever;

Who executes justice for the oppressed; who gives food to the hungry.

The LORD sets the prisoners free; the LORD opens the eyes of the blind.

The LORD lifts up those who are bowed down; the LORD loves the righteous.

The LORD watches over the strangers; he upholds the orphan and the widow, but the way of the wicked he brings to ruin.

The thought of my affliction and my homelessness is wormwood and gall!

My soul continually thinks of it and is bowed down within me. But this I call to mind, and therefore I have hope:

The steadfast love of the LORD never ceases, his mercies never come to an end; they are new every morning; great is your faithfulness.

"The LORD is my portion," says my soul, "therefore I will hope in him."

Blessed be the God and Father of our Lord Jesus Christ! By his great mercy he has given us a new birth into a living hope through the resurrection of Jesus Christ from the dead.

And we want each one of you to show the same diligence so as to realize the full assurance of hope to the very end, so that you may not become sluggish, but imitators of those who through faith and patience inherit the promises.

We have this hope, a sure and steadfast anchor of the soul, a hope that enters the inner shrine behind the curtain, where Jesus, a forerunner on our behalf, has entered, having become a high priest forever according to the order of Melchizedek.

The mystery that has been hidden throughout the ages and generations but has now been revealed to his saints. To them God chose to make known how great among the Gentiles are the riches of the glory of this mystery, which is Christ in you, the hope of glory.

I pray that the God of our Lord Jesus Christ, the Father of glory, may give you a spirit of wisdom and revelation as you come to know him, so that, with the eyes of your heart enlightened, you may know what is the hope to which he has called you,

What are the riches of his glorious inheritance among the saints, and what is the immeasurable greatness of his power for us who believe, according to the working of his great power. May the God of hope fill you with all joy and peace in believing, so that you may abound in hope by the power of the Holy Spirit.

25. HUMILITY

Old Testament: 2 Chr. 7:14; Prov. 15:32-33; Ps. 34:2; Prov. 16:25, 20:24, 18:12, 22:3-4; Mic. 6:8; Zeph. 2:3

New Testament: Jas. 4:6-7; Lk. 14:11; Jas. 4:10; Phil. 2:3, 5-8; 2 Cor. 12:10; Mt. 18:4; 1 Pet. 5:6

If my people who are called by my name humble themselves, pray, seek my face, and turn from their wicked ways, then I will hear from heaven, and will forgive their sin and heal their land.

God opposes the proud, but gives grace to the humble.

Those who ignore instruction despise themselves, but those who heed admonition gain understanding.

Submit yourselves therefore to God. Resist the devil, and he will flee from you.

The fear of the LORD is instruction in wisdom, and humility goes before honor.

For all who exalt themselves will be humbled, and those who humble themselves will be exalted. Humble yourselves before the Lord, and he will exalt you.

My soul makes its boast in the LORD; let the humble hear and be glad.

Do nothing from selfish ambition or conceit, but in humility regard others as better than yourselves.

Sometimes there is a way that seems to be right, but in the end it is the way to death.

All our steps are ordered by the LORD; how then can we understand our own ways?

Let the same mind be in you that was in Christ Jesus, who, though he was in the form of God, did not regard equality with God as something to be exploited,

Before destruction one's heart is haughty, but humility goes before honor.

But emptied himself, taking the form of a slave, being born in human likeness.

The clever see danger and hide; but the simple go on, and suffer for it. The reward for humility and fear of the LORD is riches and honor and life.

And being found in human form, he humbled himself and became obedient to the point of death—even death on a cross.

He has told you, O mortal, what is good; and what does the LORD require of you but to do justice, and to love kindness, and to walk humbly with your God?

Therefore I am content with weaknesses, insults, hardships, persecutions, and calamities for the sake of Christ; for whenever I am weak, then I am strong.

Seek the LORD, all you humble of the land, who do his commands; seek righteousness, seek humility; perhaps you may be hidden on the day of the LORD's wrath.

Whoever becomes humble like this child is the greatest in the kingdom of heaven.

Humble yourselves therefore under the mighty hand of God, so that he may exalt you in due time.

26. JOY

Old Testament: Ps. 98:4-9, 16:11; Isa. 35:10; Jer. 31:12; Ps. 30:4-5

New Testament: Mt. 2:9-10, 13:44; Lk. 15:7; Rom. 14:17; Jn. 15:9-11; Jas. 1:2-4; Heb. 12:2

Make a joyful noise to the LORD, all the earth; break forth into joyous song and sing praises. Sing praises to the LORD with the lyre, with the lyre and the sound of melody.

With trumpets and the sound of the horn make a joyful noise before the King, the LORD.

Let the sea roar, and all that fills it; the world and those who live in it. Let the floods clap their hands;

Let the hills sing together for joy at the presence of the LORD, for he is coming to judge the earth.

He will judge the world with righteousness, and the peoples with equity.

You show me the path of life. In your presence there is fullness of joy; in your right hand are pleasures forevermore.

And the ransomed of the LORD shall return, and come to Zion with singing; everlasting joy shall be upon their heads;

They shall obtain joy and gladness, and sorrow and sighing shall flee away.

They shall come and sing aloud on the height of Zion, and they shall be radiant over the goodness of the LORD, over the grain, the wine, and the oil, and over the young of the flock and the herd;

Their life shall become like a watered garden, and they shall never languish again.

Sing praises to the LORD, O you his faithful ones, and give thanks to his holy name. For his anger is but for a moment; his favor is for a lifetime.

Weeping may linger for the night, but joy comes with the morning.

When they had heard the king, they set out; and there, ahead of them, went the star that they had seen at its rising, until it stopped over the place where the child was.

When they saw that the star had stopped, they were overwhelmed with joy.

The kingdom of heaven is like treasure hidden in a field, which someone found and hid; then in his joy he goes and sells all that he has and buys that field.

Just so, I tell you, there will be more joy in heaven over one sinner who repents than over ninety-nine righteous persons who need no repentance.

For the kingdom of God is not food and drink but righteousness and peace and joy in the Holy Spirit.

As the Father has loved me, so I have loved you; abide in my love.

If you keep my commandments, you will abide in my love, just as I have kept my Father's commandments and abide in his love.

I have said these things to you so that my joy may be in you, and that your joy may be complete.

My brothers and sisters, whenever you face trials of any kind, consider it nothing but joy, because you know that the testing of your faith produces endurance;

And let endurance have its full effect, so that you may be mature and complete, lacking in nothing.

Looking to Jesus the pioneer and perfecter of our faith, who for the sake of the joy that was set before him endured the cross,

Disregarding its shame, and has taken his seat at the right hand of the throne of God.

27. JESUS CHRIST

Old Testament: Isa. 9:6-7, 11:1-3, 53:4-7

New Testament: Jn. 1:29, 13:34-35, 8:12, 11:25-26; 1 Jn. 2:1-2; Phil. 2:9-11

For a child has been born for us, a son given to us; authority rests upon his shoulders; and he is named Wonderful Counselor, Mighty God, Everlasting Father, Prince of Peace.

His authority shall grow continually, and there shall be endless peace for the throne of David and his kingdom.

He will establish and uphold it with justice and with righteousness from this time onward and forevermore. The zeal of the LORD of hosts will do this.

A shoot shall come out from the stump of Jesse, and a branch shall grow out of his roots.

The spirit of the LORD shall rest on him, the spirit of wisdom and understanding, the spirit of counsel and might, the spirit of knowledge and the fear of the LORD.

His delight shall be in the fear of the LORD.

Surely he has borne our infirmities and carried our diseases; yet we accounted him stricken, struck down by God, and afflicted.

But he was wounded for our transgressions, crushed for our iniquities; upon him was the punishment that made us whole, and by his bruises we are healed.

All we like sheep have gone astray; we have all turned to our own way, and the LORD has laid on him the iniquity of us all.

He was oppressed, and he was afflicted, yet he did not open his mouth; like a lamb that is led to the slaughter, and like a sheep that before its shearers is silent, so he did not open his mouth.

He saw Jesus coming toward him and declared, "Here is the Lamb of God who takes away the sin of the world!

I give you a new commandment, that you love one another. Just as I have loved you, you also should love one another.

By this everyone will know that you are my disciples, if you have love for one another."

Again Jesus spoke to them, saying, "I am the light of the world. Whoever follows me will never walk in darkness but will have the light of life."

Jesus said to her, "I am the resurrection and the life. Those who believe in me, even though they die, will live, and everyone who lives and believes in me will never die. Do you believe this?"

My little children, I am writing these things to you so that you may not sin. But if anyone does sin, we have an advocate with the Father,

Jesus Christ the righteous; and he is the atoning sacrifice for our sins, and not for ours only but also for the sins of the whole world.

Therefore God also highly exalted him and gave him the name that is above every name,

So that at the name of Jesus every knee should bend, in heaven and on earth and under the earth, and every tongue should confess that Jesus Christ is Lord,

To the glory of God the Father.

28. JUSTICE

Old Testament: Ps. 89:14, 140:12, 146:5-7; Isa. 56:1, 59:14, 61:8; Am. 5:21-24; Mic. 6:8

New Testament: Lk. 18:7-8, 11:42; Mt. 12:18-21; Rom. 1:16-17, 8:31-33

Righteousness and justice are the foundation of your throne; steadfast love and faithfulness go before you. I know that the LORD maintains the cause of the needy, and executes justice for the poor.

Happy are those whose help is the God of Jacob, whose hope is in the LORD their God, who made heaven and earth, the sea, and all that is in them;

Who keeps faith forever; who executes justice for the oppressed; who gives food to the hungry.

Thus says the LORD: Maintain justice, and do what is right, for soon my salvation will come, and my deliverance be revealed.

Justice is turned back, and righteousness stands at a distance; for truth stumbles in the public square, and uprightness cannot enter.

For I the LORD love justice, I hate robbery and wrongdoing; I will faithfully give them their recompense, and I will make an everlasting covenant with them.

I hate, I despise your festivals, and I take no delight in your solemn assemblies. Even though you offer me your burnt offerings and grain offerings,

I will not accept them; and the offerings of well-being of your fatted animals I will not look upon.

Take away from me the noise of your songs; I will not listen to the melody of your harps. But let justice roll down like waters, and righteousness like an ever-flowing stream.

He has told you, O mortal, what is good; and what does the LORD require of you but to do justice, and to love kindness, and to walk humbly with your God?

And will not God grant justice to his chosen ones who cry to him day and night? Will he delay long in helping them? I tell you, he will quickly grant justice to them.

And yet, when the Son of Man comes, will he find faith on earth?

But woe to you Pharisees! For you tithe mint and rue and herbs of all kinds, and neglect justice and the love of God; it is these you ought to have practiced, without neglecting the others.

Here is my servant, whom I have chosen, my beloved, with whom my soul is well pleased. I will put my Spirit upon him, and he will proclaim justice to the Gentiles.

He will not wrangle or cry aloud, nor will anyone hear his voice in the streets.

He will not break a bruised reed or quench a smoldering wick until he brings justice to victory. And in his name the Gentiles will hope.

For I am not ashamed of the gospel; it is the power of God for salvation to everyone who has faith, to the Jew first and also to the Greek.

For in it the righteousness of God is revealed through faith for faith; as it is written, "The one who is righteous will live by faith."

What then are we to say about these things? If God is for us, who is against us? He who did not withhold his own Son, but gave him up for all of us, will he not with him also give us everything else?

Who will bring any charge against God's elect? It is God who justifies.

29. KINGDOM OF GOD

Old Testament: Isa. 29:18-21, 35:10; Ps. 93:1-2, 99:4-5, 145:11-13

New Testament: Mt. 7:21-23, 13:44-50, 18:1-5; Rom. 14:17

On that day the deaf shall hear the words of a scroll, and out of their gloom and darkness the eyes of the blind shall see.

The meek shall obtain fresh joy in the LORD, and the neediest people shall exult in the Holy One of Israel.

For the tyrant shall be no more, and the scoffer shall cease to be; all those alert to do evil shall be cut off—

Those who cause a person to lose a lawsuit, who set a trap for the arbiter in the gate, and without grounds deny justice to the one in the right.

And the ransomed of the LORD shall return, and come to Zion with singing; everlasting joy shall be upon their heads;

They shall obtain joy and gladness, and sorrow and sighing shall flee away.

The LORD is king, he is robed in majesty; the LORD is robed, he is girded with strength.

He has established the world; it shall never be moved; your throne is established from of old; you are from everlasting.

Mighty King, lover of justice, you have established equity; you have executed justice and righteousness in Jacob.

Extol the LORD our God; worship at his footstool. Holy is he!

They shall speak of the glory of your kingdom, and tell of your power, to make known to all people your mighty deeds, and the glorious splendor of your kingdom.

Your kingdom is an everlasting kingdom, and your dominion endures throughout all generations.

Not everyone who says to me, 'Lord, Lord,' will enter the kingdom of heaven, but only the one who does the will of my Father in heaven. On that day many will say to me, 'Lord, Lord, did we not prophesy in your name, and cast out demons in your name, and do many deeds of power in your name?'

Then I will declare to them, 'I never knew you; go away from me, you evildoers.'

The kingdom of heaven is like treasure hidden in a field, which someone found and hid; then in his joy he goes and sells all that he has and buys that field.

Again, the kingdom of heaven is like a merchant in search of fine pearls; on finding one pearl of great value, he went and sold all that he had and bought it.

Again, the kingdom of heaven is like a net that was thrown into the sea and caught fish of every kind; when it was full, they drew it ashore, sat down, and put the good into baskets but threw out the bad.

So it will be at the end of the age. The angels will come out and separate the evil from the righteous and throw them into the furnace of fire, where there will be weeping and gnashing of teeth.

At that time the disciples came to Jesus and asked, "Who is the greatest in the kingdom of heaven?"

He called a child, whom he put among them, and said, "Truly I tell you, unless you change and become like children, you will never enter the kingdom of heaven.

Whoever becomes humble like this child is the greatest in the kingdom of heaven. Whoever welcomes one such child in my name welcomes me.

For the kingdom of God is not food and drink but righteousness and peace and joy in the Holy Spirit.

30. LIBERATION

Old Testament: Ex. 3:7-10; Lev. 25:13, 18; Isa. 61:1-3; Ps. 18:2

New Testament: Jn. 8:31-32, 36; Rom. 6:17-18; 2 Cor. 3:17; Gal. 5:1, 13; Titus 3:3-5

Then the LORD said, "I have observed the misery of my people who are in Egypt; I have heard their cry on account of their taskmasters.

Indeed, I know their sufferings, and I have come down to deliver them from the Egyptians, and to bring them up out of that land to a good and broad land, a land flowing with milk and honey...

The cry of the Israelites has now come to me; I have also seen how the Egyptians oppress them.

So come, I will send you to Pharaoh to bring my people, the Israelites, out of Egypt."

In this year of jubilee you shall return, every one of you, to your property. You shall observe my statutes and faithfully keep my ordinances, so that you may live on the land securely.

The spirit of the Lord GOD is upon me, because the LORD has anointed me; he has sent me to bring good news to the oppressed,

To bind up the brokenhearted, to proclaim liberty to the captives, and release to the prisoners;

To proclaim the year of the LORD's favor, and the day of vengeance of our God; to comfort all who mourn;

To provide for those who mourn in Zion— to give them a garland instead of ashes, the oil of gladness instead of mourning, the mantle of praise instead of a faint spirit.

The LORD is my rock, my fortress, and my deliverer, my God, my rock in whom I take refuge, my shield, and the horn of my salvation, my stronghold.

Then Jesus said to the Jews who had believed in him, "If you continue in my word, you are truly my disciples; and you will know the truth, and the truth will make you free."

So if the Son makes you free, you will be free indeed.

But thanks be to God that you, having once been slaves of sin, have become obedient from the heart to the form of teaching to which you were entrusted, and that you, having been set free from sin, have become slaves of righteousness.

Now the Lord is the Spirit, and where the Spirit of the Lord is, there is freedom.

For freedom Christ has set us free. Stand firm, therefore, and do not submit again to a yoke of slavery.

For you were called to freedom, brothers and sisters; only do not use your freedom as an opportunity for self-indulgence, but through love become slaves to one another.

For we ourselves were once foolish, disobedient, led astray, slaves to various passions and pleasures, passing our days in malice and envy, despicable, hating one another.

But when the goodness and loving kindness of God our Savior appeared, he saved us, not because of any works of righteousness that we had done, but according to his mercy, through the water of rebirth and renewal by the Holy Spirit.

31. LOVE

Old Testament: Deut. 6:5-7; Ps. 136:1, 116:1-2, 100:4-5; Song 4:1, 8:6-7

New Testament: Jn. 3:16, 15:12-13; Col. 3:13-14; 1 Cor. 13:1-8, 13

You shall love the LORD your God with all your heart, and with all your soul, and with all your might.

Keep these words that I am commanding you today in your heart.

Recite them to your children and talk about them when you are at home and when you are away, when you lie down and when you rise.

O give thanks to the LORD, for he is good, for his steadfast love endures forever.

I love the LORD, because he has heard my voice and my supplications. Because he inclined his ear to me, therefore I will call on him as long as I live.

Enter his gates with thanksgiving, and his courts with praise. Give thanks to him, bless his name.

For the LORD is good; his steadfast love endures forever, and his faithfulness to all generations.

How beautiful you are, my love, how very beautiful!

Your eyes are doves behind your veil. Your hair is like a flock of goats, moving down the slopes of Gilead.

Set me as a seal upon your heart, as a seal upon your arm;

For love is strong as death, passion fierce as the grave. Its flashes are flashes of fire, a raging flame.

Many waters cannot quench love, neither can floods drown it.

For God so loved the world that he gave his only Son, so that everyone who believes in him may not perish but may have eternal life.

This is my commandment, that you love one another as I have loved you. No one has greater love than this, to lay down one's life for one's friends.

Bear with one another and, if anyone has a complaint against another, forgive each other; just as the Lord has forgiven you, so you also must forgive.

Above all, clothe yourselves with love, which binds everything together in perfect harmony.

If I speak in the tongues of mortals and of angels, but do not have love, I am a noisy gong or a clanging cymbal.

And if I have prophetic powers, and understand all mysteries and all knowledge, and if I have all faith, so as to remove mountains, but do not have love, I am nothing.

If I give away all my possessions, and if I hand over my body so that I may boast, but do not have love, I gain nothing.

Love is patient; love is kind; love is not envious or boastful or arrogant or rude. It does not insist on its own way; it is not irritable or resentful;

It does not rejoice in wrongdoing, but rejoices in the truth. It bears all things, believes all things, hopes all things, endures all things.

Love never ends. And now faith, hope, and love abide, these three; and the greatest of these is love.

32. MARRIAGE

Old Testament: Gen. 2:18, 23-24, 24:64-67, 25:20-21, 29:18-20

New Testament: Mt. 19:7-9; Heb. 13:1, 4; Eph. 5:22, 25-33

Then the LORD God said, "It is not good that the man should be alone; I will make him a helper as his partner." Then the man said, "This at last is bone of my bones and flesh of my flesh;

This one shall be called Woman, for out of Man this one was taken." Therefore a man leaves his father and his mother and clings to his wife, and they become one flesh.

And Rebekah looked up, and when she saw Isaac, she slipped quickly from the camel, and said to the servant, "Who is the man over there, walking in the field to meet us?" The servant said, "It is my master."

So she took her veil and covered herself. And the servant told Isaac all the things that he had done.

Then Isaac brought her into his mother Sarah's tent. He took Rebekah, and she became his wife; and he loved her. So Isaac was comforted after his mother's death. And Isaac was forty years old when he married Rebekah.

Isaac prayed to the LORD for his wife, because she was barren; and the LORD granted his prayer, and his wife Rebekah conceived.

Jacob loved Rachel; so he said, "I will serve you seven years for your younger daughter Rachel." Laban said, "It is better that I give her to you than that I should give her to any other man; stay with me."

So Jacob served seven years for Rachel, and they seemed to him but a few days because of the love he had for her.

They said to Jesus, "Why then did Moses command us to give a certificate of dismissal and to divorce her?"

He said to them, "It was because you were so hard-hearted that Moses allowed you to divorce your wives, but from the beginning it was not so.

And I say to you, whoever divorces his wife, except for unchastity, and marries another commits adultery."

Let mutual love continue. Let marriage be held in honor by all, and let the marriage bed be kept undefiled; for God will judge fornicators and adulterers.

Wives, be subject to your husbands as you are to the Lord. Husbands, love your wives, just as Christ loved the church and gave himself up for her,

In order to make her holy by cleansing her with the washing of water by the word,

So as to present the church to himself in splendor, without a spot or wrinkle or anything of the kind—yes, so that she may be holy and without blemish.

In the same way, husbands should love their wives as they do their own bodies. He who loves his wife loves himself.

For no one ever hates his own body, but he nourishes and tenderly cares for it, just as Christ does for the church, because we are members of his body.

For this reason a man will leave his father and mother and be joined to his wife, and the two will become one flesh.

This is a great mystery, and I am applying it to Christ and the church.

Each of you, however, should love his wife as himself, and a wife should respect her husband.

33. MERCY

Old Testament: Lam. 3:22-23; Ps. 145:8-9, 85:10; Prov. 3:3-4; Ps 103:8; Mic. 6:8; Ps. 100:5

The steadfast love of the LORD never ceases, his mercies never come to an end; they are new every morning; great is your faithfulness.

The LORD is gracious and merciful, slow to anger and abounding in steadfast love. The LORD is good to all, and his compassion is over all that he has made.

Steadfast love and faithfulness will meet; righteousness and peace will kiss each other.

Do not let loyalty and faithfulness forsake you; bind them around your neck, write them on the tablet of your heart.

So you will find favor and good repute in the sight of God and of people.

The LORD is merciful and gracious, slow to anger and abounding in steadfast love.

He has told you, O mortal, what is good; and what does the LORD require of you but to do justice, and to love kindness, and to walk humbly with your God?

For the LORD is good; his steadfast love endures forever, and his faithfulness to all generations.

New Testament: Mt. 5:7; Eph. 2:4-6; Titus 3:5; Rom. 9:16-18; Lk. 1:50; 1 Pet. 2:10; Jude 21-23; Lk. 6:36

Blessed are the merciful, for they will receive mercy.

God, who is rich in mercy, out of the great love with which he loved us even when we were dead through our trespasses, made us alive together with Christ—

By grace you have been saved—and raised us up with him and seated us with him in the heavenly places in Christ Jesus.

He saved us, not because of any works of righteousness that we had done, but according to his mercy, through the water of rebirth and renewal by the Holy Spirit.

So it depends not on human will or exertion, but on God who shows mercy.

For the scripture says to Pharaoh, "I have raised you up for the very purpose of showing my power in you, so that my name may be proclaimed in all the earth."

So then he has mercy on whomever he chooses, and he hardens the heart of whomever he chooses.

His mercy is for those who fear him from generation to generation.

Once you were not a people, but now you are God's people; once you had not received mercy, but now you have received mercy.

Keep yourselves in the love of God; look forward to the mercy of our Lord Jesus Christ that leads to eternal life.

And have mercy on some who are wavering; save others by snatching them out of the fire; and have mercy on still others with fear, hating even the tunic defiled by their bodies.

Be merciful, just as your Father is merciful.

34. MISSION

Old Testament: Gen. 12:1-3; Isa. 60:1-5, 58:7-9

New Testament: 1 Pet. 2:9, Lk. 9:1-2, 6; 10:17-20, Titus 2:11-12, Mt. 28:19-20

Now the LORD said to Abram, "Go from your country and your kindred and your father's house to the land that I will show you. I will make of you a great nation, and I will bless you, and make your name great, so that you will be a blessing.

But you are a chosen race, a royal priesthood, a holy nation, God's own people, in order that you may proclaim the mighty acts of him who called you out of darkness into his marvelous light.

I will bless those who bless you, and the one who curses you I will curse; and in you all the families of the earth shall be blessed."

Then Jesus called the twelve together and gave them power and authority over all demons and to cure diseases, and he sent them out to proclaim the kingdom of God and to heal.

Arise, shine; for your light has come, and the glory of the LORD has risen upon you.

They departed and went through the villages, bringing the good news and curing diseases everywhere.

For darkness shall cover the earth, and thick darkness the peoples; but the LORD will arise upon you, and his glory will appear over you.

The seventy returned with joy, saying, "Lord, in your name even the demons submit to us!" He said to them, "I watched Satan fall from heaven like a flash of lightning. See, I have given you authority to tread on snakes and scorpions, and over all the power of the enemy; and nothing will hurt you.

Nations shall come to your light, and kings to the brightness of your dawn.

Lift up your eyes and look around; they all gather together, they come to you; your sons shall come from far away, and your daughters shall be carried on their nurses' arms.

Nevertheless, do not rejoice at this, that the spirits submit to you, but rejoice that your names are written in heaven."

Then you shall see and be radiant; your heart shall thrill and rejoice, because the abundance of the sea shall be brought to you, the wealth of the nations shall come to you.

For the grace of God has appeared, bringing salvation to all, training us to renounce impiety and worldly passions, and in the present age to live lives that are self-controlled, upright, and godly.

Is it not to share your bread with the hungry, and bring the homeless poor into your house; when you see the naked, to cover them, and not to hide yourself from your own kin?

Go therefore and make disciples of all nations, baptizing them in the name of the Father and of the Son and of the Holy Spirit,

Then your light shall break forth like the dawn, and your healing shall spring up quickly; your vindicator shall go before you, the glory of the LORD shall be your rear guard.

And teaching them to obey everything that I have commanded you. And remember, I am with you always, to the end of the age.

Then you shall call, and the LORD will answer, you shall cry for help, and he will say, Here I am.

35. OBEDIENCE

Old Testament: Deut. 11:1, 26-28; Josh. 24:24; 1 Sam. 15:22-23; Isa. 1:18-20; Jer. 38:20

New Testament: Heb. 5;7-9, Acts 5:29-32, Jn. 3:36, 1 Pet. 1:14-15, Phil. 2:8-11

You shall love the LORD your God, therefore, and keep his charge, his decrees, his ordinances, and his commandments always.

See, I am setting before you today a blessing and a curse: the blessing, if you obey the commandments of the LORD your God that I am commanding you today;

And the curse, if you do not obey the commandments of the LORD your God.

The people said to Joshua, "The LORD our God we will serve, and him we will obey."

And Samuel said, "Has the LORD as great delight in burnt offerings and sacrifices, as in obeying the voice of the LORD? Surely, to obey is better than sacrifice, and to heed than the fat of rams.

For rebellion is no less a sin than divination, and stubbornness is like iniquity and idolatry.

Because you have rejected the word of the LORD, he has also rejected you from being king."

Come now, let us argue it out, says the LORD: though your sins are like scarlet, they shall be like snow; though they are red like crimson, they shall become like wool.

If you are willing and obedient, you shall eat the good of the land; but if you refuse and rebel, you shall be devoured by the sword.

Just obey the voice of the LORD in what I say to you, and it shall go well with you, and your life shall be spared.

In the days of his flesh, Jesus offered up prayers and supplications, with loud cries and tears, to the one who was able to save him from death, and he was heard because of his reverent submission.

Although he was a Son, he learned obedience through what he suffered; and having been made perfect, he became the source of eternal salvation for all who obey him,

But Peter and the apostles answered, "We must obey God rather than any human authority. The God of our ancestors raised up Jesus, whom you had killed by hanging him on a tree.

God exalted him at his right hand as Leader and Savior that he might give repentance to Israel and forgiveness of sins. And we are witnesses to these things, and so is the Holy Spirit whom God has given to those who obey him."

Whoever believes in the Son has eternal life; whoever disobeys the Son will not see life, but must endure God's wrath.

Like obedient children, do not be conformed to the desires that you formerly had in ignorance. Instead, as he who called you is holy, be holy yourselves in all your conduct.

He humbled himself and became obedient to the point of death—even death on a cross.

Therefore God also highly exalted him and gave him the name that is above every name,

So that at the name of Jesus every knee should bend, in heaven and on earth and under the earth, and every tongue should confess that Jesus Christ is Lord,

To the glory of God the Father.

36. PATIENCE

Old Testament: Ps. 62:1-2; Eccl. 7:8-9; Ps. 37:7-9, 40:1-3, 27:13-14

New Testament: Gal. 5:22-23; Rom. 5:3-5; 1 Thess. 5:14; Jas. 5:7-11

For God alone my soul waits in silence; from him comes my salvation.

He alone is my rock and my salvation, my fortress; I shall never be shaken.

Better is the end of a thing than its beginning; the patient in spirit are better than the proud in spirit.

Do not be quick to anger, for anger lodges in the bosom of fools.

Be still before the LORD, and wait patiently for him; do not fret over those who prosper in their way, over those who carry out evil devices.

Refrain from anger, and forsake wrath. Do not fret—it leads only to evil.

For the wicked shall be cut off,

But those who wait for the LORD shall inherit the land.

I waited patiently for the LORD; he inclined to me and heard my cry. He drew me up from the desolate pit, out of the miry bog, and set my feet upon a rock, making my steps secure.

He put a new song in my mouth, a song of praise to our God. Many will see and fear, and put their trust in the LORD.

I believe that I shall see the goodness of the LORD in the land of the living.

Wait for the LORD; be strong, and let your heart take courage; wait for the LORD!

The fruit of the Spirit is love, joy, peace, patience, kindness, generosity, faithfulness, gentleness, and self-control.

And not only that, but we also boast in our sufferings, knowing that suffering produces endurance, and endurance produces character, and character produces hope,

And hope does not disappoint us, because God's love has been poured into our hearts through the Holy Spirit that has been given to us.

And we urge you, beloved, to admonish the idlers, encourage the faint hearted, help the weak, be patient with all of them.

Be patient, therefore, beloved, until the coming of the Lord.

The farmer waits for the precious crop from the earth, being patient with it until it receives the early and the late rains.

You also must be patient. Strengthen your hearts, for the coming of the Lord is near.

Beloved, do not grumble against one another, so that you may not be judged. See, the Judge is standing at the doors!

As an example of suffering and patience, beloved, take the prophets who spoke in the name of the Lord. Indeed we call blessed those who showed endurance.

You have heard of the endurance of Job, and you have seen the purpose of the Lord, how the Lord is compassionate and merciful.

37. PEACE

Old Testament: Ps. 85:8-10; Isa. 52:7; Ps. 119:164-165; Prov. 16:7-9; 1 Kings 5:4-5; Isa. 32:18

New Testament: Jn. 14:27; Mt. 5:9; Eph. 2:13-15; Col. 3:15; Heb. 12:14-15; 2 Thess. 3:16

Let me hear what God the LORD will speak, for he will speak peace to his people, to his faithful, to those who turn to him in their hearts.

Surely his salvation is at hand for those who fear him, that his glory may dwell in our land.

Steadfast love and faithfulness will meet; righteousness and peace will kiss each other.

How beautiful upon the mountains are the feet of the messenger who announces peace, who brings good news, who announces salvation, who says to Zion, "Your God reigns."

Seven times a day I praise you for your righteous ordinances.

Great peace have those who love your law; nothing can make them stumble.

When the ways of people please the LORD, he causes even their enemies to be at peace with them.

Better is a little with righteousness than large income with injustice.

The human mind plans the way, but the LORD directs the steps.

But now the LORD my God has given me rest on every side; there is neither adversary nor misfortune.

So I intend to build a house for the name of the LORD my God.

My people will abide in a peaceful habitation, in secure dwellings, and in quiet resting places.

Peace I leave with you; my peace I give to you. I do not give to you as the world gives. Do not let your hearts be troubled, and do not let them be afraid.

Blessed are the peacemakers, for they will be called children of God.

But now in Christ Jesus you who once were far off have been brought near by the blood of Christ.

For he is our peace; in his flesh he has made both groups into one and has broken down the dividing wall, that is, the hostility between us.

He has abolished the law with its commandments and ordinances, that he might create in himself one new humanity in place of the two, thus making peace.

And let the peace of Christ rule in your hearts, to which indeed you were called in the one body. And be thankful.

Pursue peace with everyone, and the holiness without which no one will see the Lord.

See to it that no one fails to obtain the grace of God; that no root of bitterness springs up and causes trouble, and through it many become defiled.

Now may the Lord of peace himself give you peace at all times in all ways.

The Lord be with all of you.

38. POWER

Old Testament: Ex. 15:2, 11, 17-18; Deut. 8:18; Jer. 10:12-13; Isa. 40:12, 29

New Testament: 1 Cor. 1:18, 22-25; Rom. 1:20; Col. 1:15-18; Acts 1:8

The LORD is my strength and my might, and he has become my salvation; this is my God, and I will praise him, my father's God, and I will exalt him.

Who is like you, O LORD, among the gods? Who is like you, majestic in holiness, awesome in splendor, doing wonders?

You brought them in and planted them on the mountain of your own possession,

The place, O LORD, that you made your abode, the sanctuary, O LORD, that your hands have established.

The LORD will reign forever and ever.

But remember the LORD your God, for it is he who gives you power to get wealth, so that he may confirm his covenant that he swore to your ancestors, as he is doing today.

It is he who made the earth by his power, who established the world by his wisdom, and by his understanding stretched out the heavens.

When he utters his voice, there is a tumult of waters in the heavens, and he makes the mist rise from the ends of the earth.

He makes lightnings for the rain, and he brings out the wind from his storehouses.

Who has measured the waters in the hollow of his hand and marked off the heavens with a span, enclosed the dust of the earth in a measure,

And weighed the mountains in scales and the hills in a balance?

He gives power to the faint, and strengthens the powerless.

For the message about the cross is foolishness to those who are perishing, but to us who are being saved it is the power of God.

For Jews demand signs and Greeks desire wisdom, but we proclaim Christ crucified, a stumbling block to Jews and foolishness to Gentiles,

But to those who are the called, both Jews and Greeks, Christ the power of God and the wisdom of God. For God's foolishness is wiser than human wisdom, and God's weakness is stronger than human strength.

Ever since the creation of the world his eternal power and divine nature, invisible though they are, have been understood and seen through the things he has made.

He is the image of the invisible God, the firstborn of all creation; for in him all things in heaven and on earth were created,

Things visible and invisible, whether thrones or dominions or rulers or powers—all things have been created through him and for him.

He himself is before all things, and in him all things hold together. He is the head of the body, the church; he is the beginning, the firstborn from the dead, so that he might come to have first place in everything.

But you will receive power when the Holy Spirit has come upon you; and you will be my witnesses in Jerusalem, in all Judea and Samaria, and to the ends of the earth.

39. PRAISE

Old Testament: Ps. 146:1-2; 2 Chr. 5:13-14; Ps. 34:1-3, 150

New Testament: Phil. 4:4-7; Rom. 15:8-11; Heb. 13:15-16; Rev. 19:1, 6

Praise the LORD! Praise the LORD, O my soul! I will praise the LORD as long as I live;

I will sing praises to my God all my life long.

It was the duty of the trumpeters and singers to make themselves heard in unison in praise and thanksgiving to the LORD, and when the song was raised,

With trumpets and cymbals and other musical instruments, in praise to the LORD, "For he is good, for his steadfast love endures forever,"

The house, the house of the LORD, was filled with a cloud, so that the priests could not stand to minister because of the cloud; for the glory of the LORD filled the house of God.

I will bless the LORD at all times; his praise shall continually be in my mouth.

My soul makes its boast in the LORD; let the humble hear and be glad.

O magnify the LORD with me, and let us exalt his name together.

Praise the LORD! Praise God in his sanctuary; praise him in his mighty firmament!

Praise him for his mighty deeds; praise him according to his surpassing greatness!

Praise him with trumpet sound; praise him with lute and harp!

Praise him with tambourine and dance; praise him with strings and pipe!

Praise him with clanging cymbals; praise him with loud clashing cymbals!

Let everything that breathes praise the LORD! Praise the LORD!

Rejoice in the Lord always; again I will say, Rejoice. Let your gentleness be known to everyone. The Lord is near.

Do not worry about anything, but in everything by prayer and supplication with thanksgiving let your requests be made known to God.

And the peace of God, which surpasses all understanding, will guard your hearts and your minds in Christ Jesus.

For I tell you that Christ has become a servant of the circumcised on behalf of the truth of God in order that he might confirm the promises given to the patriarchs,

And in order that the Gentiles might glorify God for his mercy. As it is written,

"Therefore I will confess you among the Gentiles, and sing praises to your name";

And again he says, "Rejoice, O Gentiles, with his people"; and again, "Praise the Lord, all you Gentiles, and let all the peoples praise him".

Through him, then, let us continually offer a sacrifice of praise to God, that is, the fruit of lips that confess his name.

Do not neglect to do good and to share what you have, for such sacrifices are pleasing to God.

After this I heard what seemed to be the loud voice of a great multitude in heaven, saying, "Hallelujah! Salvation and glory and power to our God."

Then I heard what seemed to be the voice of a great multitude, like the sound of many waters and like the sound of mighty thunderpeals, crying out,

"Hallelujah! For the Lord our God the Almighty reigns."

40. PRAYER

Old Testament: Ps. 39:12; 2 Chr. 7:14; 1 Sam. 12:19, 23, 7:9; Job 42:8-9; 1 Kings 8:22-23; Ps. 66:18-19; Prov. 15:29

Hear my prayer, O LORD, and give ear to my cry; do not hold your peace at my tears.

If my people who are called by my name humble themselves, pray, seek my face, and turn from their wicked ways, then I will hear from heaven, and will forgive their sin and heal their land.

All the people said to Samuel, "Pray to the LORD your God for your servants, so that we may not die; for we have added to all our sins the evil of demanding a king for ourselves."

And Samuel answered, "Far be it from me that I should sin against the LORD by ceasing to pray for you; and I will instruct you in the good and the right way."

Samuel cried out to the LORD for Israel, and the LORD answered him.

Now therefore take seven bulls and seven rams, and go to my servant Job, and offer up for yourselves a burnt offering; and my servant Job shall pray for you, for I will accept his prayer not to deal with you according to your folly; for you have not spoken of me what is right, as my servant Job has done.

So Eliphaz the Temanite and Bildad the Shuhite and Zophar the Naamathite went and did what the LORD had told them; and the LORD accepted Job's prayer.

Then Solomon stood before the altar of the LORD in the presence of all the assembly of Israel, and spread out his hands to heaven.

He said, "O LORD, God of Israel, there is no God like you in heaven above or on earth beneath, keeping covenant and steadfast love for your servants who walk before you with all their heart."

If I had cherished iniquity in my heart, the Lord would not have listened.

But truly God has listened; he has given heed to the words of my prayer.

The LORD is far from the wicked, but he hears the prayer of the righteous.

New Testament: 1 Thess. 5:16-18; Mt. 21:22; Jas. 5:16; Lk. 18:7-8; Mt. 6:6-13

Rejoice always, pray without ceasing, give thanks in all circumstances; for this is the will of God in Christ Jesus for you.

Whatever you ask for in prayer with faith, you will receive.

Therefore confess your sins to one another, and pray for one another, so that you may be healed. The prayer of the righteous is powerful and effective.

And will not God grant justice to his chosen ones who cry to him day and night? Will he delay long in helping them? I tell you, he will quickly grant justice to them. And yet, when the Son of Man comes, will he find faith on earth?

But whenever you pray, go into your room and shut the door and pray to your Father who is in secret; and your Father who sees in secret will reward you.

When you are praying, do not heap up empty phrases as the Gentiles do; for they think that they will be heard because of their many words. Do not be like them, for your Father knows what you need before you ask him.

Pray then in this way:

Our Father in heaven, hallowed be your name. Your kingdom come. Your will be done, on earth as it is in heaven. Give us this day our daily bread. And forgive us our debts, as we also have forgiven our debtors. And do not bring us to the time of trial, but rescue us from the evil one.

41. PRESENCE OF GOD

Old Testament: Ps. 139:7-10, 51:11; Ex. 13:21-22, 19:4; Deut. 31:8; Ps. 16:11; Isa. 6:1, 5; Ps. 15:1-2

Where can I go from your spirit? Or where can I flee from your presence?

If I ascend to heaven, you are there; if I make my bed in Sheol, you are there.

If I take the wings of the morning and settle at the farthest limits of the sea, even there your hand shall lead me, and your right hand shall hold me fast.

Do not cast me away from your presence, and do not take your holy spirit from me.

The LORD went in front of them in a pillar of cloud by day, to lead them along the way, and in a pillar of fire by night, to give them light, so that they might travel by day and by night.

Neither the pillar of cloud by day nor the pillar of fire by night left its place in front of the people.

You have seen what I did to the Egyptians, and how I bore you on eagles' wings and brought you to myself. It is the LORD who goes before you. He will be with you; he will not fail you or forsake you. Do not fear or be dismayed.

You show me the path of life. In your presence there is fullness of joy; in your right hand are pleasures forevermore.

In the year that King Uzziah died, I saw the Lord sitting on a throne, high and lofty; and the hem of his robe filled the temple.

And I said: "Woe is me! I am lost, for I am a man of unclean lips, and I live among a people of unclean lips; yet my eyes have seen the King, the LORD of hosts!"

O LORD, who may abide in your tent? Who may dwell on your holy hill?

Those who walk blamelessly, and do what is right, and speak the truth from their heart.

New Testament: Jn. 1:1-2, 14, 8:28-29; Acts 17:26-28; Rom. 8:9; 1 Cor. 3:16; Eph. 2:21-22

In the beginning was the Word, and the Word was with God, and the Word was God. He was in the beginning with God.

And the Word became flesh and lived among us, and we have seen his glory, the glory as of a father's only son, full of grace and truth.

So Jesus said, "When you have lifted up the Son of Man, then you will realize that I am he, and that I do nothing on my own,

But I speak these things as the Father instructed me. And the one who sent me is with me; he has not left me alone, for I always do what is pleasing to him."

From one ancestor he made all nations to inhabit the whole earth, and he allotted the times of their existence and the boundaries of the places where they would live,

So that they would search for God and perhaps grope for him and find him — though indeed he is not far from each one of us.

For 'in him we live and move and have our being'.

But you are not in the flesh; you are in the Spirit, since the Spirit of God dwells in you.

Do you not know that you are God's temple and that God's Spirit dwells in you?

In him the whole structure is joined together and grows into a holy temple in the Lord; in whom you also are built together spiritually into a dwelling place for God.

42. PROMISES OF GOD

Old Testament: Gen. 28:13-15; 2 Chr. 7:14; Ps. 91:9-11; Ezek. 34:27-28; Isa. 25:7-8; Num. 23:19

New Testament: Heb. 4:1, 9-10; Acts 2:15-17, 38-39; Jn. 14:1-3; Rev. 22:2

I am the LORD, the God of Abraham your father and the God of Isaac;

The land on which you lie I will give to you and to your offspring;

And your offspring shall be like the dust of the earth, and you shall spread abroad to the west and to the east and to the north and to the south;

Know that I am with you and will keep you wherever you go, and will bring you back to this land; for I will not leave you until I have done what I have promised you.

If my people who are called by my name humble themselves, pray, seek my face, and turn from their wicked ways, then I will hear from heaven, and will forgive their sin and heal their land.

Because you have made the LORD your refuge, the Most High your dwelling place, no evil shall befall you, no scourge come near your tent.

For he will command his angels concerning you to guard you in all your ways.

They shall know that I am the LORD, when I break the bars of their yoke,

And save them from the hands of those who enslaved them. They shall live in safety, and no one shall make them afraid.

And he will destroy on this mountain the shroud that is cast over all peoples, he will swallow up death forever.

Then the Lord GOD will wipe away the tears from all faces, and the disgrace of his people he will take away from all the earth, for the LORD has spoken.

God is not a human being, that he should lie, or a mortal, that he should change his mind. Has he promised, and will he not do it?

Therefore, while the promise of entering his rest is still open, let us take care that none of you should seem to have failed to reach it.

So then, a sabbath rest still remains for the people of God; for those who enter God's rest also cease from their labors as God did from his.

Indeed, these are not drunk, as you suppose, for it is only nine o'clock in the morning. No, this is what was spoken through the prophet Joel:

'In the last days it will be, God declares, that I will pour out my Spirit upon all flesh, and your sons and your daughters shall prophesy, and your young men shall see visions, and your old men shall dream dreams.'

Peter said to them, "Repent, and be baptized every one of you in the name of Jesus Christ so that your sins may be forgiven; and you will receive the gift of the Holy Spirit.

For the promise is for you, for your children, and for all who are far away, everyone whom the Lord our God calls to him."

Do not let your hearts be troubled. Believe in God, believe also in me. In my Father's house there are many dwelling places.

If it were not so, would I have told you that I go to prepare a place for you?

And if I go and prepare a place for you, I will come again and will take you to myself, so that where I am, there you may be also.

On either side of the river is the tree of life with its twelve kinds of fruit, producing its fruit each month; and the leaves of the tree are for the healing of the nations.

43. RECONCILIATION

Old Testament: Gen. 27:41, 28:1, 3, 5, 31:41, 42, 32:3-7, 33:1, 3, 4

New Testament: Mt. 18:21-22, 5:23-24, 6:14-15; Eph. 4:31-32; 2 Cor. 5:18-20; Col. 1:19-21

Now Esau hated Jacob because of the blessing with which his father had blessed him

And Esau said to himself, "...I will kill my brother Jacob."

Then Isaac called Jacob and blessed him, and charged him, "...Go at once to Paddan-aram to the house of Bethuel...and take as wife from there one of the daughters of Laban... May God Almighty bless you and make you fruitful and numerous... May he give to you the blessing of Abraham, to you and to your offspring..."

Thus Isaac sent Jacob away; and he went to Paddan-aram.

Jacob said to Laban, "...These twenty years I have been in your house; I served you fourteen years for your two daughters, and six years for your flock...

God saw my affliction and the labor of my hands..."

Jacob sent messengers before him to his brother Esau... instructing them, "Thus you shall say to my lord Esau: Thus says your servant Jacob, 'I have lived with Laban as an alien, and stayed until now; and I have oxen, donkeys, flocks, male and female slaves; ...in order that I may find favor in your sight.' "

The messengers returned to Jacob, saying, "We came to your brother Esau, and he is coming to meet you, and four hundred men are with him." Then Jacob was greatly afraid and distressed.

Now Jacob looked up and saw Esau coming, and four hundred men with him... He himself went on ahead of them, bowing himself to the ground seven times, until he came near his brother.

But Esau ran to meet him, and embraced him, and fell on his neck and kissed him, and they wept.

Then Peter came and said to him, "Lord, if another member of the church sins against me, how often should I forgive? As many as seven times?"

Jesus said to him, "Not seven times, but, I tell you, seventy-seven times.

So when you are offering your gift at the altar, if you remember that your brother or sister has something against you,

Leave your gift there before the altar and go; first be reconciled to your brother or sister, and then come and offer your gift.

For if you forgive others their trespasses, your heavenly Father will also forgive you;

But if you do not forgive others, neither will your Father forgive your trespasses."

Put away from you all bitterness and wrath and anger and wrangling and slander, together with all malice, and be kind to one another,

Tenderhearted, forgiving one another, as God in Christ has forgiven you.

All this is from God, who reconciled us to himself through Christ, and has given us the ministry of reconciliation;

That is, in Christ God was reconciling the world to himself, not counting their trespasses against them, and entrusting the message of reconciliation to us.

So we are ambassadors for Christ, since God is making his appeal through us; we entreat you on behalf of Christ, be reconciled to God.

For in him all the fullness of God was pleased to dwell, and through him God was pleased to reconcile to himself all things... by making peace through the blood of his cross.

44. REPENTANCE

Old Testament: Ps. 51:1-4, 6, 9-13; Ezek. 18:27-28

Have mercy on me, O God, according to your steadfast love; according to your abundant mercy blot out my transgressions.

Wash me thoroughly from my iniquity, and cleanse me from my sin.

For I know my transgressions, and my sin is ever before me.

Against you, you alone, have I sinned, and done what is evil in your sight, so that you are justified in your sentence and blameless when you pass judgment.

You desire truth in the inward being; therefore teach me wisdom in my secret heart.

Hide your face from my sins, and blot out all my iniquities.

Create in me a clean heart, O God, and put a new and right spirit within me.

Do not cast me away from your presence, and do not take your holy spirit from me.

Restore to me the joy of your salvation, and sustain in me a willing spirit.

Then I will teach transgressors your ways, and sinners will return to you.

Again, when the wicked turn away from the wickedness they have committed and do what is lawful and right, they shall save their life.

Because they considered and turned away from all the transgressions that they had committed, they shall surely live; they shall not die.

New Testament: Mt. 3:2; Jn. 3:3; Lk. 5:30-32, 15:10; Acts 5:31-32; 2 Pet. 3:9; Lk. 24:44-48

Repent, for the kingdom of heaven has come near.

Jesus answered him, "Very truly, I tell you, no one can see the kingdom of God without being born from above."

The Pharisees and their scribes were complaining to his disciples, saying, "Why do you eat and drink with tax collectors and sinners?" Jesus answered, "Those who are well have no need of a physician, but those who are sick;

I have come to call not the righteous but sinners to repentance."

Just so, I tell you, there is joy in the presence of the angels of God over one sinner who repents.

God exalted him at his right hand as Leader and Savior that he might give repentance to Israel and forgiveness of sins. And we are witnesses to these things, and so is the Holy Spirit whom God has given to those who obey him.

The Lord is not slow about his promise, as some think of slowness, but is patient with you, not wanting any to perish, but all to come to repentance.

Then he said to them, "These are my words that I spoke to you while I was still with you—that everything written about me in the law of Moses, the prophets, and the psalms must be fulfilled."

Then he opened their minds to understand the scriptures, and he said to them, "Thus it is written, that the Messiah is to suffer and to rise from the dead on the third day,

And that repentance and forgiveness of sins is to be proclaimed in his name to all nations, beginning from Jerusalem. You are witnesses of these things."

45. SALVATION

Old Testament: Ps. 27:1, 95:1; Isa. 55:1-2, 6-7;
Hos. 13:4; Isa. 35:4; 2 Chr. 20:17

The LORD is my light and my salvation; whom shall I fear? The LORD is the stronghold of my life; of whom shall I be afraid?

O come, let us sing to the LORD; let us make a joyful noise to the rock of our salvation!

Ho, everyone who thirsts, come to the waters; and you that have no money, come, buy and eat! Come, buy wine and milk without money and without price.

Why do you spend your money for that which is not bread, and your labor for that which does not satisfy?

Seek the LORD while he may be found, call upon him while he is near; let the wicked forsake their way, and the unrighteous their thoughts;

Let them return to the LORD, that he may have mercy on them, and to our God, for he will abundantly pardon.

Yet I have been the LORD your God ever since the land of Egypt; you know no God but me, and besides me there is no savior.

Say to those who are of a fearful heart, "Be strong, do not fear! Here is your God. He will come with vengeance, with terrible recompense. He will come and save you."

This battle is not for you to fight; take your position, stand still, and see the victory of the LORD on your behalf, O Judah and Jerusalem.

Do not fear or be dismayed; tomorrow go out against them, and the LORD will be with you.

New Testament: Lk. 2:11; Jn. 3:16-17; Acts 4:12;
Rom. 1:16, 5:10, 10:13; 1 Tim. 4:10; 2 Cor. 6:2;
Jude 25

To you is born this day in the city of David a Savior, who is the Messiah, the Lord.

For God so loved the world that he gave his only Son, so that everyone who believes in him may not perish but may have eternal life.

Indeed, God did not send the Son into the world to condemn the world, but in order that the world might be saved through him.

There is salvation in no one else, for there is no other name under heaven given among mortals by which we must be saved.

For I am not ashamed of the gospel; it is the power of God for salvation to everyone who has faith, to the Jew first and also to the Greek.

For if while we were enemies, we were reconciled to God through the death of his Son, much more surely, having been reconciled, will we be saved by his life.

For, "Everyone who calls on the name of the Lord shall be saved."

For to this end we toil and struggle, because we have our hope set on the living God, who is the Savior of all people, especially of those who believe.

See, now is the acceptable time; see, now is the day of salvation!

To the only God our Savior, through Jesus Christ our Lord, be glory, majesty, power, and authority, before all time and now and forever. Amen.

46. SANCTIFICATION

Old Testament: Ps. 15:1-5; Ex. 19:5-6, 31:13; Ps. 24:3-4; Lev. 20:7-8

New Testament: 1 Thess. 4:3-5; 2 Thess. 2:13; 2 Cor. 6:14-18, 7:1

O LORD, who may abide in your tent? Who may dwell on your holy hill?

Those who walk blamelessly, and do what is right, and speak the truth from their heart;

Who do not slander with their tongue, and do no evil to their friends,

Nor take up a reproach against their neighbors; in whose eyes the wicked are despised, but who honor those who fear the LORD;

Who stand by their oath even to their hurt, who do not lend money at interest, and do not take a bribe against the innocent.

Those who do these things shall never be moved.

If you obey my voice and keep my covenant, you shall be my treasured possession out of all the peoples.

Indeed, the whole earth is mine, but you shall be for me a priestly kingdom and a holy nation.

You shall keep my sabbaths, for this is a sign between me and you throughout your generations, that you may know that I, the LORD, sanctify you.

Who shall ascend the hill of the LORD? And who shall stand in his holy place?

Those who have clean hands and pure hearts,

Who do not lift up their souls to what is false, and do not swear deceitfully.

Consecrate yourselves therefore, and be holy; for I am the LORD your God.

Keep my statutes, and observe them; I am the LORD; I sanctify you.

For this is the will of God, your sanctification: that you abstain from fornication;

That each one of you know how to control your own body in holiness and honor, not with lustful passion, like the Gentiles who do not know God.

But we must always give thanks to God for you, brothers and sisters beloved by the Lord, because God chose you as the first fruits for salvation through sanctification by the Spirit and through belief in the truth.

Do not be mismatched with unbelievers.

For what partnership is there between righteousness and lawlessness? Or what fellowship is there between light and darkness?

What agreement does Christ have with Beliar? Or what does a believer share with an unbeliever? What agreement has the temple of God with idols?

For we are the temple of the living God; as God said, "I will live in them and walk among them, and I will be their God, and they shall be my people.

Therefore come out from them, and be separate from them, says the Lord, and touch nothing unclean; then I will welcome you,

And I will be your father, and you shall be my sons and daughters, says the Lord Almighty."

Since we have these promises, beloved, let us cleanse ourselves from every defilement of body and of spirit, making holiness perfect in the fear of God.

47. SUFFERING

Old Testament: Ex. 3:7-8; Ps. 55:1-2, 5-8, 16, 22; Lam. 3:16-17, 20-23; Ps. 34:19

New Testament: 1 Pet. 4:12-13, 19; Rom. 8:18, 5:3-4; Lk. 22:41-42, 44; Rev. 7:13-15, 17

Then the LORD said, "I have observed the misery of my people who are in Egypt; I have heard their cry on account of their taskmasters. Indeed, I know their sufferings,

And I have come down to deliver them from the Egyptians, and to bring them up out of that land to a good and broad land, a land flowing with milk and honey."

Give ear to my prayer, O God; do not hide yourself from my supplication. Attend to me, and answer me; I am troubled in my complaint. I am distraught. Fear and trembling come upon me, and horror overwhelms me.

And I say, "O that I had wings like a dove! I would fly away and be at rest; truly, I would flee far away;

I would lodge in the wilderness; I would hurry to find a shelter for myself from the raging wind and tempest." But I call upon God, and the LORD will save me.

Cast your burden on the LORD, and he will sustain you; he will never permit the righteous to be moved.

He has made my teeth grind on gravel, and made me cower in ashes; my soul is bereft of peace; I have forgotten what happiness is.

My soul continually thinks of it and is bowed down within me. But this I call to mind, and therefore I have hope:

The steadfast love of the LORD never ceases, his mercies never come to an end; they are new every morning; great is your faithfulness.

Many are the afflictions of the righteous, but the LORD rescues them from them all.

Beloved, do not be surprised at the fiery ordeal that is taking place among you to test you, as though something strange were happening to you.

But rejoice insofar as you are sharing Christ's sufferings, so that you may also be glad and shout for joy when his glory is revealed.

Therefore, let those suffering in accordance with God's will entrust themselves to a faithful Creator, while continuing to do good.

I consider that the sufferings of this present time are not worth comparing with the glory about to be revealed to us.

And not only that, but we also boast in our sufferings, knowing that suffering produces endurance, and endurance produces character, and character produces hope.

Then he withdrew from them about a stone's throw, knelt down, and prayed, "Father, if you are willing, remove this cup from me; yet, not my will but yours be done."

In his anguish he prayed more earnestly, and his sweat became like great drops of blood falling down on the ground.

Who are these, robed in white, and where have they come from? These are they who have come out of the great ordeal; they have washed their robes and made them white in the blood of the Lamb.

For this reason they are before the throne of God, and worship him day and night within his temple,

And the one who is seated on the throne will shelter them. And God will wipe away every tear from their eyes.

48. THANKSGIVING

Old Testament: Ps. 92:1-4; Ezra 3:10-11; 1 Chr. 29:10-13

New Testament: 1 Thess. 5:18; 1 Tim. 4:4-5; Col. 2:6-7; Phil. 4:6-7; 1 Cor. 1:4-7; 2 Cor. 2:14-15

It is good to give thanks to the LORD, to sing praises to your name, O Most High; to declare your steadfast love in the morning, and your faithfulness by night, to the music of the lute and the harp, to the melody of the lyre.

For you, O LORD, have made me glad by your work; at the works of your hands I sing for joy.

When the builders laid the foundation of the temple of the LORD, the priests in their vestments were stationed to praise the LORD with trumpets,

And the Levites, the sons of Asaph, with cymbals, according to the directions of King David of Israel;

And they sang responsively, praising and giving thanks to the LORD, "For he is good, for his steadfast love endures forever toward Israel."

And all the people responded with a great shout when they praised the LORD, because the foundation of the house of the LORD was laid.

Then David blessed the LORD in the presence of all the assembly; David said: "Blessed are you, O LORD, the God of our ancestor Israel, forever and ever.

Yours, O LORD, are the greatness, the power, the glory, the victory, and the majesty; for all that is in the heavens and on the earth is yours;

Yours is the kingdom, O LORD, and you are exalted as head above all. Riches and honor come from you, and you rule over all. In your hand are power and might;

And it is in your hand to make great and to give strength to all. And now, our God, we give thanks to you and praise your glorious name.

Give thanks in all circumstances; for this is the will of God in Christ Jesus for you.

For everything created by God is good, and nothing is to be rejected, provided it is received with thanksgiving; for it is sanctified by God's word and by prayer.

As you therefore have received Christ Jesus the Lord, continue to live your lives in him,

Rooted and built up in him and established in the faith, just as you were taught, abounding in thanksgiving.

Do not worry about anything, but in everything by prayer and supplication with thanksgiving let your requests be made known to God.

And the peace of God, which surpasses all understanding, will guard your hearts and your minds in Christ Jesus.

I give thanks to my God always for you because of the grace of God that has been given you in Christ Jesus, for in every way you have been enriched in him,

In speech and knowledge of every kind— just as the testimony of Christ has been strengthened among you—so that you are not lacking in any spiritual gift as you wait for the revealing of our Lord Jesus Christ.

But thanks be to God, who in Christ always leads us in triumphal procession, and through us spreads in every place the fragrance that comes from knowing him.

For we are the aroma of Christ to God among those who are being saved and among those who are perishing.

49. UNITY

Old Testament: Gen. 2:21-24; Ruth 1:16-17; Eccl. 4:9-10; 1 Chr. 13:2-4; Ps. 133:1

New Testament: Jn. 17:11; Acts 2:1-4; 1 Cor. 12:12-13; Eph. 4:1-6; 2 Cor. 13:11

So the LORD God caused a deep sleep to fall upon the man, and he slept; then he took one of his ribs and closed up its place with flesh.

And the rib that the LORD God had taken from the man he made into a woman and brought her to the man.

Then the man said, "This at last is bone of my bones and flesh of my flesh; this one shall be called Woman, for out of Man this one was taken."

Therefore a man leaves his father and his mother and clings to his wife, and they become one flesh.

But Ruth said, "Do not press me to leave you or to turn back from following you! Where you go, I will go; where you lodge, I will lodge;

Your people shall be my people, and your God my God. Where you die, I will die— there will I be buried."

Two are better than one, because they have a good reward for their toil. For if they fall, one will lift up the other; but woe to one who is alone and falls and does not have another to help.

David said to the whole assembly of Israel, "If it seems good to you, and if it is the will of the LORD our God, let us send abroad to our kindred who remain in all the land of Israel.

Then let us bring again the ark of our God to us; for we did not turn to it in the days of Saul." The whole assembly agreed to do so, for the thing pleased all the people.

How very good and pleasant it is when kindred live together in unity!

I am coming to you. Holy Father, protect them in your name that you have given me, so that they may be one, as we are one.

When the day of Pentecost had come, they were all together in one place.

And suddenly from heaven there came a sound like the rush of a violent wind, and it filled the entire house where they were sitting.

Divided tongues, as of fire, appeared among them, and a tongue rested on each of them. All of them were filled with the Holy Spirit and began to speak in other languages, as the Spirit gave them ability.

For just as the body is one and has many members, and all the members of the body, though many, are one body, so it is with Christ.

For in the one Spirit we were all baptized into one body—Jews or Greeks, slaves or free—and we were all made to drink of one Spirit.

I therefore, the prisoner in the Lord, beg you to lead a life worthy of the calling to which you have been called, with all humility and gentleness, with patience, bearing with one another in love,

Making every effort to maintain the unity of the Spirit in the bond of peace.

There is one body and one Spirit, just as you were called to the one hope of your calling, one Lord, one faith, one baptism, one God and Father of all, who is above all and through all and in all.

Finally, brothers and sisters, farewell. Put things in order, listen to my appeal, agree with one another, live in peace; and the God of love and peace will be with you.

50. VICTORY

Old Testament: Ps. 98:1-3; Ex. 15:6; 1 Chr. 29:11; Ex. 15:11; Ps. 21:13; Ex. 15:1, 18

New Testament: Lk. 1:46-49, 51-52; 1 Cor. 15:55-58; Rom. 8:38-39, 37

O sing to the LORD a new song, for he has done marvelous things.

His right hand and his holy arm have gotten him victory.

The LORD has made known his victory; he has revealed his vindication in the sight of the nations.

He has remembered his steadfast love and faithfulness to the house of Israel.

All the ends of the earth have seen the victory of our God.

Your right hand, O LORD, glorious in power—your right hand, O LORD, shattered the enemy.

Yours, O LORD, are the greatness, the power, the glory, the victory, and the majesty.

Who is like you, O LORD, among the gods?

Who is like you, majestic in holiness, awesome in splendor, doing wonders?

Be exalted, O LORD, in your strength! We will sing and praise your power.

I will sing to the LORD, for he has triumphed gloriously.

The LORD will reign forever and ever.

My soul magnifies the Lord, and my spirit rejoices in God my Savior,

For he has looked with favor on the lowliness of his servant.

For the Mighty One has done great things for me, and holy is his name.

He has shown strength with his arm; he has scattered the proud in the thoughts of their hearts.

He has brought down the powerful from their thrones, and lifted up the lowly.

Where, O death, is your victory? Where, O death, is your sting?

The sting of death is sin, and the power of sin is the law.

But thanks be to God, who gives us the victory through our Lord Jesus Christ.

Therefore, my beloved, be steadfast, immovable, always excelling in the work of the Lord, because you know that in the Lord your labor is not in vain.

For I am convinced that neither death, nor life, nor angels, nor rulers, nor principalities, nor things present, nor things to come, nor powers,

Nor height, nor depth, nor anything else in all creation, will be able to separate us from the love of God in Christ Jesus our Lord.

In all these things we are more than conquerors through him who loved us.

51. WILL OF GOD

Old Testament: Ps. 119:33-34, 143:10, 37:23-24; Mic. 6:8; Prov. 14:12, 3:5-6; Jer. 29:11

New Testament: Rom. 12:1-2; Col. 1:9-10; Mk. 3:31-35, 14:36

Teach me, O LORD, the way of your statutes, and I will observe it to the end.

Give me understanding, that I may keep your law and observe it with my whole heart.

Teach me to do your will, for you are my God. Let your good spirit lead me on a level path.

Our steps are made firm by the LORD, when he delights in our way;

Though we stumble, we shall not fall headlong, for the LORD holds us by the hand.

What does the LORD require of you but to do justice, and to love kindness, and to walk humbly with your God?

There is a way that seems right to a person, but its end is the way to death.

Trust in the LORD with all your heart, and do not rely on your own insight.

In all your ways acknowledge him, and he will make straight your paths.

For surely I know the plans I have for you, says the LORD, plans for your welfare and not for harm, to give you a future with hope.

I appeal to you therefore, brothers and sisters, by the mercies of God, to present your bodies as a living sacrifice, holy and acceptable to God, which is your spiritual worship.

Do not be conformed to this world, but be transformed by the renewing of your minds, so that you may discern what is the will of God—what is good and acceptable and perfect.

For this reason, since the day we heard it, we have not ceased praying for you and asking that you may be filled with the knowledge of God's will in all spiritual wisdom and understanding,

So that you may lead lives worthy of the Lord, fully pleasing to him, as you bear fruit in every good work and as you grow in the knowledge of God.

Jesus' mother and brothers came; and standing outside, they sent to him and called him.

A crowd was sitting around him; and they said to him, "Your mother and your brothers and sisters are outside, asking for you."

And he replied, "Who are my mother and my brothers?" And looking at those who sat around him, he said, "Here are my mother and my brothers!

Whoever does the will of God is my brother and sister and mother."

Abba, Father, for you all things are possible; remove this cup from me;

Yet, not what I want, but what you want.

52. WISDOM

Old Testament: Ps. 111:10; Prov. 3:5-8, 1 Kings 4:29, 32, 10:1, 3; Dan. 2:20-21; Prov. 3:13-18

New Testament: Col. 3:16; 1 Cor. 1:20-21, 30-31; Jas. 1:5, 3:13-14, 17; Rom. 11:33

The fear of the LORD is the beginning of wisdom; all those who practice it have a good understanding. His praise endures forever.

Trust in the LORD with all your heart, and do not rely on your own insight. In all your ways acknowledge him, and he will make straight your paths.

Do not be wise in your own eyes; fear the LORD, and turn away from evil. It will be a healing for your flesh and a refreshment for your body.

God gave Solomon very great wisdom, discernment, and breadth of understanding as vast as the sand on the seashore. He composed three thousand proverbs, and his songs numbered a thousand and five.

When the queen of Sheba heard of the fame of Solomon, (fame due to the name of the LORD), she came to test him with hard questions.

Solomon answered all her questions; there was nothing hidden from the king that he could not explain to her.

Daniel said: "Blessed be the name of God from age to age, for wisdom and power are his. He changes times and seasons, deposes kings and sets up kings; he gives wisdom to the wise and knowledge to those who have understanding."

Happy are those who find wisdom, and those who get understanding, for her income is better than silver, and her revenue better than gold.

She is more precious than jewels, and nothing you desire can compare with her. Long life is in her right hand; in her left hand are riches and honor.

Her ways are ways of pleasantness, and all her paths are peace. She is a tree of life to those who lay hold of her; those who hold her fast are called happy.

Let the word of Christ dwell in you richly; teach and admonish one another in all wisdom.

Where is the one who is wise? Where is the scribe? Where is the debater of this age? Has not God made foolish the wisdom of the world?

For since, in the wisdom of God, the world did not know God through wisdom, God decided, through the foolishness of our proclamation, to save those who believe.

He is the source of your life in Christ Jesus, who became for us wisdom from God, and righteousness and sanctification and redemption,

In order that, as it is written, "Let the one who boasts, boast in the Lord."

If any of you is lacking in wisdom, ask God, who gives to all generously and ungrudgingly, and it will be given you.

Who is wise and understanding among you? Show by your good life that your works are done with gentleness born of wisdom.

But if you have bitter envy and selfish ambition in your hearts, do not be boastful and false to the truth.

But the wisdom from above is first pure, then peaceable, gentle, willing to yield, full of mercy and good fruits, without a trace of partiality or hypocrisy.

O the depth of the riches and wisdom and knowledge of God! How unsearchable are his judgments and how inscrutable his ways!

53. EMANCIPATION DAY (JANUARY 1)

O Lord, we celebrate your strong hand of deliverance. We have seen your grace in the midst of life's burdens.

Lord God of Hosts, on the anniversary of our freedom from slavery, we know that we can do all things through Christ, who strengthens us. (see Phil. 4:13)

The Emancipation Proclamation freed African slaves in the United States on New Year's Day in 1863. But actual freedom for the last slaves did not come until a June day two and a half years later. This Juneteenth milestone reminds us of the triumph of the human spirit.

Lord God of Hosts, be with us always, as you were with Harriett Tubman.

The Constitution once defined African Americans as three-fifths human. But we have labored and died as whole men and women.

Lord God of Hosts, be with us always, as you were with Frederick Douglas.

The Thirteenth Amendment abolished the heinous institution of slavery, but we still struggle against the chains of racial discrimination.

Lord God of Hosts, be with us always, as you were with Vernon Johns.

The Fourteenth Amendment made us citizens by legislation because our blood, sweat, and tears helped to build this nation.

Lord God of Hosts, be with us always, as you were with Thurgood Marshall.

The Fifteenth Amendment said we could not be denied the right to vote because of our color; yet we have faced systematic exclusion from the political process, and we continue to struggle for full inclusion.

Lord God of Hosts, be with us always, as you were with Barbara Jordan.

The Twenty-fourth Amendment abolished poll taxes, voting tests, and other restrictions upon our right to vote; but these soon were replaced by gerrymandering and political apathy.

Lord God of Hosts, be with us always, as you were with Benjamin Quarles.

The Civil Rights Act of 1964 translated into law most of the goals of the Civil Rights Movement, protecting all citizens from racial segregation and discrimination. Let us remain ever vigilant in our commitment to proactive citizenship.

Lord God of Hosts, be with us always, as you were with Stokely Carmichael.

Our hopes soar to heights of joy when we remember the emancipation of Nelson Mandela in 1990, and his ascendancy to President of South Africa after twenty-six long years in prison. Blessed are the righteous.

Lord God of Hosts, be with us always, as you are with Desmond Tutu.

Let us leave behind those sins that pulled us down in the old year, and answer the high calling of your will for our lives in the new year.

Lord God of Hosts, on the anniversary of our freedom from slavery, we know that we can do all things through Christ, who strengthens us.

54. REV. DR. MARTIN LUTHER KING JR.

In every era, God has chosen men and women to serve the needs of his people. Such a servant was Martin Luther King, Jr., whose birth we celebrate. We are deeply thankful for the life of this twentieth century prophet.

May the wisdom and words of Martin Luther King rekindle our faith.

May the deep love that Dr. King had for all people be released in us, that we too might work miracles in the lives of those who continue to hate.

Dr. King taught that only love can overcome hatred, bitterness and fear.

May his struggle for social transformation continue in this generation. May all people come to believe that with perseverance, "We Shall Overcome".

"But let justice roll down like waters, and righteousness like an everflowing stream." (Am. 5:24)

May the work of Dr. King continue to eradicate racial injustice and its ungodly consequences.

Dr. King pursued his dream for racial equality by appealing to the conscience of his enemies.

May we continue to cultivate the nonviolent discipline of Dr. King, abandoning unrestrained acts of force.

He taught us that a heart full of grace and love is just as important as an education.

May the spirit of Dr. King continue to flow through our daily living.

He believed in self-respect and dignity, even though he knew that there would be difficult days ahead.

May we have the courage of Dr. King as we continue to stand up for justice, reconciliation and truth, despite challenge and controversy.

Dr. King said that war is never a victory, regardless of the outcome.

May the peace of the risen Christ cause the fury of war to vanish from the face of the earth.

Dr. King went to the mountain top; he saw the Promised Land; and he reassured us that we will get there one day. God of Glory, be with us on the journey.

55. INSTALLATION OF CHURCH LEADERS

You have accepted the office to which you have been elected or appointed. Do you promise, with the Lord as your helper, to faithfully fulfill its duties?

We do, and we ask all other officers to receive us as fellow laborers with God.

Pray now for the faith and compassion of our Lord Jesus Christ, for the boldness of Peter, for the evangelistic zeal of Philip, for the administrative insight of Priscilla and Aquila, and for the wisdom of Paul.

Jethro counseled Moses that the task before him was too enormous for him alone. We acknowledge the same. We ask for your prayers, support, encouragement and cooperation.

God has endowed each of us with unique gifts and talents for the edification of the church and the work of ministry. Will you accept this church office in proportion to your faith to prophesy, to minister, to teach, to exhort, to give liberally, to lead with diligence, and to show mercy with cheerfulness?

We accept our offices with every intention to use our talents to lead God's people according to our discernment of God's will.

Remember those who were judges in Israel and leaders in the New Testament church. Remember our mothers and fathers in the faith, our ancestors who built and carried the church. They accomplished much, for they were rich in faith, wisdom, and courage.

We give thanks for their example, their competence, and their steadfast commitment.

Do you covenant and promise that you will walk together in love for one another, and exercise affectionate care and watchfulness over all those given to your charge?

We will faithfully admonish and entreat one another as occasion may require. We will not forsake the assembling of ourselves together, nor neglect to pray for ourselves and others. We will strive to maintain the high standards of our offices so that the ministries of our church may be strengthened.

Will you, according to your abilities and opportunities, show good to all, especially in helping to extend the gospel in its purity and power to the whole human family? Will you regularly support the work of the church by systematic contributions both spiritual and financial?

We will support our church amid good and ill report. We will humbly and earnestly seek to live to the glory of God, and to be directed by the Holy Spirit.

May God uphold you and direct you as you go forth!

Praise be to God!

56. EPIPHANY

We come celebrating the Epiphany feast, the manifestation of God in Jesus Christ.

Just as the shepherds and magi first came to adore and worship the newborn King, we come in faith, joy, hope, anticipation, and renewal.

Glory to God! Rejoice, and give thanks, for Christ has come.

Hallelujah, Redemption Incarnate has come for all.

We rise, we shine in the light of God's glory.

The Light of the world, Jesus Christ as manifested love, is here.

We know the Light has come "For we observed his star at its rising and have come to pay him homage." (Matt. 2:2)

King Herod heard this and was frightened. He called together all the chief priests and scribes. Herod asked them where the Messiah was to be born.

We come, not in fear, but in joy. For Immanuel has come to ransom Israel, to ransom the lost, the lonely, and the misunderstood.

Jesus has come to ransom those imprisoned to substances, greed, abuse, low self-esteem, hate, anger, to any oppressive force, thought or deed. Jesus has come to liberate communities and individuals. He has come to free us!

We seek the Christ child boldly. Like the magi, we see the star and stop to praise.

We have come to participate in bringing Jesus, the Light of the world, into the world.

We, too, see the child with Mary and Joseph. We kneel and worship Jesus. We offer our gifts of tithes, service, and thanksgiving.

Jesus is the Light that illumines our path, the incarnated goodness and mercy that accompanies us each and every day of our lives.

We look to see Christ in every child of God, as we celebrate, honor, and live in the hope and peace of this blessed revelation.

How blessed we are to see, to believe, and to receive this bounteous gift of God.

57. BLACK HISTORY OBSERVANCE

Oh God, you have heard the anguished cries of our ancestors. Their sounds echo and penetrate time to remind us of our foreparents who were brutally captured and forcibly enslaved, as they left the peaceful womb of their African homeland.

"Stony the road we trod."

Oh God, you have seen the millions of dark bodies buried beneath the tumultuous waves of the deep. Bodies of African men and women who held the seeds of greatness. You have seen women's dreams for a united family vanish as they were sold at auction blocks. You have seen the legacy of the African American family decimated and demeaned by those who have attempted to control our destiny.

"Bitter the chastening rod, felt in the days when hope unborn had died."

Oh God, you have ignited the sparks within us into a blazing demand for freedom, equality and justice. This quest cost Harriet Tubman sleepless nights, as she led her people to freedom; it was an equality that Rosa Parks and civil rights activists fought for and gave their lives for; it was a justice that Martin Luther King, Jr. stood for, as thousands stood with him at the Lincoln Memorial.

"Yet with a steady beat, have not our weary feet, come to the place for which our fathers sighed?"

Oh God, you have seen our tears. You have been pained by the evil of human hearts. Yet, you loved humanity enough that you sent your only Son to identify with the outcast, marginalized and rejected. As the cries of Jesus pierced your heart, so have the cries of your people—cries from different cultures and in different languages.

"God of our weary years, God of our silent tears."

O God, you answered us during our exodus from Africa. You wiped every teardrop during our exile in captivity. Our foreparents dared to dream that one day, on these shores, we would become politicians, preachers, educators, doctors, writers, scientists, artists, and so much more.

"Lest our feet stray from the places, our God, where we met Thee."

Our ancestors' hard work, their courage, their convictions, and their belief in you paved the way for our emancipation and education. But it is clear, you have liberated us. You have set us free. "Free at last, free at last, thank God Almighty, I'm free at last!"

"Lest our hearts drunk with the wine of the world we forget Thee. Shadowed beneath Thy hand, may we forever stand. True to our God and true to our native land."

58. CHURCH ANNIVERSARY

Be with us, O God, as we celebrate this day and the years of Christian fellowship that we have shared as a congregation.

For such a time as this, you have called the church to be at its best.

Quicken our memories of those whose wisdom and love established this church and whose faith and steadfastness glorified you through its life.

For those who laid the foundations of this household of faith, we give thanks.

Make vivid to us the glorious victories that have been won in your name and the continuing fellowship, which has revealed your Spirit through these years.

For this rich inheritance of the Church of Jesus Christ, we give thanks.

Crown our joy in this hour with a fresh awareness of the vast company of Christians who share our celebration and who urge us to yet greater achievements in Christ's name.

For those who make common cause with us, we give thanks.

May we be worthy of the faith of our ancestors and eager to win new victories for righteousness' sake.

For the "invisible institution" of black slaves we give you thanks. For the emergence of the Black Church, solidified by shared suffering and deliverance, we give thanks.

We remember with gratitude and awe their creative appropriation of the Bible, and their centuries-long struggle for freedom all alone.

For the Quakers who took a firm stand against slavery in 1688, we give thanks.

Fill us with an ever-increasing knowledge of truth, and with an ever-growing awareness of need. Give us a more generous spirit.

For the assurance of new opportunities to serve you better, we give thanks.

O God, our help in ages past, our hope for years to come, renew our faith and increase our strength. May we be worthy recipients of past blessings and ready helpers in the tasks that lie ahead.

Come, Lord Jesus, empower and hold our church to your heart.

Unite us in common commitment to the Lordship of Jesus Christ, that the world may see our dedication to follow your teachings and to fulfill your will for this church.

May your kingdom come and your will be done in splendid, perfect fellowship. Continue to guide us in the future, as you have in the past.

59. BAPTISM

Come, Holy Spirit, come, Heavenly Dove. As we approach baptism, let us be mindful of our brokenness and be grateful for our redemption through Christ Jesus.

Lord, cleanse us from sin and make us wholly yours.

Baptism marks the beginning of our Christian journey. It is a time of initiation into responsibility and commitment to Christ. Through the symbolic cleansing of the water, we lay down our old selves and are born again as new creations in Christ.

Come, Holy Spirit. Take our lives and make them new in your name.

In the Jordan River, Christ was baptized by John. Come, Holy Spirit, come. Trouble the water, sanctify it that all who are baptized here may begin new lives of obedience to God.

You are the refreshing spring, the living water that never runs dry. In you, we thirst not.

Through baptism we are buried with Christ into death. As Christ was raised from the dead by the glory of God, we, too, are raised from the baptismal waters to walk in the newness of life.

Make of our lives an acceptable sacrifice and of our witness refreshing pools for others.

Our ancestors waded in the chilly waters of the South. Through baptism they were made new and free creatures in Christ.

"Jordan River is chilly and cold. It chilled my body, but not my soul."

Today is a day of recommitment. On this day and every day we give you thanks. Through baptism, the Lord's Supper, and the gift of the Holy Spirit, we are offered opportunities for our sins to be washed away in the cleansing blood of the Lamb.

There is one faith, one Lord, one baptism, one Body, one Spirit, one God and Father of us all. Through baptism we are united eternally with Christ. Make us worthy, dear Lord.

60. THE CIVIL RIGHTS MOVEMENT

When God created man and woman, the freedom of persons was already established.

We are made in the image of God, African Americans, as well as all others. From one blood has God created all the races and nations of the earth.

Galatians declares that in Christ, regarding freedom and equality, there is no longer Jew or Greek, slave or free, male and female. (see Gal. 3:28)

Likewise, during the founding of the United States of America, the writers of our Constitution proclaimed human rights for all.

However these rights were not granted to most African Americans.

In the 1950's and 60's, we experienced one of the proudest times in our history, the modern civil rights movement.

The promise of freedom, the vote, and equality, affirmed in the Thirteenth, Fourteenth, and Fifteenth Amendments, became more achievable for African Americans.

We are thankful for Rosa Parks, Medgar Evers, James Farmer, and Fannie Lou Hamer. Nothing could quench their thirst for freedom. It was their time and they would not be denied.

The events associated with the Southern Christian Leadership Conference, the Montgomery Bus Boycott, the Student Non-Violent Coordinating Committee, and the Congress of Racial Equality have changed our lives.

During this time, Brown vs. The Board of Education, the NAACP, the March on Washington, the work of the National Urban League, the Black Church, and other religious communities united people against racial injustice.

Media coverage of the brutal treatment of black Americans awakened the conscience of America that lead to the 1964 Civil Rights Act. We would not be moved even though confronted by police dogs and water hoses.

May God help us to exercise more seriously our right to vote and our pursuit of equality. God strengthen us in the ongoing struggle for freedom, civil rights, and justice.

61. RITES OF PASSAGE FOR YOUTH

God bless our youth that they may grow into men and women who honor you, and reflect the best of their families and communities.

As they experience the difficult task of becoming adults, guide them in the pursuit of faith, identity, and purpose.

Above all may they come to know you and love you with all their hearts, minds and souls. Let them know that you are always with them, helping them fulfill the plan, which you have designed for their lives. May they keep your commandments, and search out your will.

Wherever life takes them, may they never cease to praise you, to pray, and to study your Holy Word.

God, save them from negative self images, from feelings of hopelessness, and from peer pressure that contradicts the values which their families and churches have instilled in them.

As Jesus increased in wisdom and favor, grant that young people may also attain spiritual and human maturity. (see Lk. 2:52)

May they understand the responsibility and sensitivity necessary to become a friend, a leader, a spouse, and a parent.

Lord, give them role models and mentors. Grant them spiritual immunity from the brokenness and meanness of life. Help them to develop good relationships with others.

May they acquire knowledge of their ancestry, master contemporary life skills, and understand the multicultural dimensions of our world.

May they begin the adult journey by remembering the history of their people. May they travel with confidence.

May they value education and see themselves as an important part of their nation. Bless them to choose and prepare for careers and vocations that enrich their lives and the lives of others.

As they set personal and career goals, give them the knowledge and capability to achieve them. Help them to aim high, embrace good health, moral principles, respect for life and property, and a desire to serve others.

May they feel connected to every village and nation of the world, and understand the importance of participating in many arenas of life.

God of our past, present, and future, let our youth see visions, discern problems and search for solutions. Make them and shape them into strong African American men and women.

62. HUNGER AWARENESS

Jacob sent his sons into Pharaoh's land in search of food because of hunger. When David and his companions were hungry, they "entered the house of God and ate the bread of the Presence, which it was not lawful for him or his companions to eat, but only for the priests." (Matt. 12:3-4)

We acknowledge that often the teachings of Jesus were at the table, before, after or during a meal. Bread and wine are sacramental symbols of his abiding presence with us, and of his anticipated return.

Whether for food or fellowship, nourishment and nurture are set at the family table.

Lord God make us aware of hunger in the world - of children who are deprived of an adequate breakfast and of seniors who do not have the income necessary for an adequate diet.

As we give thanks for your provision, may we do our part in responding to human need.

May we become concerned and involved in the alleviation of hunger, wherever it is found. Help us to realize that there is much more that we can do.

May we open our hearts and use our resources to ease pain and hurt.

May we continue to be participants in the struggle to end world hunger, that all may receive sustenence and their share of God's daily bread.

63. A CALL TO FAST

There are seasons of fasting throughout the church year. In these seasons we practice restraint from distractions and indulge in undivided attention to God.

Fasting returns us to the simplicity of enjoying an intimate relationship with God. It takes us back to the basics of studying the Word, praying, fellowshipping with believers and meditating on godly things.

Let us fast from selfishness, jealousy, anger and pride.

Let us feast on gratitude, appreciation, compassion, and prayerful silence.

Let us anoint our heads and wash our hands and faces. Let not our fasting appear evident to others, but only to you, Lord.

Our people have endured long periods of affliction, hardship and suffering. We are surrounded by a great cloud of witnesses who have traveled hard roads before us.

O Lord, the road we follow is still stony, and the rod of our chastening is still bitter.

God of plenty and fullness, empty us of everything that is not yours. Refill us with your bounty for evermore.

Let us run with patience the race that is set before us.

Now let us fast, as did Jesus, Elijah, and Moses to gain a closer communion with you.

64. CLERGY APPRECIATION

Good Shepherd of the sheep, you have appointed some to be pastors and teachers, under-shepherds of our souls. For this we give thanks.

We rejoice that they follow in the tradition of the apostles and prophets of old.

Apostles are commissioned as delegates of the Lord Jesus Christ to bring the Word of God to the unbelieving.

They proclaim the good news of the death and resurrection of Jesus Christ.

After Jesus prayed, he then selected the initial twelve apostles to further his teaching.

They were trained by his example to carry on his ministry after his departure.

Jesus commissioned seventy more apostles, representing all the nations of the world.

After his departure, the apostles testified to his resurrection. Barnabas and Andronicus, Junia and Paul, were added to this group.

The prophets are messengers to the believing Church, discerned as instruments of fresh revelations.

They included Anna and Simeon, the prophets at Antioch and Jerusalem, and finally, Philip's daughters.

Prophets give inspired instruction in moral and religious truth. Some are endowed with literary powers, and commit their visions and revelations to writing.

Prophets edify, comfort, and counsel God's people.

Among the apostles and prophets whom we honor today are Richard Allen and Absolam Jones, Jarena Lee, Lemuel Haynes, Sojourner Truth, and Bishops Mason and Lawson.

Thanks be to God!

We also honor Adam Clayton Powell, Benjamin Mays, Howard Thurman, Pauli Murray, Martin Luther King Jr., C. L. Franklin, J. H. Jackson, and Samuel Procter. We give thanks for unnamed servants of the Lord, women and men of the past, as well as those who serve us today.

Thanks be to God!

Our clergy announce God's will with authority, honoring the Apostle and High Priest of our profession, Christ Jesus. They take heed to build carefully upon his foundation, studying and rightly dividing the word of truth.

Thanks be to God for the diligent efforts of our clergy!

65. MARRIAGE IN CHRIST

From the beginning of creation, God made us male and female. Jesus said, "For this reason a man shall leave his father and mother and be joined to his wife, and the two shall become one flesh. So they are no longer two, but one flesh." (Matt. 19:5)

A successful marriage is not an accident. A successful marriage is the result of hard work.

Marriage is not to be entered into lightly, but prayerfully and reverently.

Give your children wisdom in choosing marriage partners. Help them to see the value of being equally yoked.

While both marriage and singleness are acceptable to you, O God, many crave the intimacy of oneness and companionship. Because this is according to your design, keep marriages strong. Give husbands and wives good listening skills, maturity, honesty and humility.

Deep affection and mutual respect are spiritual qualities motivated by our reverence for Christ. As we become more Christ-like, we become better wives and husbands.

O God, build marriages upon foundations that are far deeper than emotional infatuations so that they may have staying power, with husbands and wives learning how to serve and be served.

As Christ leads and feeds the Church, may husbands feed and care for their wives. May they love their wives as they do their own bodies. (see Eph. 5:28)

As wives submit to their husbands, so husbands should submit to their wives. May they do so in recognition that Christ is the head of both. May they acknowledge that mutual submission never denies wife or husband the freedom of choice or expression.

We realize that many marriages are under constant attack. Help us to preserve marriage as a faithful covenant, guided by steadfast love and closeness of soul.

May we avoid preoccupation with things, spend more time with our family, and give to those in need. Help us to save more and to spend less.

O God, help couples to be content when their material needs are met. May money alone never be their goal. Deliver us all from credit cards and impulse buying. For these are traps that lead to ruin.

May couples not keep an account of wrongs and not show rudeness or selfishness. May they not be easily angered, but be easily affirmed.

O Lord, we need your help.

Words can either nourish or crush the spirit. May we strive to speak words of encouragement.

"Live in harmony with one another in accordance with Christ Jesus, that you may with one voice glorify the God of the Lord Jesus Christ." (Rom. 15:6).

66. TRIUMPHANT ENTRY (PALM SUNDAY)

"Hosanna! Blessed is the one who comes in the name of the Lord!" Today we celebrate Jesus' triumphal entry into Jerusalem.

Hosanna! Hosanna! Blessed is he who comes in the name of the Lord!

Jesus humbly rode into Jerusalem on a donkey for the Feast of the Passover. The crowds spread their cloaks on the road and others laid palms to prepare the way for his victorious coming.

Rejoice! Rejoice! The King arrives!

Five hundred years before Jesus, the prophet Zechariah told of the Messiah's coming in humility and peace. (see Zech. 9:9)

Rejoice! Rejoice! The triumphant King has come!

On the journey to liberation from sin, we celebrate Christ's victories, sorrowfully contemplate his sacrifice, and we revel in his resurrection, the ultimate victory.

We remember the long road to freedom that our ancestors traveled, filled with triumphs, death, and new life.

Ride on, King Jesus! Ride on, conquering King!

Jesus came "to bring good news to the poor; to proclaim release to the captives and recovery of sight to the blind; and to let the oppressed go free." (Lk. 4:18)

With excitement and joy we welcome you into our lives. With loud hosannas we join you on your march toward liberation, justice, and love for all people.

Rejoice! Rejoice! The triumphant King has come!

67. HOLY WEEK

Lord, we celebrate this Holy Week by tracing your steps from Palm Sunday to Easter Sunday. Amid the waving of palms and the spreading of garments, you rode into Jerusalem. Your triumphant entry into the city marked the beginning of our redemption.

O blessed Savior, we thank you for our redemption.

Lord, on that Monday, you rebuked and confronted unrighteousness by cleansing the temple.

O Holy and Righteous One, we thank you for our redemption.

Lord, on Tuesday and Wednesday, you proclaimed that when you are lifted up from the earth, you will draw all people to you.

Lord Jesus, we thank you for our redemption.

Lord, on Thursday, you celebrated the Passover and instituted the supper that has become our Eucharist. You washed the disciples' feet, promised the Holy Spirit, and healed the ear of Malchus, because of your love for humankind.

O Great Healer, we thank you for our redemption.

Lord, on that same day Judas betrayed you for thirty pieces of silver. You were arrested and brought before Caiaphas, the high priest, but showed no anger against these men.

Forgiving God, we thank you for our redemption.

Lord, on Friday Peter denied you three times. Pilate did not want any part of your crucifixion. You were mocked and spat upon and Judas hanged himself because of his betrayal. Lord, you even accepted the thief on the cross and died at Calvary because of your love for us.

"Were you there when they crucified my Lord? Sometimes it causes me to tremble, tremble, tremble."

Lord, when you died on the hill on Calvary, darkness covered the whole land, the earth shook, the veil of the temple split in two, the thunder rumbled, and the graves opened. The centurion was heard saying, "Certainly this man was innocent." (Lk. 23:47)

"Were you there when they pierced him in his side? Sometimes it causes me to tremble, tremble, tremble."

Lord, come Sunday, people all over the world will join together to thank you for the power of your resurrection. We know the pain and suffering of Good Friday, and thank you for helping us to experience the joy of Easter. Because you live we can face tomorrow.

Lord Jesus, we thank you for paying the cost of righteousness.

68. RESURRECTION SUNDAY (EASTER)

On that first Easter morning, as the sun was dawning, Jesus rose triumphantly from the dead. The earth shook as the angel rolled the stone away.

No grave could hold his body down. He is risen. He is risen indeed!

As Mary Magdalene and the other Mary looked on in fear, the Risen Lord revealed himself to them, and they departed with great joy.

Rejoice! And again I say rejoice! For Christ Jesus has broken the curse of death and destroyed the power that it once had over us.

Although we live in a world filled with moral decay and violence, and although we were stripped of our original culture and our past as a people, we, like Christ, can be resurrected.

Give glory to God, who humbled himself, even to death on a cross. Give glory to the exalted Christ!

The same power that raised Jesus from the dead is now given to each of us and to all those who believe on him.

Let us receive this spiritual power and use it wisely for the liberation of all God's people!

Let us make a joyful noise unto the Lord. For there is none like him who can break the chain of oppression, evil, and the grave. He is risen and is seated at the right hand of God.

"Worthy is the Lamb that was slaughtered to receive power and wealth and wisdom and might and honor and glory and blessing!" (Rev. 5:12)

Who is worthy? Christ is worthy. "Because he lives, I can face tomorrow. Because he lives, all fear is gone. Because I know he holds the future and life is worth the living just because he lives."

"Who is worthy? The Lion of the tribe of Judah, the Root of David, conquered, so that he can open the scroll and its seven seals." (Rev. 5:13)

Who is worthy? The One seated on the throne and the Lamb. To them be all blessing and honor and glory and might!

He is worthy! The Risen Christ! The Resurrected One! Praise him! Praise his Holy Name!

69. PENTECOST SUNDAY

"When the day of Pentecost had come, they were all together in one place. Suddenly, from heaven, there came a sound like the rush of a violent wind, and it filled the entire house where they were sitting.

Divided tongues, as of fire, appeared among them, and a tongue rested on each of them. They were all filled with the Holy Spirit and began to speak in other languages, as the Spirit gave them ability." (Acts 2)

And they heard one another in their own languages. Egyptians understood Judeans, and Judeans understood Asians and Asians understood Arabs. They heard each other declare, in their native tongues, the wonderful works of God.

Thus, the Church was born on Pentecost Day. We pray for the continued outpouring of your Spirit upon the church so that the fires of Pentecost may anoint us to take the gospel of Jesus Christ to all the world.

Thank you for African American churches which have kept the spirit of Pentecost in the forefront of their teaching and religious expression. We remember the Azusa Street revival of Los Angeles, conducted by William J. Seymour. This great revival gave birth to modern day Pentecostalism.

Bishop Mason, founder of the Church of God in Christ, said, "I prayed earnestly that God would give me above all things a religion like the one I had heard about from the old slaves, and seen demonstrated in their lives."

Jesus said, "You will receive power when the Holy Spirit has come upon you, and you will be my witnesses."

Lord, as witnesses, we thank you for all the gifts of the Holy Spirit. We thank you for fire shut up in our bones. (see Jer. 20:9)

You have done marvelous things. May your Spirit continually fall fresh on us.

Holy Spirit, we welcome you in this place, in our hearts, in our homes, in our lives and in our world.

Help us to release the anointing of the Holy Spirit which dwells within us. Let us pour your blessing into the lives of others.

Let us lift up the name of Jesus with power from on high.

70. BLACK WOMEN

Today, O Lord, we honor black women—carriers and cultivators of culture. In a lush African garden, your hands fashioned her as Mother of Creation. Bless her now as she continues to pass culture on to future generations.

Thank you for black women, Lord. Their descendents have blessed the earth.

We remember some of the African queens: Hatshepsut, Nefertiti, Makeda, Nzingha, and Yaa Asantewa. Through the centuries they grew in wisdom and strength. Fertile minds were formed at their knee. They nurtured kingdoms as queen rulers of mighty nations. Bless black women now, Lord, as they continue to educate and lead their people.

Strengthen black women, Lord. Their genius has enriched the earth.

We remember Harriet Tubman, Sojourner Truth, Pauli Murray and Rosa Parks. The black woman was treated as property during enslavement and the Middle Passage. Yet she survived and her vision of freedom ignited a determination to struggle for human and civil rights. Bless black women now, Lord, as they fight against injustice through strategies for hope, survival, and advancement.

Empower black women, Lord. Their bravery has ennobled the earth.

We remember Augusta Savage, Katherine Dunham, Marian Anderson, Mahalia Jackson, and Meta Warrick Fuller. They birthed black literary and artistic traditions. Through autobiography, quilts, sculpture, dance, song and poetry, the once muffled voices of black women ring clear with creative power. Bless them now, Lord, as their moans and hums, whispers and shouts make our land beautiful.

Inspire black women, Lord. Their beauty has adorned the earth.

We remember Rahab, Zipporah, Jarena Lee, Julia Foote, and Zilpha Elaw. Black women prayed and preached, healed and helped faithfully at all times. As prayer warriors, they knew how to trust you, O God, especially in times of trouble. Their triumph has sparked fire in our souls. May the light that radiates from you today cast beautiful patterns on our lives through them.

We rejoice now, O Lord, with black women everywhere. Thank you, Lord. Their work blesses the earth.

71. BLACK MOTHERS

All knowing God, who sees and helps to bear the pains and disappointments of every black mother, we ask that you extend to our mothers comfort and strength.

We pray for black mothers everywhere. They give us life and love and hold our families together. Amid changing family structures we remember mothers young and old, single mothers and fathers, homeless mothers, grandmothers, godmothers, and surrogate mothers.

We pray for black mothers who suffer due to unemployment, insufficient housing and poor healthcare. Heal black mothers, Lord, as they have often experienced mistreatment and witnessed the harsh abuse of their children, husbands, siblings and parents.

Divine Nurturer, fortify our mothers. Continue to make them a refuge in the time of trouble.

We pray for mothers and their children, as violent crimes and drug abuse conspire to tear the fiber of black families.

We pray for black mothers of old who have bent their backs cleaning homes, picking cotton and working by the sweat of their brow. We thank them for their determination and their belief that education is a door to liberation and success.

God, empower black mothers to enrich the lives of their families. Aid them as they teach sons and daughters determination and the value of investing in the future.

Mothers have always been activists and leaders, teaching us how to live and making our communities better. We remember poet and writer Frances E. W. Harper who birthed a crusade against lynching during Reconstruction.

We remember Rosa Parks who birthed a bus boycott, and Shirley Chisholm who blazed the trail to high public office for black women.

We cherish mothers who teach, write or preach the truth and who open the minds of children to limitless possibility. We celebrate mothers who are homemakers, educators, authors and pastors, who formulate ideas, expend creative energy and inspire young people to become leaders.

They have been a loving presence in business and play, in the arts and in all of life.

Because our mothers taught us that "the Lord will make a way out of no way", we have the inheritance of a powerful spiritual legacy. We give black mothers bouquets of gratitude and honor. Kind and Gentle Savior, ever bless them.

72. MEN'S DAY

"How good and how pleasant it is when brothers live together in unity! It is like precious oil poured on the head ... For there the Lord bestows his blessing, even life forevermore." (Ps. 133:1)

We are one in the Spirit; we are one in the Lord.

From the depths of shame and degradation, we have been raised to bask in the light of divine love. We wear the righteousness of Christ Jesus for all the world to see. We are black men redeemed, renewed, and regenerated.

Praise God for redemption full and free.

We call to remembrance the spirit and intellect of our ancient African ancestors. Their civilizations reveal the rich endowments of their culture. Their blood courses through our veins, and reminds us that we are creative, capable, and strong.

We stand on the shoulders of our forefathers. They survived the passage on crowded slave ships, the humiliation of slavery, the tearing away of wives and children, the ravages of racism, unemployment and underemployment.

We honor the memory of both named and unnamed black men, who gave their lives in the fight for freedom and peace.

Thank you, God, that our lives are enriched because of their sacrifices.

We recognize the contributions of extraordinary African American men such as Frederick Douglas and Ralph Bunch, Jesse Owens, Jackie Robinson, Arthur Ashe, George Pullman, the Tuskegee Airmen, Richard Wright, Alex Haley, Adam Clayton Powell, and Richard Allen.

Many more black male achievers such as these have inspired and motivated us.

With perseverance and much determination, black men have overcome many economic, political, and psychological obstacles.

Lord, lift us out of complacency. Help us protect, love, and support our families.

O God, remove all hatred, animosity, and anger from our souls. Keep us from the snare of the enemy. Envelop us in your undying love.

Through Jesus Christ, the way to abundant love has been paved for us.

We now dedicate ourselves to the task of continuing the legacy of great black men. To God we will be true and faithful. To our church we give our time, our talent and our treasure. To our community we pledge our hearts and hands.

God, our Protector, we pray for solidarity among black men, united, courageous and responsible, strong in the power of your Spirit. Thanks be to you.

73. MEMORIAL DAY

Today we celebrate the men and women who lost their lives after heeding the clarion call of their country to military duty. We especially raise up the African Americans whose contributions have often been ignored, devalued and forgotten. We honor those whose lives were lost beginning with the Revolutionary War and in each subsequent military encounter. We remember our fallen loved ones, relatives, friends and neighbors.

Let our tribute rise. Let it echo in the halls of memory. Let it resound throughout eternity. Accept our praise, O God, our Fortress and our Refuge.

We celebrate their patriotism. Although they were sometimes systematically denied full participation in the democratic process, our African American brothers and sisters loved America. They fought for the franchisement of all people, for life, liberty, and the pursuit of happiness.

Let our tribute rise. Let it echo in the halls of memory. Let it resound throughout eternity. Accept our praise our Rock and Defender.

We celebrate their courage. Defying stereotypical assertions of cowardice and fear, blacks demonstrated bravery and resourcefulness in times of duress and chaos, performing heroic rescues, launching aggressive attacks, and defending their positions. We salute them.

Let our tribute rise. Let it echo in the halls of memory. Let it resound throughout eternity. Accept our praise our Sword and Shield.

We celebrate their discipline. With polished precision our brothers and sisters performed their duties, many times not receiving the promotions to which they were entitled. Even though they were sometimes hated and abused by fellow soldiers, they worked and fought heroically.

Let our tribute rise. Let it echo in the halls of memory. Let it resound throughout eternity. Accept our praise, O God, our Leader and our Guide.

We celebrate their dignity. Our African American soldiers wore their uniforms proudly. With honor and distinction they died on behalf of America. No sacrifice, even the giving of their lives, was too great to offer in the belief of freedom for all. In memory thereof, we call their names...

(Members of the congregation may call out names of relatives and friends who have given their lives in military service.)

Sustained by undying faith in the God of the universe, our African American brothers and sisters never lost hope that God's kingdom would come, that God's will would be done through their patriotism.

Let our tribute rise. Let it echo in the halls of memory. Let it resound throughout eternity. Accept our praise, Lord Jesus, our soon coming King.

74. HOLY COMMUNION (THE LORD'S SUPPER)

As we come to the Lord's table, let us come with a spirit of humility and penitence.

Compassionate God, have mercy on us we pray.

Let us examine ourselves: our thoughts, our actions, our motives, and our attitudes toward others.

O Holy God, have mercy and forgive us our shortcomings.

Help us to remember our responsibility to our families and our neighbors, our stewardship to you, and the work you have given to our hands.

O Living God, we stand in need of your grace, strength, and mercy.

As we eat the bread, which represents your body, which is the True and Living Bread, open our eyes to recognize the intimacy that you yearn to share with us.

O Loving God, teach us to love you above all else.

As we drink the cup, which represents Christ's blood shed for us, we thank you for the new covenant, "Love ye one another", which is written on our hearts. Let us rejoice because our names are written in heaven. (see Matt. 13:34)

Tender Father and Mother, may your great sacrifice of redeeming love renew us for loving service and sacrifice for others.

May this Lord's Supper energize every area of our lives and enable us to transcend our circumstances, our inadequacies, and our enemies.

God who sees us, touch and empower us so that our lives will be renewed.

We praise you, O God, who made us your own people through the death and resurrection of your Son, our Lord.

Abide in us, Savior and Redeemer. Fill us with the life-giving power of your Spirit, now and forever.

75. OUR ELDERS

Sovereign God, we remember our elders of African descent. They fought courageously during times of war and peace. They built much of the United States of America with the knowledge, skill, and sweat of their brows. They also built their own institutions when denied admission to the institutions of others. They cared for their own needs and the needs of others. Despite many hardships, they sustained their families and communities.

We remember our elders today with pride.

They loved God. They created new means of expressing that love in their preaching and praying, in their spirituals and gospel music. They built churches and religious organizations, and expressed their faith in the lives they lived.

We remember our elders today with faith and reverence.

They gave us birth. They loved and cared for us. They passed a cherished heritage on to us. Our elders educated us and opened our eyes to the beauty of our past and the hopefulness of our future. They taught us to love ourselves and one another.

We remember our elders today with love and gratitude.

They filled their lives with art, poetry and literature. They excelled whenever they were given the opportunity. They were brilliant, creative and inventive. They painted, tapped, sculpted, drummed, hummed, sang and shouted, leaving us a rich, imaginative legacy.

We remember our elders today with respect and appreciation.

Now let us call the names of some of them: Absolom Jones, Lemuel Haynes, Richard Allen, David Walker, Maria Stewart, Sojourner Truth, and Jarena Lee,

Daniel Payne, Frederick Douglas, Mary Pleasant, Harriett Tubman, Nannie Helen Burroughs, and Booker T. Washington,

Anna Julia Cooper, William O. Tanner, Ida B. Wells, Mary Church Terrell, George Washington Carver, Adam Clayton Powell, and William E. B. DuBois,

Paul Lawrence Dunbar, Carter G. Woodson, Mary McLeod Bethune, Marcus Garvey, Paul Robeson, Duke Ellington, and Howard Thurman.

Now let us be mindful of those elders whose names are lost to us in history, those who were washed away in the Middle Passage. Let us remember them before God.

(Silence)

Let us now call the names of the elders, living and departed, who in our lifetime have positively influenced our homes, churches, communities and the world.

(Naming of elders by the congregation.)

We thank you, O God, for the elders you have given us.

Thanks be to God!

76. BLACK CHILDREN

Children are precious gifts from God and we love them. Let us remind ourselves that it takes a whole village to raise a child to compassion, competence, and character.

We celebrate their gifts and strengths. We pray for them. Lord, help us to hear the dreams and concerns of children, and to never give up on them.

We thank you for David, who found favor with you and was anointed king in his youth. We also thank you for Josiah who became king at eight years of age, and whose reign was pleasing to you.

We thank you for the young maiden who instructed Naaman to seek the prophet. We also thank you for Miriam who led with her brother Moses, for Jeremiah who was called from his mother's womb, and for Jesus who confounded the chief priests and scribes at the age of twelve.

We remember Emmit Till whose murder in Money, Mississippi shed light on the atrocities of racism. We remember the Little Rock Arkansas Nine, who risked their lives so that black children could receive an equal education. We remember the four young ladies who lost their lives in a Birmingham church during Sunday School.

In the twentieth century, many black children were still in desperate need. Every day seven hundred of them were born in poverty, seven were killed by guns, twenty eight never reached their first birthday and others died daily from HIV infection and drugs.

Some children are suspended from school, arrested, and incarcerated. Some are unmarried mothers. O Lord, rescue and deliver them all. Help them to become beacons of hope and agents of change in America and in the world.

As the lives of children and youth are channeled to schooling and career preparation, help them find the time to read and to understand your commandments, to know and to love Jesus Christ, and to be witnesses of your saving grace to their own generation.

O Lord, position significant and caring adults in their lives to guide them to discover the unique potential which you have placed within them.

Shield them from all hurt, harm, and danger. Shelter them from abuse, low self esteem, drugs, pornography, prostitution, and poverty.

May you help them to stay in school, to obey their parents, and to resist negative peer pressure. Give them important roles to play in the home, church, school, and community. Give every family and community assets that ensure the positive development of black children.

Our hope for the future resides in our children. We pray that they thrive according to your purpose.

77. FATHER'S DAY

God of our fathers and Creator of us all, we treasure our Christian fathers who are guardians of your creation. They have endeavored to be models of faith, freedom and strength for our families.

God of Abraham, Isaac, and Jacob, we thank you for our fathers and for the care they have given your creation.

As the Father of Jesus, you, God, are the model of perfect love and nurture. We will ever look to you for guidance and direction. We celebrate Joseph, Jesus' earthly father, who assumed unexpected responsibilities with grace and dedication.

Abba Father, Great Teacher, instruct our fathers in the ways of perfect love.

We mourn the many fathers lost in the Middle Passage, and those who were ripped away from their families during slavery. We vow to continue the process of reconciling black families, binding them together in love.

O Great Physician, teach us how to mend the family ties that have been severed.

We remember the weathered hands and gentle spirits of our own fathers. With proud yet humble hearts, they were cast down but not destroyed.

In the name of the fathers who have loved and raised us, we give thanks.

Our fathers have been warrior kings, leaders of nations and pillars of faith in church and society.

Strengthen their minds, bodies and spirits so that they may faithfully serve you. Help today's fathers, O God, to become wiser managers of their households.

Black fathers have distinguished themselves in every profession, at home and abroad. They have taught us strength in adversity and have led us in work and at play, in sports, in fishing, in building and trades.

"Faith of our fathers, living still in spite of dungeon, fire and sword. Faith of our fathers, holy faith. We will be true to you till death!"

78. URBAN MINISTRY

God tells us to spread the good news on the mountains, over the valleys, in the "hood", on street corners, in sanctuaries, in our homes, everywhere.

We go in faith and joy to tell the good news of God's unconditional love for all people.

God calls us to be in covenant relationships and covenant ministries:

To love and care, to share and clothe, to feed and nurture, to counsel and teach, to be committed to the health and well-being of our communities.

We are called to be the living church in the world.

The Church is the body of Christ, beyond these walls. We go in faith to minister in hospitals, prisons, schools, in places where people gather.

Gracious God, in all that is beautiful and right, fix our hearts so that our own doubts, fears, and judgmental nature will not impede our service.

God, prepare minds and souls to be your vessels, ever respectful and loving of others and ourselves.

Blessed be every child of God. Blessed be the gift of life, that we are the salt of the earth and the light of the world.

Our light is the light of Christ. God calls us to be beacons of hope, to help those in distress, following the model of the beloved Son, Jesus. Our church homes are to be havens for those needing refuge.

In the midst of domestic violence, gang unrest, drug and substance abuse, depression, adultery, loneliness, hate, and greed, help us live the option of love before your people.

O God, lead our communities to wholesome spiritual, social, political, and financial action.

Anoint us to step out boldly in courage to affect healing, renewal, opportunity, and hope.

We pledge our support to develop new, meaningful ministries. We open our eyes, by God's grace, to see all of creation in new ways.

Rather than demonize differences, may we respect and celebrate them. We open ourselves totally to do the work of love and mercy throughout our community.

Open our eyes that we may see the needs of your people; open our hearts and souls that we may serve with dignity and in peace.

79. NATION BUILDING (FOURTH OF JULY)

As we pray, Lord, we meditate upon the independence of the United States of America. We remember the contributions of African Americans in the building of this nation.

We begin with Crispus Attucks, a runaway slave, who was killed in Boston in 1770. He was the first martyr of the American Revolution.

Our country has set aside this day to commemorate our national freedom and the signing of the Declaration of Independence.

We, however, as African Americans, are conscious of the liberty and justice historically denied to our race, even by the framers of the Constitution. Lord, have mercy.

What these men achieved in freeing our nation was a great accomplishment, even though many were slave holders.

Thanks be to you, that the evils of slavery did not prevent us from making creative and constructive contributions to America, the great experiment in democracy.

As African Americans we are conscious of the hypocricy of this nation's founding fathers, yet proud of the struggles of our own heroic ancestors.

As W. E. B. Dubois described, we live with the double consciousness of being both black and American.

Gracious God, thank you for the many opportunities made available to us. But still we have a keen awareness of continuing prejudice and discrimination.

Let us not forget that African American men, women and children are to be included when the names of our nation builders are called.

May we never forget the labor and struggle of our brothers and sisters in the building of the land of the free and the home of the brave.

Almighty God, we pray that modern patriots will continue the pursuit of freedom for all as we continue to build this great nation.

80. BLACK SACRED MUSIC

Colossians instructs us to sing "psalms and hymns and spiritual songs", making melody in our hearts. (Col. 3:16)

David also commanded the chiefs of the Levites to appoint singers to play on musical instruments, on harps and lyres and cymbals, to raise loud sounds of joy. (see 1 Chr. 15:16)

Within our veins flow the rhythm, timing, and cadence of worship. We praise the Creator with our minds, hearts, souls and feet!

Our people have long been sustained by Negro spirituals, Watts and Tindley hymns, gospel songs of Dorsey and Cleveland and contemporary sounds by Hawkins and Smallwood.

What would the Black Church be without "Ride On, King Jesus," "Hush, Hush, Somebody's Calling My Name," "Were You There," "Go Tell It on the Mountain," "Jesus Keep Me Near the Cross," and "Precious Lord"?

What would our lives be without "Roll, Jordon Roll," "O Freedom," "I'll Fly Away," "Blessed Assurance," "Leaning On the Everlasting Arm," "Great Is Thy Faithfulness," and "Jesus You're the Center of My Joy"?

African Saint Augustine wrote that when we sing, we pray twice.

O God, you taught our ancestors to sing the songs of Zion from their souls, even as their hearts were breaking. Through our music we persevered, we pressed forward, we trusted you, and sang your praises, even in a strange land.

Through years of adversity, our music has lifted our vision and given us the strength to endure.

With the spirituals and hymns of the Black Church, we have moaned, hummed, sung and shouted to your glory.

"I will sing praise with the spirit, but I will sing praise with the mind also." (1 Cor. 14:15)

For us, there has been no liberation movement without a song. From across the continent of Africa and throughout the Diaspora, let us lift every voice and sing!

Praise him with tambourine and dance,

Praise him with trumpet sound,

Praise him with resounding cymbals,

Let everything that has breath, praise the Lord! (Ps. 150:6)

81. BLACK FAMILY

O God of Abraham, Isaac and Jacob, Creator and Sustainer of the universe, Maker of all there is, we recognize the multitude of challenges facing families as we celebrate the bonds of kinship established through your love.

We celebrate strong black families everywhere and their future generations.

We understand the negative impact of poverty, poor education, crime and substance abuse, premature sexual activity, inadequate housing, and unemployment on the black family.

We acknowledge that of ourselves we can do nothing, but with you all things are possible.

We declare our interest in and commitment to the survival of the black family.

We pray for black families everywhere and for future generations.

Now, therefore, we affirm for every black family faith, strength, and love.

We pray for faith, strength, and love for black families everywhere and for future generations.

We further pray for every black family understanding, wisdom, and power.

We pray for understanding, wisdom, and power for black families everywhere and for future generations.

We pray for the inner strength of every black family member—every parent, every spouse, every child, every sibling, and every caregiver—that they may never forget your promise to strengthen them and cause them to stand, upheld by your righteous, omnipotent hand.

Our prayer is that you would renew our minds, uplift our hearts, and create a growing spiritual life for our people today and for future generations.

"When we asunder part, it gives us inward pain; but we shall still be joined in heart, and hope to meet again."

"Blest be the tie that binds, our hearts in Christian love! The fellowship of kindred minds is like to that above."

82. CHRISTIAN EDUCATION

Christian education is our invitation to equip God's people with the teachings of Jesus, who has commissioned us to go into all the world, making disciples, teaching them to observe all that he commanded. (see Matt. 28:19)

Help us wise and omniscient God, to encourage men and women, boys and girls to seek to know you and to make known the gospel of your Son, Jesus Christ.

Help us to nurture and instruct in the ways of the Lord, for that is the chief responsibility of the church and family. Grant us grace to fulfill this high calling.

Beginning with the study of Holy Scripture, may we find one another exploring your love and justice in Sunday School, Vacation Bible School, Bible class, Christian higher education and graduate theological education.

Thank you, Lord, for all those who taught us your Word and lived a life which made your teaching real for us. We follow the example of Jesus Christ and seek to emulate these persons, who rightly taught us and lit the flame of excellence within us.

May the visual images that we use help us to imagine your omnipotence and to affirm our likeness to you.

Teach us your ways, O Lord, that we may not lean to our own understanding, but rather trust in you. As we honor and worship you, teach us to respect one another. Help us to maintain a sound, disciplined mind and give us obedient, compassionate hearts.

As we aspire to live more virtuous lives, help us to overcome ignorance, hesitancy and compromise.

We remember great schoolmasters like Booker T. Washington, W. E. B. DuBois, Frances Coppin, Mary McLeod Bethune, Benjamin Mays, and Marva Collins.

Thank you for the capacity to think. May we use the lights of exploration and discovery to improve our homes, neighborhoods, municipalities and world.

May we always study to show ourselves approved of you, even as we use media and technology in your service.

We thank you, God, for biblical translations through which we revisit the law and the prophets, the wisdom of the proverbs, the poetry of the psalms, the gospel of our Lord Jesus Christ, and the history of the apostles.

Thank you, God, for religious scholars who have helped us understand and identify the choices we can make in response to your revelation in human history.

As the old hymn proclaims, "A charge to keep we have, a God to glorify, a never dying soul to save, and fitted for the sky."

83. BLACK MARTYRS

"When he opened the fifth seal, I saw under the altar the souls of those who had been slaughtered for the word of God, and for the testimony they had given." (Rev. 6:9)

With grateful hearts and uplifted voices, we remember those who held to the faith, for they gave their lives in the struggle to be free.

Thank you, God, for black martyrs. Because of them, we are blessed.

Blessed are those mighty men and women of strength, who set a path for others to follow.

Lord, help us, that when our time comes, we too may face persecution and even death, with pride and dignity.

"Blessed are those who are persecuted for righteousness' sake, for theirs is the kingdom of heaven." (Matt. 5:10)

Nubian queens and great kings foresaw the plight of slavery to be one of oppression and cruelty. They resisted, preferring death.

Blessed are those who threw off the shackles of powerlessness and looked to a better day.

Crispus Attucks, Nat Turner, John Brown, the Scottsboro boys, Robert Brown Elliott, Brothers Martin, Malcolm and Medgar, as well as Steve Biko responded to cruel injustice with their lives.

In the spirit of Denmark Veasey, we long to see the promise of freedom blossom in the land of the living.

The flowers of freedom are watered with the blood, sweat and tears of our ancestors who never gave up the fight!

O Lord, have mercy on our world. It has embarked on a journey that is in great need of your intervention.

In the spirit of Cynthia Wesley, Addie Mae Collins, Carole Robertson, and Denise McNair, four girls murdered in the Sixteenth Street Baptist Church in Birmingham,

We will not shrink in the face of duty. We will not meander in the maze of mediocrity.

Black martyrdom wears many faces, but the response to the call is the same. God, we know that we will be victorious. We claim victory in your name.

As martyrdom knocks on our hearts even now, may we be willing to sacrifice everything to insure freedom and deliverance. We give thanks to God, who leads and guides us all.

84. RACIAL RECONCILIATION

Lord God, it was in an African garden that you created the human family.

In Eden, waters freely ran; plants, animals and all of nature were one.

Who are we that you should have made us in your image, crowned us with your glory and given us the freedom to make choices?

Through human freedom your original intent was intruded upon and violated.

From that moment of transgression and separation, you have constantly sought to find us, to forgive us, and to bring us back to you.

Lord Kyrios, forgive our disobedience.

Under watchful eye, Moses led your people out of Egypt while you guided your children through the wilderness. The Hebrew boys escaped the fiery furnace. Likewise, you guided African Americans through the perils of enslavement and brutality.

Forgive those who accept ideas of racial inferiority and prejudice.

Our leaders have taught us how to love in the face of hatred. We therefore seek reconciliation, and not revenge.

We extend love and fellowship to all who, like us, are created in your image.

God, you sought to repair the damage done in the garden by sending your Son, Jesus Christ to reconcile us to you and to each other.

Thank you for the ministry of reconciliation that lifts our spirits and changes our hearts.

Help us to forgive those who need peace and healing, and grant us a clearer understanding of your truth.

Give us courage to stand against those who would continue to sow evil. And may our lives point others to respect, equality, and dignity.

85. AN AWESOME GOD

How awesome is the Lord Most High, the great King over all the earth. God is on the move! All of those who serve the Lord will be blessed! (Ps. 47:2)

Come we who love the Lord and let our joys be known!

There is a song in our hearts. There are untold melodies on our lips. For our God is worthy of songs of praise and delight!

The neglected and the orphan have a new song to sing; for God cares for the down-trodden and the forgotten ones of the world.

The homeless and the wayward have a shelter. The captives to addictions and compulsions have a way up and out.

Before the beginning, God was at work, making provisions for us, taking the desolate and void, making a place of wonder and delight for our habitation.

"And he set that sun a-blazing in the heavens..."

Our God is an awesome God!

"Then down between the darkness and the light he hurled the world..."

Our God is an awesome God!

The rich, black soil was dense and the mountain ranges high as God spoke the Motherland into existence. The God of Africa, the High God, reigned in splendor.

God has helped us to preserve our heritage, even in exile.

In strange lands, we have been made to dwell. In different climates, we have learned to adjust. In different cultures, we have remained distinct. God's goodness provided for our needs.

From around the world, we of the Diaspora continue to lift our sounds of exultation to our God.

O Lord, our Lord, how majestic is your name in all the earth. (Ps. 8:11)

Regal Power and Sovereign Majesty is the name of our God.

God is in this house! God reigns with power and love!

Our God is an Awesome God!

86. BLACK SCIENTISTS AND INVENTORS

We thank you, O God, for the scientific ingenuity of African Americans, which has often gone unrecognized in the histories of the world. We have discovered that black men and women are among the world's greatest inventors.

O God, you have made African Americans great achievers. We are physicians, astronauts, pharmacists and technical professionals. Our ancestral past is distinguished by scientists and mathematicians who built pyramids and laid the foundations of modern medicine.

Benjamin Banneker was a self-taught mathematician and astronomer who received international recognition for his almanacs. He also designed the layout of Washington, D.C., our nation's capital.

Our chemists, biologists and botanists populate universities and other institutions throughout the world.

We are inventors. George Washington Carver suffered through slavery and childhood illness to later fashion an abundance of products from the peanut and sweet potato. While at Tuskegee University, he received patents for many of his unique discoveries. He also prayed each morning and taught a Bible class.

Black inventors have improved the quality of life for all Americans. Labor-saving devices and other inventions have helped both our agricultural and urban centers. These range from the elevator to the fire extinguisher, from the traffic signal to the pencil sharpener.

M. C. Harney, L. S. Buridge, N. R. Marshman, W. B. Purvis, H. Blair and G. E. Beckett gave this country the lamp, the typewriter, the fountain pen, the corn harvester and the mail box.

O God, you are the Maker of miracles. We celebrate black inventions that have made our lives better.

We are doctors. Dr. Charles R. Drew helped make blood banks possible by determining that plasma can be preserved and stored for later use. Dr. T. K. Lawless discovered cures for many skin diseases.

We are scientists. Ernest Everett Just was a leader in microbiology, researching the cell, the embryo and the fertilization process at Howard University.

Black scientists and inventors have served as God's hands on earth. Now, O God, may we work with diligence, utilizing our talents to bring to fruition the future you have already promised us.

Gracious Majesty, we see the order and design of your creation, the heavens, earth and life therein. We respond in awesome wonder. All praise be to you!

87. A FUNERAL PRAYER

God knows our frame; God remembers that we are dust. Blessed are the dead who die in the Lord. May they rest from their labors and may their works follow them.

Creator God, from whom we all have come, unto whom we shall return and in whom we live, move and have our being, we praise you for your good gift of life.

We thank you for the loving patience with which you teach us your truth, and for the deeper meanings of life which lies hidden in sorrow, loss, and grief.

Preserve us from faithless doubts and anxieties and grant that no clouds of this mortal life may hide from us the light of your unchanging love.

O Lord, guide us all the day long in this troublesome life, until the shadows lengthen and the evening comes, and the busy world is hushed. Support us until the fever of life is over and our work is done. Then, of your mercy, grant us a safe lodging and holy rest in that place you have prepared for us.

May we show forth our thankfulness to you in trustful, courageous lives.

We give thanks for the life of your child _____*(first name of the deceased)*. We recall the qualities in _____ that made us love (him/her). We thank you for all the good influences (he/she) made upon the lives of others. We thank you for the truth that has passed from (his/her) life into the lives of others. Their lives are richer because of it.

Open wide your gates, O Lord, and receive the spirit of _____. Grant him/her everlasting life and comfort the bereaved family and friends.

We praise your name for the revelation of your love in our Lord Jesus Christ, and for the hope set before us in the gospel. We know that deep in the human heart there is a trust that life does not end with death.

Thank you, O God, for the faith that you will not leave us in the dust, but will care for us beyond what we can see, even as you have cared for us in this earthly life.

Lift us into the light of your countenance. Cause your light to shine upon us so that our sorrow can be turned into prayer. As is your majesty, so is your mercy. In your will is our peace. May this faith grow in us until the wounds of parting are healed by the assurance of reunion. Lead us by the still waters and sit us in pastures of grace.

"Death has been swallowed up in victory. Where, O death, is your victory? O death, where is your sting?" (1 Cor. 15:54-55)

88. EDUCATION

Let us remember that "the fear of the Lord is the beginning of all wisdom; all those who practice it have a good understanding." (Ps. 111:10)

Lord God, Giver of wisdom, hear our prayer.

Thank you, God, for the education we have received and for opportunities to increase our knowledge. We bless our parents who introduced us to reading, relationships, and lifeskills.

"Train children in the right way and when old, they will not stray." (Prov. 22:6)

We thank you, God, for good teachers, good books, public libraries, and the educational programs of television and radio.

"Whoever loves discipline loves knowledge, but those who hate to be rebuked are stupid." (Prov. 12:1)

We pray for our pre-schools, for the teachers, the students and the workers.

God of steadfast love, hear our prayer.

We pray for the members of this congregation who are involved in all aspects of education: teachers, counselors, principals and other administrators, board members, secretaries, custodians and nurses.

"Trust in the Lord with all your heart and do not rely on your own insight. In all your ways acknowledge him, and he will make straight your paths." (Prov. 3:5-6)

We pray for universities, colleges, and other institutions of adult learning. We pray for their students. Make us aware of the injustices in our society about which so many students complain.

We pray for those in developing countries who do not enjoy the tremendous educational opportunities of this nation. Expand their educational enterprise.

We pray for literacy programs, for Bible societies and distributors of Christian literature at home and abroad.

"There are six things that the Lord hates, seven that are an abomination to him: haughty eyes, a lying tongue, and hands that shed innocent blood, a heart that devises wicked plans, feet that hurry to run to evil, a lying witness who testifies falsely, and one who sows discord in a family." (Prov. 6:16-19)

We pray for the teaching and preaching ministries of our congregation. Create in those who are called to instruct your people, a mind and a heart committed to studying your Word.

May these ministries improve relationships and inspire greater entrepeneurship.

We pray that the increase of knowledge and education may not make us intellectually proud or spiritually barren.

God, Creator of all wisdom and knowledge, make us productive citizens and responsible stewards of your gifts and graces.

89. LABOR DAY BLESSINGS

We rejoice this day to worship you, O God, and give thanks, as we take rest from our labors.

For we are saints in Caesar's house—shining lights—witnesses for our Lord. (see Phil. 4:22)

Let us remember that the first recorded command given to humankind was to work. Our ability to work is a gift from God.

We acknowledge the role of African Americans in building this country. We recognize their sweat, sacrifice and struggle.

Not all slaves were relegated to the fields and "the big house." Some were skilled tradesmen, blacksmiths, carpenters, brickmasons and iron workers. Others worked in copper and gold mines, tobacco factories and textile mills.

We pray for all who are employed, that they might give good and honest work. We pray for all employers that they may carry out their responsibilities with justice and integrity. We pray for the unemployed and those who cannot work.

We pray for those whose work is dull, monotonous or dangerous. We also pray for those whose work presents them with great temptation or separates them for long periods from their families.

O God, as we continue to work toward building a future for ourselves and our children, make us ever mindful of your importance in our lives. May we seek above all to please you in our work.

We pray for the labor union movement and are thankful for the better working conditions and fairer wages which it has achieved. With admiration, we remember A. Philip Randolph who founded the first union of black workers. May all union workers use their powers wisely and responsibly.

As we labor, may we remember our brothers and sisters in need.

We pray for those who are denied employment opportunities because of ethnicity, religious affiliations, physical disabilities or gender. We pray for those who are self-employed and for small business owners. We also pray for those who are retired.

Lord, hear our prayer.

May African Americans prosper in blue collar trades, in service industries, in business, and in the professions so that they may achieve self-determination and reach their personal and professional goals.

Help us to model the life of your Son before our co-workers and employers. For we reveal in our work that we are shining lights witnessing for our Lord.

90. HEALTH AND WELLNESS

History bears witness that God has chosen the fragile vessels of people to be vehicles of grace and messengers of his ministering presence and mercy.

We bear the mark of God's image. We have been created as unique and special individuals, knowing that our bodies are temples of the Holy Spirit.

We live in a medical age unprecedented in history. We have eliminated many of the scourges and plagues that haunted the world through the ages.

We thank you, God. You are the Comforter and Healer of all sickness and affliction. We depend on you to give us insight and wisdom for greater cures, therapies, and techniques to conquer diseases and mental afflictions.

Bless all health practitioners, the methods they use and medicines they prescribe. Give us the faith and trust to cooperate with the revealed truth which you have given them to help us attain wholeness of body and mind.

Heal your people through the hands of research, surgery, and touch. Relieve the pain of many who are languishing in despair. Give them the strength to endure and the faith to overcome whatever ails them.

Today we take responsibility for our own health and wellness by learning how to practice good habits and how to respond to our body's warning signs.

We take responsibility for our diet, exercise and health care. Lord, give us a balanced life of work and relaxation.

Pressures, demands, and worries fill us with disease. We take responsibility to keep them within manageable limits. Illness is often associated with the need for inner healing. Therefore, we take responsibility to confess our sins before God, and to be reconciled to our brothers and sisters.

Wellness is a state of mind, body and soul. We take responsibility to view health and wholeness as an important part of our salvation. Jesus said, "For which is easier to say, 'Your sins are forgiven' or to say, 'Stand up and walk?'" (Matt. 9:5)

We pray that all people may have access to quality health care, regardless of economic status or family situation.

Jesus was concerned with the sick and he was attentive to the mind and spirit of those who suffered. May we do the same in daily service, reminding others that the healing power of the Holy Spirit is within every true believer.

91. THE MIDDLE PASSAGE (THE MAAFA)

Eternal God, our Creator, the descendants of earth's firstborn ancestors come to you in remembrance of tragic death.

We have often spoken and acted in ignorance of our history, but today we remember the sufferings of the past. We grieve for those who made the long transatlantic crossing on slave ships.

We remember those dark-hued kings and queens, chiefs and warriors who were stolen, shackled, and sold from African soil and kindred.

In the Middle Passage from Africa to the New World, they traveled cramped in spaces too small for them to turn.

We remember those who died from exhaustion, and cruel conditions; we remember those who were killed for their resistance.

We remember our brothers and sisters whose bodies were beaten, broken and violated. We remember our sisters who bore their young, only to be torn from them. We remember the ones who found freedom's final rest hanging from a tree. May we never see this sort of atrocity again.

We remember the cries of children whose tears were never comforted, and whose hearts were never warmed by the embrace of their mothers and fathers; and who were afflicted with the diseases of their oppressors.

Africa, our Africa, we may never have known you, but our faces are full of your blood. We, your children, cry, "God have mercy." May the world never see this atrocity again.

May faith in Christ sustain us as we forgive the trespassers of our past.

We vow to remember and to honor the resistance and endurance of our ancestors. We thank you, God, for bringing us to freedom and for showing us the pathway to hope.

92. SUBSTANCE ABUSE AWARENESS

O God, you are great, and your name is great in all the earth! Speak to us of your creation and of the purpose for which you have created us. Speak to us with urgency as we desperately search for answers to the plague of substance abuse.

Speak to us Lord with words of healing and victory.

Contemplating the global plight of drug abuse and addiction leaves us wounded and confused. The death and destruction that this plague brings humbles us and menaces the health and survival of many who love and care for us.

In the beginning, God created the heavens and the earth; and it was good. We are marvelously and wonderfully made.

Rescue us from the hand of the wicked and cruel who profit from the demise of others. Blessed is the nation whose God is the Lord, the people whom the Lord has chosen as his heritage.

Happy are those who take refuge in God instead of in the things of this world.

Cigarettes, alcohol, prescription drugs, marijuana, heroin, cocaine, and crack: the abuse of these and other substances defeat the glorious purpose for which we were made.

The use of drugs among mothers of unborn and newborn babies cripple the children of the next generation. Their prospects for a healthy future are diminished.

We know that our bodies are God's temple and that God's Spirit lives in us. God help us not to destroy these temples, earthen vessels though they be.

Drug abuse occurs in rich and poor, in educated and uneducated, in church folk and unchurched, in all ethnic groups, classes, professions, neighborhoods, and homes.

Lord God, in the name and Spirit of Jesus, make us ready to accept the challenge of social wholeness as a high priority. Set the captives free and deliver your people from all that is against them.

Greater is he that is in me than he that is in the world. Let God arise and his enemies be defeated. We bind addictions of all kind and we release life-affirming love on earth and in heaven. (See 1 Jn. 4:4, Matt. 18:18)

93. GLOBAL MISSION

God, who judges the nations of the world, we heed your Son's great commission to go into all the world making disciples of all, baptizing them in the name of the Father, the Son, and the Holy Spirit, teaching them to observe all things whatsoever you have commanded. (See Matt. 28:19)

May we respond with glad hearts to spread the good news of the gospel near and far.

May we see in all people the deeper expressions of true humanity, affirming our many similarities and overcoming our differences.

As we go, may we be equipped to understand various cultures and languages. May we go with open minds and hearts responding to the many needs of your children who suffer in many lands.

May we learn their history and be sensitive to the destinies of cultures different from our own. May we go not only to give but also to learn and to receive. Let us not impose restrictions upon the activity of your Holy Spirit moving in their midst.

May we share, from our struggles and triumphs, the possibilities that we have experienced and envisioned in Christ Jesus. Make us friends to all the world; a world which you loved so dearly that you gave your Son for its salvation.

We thank you for the privileges and comforts which we enjoy in our land. We pray for security and justice in all lands.

We pray a special blessing upon our motherland, the continent of Africa, where poverty abounds. We pray that tribalism, war, and dictatorship may give way to equality and freedom. Remove the vestiges of slavery and colonialism.

Lord, we realize that there are no poor countries, only poor people. Grant redemption by feeding the hungry, clothing the naked, and establishing democratic government. Eliminate disease and high international debt.

Today, a few of the world's citizens consume most of the world's resources. Remove this imbalance and give everyone a fair chance, an equal start, and a level playing field.

Help us to educate the illiterate, to affirm technological and agricultural self-sufficiency, and to establish sustainable environments.

Thank you for new models of international reconciliation and truth-telling. Rid the world of "ethnic cleansing." May technology and telecommunications work together for the good of all.

Lord, may we ever obey your call to unfamiliar places, both at home and abroad, from our doorsteps to the ends of the earth.

Knowing that you are with us always, let us go with love rejoicing.

94. REVIVAL

The pathway to the burning fire and refreshing springs of revival is faith. We remember that in the antebellum South, American slaves of African ancestry stole away in the darkness of night to celebrate salvation in Jesus!

Lord God, your people are still in need of repentance and renewal. They are seeking sacred hiding places in the hope of finding you.

Like Moses who approached you through a bush which burned but was not consumed, we desire to draw closer to you during this revival.

God of Strength, the power of your divine presence enlightens our vision, empowers our mission, directs our ministries, renews our spirit, transforms our minds, heals our sufferings and cleanses our souls.

When Joshua battled the Amorites, you caused the sun to stand still over Gibeon. Before David slew the Philistine giant and King Jehoshaphat defeated both the Moabites and the Ammonites, you said, "The battle is not yours, but the Lord's." (see 2 Chr. 20:15, Josh. 10:12)

God of Victory, we confess that your strength is seen in our weakness, and that our best efforts are feeble attempts unless your divine presence and eternal wisdom are called upon.

Through the faith of a Hebrew maiden, the Israelites secured a leader—Moses; through faith Ruth clung to Naomi and God redeemed the future of all generations; Rahab's faith provided safety for two of Joshua's spies.

Through faith a widow provided food for Elijah when the brook of Cherith dried up; through faith Hannah gave Samuel to the Lord; through faith Mary, a young virgin, trusted that the life within her was indeed of the Holy Spirit!

"As a deer longs for flowing streams" we stand before the altars of our hearts asking for an outpouring of your Holy Spirit. Miracle-working, Supernatural God, stir up our faith to such an extent that we may fulfill your purpose at this time. (Ps. 42:1)

God, who has answered by fire, send again the wind and the fire of your Spirit. On your people pour your power. "Lord, let there be a revival and let it begin with me!"

95. BEING SINGLE

God bless the widowed, divorced, and unmarried in our midst. May your love enfold them and the community of faith affirm them in their singleness.

Being single is to know the joy and fulfillment of God's consuming and unconditional love for us. It is full; it is blessed; it is beautiful.

Being single is the ability to enjoy ourselves and to acknowledge our limitations. Sometimes it allows intimacy with God without distraction.

Being single is the freedom to be alone and not lonely, to be at peace with nature, and to be complete with friends and family.

Being single is the ability to pray in the name of Jesus and to dance freely before him, knowing that he cares not if we sing off key or dance to a different beat.

Being single is having the ability to shed tears at night knowing that when we need to be comforted, we will be rocked in the cradle of God's arms.

Being single is being a proud black man and black woman who respects others who share in his or her life.

Being single is a shared dinner with friends on Saturday night and communion with the saints on Sunday morning.

Being single is listening to the preached Word and allowing it to validate, encourage and strengthen.

Being single is walking through a storm uncertain and scared, and later singing, "My soul looks back and 'knows' how I got over."

Being single is knowing that others before us have run this race and allowing them to encourage us in the midnight hour of our soul. Being single is giving to God freely of our time, talent and treasure.

Lord, we thank you for the contributions of single persons to our church and community.

96. BLACK COLLEGES

African Americans have long valued education as the key to greater achievement. No sacrifice was too great for our parents to make for our education.

They told us: "Education is the key. No one can take that away from you."

Many black parents didn't have the means to send their children to college. Some of these children worked their way through college washing dishes in the cafeteria, mowing lawns, working as maids, pumping gas, scrubbing floors and performing other menial tasks.

Thank you Lord for making a way out of no way.

We thank God for people who bestowed institutions of higher education to their children. There are over one hundred historically black colleges and universities in the United States. Cheyney State is the oldest black college, founded in 1837.

We also cherish Lincoln, Shaw, Virginia Union, Fisk, Howard, Hampton, Morehouse, Tougaloo, Clark-Atlanta, Alcorn, Houston-Tillotson, Spelman and Tuskegee, as well as other unnamed institutions which we now call out. (Pause)

(Silently remember the black college which you attended and call out its name if it does not appear above.)

We remember the founding of black fraternities and sororities and their contribution to our communities. We remember professors and administrators of vision. They filled us with knowledge and they taught us black history.

A people without knowledge of their own history is like a tree without roots.

In 1943, the President of Tuskegee Institute, Dr. Frederick D. Patterson, initiated the United Negro College Fund to raise money to support black colleges.

The saying, "A mind is a terrible thing to waste," draws national attention to the educational needs of black students.

The majority of black college graduates have attended historically black colleges and universities. Often these students were the first members of their families to attend college.

People are destroyed for lack of knowledge and perish where there is no vision to light the way.

We are called upon to sustain institutions of higher education for future generations. Dr. Benjamin Mays believed that the primary task of black colleges is to build character. God help us to remain ever conscious of the quality of fruit our people bear.

Blessed Teacher, African Americans will not perish because we shall continue to support and strengthen black students, black colleges and universities. Thanks be to you!

97. INTERFAITH DAY

This is the day that we honor all religious faiths that give glory to God.

Lord, grant us peace and unity in your Spirit.

Grant that people of all faiths and denominations will look to you for guidance and direction.

Holy Parent of us all, grant us peace and unity in your Spirit.

Break down the walls of suspicion, bigotry, and exclusivity that divide us.

Lord, grant us peace and unity in your Spirit.

Help us to see the beauty, wonder, glory and joy of all religious faiths that recognize the Creator of life and love.

God of glory, grant us peace and unity in your Spirit.

On this day, we pay tribute to the giver of life and truth as we remember that there is only one true and living God. The presence of your Spirit is felt by your followers all over the world.

Marvelous God, grant us peace and unity in your Spirit.

As we weave our religious banners into garments of peace, weave us together, O Lord, as one.

God of love, grant us peace and unity in your Spirit.

Let us not stray from our real purpose. As we acknowledge you in our lives, lead, guide and direct our paths.

Good Shepherd, grant us peace and unity in your Spirit.

As we discover the greater depths of the encompassing love you have for us, bind us together as one in the ever present need to assist you in the work of bringing world peace, joy, and harmony.

We are your people, and the sheep of your pastures. Grant us peace and unity as we venture forth in your name.

98. BLACK LITERATURE

God of creative expression and giver of every good gift, we thank you for black authors, our storytellers who have documented what has been done to us, what we have accomplished, and how we have accomplished it.

We gather today in God's presence to celebrate the richness of black literature.

From slave narrative to fiction, in poetry and drama, African Americans have captured the joys, pains, triumphs, and defeats of our people through their literary gifts.

They have declared to the world how, with your help, we have survived.

They have used their God-given ability to inspire us through language and rhythm, striking imagery and metaphor. Some wrote sermons; others wrote poems, songs, stories and plays full of happiness and humor, sadness and despair.

They have been the distinctive voices of a multifaceted people. They have spoken of our conflicts and struggles, our hopes and dreams.

We remember Countee Cullen, Langston Hughes, Sterling Brown, and James Baldwin. They often wrote of Jesus and the church. We remember Phyllis Wheatley, Arna Bontemps, Walter White, Jessie Fauset, Wallace Thurman, and E. Franklin Frazier.

They helped to lay the foundation for Negro group expression and our national identity.

Some were journalists, like Frederick Douglas and Ida B. Wells Barnett who issued the clarion call away from apathy and the wake-up call to freedom and its cost. Some, like Maria Stewart, wrote political speeches that gave us the will to believe that change was imperative. They reinforced in us the courage to stand up for truth, justice, and righteousness.

They produced creative masterpieces, which reflected the African American experience, and became God's modern day prophets.

Lord, we thank you for W. E. B. DuBois, who uncovered *The Souls of Black Folk*. We thank you for Ralph Ellison, who revealed the struggles of *The Invisible Man*. We thank you for Richard Wright, who wrote *Native Son*. We thank you for Alex Haley, who traced our *Roots*.

Drawing upon the legacy of the insidious effects of slavery, African American writers defined the complexities of being black in America.

We remember James Weldon Johnson, Paul Lawrence Dunbar, Claude McKay, and Jean Toomer. We remember Lorraine Hansberry, Zora Neale Hurston, and Nella Larson.

We praise you, O God, for those writers who so eloquently used their pens. Thank you, God, for the insights they have shared with us.

99. THANKSGIVING

All praise be to God for the birds of the air, the fruit of the field, and interstellar space. We praise you for all that is past and trust in you for all that is to come. For our history and our future we give thanks unto the Lord.

All praise be to God for the harvest. May we be good stewards of your bounty.

Thankfulness should be a constant state of being, but during this season of Thanksgiving, we take special pause to give thanks. All love comes from you, O Lord. Teach us to love. For our families and all who work to knit us in love, we are grateful.

All praise be to the Living God. May we be good stewards of your bounty.

God, our Provider, we give thanks for the places we call home. For nations and mother-lands, cities and neighborhoods, places to lay our heads and tables blessed with food, we give you thanks.

All praise be to the Loving God. May we be good stewards of your bounty.

We are a colorful nation of workers and dreamers, whether we came willingly or in chains. Aid us Lord, as we continue to challenge this nation to live up to its promises of freedom, opportunity and equality. Help us as we continue to be the conscience of our land, guardians of civil rights and human dignity.

All praise be to the Holy God. May we be good stewards of your bounty.

Thank you for jobs and the possibility of jobs. Thank you for well-being and the guardians of our well-being. Thank you for your church and our church family, for our pastor, minis-ters and elders. For laughter, joy and the beauty of the earth, we give thanks.

All praise be to the Most High God. May we be good stewards of your bounty.

Now unto your Son, who made one perfect sacrifice for all, we give triumphant thanks. For his shed blood and its redemptive power, we rejoice. We are grateful that from your hand we receive daily sustenance and love that is more than we expect or deserve.

All praise be to God for the harvest. We give thanks to him. For God has done great things. "For the Lord is good; his steadfast love endures forever, and his faithfulness to all generations." (Ps. 100:5)

100. ADVENT

While we were yet sinners, Jesus came at the right time, after forty two generations.

During this Advent season the whole church, the Body of Christ, looks forward to the second coming of the promised Messiah, Jesus, our Lord.

God sent the angel Gabriel to Nazareth to announce to the virgin Mary that she had found favor with God. Her cousin, Elizabeth, said, "Blessed are you among women, and blessed is the fruit of your womb." (Lk. 1:42)

As the Word made flesh, Jesus came to an unprepared people in an unprepared place.

We remember our Savior's humble and obscure entry into our world.

O God, we remember your love for your creation and thank you for Jesus, your only begotten Son.

God, help us to understand and appreciate the ways in which you use the forgotten, the marginalized, the outcast, the weak, the poor, the imprisoned and the afflicted to proclaim the presence of your kingdom.

At the birth of our Savior, angels sang with jubilation and shepherds praised Jesus and glorified God!

Lord Jesus, as we reflect upon the joyous miracle of your birth, deepen our understanding of the purpose of your coming.

When you came as a tender baby to save a fallen world, Mary wrapped you in swaddling clothes.

And when you died upon a cross at Calvary to redeem and restore a lost creation, Joseph of Arimathaea wrapped you in burial clothes.

And when you ascended to your Father in Heaven, God clothed you with all power in heaven and on earth!

You told your disciples you would come again to receive us unto yourself. Thus, every day we look forward to your second coming with great anticipation.

We herald your coming, Wonderful Counselor, for you are the King of kings, Lord of lords, the Mighty God, Everlasting Father, the Prince of Peace. We love you. We adore you. You alone are worthy of all our praise! (see Is. 9:6)

101. STEWARDSHIP

O God, we desire to be good stewards of all that you have made: the earth, the world, and all that dwells therein. All that we have comes as a trust from you.

God, Elohim, we give thanks for your gifts to us.

We are called by God to use whatever gifts we have been given in service to others.

As you have so freely given to us and lovingly made us what we are, we now freely give back to you the substance of our lives—our time, talent and money.

We are reminded in the gospel that from the poverty of the cross we have gained the richness of life.

Thank you, Lord, for allowing us to give to the work you have assigned our hands to do in this your earthly kingdom.

You have put your divine stamp upon us, endowed us with honor, and created us in your likeness. We are fearfully and wonderfully made. Through providence and grace we offer our tithes and offerings on your altar.

Lord, Adonai, where our hearts and hands are closed, open them. Where our resolve is weak, strengthen us.

Our health and strength have come from you and it is you who make our financial resources possible.

Teach us to give as we have received. Remind us that what we claim as ours is really yours. Without your gifts to us we have nothing.

We are called by you, O Lord, to be good stewards of all that has been entrusted in our care. You have called us to honor your name with our presence and our service.

Gracious God, our prayer is that we may give a good accounting of our stewardship.

We have received the glorious gospel of Jesus Christ as a gift, and we have been made his disciples.

We pray that we shall be good and faithful stewards, sharing with others the light that Jesus has given to us, ever giving and serving from a willing heart. We have freely received, now let us freely give!

102. CHRISTMAS

"The people who walked in darkness have seen a great light; those who dwelt in a land of deep darkness, on them light has shined." This is the good news: the Anointed Messiah has come, and with him is the triumph of redeeming love. (Is. 9:2)

Thanks be to God, for the gift of your Son, Jesus, the light in darkness and hope of the world, whom you have sent to save humanity.

"And she gave birth to her firstborn son and wrapped him in bands of cloth, and laid him in a manger, because there was no place for them in the inn." His name shall be called Immanuel, meaning, "God with us." (Lk. 2:7)

"Do not be afraid, for I am bringing you good news of a great joy for all people: for to you is born this day in the city of David a Savior, who is the Messiah, the Lord." (Lk 2:10-11)

With all the angels, we praise your name, and tell the world the wondrous story of your birth.

"Sweet little Jesus boy, born in a manger, Sweet little holy child, We didn't know who you was."

Quietly you came to us. You came with power that we may share your power; humble, that the poor and lowly might see their greatness; destined for a cross, that all might have life eternal.

God so loved the world that he gave his only begotten Son. (see Jn. 3:16)

The work of Christmas is to find the lost, heal the broken, feed the hungry, release the captive, rebuild the nations, bring peace among the people, and make music in the heart.

Come celebrate, sing carols, decorate trees, and prepare a feast. Glory, glory to the new-born King! "O come let us adore him. O come let us adore him, Christ, the Lord."

103. KWANZAA

Bless us, O Lord, as we gather here to give you praise. Bless these symbols of African tradition. Bless these candles which represent the values of our motherland, codified by Ron Karenga in 1966. We now make these values part of our lives.

Give us understanding and wisdom, O God, as to how we can free our brothers and sisters from misguided values. Help us to embody true community.

O Ancient of Days, as we recall the seven principles of Kwanzaa, we request your presence. We call first UMOJA, the Kwanzaa principle of *unity:*

Umoja—May we strive for unity in the family, community, nation and race.

We call second KUJICHAGULIA, the Kwanzaa principle of *self-determination:*

Kujichagulia—may we define ourselves, create for ourselves, and speak for ourselves.

We call third UJIMA, the Kwanzaa principle of *collective work and responsibility:*

Ujima—may we build and maintain our community together, make our brothers' and sisters' problems our problems, and solve them together.

We call fourth UJAMAA, the Kwanzaa principle of *cooperative economics:*

Ujamaa—may we build and maintain our own stores, shops, and other businesses, and profit from them together.

We call fifth NIA, the Kwanzaa principle of *purpose:*

Nia—may we make as our collective vocation the building and developing of our community in order to restore our people to their traditional greatness.

We call sixth KUUMBA, the Kwanzaa principle of *creativity:*

Kuumba—may we do always as much as we can in the way we can to leave our community more beautiful and beneficial than when we inherited it.

We call seventh IMANI, the Kwanzaa principle of *faith:*

Imani—may we believe with all our heart in our parents, our teachers, our leaders, our people and our God, and in the righteousness and victory of our struggle.

By affirming these values, we continue the tradition and wisdom of our African ancestors.

Lord God, let us continue to remember the glory of our African past. Bless our efforts today and may your divine hand lead and guide us to the Beloved community.

104. WATCH NIGHT SERVICE

O God, as was customary of our parents and ancestors, we come to this Watch Night vigil to be with you, in your house, as we usher out the old year and welcome the dawning of a new year.

We come, thanking you for guidance and direction. Go before us, O God, and draw us into the future where you are.

Our slave ancestors watched that night long ago for the signing of the Emanicpation Proclamation. Lord, keep us awake and alert as we follow in the light of your Word, searching for the good news of the gospel, and the comforting signs of your love in this world.

We thank you for watching over us and caring for us through the old year, as we walked in the light of your love. We thank you for your promises of peace, healing, and justice.

We come, O God, with great expectations and great hopes. Keep these fires kindled within us that we may watch and wait, and once more feel your presence. Let us know your power as we embark upon this journey.

You have led us in the past. Guide us now, and always, that we might choose to do your will and follow your way. We are pilgrims in a barren land.

We give you praise, O God, for your goodness and mercy; for life, health and friends, and for the many blessings you always send. Above all, we thank you for Jesus Christ, who lifts our hopes, guides us in the Way, in this new year, and in years to come.

All praise, honor, glory, and thanks to you, our God, through Jesus Christ our risen Savior and Lord.

BLESS THE LORD   105

Bless the LORD O my soul, and all that is within me, bless His holy name.
Psalm 103:1

Text: Psalm 103:1
Tune: Andraé Crouch, b.1945, © Bud John Songs, Inc.; arr. by Nolan Williams, Jr., b.1969

106 IN THE BEAUTY OF HOLINESS

...be holy yourselves in all your conduct; for it is written, "You shall be holy, for I am holy."
1 Peter 1:15-16

Come let us wor-ship the Lord in the beau - ty of

ho - li-ness. Come let us wor-ship the Lord

in the beau-ty of ho - li-ness. Give Him the hon-

or. Give Him the praise.

Come let us wor-ship the Lord; Let's give Him the praise.

107 WE'VE COME TO WORSHIP YOU

Thus says the LORD: "Let my people go, so that they may worship me."
Exodus 8:1

1. Lord, we've come to wor - ship You.
2. Lord, we've come to give You thanks.
3. Lord, we've come to give You praise.

Lord, we've come to wor - ship You, for we
Lord, we've come to give You thanks, for we
Lord, we've come to give You praise, for we

know that Your name is wor - thy, oh Lord, and we've
know that Your name is wor - thy, oh Lord, and we've
know that Your name is wor - thy, oh Lord, and we've

come to wor - ship You.
come to give You thanks.
come to give You praise.

Text: Stephen Key
Tune: Stephen Key
© 1993, StepKey Music

This Is the Day 108

This is the day that the LORD has made; let us rejoice and be glad in it.
Psalm 118:24

This is the day, This is the day that the Lord has made, that the

Lord has made. I will re-joice, I will re-joice and be

glad in it, and be glad in it. This is the day that the

Lord has made. I will re-joice and be glad in it.

This is the day, This is the day that the Lord has made.

Text: Psalm 118:24
Tune: Les Garrett, b.1944, © 1967, Scripture in Song, a div. of Integrity Music, Inc.; arr. by Stephen Key

109 I Will Call Upon the Lord

Because He inclined his ear to me, therefore I will call on Him as long as I live.
Psalm 116:2

I will call up-on the Lord, For

I will call up-on the

He is wor-thy to be praised.

Lord, For He is wor-thy to be

alt - ed. The Lord   liv-eth, and bless-ed be the Rock;

And let the God   of my sal-va - tion be ex - alt - ed.

Text : Psalm 18:2, 2 Samuel 22:47; Michael O'Shields, © 1981, Sound III
Tune: Michael O'Shields, © 1981, Sound III; arr. by Joseph Joubert, © 2000, GIA Publications, Inc.

PRAISE YOU 110

Upon You I have leaned from my birth; ...You who took me from my mother's womb. My praise is continually of You.
Psalm 71:6

Text: Elizabeth Goodine, b.1962
Tune: Elizabeth Goodine, b.1962

111 MY TRIBUTE

What shall I return to the LORD for all His bounty to me?
Psalm 116:12

How can I say thanks for the things You have done for me— Things so un-de - served, Yet You give to prove Your love for me? The voic - es of a mil-lion an - gels could not ex - press my grat-i - tude— All that I am and ev - er hope to be, I owe it all to Thee.

Just let me live my life— Let it be pleas-ing, Lord, to Thee; And should I gain an-y praise, Let it go to Cal - va - ry. With His

D.S.

Text: Andraé Crouch, b.1945
Tune: MY TRIBUTE; Andraé Crouch, b.1945
© 1971, Bud John Songs, Inc. (ASCAP)

WHEN, IN OUR MUSIC, GOD IS GLORIFIED 112

I will sing to the Lord, for He has triumphed gloriously.
Exodus 15:1

1. When, in our mu - sic, God is glo - ri - fied,
2. How of - ten, mak - ing mu - sic, we have found
3. So has the Church, in lit - ur - gy and song,
4. And did not Je - sus sing a psalm that night
5. Let ev - 'ry in - stru-ment be tuned for praise!

And ad - o - ra - tion leaves no room for pride,
A new di - men - sion in the world of sound,
In faith and love, through cen - tu - ries of wrong,
When ut - most e - vil strove a - gainst the Light?
Let all re - joice who have a voice to raise!

It is as though the whole cre - a - tion cried:
As wor - ship moved us to a more pro - found
Borne wit - ness to the truth in ev - 'ry tongue:
Then let us sing, for whom he won the fight:
And may God give us faith to sing al - ways:

1.-4.
Al - le - lu - ia!

5.
Al - le - lu - ia!

Text: Mark 14:26; Fred Pratt Green, 1903-2000, © 1972, Hope Publishing Co.
Tune: ENGELBERG, 10 10 10 with alleluia; Charles V. Stanford, 1852-1924

113 TOTAL PRAISE

I lift up my eyes to the hills—from where will my help come?
Psalm 121:1

Lord, I will lift mine eyes to the hills

know - ing my help is com - ing from You.

Your peace You give me in time of the storm.

You are the source of my strength.

You are the strength of my life.

I lift my hands in to-tal praise to You.

Text: Richard Smallwood
Tune: Richard Smallwood; arr. by Stephen Key
© 1996, Zomba Songs, Inc. and T. Autumn Music; admin. by Zomba Songs, Inc.

114 WELCOME INTO THIS PLACE

I was glad when they said to me, "Let us go to the house of the LORD!"
Psalm 122:1

Wel-come in-to this place. Wel-come in-to this bro-ken ves-sel. You de-sire to a-bide in the prais-es of Your peo-ple, so we lift our hands and we lift our hearts as we of-fer up this praise un-to Your name.

Text: Orlando Jaurez
Tune: Orlando Jaurez; arr. by Jimmie Abbington

DAY AND NIGHT PRAISE 115

Day and night without ceasing they sing, "Holy, holy, holy, the Lord God the Almighty..."
Revelation 4:8

Text: Margaret Pleasant Douroux, b.1941, ©
Tune: Margaret Pleasant Douroux, b.1941, ©; harm. by Stanley Thurston, © 2000, GIA Publications, Inc.

116 O King, O Lord, O Love

Blessed be the LORD, the God of Israel, from everlasting to everlasting. And let all the people say, "Amen."
Psalm 106:48

O King, O Lord, O Love, High Priest of praise, we come to wor-ship You, to com-mune with You, to bow be-fore Your throne.

El Shad - dai, we a - dore You, as our lives we lay be - fore You: to wor - ship You, com-mune with You, O King, O Lord, O Love!

Text: Timothy Watson, © 1996
Tune: Timothy Watson, © 1996; arr. by Nolan Williams, Jr., b.1969, © 2000, GIA Publications, Inc.

117 PRAISE TO THE LORD, THE ALMIGHTY

Blessed be His glorious name forever; may His glory fill the whole earth. Amen and Amen.
Psalm 72:19

1. Praise to the Lord, the Al-might-y, the King of cre-a - - tion! O my soul, praise Him, for He is thy health and sal-va - - tion! All ye who hear, Now to His tem-ple draw near; Praise Him in glad ad-o-ra - tion.

2. Praise to the Lord, who o'er all things so won-drous-ly reign - eth, Shel-ters thee un - der His wings, yea, so gent-ly sus-tain - eth! Hast thou not seen How thy de-sires e'er have been Grant-ed in what He or-dain - eth?

3. Praise to the Lord, who doth pros-per thy work and de-fend thee; Sure-ly His good - ness and mer-cy here dai - ly at-tend thee. Pon-der a - new What the Al-might-y can do, If with His love He be-friend thee.

4. Praise to the Lord, O let all that is in me a-dore Him! All that hath life and breath, come now with prais-es be-fore Him. Let the A - men Sound from His peo-ple a-gain, For-ev-er-more we a-dore Him.

Text: German Hymn, Joachim Neander, 1650-1680; tr. by Catherine Winkworth, 1827-1878
Tune: LOBE DEN HERREN, 14 14 47 8, *Stralsund Gesangbuch*, 1665; harm. by W. Sterndale Bennett, 1816-1875

HALLELUJAH, AMEN 118

Hallelujah! For the Lord our God the Almighty reigns.
Revelation 19:6

Hal-le - lu-jah, hal-le - lu - jah, hal-le - lu-jah, a - men! In all I say and I do: Hal-le - lu - jah, a - men! Hal-le -

* Begin with soprano line, then add each part one at a time, increasing in volume and
  intensity.

119 Thou Art Worthy

Worthy is the Lamb that was slaughtered to receive... wisdom and might and honor and glory and blessing!
Revelation 5:12

Thou art wor-thy, Thou art wor-thy,

Thou art wor-thy, O Lord.

To re-ceive glo-ry, glo-ry and hon-or,

Glo-ry and hon-or and pow'r. For

Text: Revelation 4:11, 5:9; Pauline M. Mills, 1898-1995
Tune: Pauline M. Mills, 1898-1995
© 1963, 1975, 1993, Fred Bock Music Company

120 Joyful, Joyful, We Adore You

For the kingdom of God is not food and drink but righteousness and peace and joy in the Holy Spirit.
Romans 14:17

1. Joy - ful, joy - ful, we a - dore You, God of glo - ry,
2. All Your works with joy sur - round You, Earth and heav'n re -
3. Al - ways giv - ing and for - giv - ing, Ev - er bless - ing,
4. Mor - tals join the might - y cho - rus, Which the morn - ing

Lord of love; Hearts un - fold like flow'rs be - fore You,
flect Your rays, Stars and an - gels sing a - round You,
ev - er blest, Well - spring of the joy of liv - ing,
stars be - gan; God's own love is reign - ing o'er us,

O - p'ning to the sun a - bove. Melt the clouds of
Cen - ter of un - bro - ken praise; Field and for - est,
O - cean depth of hap - py rest! Lov - ing Fa - ther,
Join - ing peo - ple hand in hand. Ev - er sing - ing,

sin and sad - ness; Drive the dark of doubt a - way;
vale and moun - tain, Flow - 'ry mead - ow, flash - ing sea,
Christ our Broth - er, Let Your light up - on us shine;
march we on - ward, Vic - tors in the midst of strife;

Giv - er of im - mor - tal glad - ness, Fill us with the light of day!
Chant-ing bird and flow-ing foun - tain, Prais-ing You e - ter-nal - ly!
Teach us how to love each oth - er, Lift us to the joy di-vine.
Joy - ful mu - sic leads us sun - ward In the tri-umph song of life.

Tune: Henry van Dyke, 1852-1933, alt.
Tune: HYMN TO JOY, 8 7 8 7 D; arr. from Ludwig van Beethoven, 1770-1827, by Edward Hodges, 1796-1867

I WILL BLESS THE LORD 121

I will bless the LORD at all times; His praise shall continually be in my mouth.
Psalm 34:1

I will bless the Lord at all times. His praise shall con-

tin - u - al - ly be in my mouth. | 1. be in my mouth. | 2. In my mouth,

in my mouth, His praise shall con-tin - u - al - ly be in my mouth.

Text: Psalm 34:1
Tune: Shirley M. K. Berkeley; arr. by Valeria A. Foster, © 2000, GIA Publications, Inc.

122 AMEN SIAKUDUMISA

...all the people answered, "Amen, Amen." Then they... worshipped the LORD with their faces to the ground.
Nehemiah 8:6

Ma - si - thi.   Ma - si - thi.
O sing now.   *O sing now.*

A - men si - a - ku - du - mi - sa.
A - men sing prais - es to the Lord.

Si - a - ku - du - mi - sa.
Sing prais - es to the Lord.

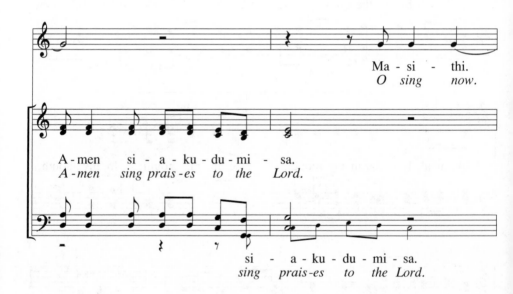

Ma - si - thi.
O sing now.

A - men si - a - ku - du - mi - sa.
A - men sing prais - es to the Lord.

si - a - ku - du - mi - sa.
sing prais - es to the Lord.

African phonetics:
Mah-see-tee
Amen see-ah-koo-doo-mee-sah

Text: *Amen. Praise the name of the Lord.* South African traditional (Xhosa); English text, Hymnal Version
Tune: Attr. to S. C. Molefe as taught by George Mxadana; arr. by John L. Bell, b.1949, © 1990, Iona Community, GIA Publications, Inc., agent

123 WE'LL PRAISE THE LORD

Let everything that breathes praise the LORD! Praise the LORD!
Psalm 150:6

1. We'll praise the Lord for He is great, And in His
2. We'll praise the Lord for He is wise; His wis-dom
3. We'll praise the Lord for He is just, And in Him
4. We'll praise the Lord for He is true; His word the
5. Oh, praise Him for His name is Love, And from His

pres - ence an - gels wait; All heav'n is swell-ing with His
shines through all the skies; The earth He meas-ures with a
we may ev - er trust; Princ - es and kings may turn a-
same all a - ges through; Earth, sea and sky may pass a-
glo - rious throne a - bove, He bends to wel-come our weak

praise— Shall we not, too, our an - thems raise?
span, And crowns us with His im - age: man.
side, But God by right will e'er a - bide.
way, But firm, God's truth will ev - er stay.
praise, Shall we not, then, our an - them raise?

Oh, we will praise Him, Oh, we will praise Him, Oh, we will

praise Him, praise Him,

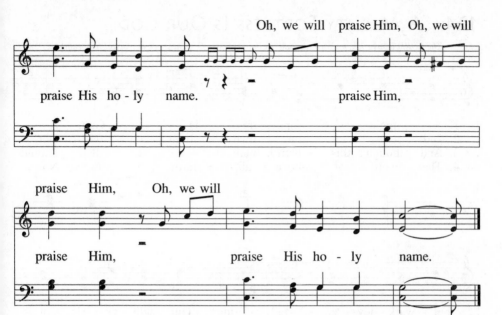

Text: T. G. Steward
Tune: NAZREY, LM with refrain; J. T. Layton

124 A Mighty Fortress Is Our God

The LORD is my rock, my fortress, and my deliverer, my God, my rock in whom I take refuge...
Psalm 18:2

1. A might - y for - tress is our God, A
2. Did we in our own strength con - fide, Our
3. And though this world, with dev - ils filled, Should
4. That word a - bove all earth - ly pow'rs, No

bul - wark nev - er fail - ing; Our help - er He a -
striv - ing would be los - ing; Were not the right One
threat - en to un - do us, We will not fear, for
thanks to them, a - bid - eth; The Spir - it and the

mid the flood Of mor - tal ills pre - vail - ing. For
on our side, The One of God's own choos - ing. Dost
God hath willed His truth to tri - umph through us. The
gifts are ours Through Him who with us sid - eth; Let

still our an - cient foe Doth seek to work us woe; His
ask who that may be? Christ Je - sus, it is He, Lord
prince of dark - ness grim, We trem - ble not for him; His
goods and kin - dred go, This mor - tal life al - so; The

craft and pow'r are great, And, armed with cru - el
Sab - a - oth His name, From age to age the
rage we can en - dure, For lo! his doom is
bod - y they may kill, God's truth a - bid - eth

hate, On earth is not his e - qual.
same, And He must win the bat - tle.
sure, One lit - tle word shall fell him.
still, His king - dom is for - ev - er.

Text: Martin Luther, 1483-1546; tr. by Frederick H. Hedge, 1805-1890
Tune: EIN' FESTE BURG, 87 87 66 66 7; Martin Luther, 1483-1546

125 A Child of the King

"And I will be your Father and you shall be my sons and daughters," says the Lord Almighty.
2 Corinthians 6:18

1. My Fa - ther is rich in hous - es and land, He hold - eth the wealth of the world in His hands! Of ru - bies and dia - monds, of sil - ver and gold, His cof - fers are full, He has rich - es un - told.

2. My Fa - ther's own Son, the Sav - ior of men, Once wan - dered on earth as the poor - est of them; But now He is reign - ing for ev - er on high, And will give me a home in heav'n by and by.

3. I once was an out - cast stran - ger on earth, A sin - ner by choice and an a - lien by birth; But I've been a - dopt - ed, my name's writ - ten down, An heir to a man - sion, a robe and a crown.

4. A tent or a cot - tage, why should I care? They're build - ing a pal - ace for me o - ver there; Though ex - iled from home, yet still I may sing: All glo - ry to God, I'm a child of the King.

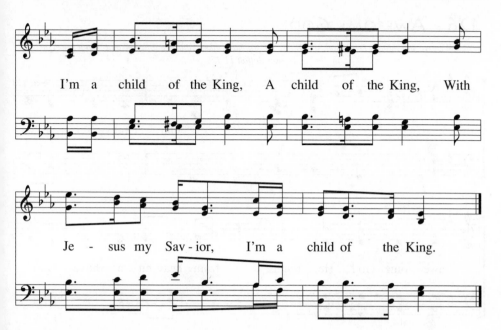

I'm a child of the King, A child of the King, With

Je - sus my Sav - ior, I'm a child of the King.

Text: Harriet E. Buell, 1834-1910
Tune: BINGHAMTON, 10 11 11 11 with refrain; John B. Sumner, 1838-1918; arr. by Valeria A. Foster, © 2000, GIA Publications, Inc.

126 AWESOME GOD

We give you thanks, Lord God Almighty... for you have taken your great power and begun to reign.
Revelation 11:17

Our God is an awe-some God. He reigns from heav-en a-bove with wis - dom, pow'r, and love. Our God is an awe-some God. Our God. He reigns! He

reigns! He reigns! Our

God is an awe - some God. He God.

Text: Rich Mullins
Tune: Rich Mullins; arr. by Nolan Williams, Jr. b.1969

127 FATHER, I STRETCH MY HANDS TO THEE

I stretch out my hands to You; my soul thirsts for You like a parched land.
Psalm 143:6-7

1. Fa - ther, I stretch my hands to Thee;
2. What did Thine on - ly Son en - dure,
3. Sure - ly Thou canst not let me die;
4. Au - thor of faith! to Thee I lift

No oth - er help I know.
Be - fore I drew my breath!
O speak and I shall live;
My wea - ry, long - ing eyes;

If Thou with - draw Thy - self from me,
What pain, what la - bor to se - cure
And here I will un - wea - ried lie,
O let me now re - ceive that gift!

O! whith - er shall I go?
My soul from end - less death!
Till Thou Thy Spir - it give.
My soul with - out it dies.

Text: Charles Wesley, 1707-1788
Tune: MARTYRDOM, CM; Hugh Wilson, 1766-1824; arr. by Nolan Williams, Jr., b.1969. © 2000, GIA Publications, Inc.

FATHER, I STRETCH MY HANDS TO THEE 128

Hear the voice of my supplication, as I cry to You for help, as I lift up my hands toward Your most holy sanctuary.
Psalm 28:2

1. Fa - ther, I stretch my hands to Thee,   Fa - ther,
2. If   Thou with-draw Thy-self from me.   If   Thou

I   stretch   my
with   -   draw   Thy   -

hands   to   Thee,   No oth - er help I
self   from   me,   Oh, whith-er shall I

know,   No   oth - er   help
go,   Oh,   whith - er   shall

I   know.
I   go.

Text: Charles Wesley, 1707-1788
Tune: Meter hymn, lined out and arr. by Evelyn Simpson-Curenton, b.1953, © 2000, GIA Publications, Inc.

129 LORD, KEEP ME DAY BY DAY

...if the earthly tent we live in is destroyed, we have a building from God, ...eternal in the heavens.
2 Corinthians 5:1

1. Lord, keep me day by day
2. Lord, keep my bod - y strong
3. I'm just a stran - ger here,

in a pure and per - fect way.
so that I can do no wrong.
trav-'ling through this bar - ren land.

I want to live
Lord, give me grace
Lord, I know

I want to
just to run this Chris-tian
there's a build-ing some-

live on
race
where,

in a build-ing not made
to a build-ing not made
a build-ing not made

by hand.
by hand.
by hand.

Last time

Text: Eddie Williams, © 1959, Martin and Morris, Inc.
Tune: Eddie Williams, © 1959, Martin and Morris, Inc.; arr. by Valeria A. Foster, © 2000, GIA Publications, Inc.

THE ANGELS KEEP A-WATCHIN' 130

For He will command His angels concerning you to guard you in all your ways.
Psalm 91:11

Text: Negro Spiritual
Tune: Negro Spiritual; arr. by Nolan Williams, Jr., b.1969, © 2000, GIA Publications, Inc.

131 GUIDE MY FEET

By the tender mercy of our God, the dawn from on high will break upon us,... to guide our feet into the way of peace.
Luke 1:78-79

1. Guide my feet
2. Hold my hand
3. Stand by me
4. I'm Your child
while I run this race,

Oh, Lord,

Guide my feet
Hold my hand
Stand by me
I'm Your child
while I run this race,

Oh, Lord,

Guide my feet
Hold my hand
Stand by me
I'm Your child
while I run this race, For I

vain.

don't want to run this race in vain, race in vain.

vain.

Text: Negro spiritual
Tune: GUIDE MY FEET, 888 10; Negro spiritual; harm. by Dr. Wendell P. Whalum, © estate of Wendell Whalum

GOD IS A WONDER TO MY SOUL 132

I came that they may have life, and have it abundantly.
John 10:10

1. God is a won-der to my soul.
2. My God's truth has set me free.
3. Now I can live a-bun-dant-ly.

God is a won-der to my soul.
My God's truth has set me free. Came in-
Now I can live a-bun-dant-ly.

to my life one day, And took all my sins a-way.

Oh, God is a won-der to my soul.
Oh, my God's truth has set me free.
Now I can live a-bun-dant-ly.

Text: Dr. Robert J. Fryson, © 1989
Tune: WONDER, 88 77 9; traditional; arr. by Valeria A. Foster, © 2000, GIA Publications, Inc.

133 BE STILL, GOD WILL FIGHT YOUR BATTLES

The LORD will fight for you, and you have only to keep still.
Exodus 14:14

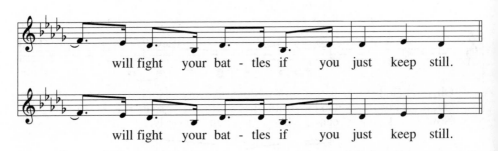

*Percussion is to be used throughout the piece.

Verse 2

2. *Keep a pray - in',   God will fight your bat-tles. Keep a

2. *Keep a pray - in',   God will fight your bat-tles.

pray - in',   God will fight your bat-tles. Keep a

Keep a pray - in',   God will fight your bat-tles.

pray - in',   God will fight your bat - tles.   God

Keep a pray - in'   God will fight your bat - tles.   God

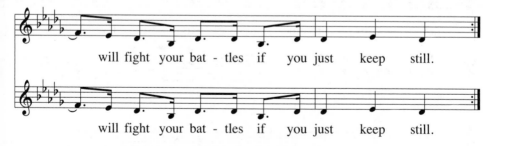

will fight your bat - tles if you just keep still.

will fight your bat - tles if you just keep still.

* 3. Keep a waitin', God will fight your battles...
4. Keep a singin', God will fight your battles...
5. I'm a witness, God will fight your battles...

Text: African-American traditional
Tune: African-American traditional; arr. by Nolan Williams, Jr., b.1969, © 2000, GIA Publications, Inc.

134 GOD IS

God is our refuge and strength, a very present help in trouble.
Psalm 46:1

Chorus

God is the joy and the strength of my life. He moves all pain, mis - er - y, and strife. He prom-ised to keep me, nev - er to leave me, He's nev - er, ev - er come short of His word. I've got to fast and pray, stay in the nar - row way. I'll keep my life clean

ev - 'ry day.   I want to go with Him when He comes back.

I've come   too far   and I'll nev-er turn back.

God   is,   God   is,   God   is,   God   is.

To repeat **D.C.**

God   is my   all   and   all.

Final ending

God   is my   all   and   all.

Text: Dr. Robert J. Fryson, © 1976
Tune: Dr. Robert J. Fryson, © 1976; arr. by Evelyn Simpson-Curenton, b.1953, and Nolan Williams, Jr., b.1969, © 2000, GIA Publications, Inc.

135 BE STILL, MY SOUL

Be still, and know that I am God! I am exalted among the nations, I am exalted in the earth.
Psalm 46:10

1. Be still, my soul— the Lord is on thy side!
2. Be still, my soul— thy God doth un - der - take
3. Be still, my soul— the hour is has - t'ning on

Bear pa - tient - ly the cross of grief or pain;
To guide the fu - ture as He has the past;
When we shall be for ev - er with the Lord,

Leave to thy God to or - der and pro - vide—
Thy hope, thy con - fi - dence let noth - ing shake—
When dis - ap - point - ment, grief, and fear are gone,

In ev - 'ry change He faith - ful will re - main.
All now mys - te - rious shall be bright at last.
Sor-row for - got, love's pur - est joys re - stored.

Be still, my soul— thy best, thy heav'n - ly Friend
Be still, my soul— the waves and winds still know
Be still, my soul— when change and tears are past,

Through thorn - y ways leads to a joy - ful end.
His voice who ruled them while He dwelt be - low.
All safe and bless - ed we shall meet at last.

Text: Katharina von Schlagel; tr. by Jane L. Borthwick, 1813-1897
Tune: FINLANDIA, 10 10 10 10 10 10; Jean Sibelius, 1865-1957

136 GOD LEADS US ALONG

He makes me lie down in green pastures; He leads me beside still waters.
Psalm 23:2

1. In shad - y, green pas - tures, so rich and so sweet,
2. Some - times on the mount where the sun shines so bright,
3. Tho' sor - rows be - fall us and Sa - tan op - pose,
4. A - way from the mire and a - way from the clay,

God leads His dear chil - dren a - long;

Where the wa - ter's cool flow bathes the wea - ry one's feet,
Some - times in the val - ley, in dark - est of night,
Thru grace we can con - quer, de - feat all our foes,
A - way up in glo - ry, e - ter - ni - ty's day,

God leads His dear chil - dren a - long.

Some thru the wa-ters, some thru the flood,

Some thru the fire, but all thru the blood;

Some thru great sor-row, but God gives a song,

In the night sea-son, and all the day long.

Text: G. A. Young, b.1903
Tune: GOD LEAD US, 11 8 11 8 with refrain; G. A. Young, b.1903

137 GOD WILL TAKE CARE OF YOU

Cast all your anxiety on Him, because He cares for you.
1 Peter 5:7

1. Be not dis - mayed what - e'er be - tide,
2. Through days of toil when heart does fail,
3. All you may need He will pro - vide,
4. No mat - ter what may be the test,

God will take care of you; Be - neath His wings of
God will take care of you; When dan - gers fierce your
God will take care of you; Noth - ing you ask will
God will take care of you; Lean, wea - ry one, up -

love a - bide, God will take care of you.
path as - sail, God will take care of you.
be de - nied, God will take care of you.
on His breast, God will take care of you.

God will take care of you, Through ev - 'ry day,

O'er all the way; He will take care of you,

of you.

God will take care take care of you.

of you.

Text: Civilla D. Martin, 1866-1948
Tune: GOD CARES, CM with refrain; W. Stillman Martin, 1862-1935

138 GUIDE ME, O THOU GREAT JEHOVAH

The LORD will guide you continually, and satisfy your needs in parched places...
Isaiah 58:11

1. Guide me, O Thou great Je-ho-vah, Pil-grim through this
2. O-pen now the crys-tal foun-tain, Whence the heal-ing
3. When I tread the verge of Jor-dan, Bid my anx-ious

bar-ren land; I am weak, but Thou art might-y;
stream doth flow; Let the fire and cloud-y pil-lar
fears sub-side; Bear me through the swel-ling cur-rent,

Hold me with Thy pow'r-ful hand; Bread of heav-en,
Lead me all my jour-ney through; Strong De-liv-'rer,
Land me safe on Ca-naan's side; Songs of prais-es,

Bread of heav-en, Feed me till I want no
strong De-liv-'rer, Be Thou still my strength and
songs of prais-es, I will ev-er give to

more,	Feed	me till	I	want no	more.
shield,	Be	Thou still	my	strength and	shield.
Thee,	I	will ev - er		give to	Thee.

Text: William Williams, 1717-1791; St. 1, tr. Peter Williams, 1722-1796
Tune: CWM RHONDDA, 8 7 8 7 8 77; John Hughes, 1873-1932

GUIDE ME, O THOU GREAT JEHOVAH 139

The LORD will guide you continually, and satisfy your needs in parched places...
Isaiah 58:11

Leader:

1. Guide	me,	oh,	Thou	Great	Je - ho - vah,
2. I	am	weak	but	Thou	art might - y,
3. Bread	of	heav - en,	Bread	of	heav - en,

All:

Pil - grims through this	bar - ren	land.	Guide	me,
Hold me	with Thy	pow'r - ful	hand.	I	am
Feed me	till I	want no	more.	Bread	of

oh, Thou	Great	Je - ho - vah,	Pil - grims
weak but	Thou	art might-y,	Hold me
heav - en,	Bread	of heav - en,	Feed me

through this	bar - ren	land.
with Thy	pow'r - ful	hand.
till I	want no	more.

Text: William Williams, 1717-1791; tr. Peter Williams, 1722-1796
Tune: Traditional, arr. Betty Gadling, © 2000, GIA Publications, Inc.

140 GUIDE ME, O THOU GREAT JEHOVAH

The LORD will guide you continually, and satisfy your needs in parched places...
Isaiah 58:11

1. Guide me, O Thou great Je - ho - vah, Pil - grim through this bar - ren land; I am weak, but Thou art might - y; Hold me with Thy pow'r - ful hand: Bread of heav - en, Feed me till I want no more; Bread of

2. O - pen now the crys - tal foun - tain, Whence the heal - ing wa - ters flow; Let the fi - ery, cloud - y pil - lar, Lead me all my jour - ney through: Strong De - liv - erer, Be Thou still my strength and shield; Strong De -

3. When I tread the verge of Jor - dan, Bid my anx - ious fears sub - side; Bear me through the swel - ling cur - rent, Land me safe on Ca - naan's side: Songs of prais - es I will ev - er give to Thee; Songs of

heav - en, Feed me till I want no more.
liv - erer, Be Thou still my strength and shield.
prais - es I will ev - er give to Thee.

Text: William Williams, 1717-1791; St. 1, tr. Peter Williams, 1722-1796
Tune: ZION, 87 87 47 47; Thomas Hastings, 1784-1872

CAST YOUR CARES 141

Cast all your anxiety on Him, because He cares for you.
1 Peter 5:7

Cast your cares up - on Him! Cast your cares up - on

Him! He knows, He cares, God real-ly cares. God cares for you!

Last time

Verse

I am learn-ing to put all my trust in Him, For He knows the

road up a-head. I must not com-

plain, I must learn to trust in His name. He knows,

He cares, God real-ly cares. God

D.S.

cares for you!

Text: Carlton Burgess, © 1994
Tune: Carlton Burgess, © 1994; arr. by Nolan Williams, Jr., b.1969, © 2000, GIA Publications, Inc.
Administered by GIA Publications, Inc.

142 HE LEADETH ME

He restores my soul. He leads me in right paths for His name's sake.
Psalm 23:3

1. He lead - eth me! O bless - ed thought! O
2. Some - times 'mid scenes of deep - est gloom, Some -
3. Lord, I would clasp Thy hand in mine, Nor
4. And when my task on earth is done, When

words with heav'n - ly com - fort fraught! What -
times where E - den's bow - ers bloom, By
ev - er mur - mur nor re - pine; Con -
by Thy grace the vic - t'ry's won, E'en

e'er I do, wher - e'er I be, Still
wa - ters still, o'er trou - bled sea, Still
tent, what - ev - er lot I see, Since
death's cold wave I will not flee, Since

'tis God's hand that lead - eth me.
'tis His hand that lead - eth me!
'tis my God that lead - eth me!
God thru Jor - dan lead - eth me.

He lead - eth me, He lead - eth me, By
His own hand He lead-eth me; His faith - ful fol-l'wer
I would be, For by His hand He lead - eth me.

Text: Joseph H. Gilmore, 1834-1918
Tune: HE LEADETH ME, LM with refrain; William B. Bradbury, 1816-1868

143 HIS EYE IS ON THE SPARROW

Look at the birds... they neither sow nor reap, yet your heavenly Father feeds them. Are you not of more value than they?
Matthew 6:26

1. Why should I feel dis - cour - aged, Why should the shad - ows
2. "Let not your heart be trou - bled," His ten - der word I
3. When ev - er I am tempt - ed, When ev - er clouds a -

come, Why should my heart be lone - ly, And
hear, And rest - ing on His good - ness, I
rise, When songs give place to sigh - ing When

long for heav'n and home; When Je - sus is my
lose my doubts and fears; Though by the path He
hope with - in me dies, I draw the clos - er

por - tion? My con - stant Friend is He:
lead - eth, But one step I may see; His
to Him, From care He sets me free;

eye is on the spar - row, And I know He watch - es me; His eye is on the spar - row, and I know He watch - es me. I sing be - cause I'm hap - py, I sing be - cause I'm free; For His eye is on the spar-row, And I know He watch-es me.

Text: Civilla D. Martin, 1866-1948
Tune: SPARROW, 7 6 7 6 7 6 7 7 7 7 with refrain; Charles H. Gabriel, 1856-1932; arr. by Horace Clarence Boyer, b.1935, © 1992

144 MY HEAVENLY FATHER WATCHES OVER ME

The LORD watches over all who love Him, but all the wicked He will destroy.
Psalm 145:20

1. I trust in God wher-ev-er I may be, Up-on the land or on the roll-ing sea; For come what may, from day to day, My heav'n-ly Fa-ther watch-es o-ver me.

2. He makes the rose an ob-ject of His care, He guides the ea-gle through the path-less air; And sure-ly He re-mem-bers me, My heav'n-ly Fa-ther watch-es o-ver me.

3. I trust in God, for, in the li-on's den, On bat-tle-field, or in the pris-on pen; Through praise or blame, through flood or flame, My heav'n-ly Fa-ther watch-es o-ver me.

4. The val-ley may be dark, the shad-ows deep, But oh, the shep-herd guards His lone-ly sheep; And through the gloom, He'll lead me home, My heav'n-ly Fa-ther watch-es o-ver me.

I trust in God, I know He cares for me, On moun-tain

bleak or on the storm-y sea; Though bil-lows

roll, He keeps my soul, My heav'n-ly

Fa-ther watch-es o - ver me.

Text: W.C. Martin
Tune: HEAVENLY FATHER, 10 10 8 10 with refrain; Charles H. Gabriel, 1856-1932; arr. J. Jefferson Cleveland, 1937-1988 and
   Verolga Nix-Allen, b.1933

145 LEAD ME, LORD

Lead me in Your truth, and teach me, for You are the God of my salvation.
Psalm 25:5

Lead me, Lord, lead me in Thy right - eous - ness,

Make Thy way plain be - fore Thy face.

Optional Ending

For it is Thou, Lord, Thou, Lord on - ly, that

mak - est me dwell in safe - ty.

Text: Psalm 5:8
Tune: Samuel Sebastian Wesley

HOW FIRM A FOUNDATION 146

For no one can lay any foundation other than the one that has been laid; that foundation is Jesus Christ.
1 Corinthians 3:11

1. How firm a foun-da-tion, ye saints of the
2. "Fear not, I am with thee, O be not dis-
3. "When through the deep wa-ters I call thee to
4. "When through fi-ery tri-als thy path-way shall
5. "The soul that on Je-sus hath leaned for re-

Lord, Is laid for your faith in His ex-cel-lent
mayed, For I am thy God, I will still give thee
go, The riv-ers of woe shall not thee o-ver-
lie, My grace, all suf-fi-cient, shall be thy suppose, I will not, I will not de-sert to his

Word! What more can He say than to you He hath
aid; I'll strength-en thee, help thee, and cause thee to
flow; For I will be with thee, thy troub-les to
ply; The flame shall not hurt thee— I on-ly de-
foes; That soul, though all hell should en-deav-or to

said, To you, who for ref-uge to Je-sus have fled?
stand, Up-held by my gra-cious, om-nip-o-tent hand.
bless, And sanc-ti-fy to thee, thy deep-est dis-tress.
sign Thy dross to con-sume and thy gold to re-fine.
shake, I'll nev-er, no nev-er, no nev-er for-sake!"

Text: 2 Peter 1:4; "K" in Rippon's *A Selection of Hymns*, 1787
Tune: FOUNDATION, 11 11 11 11; Caldwell's *Unison Harmony*, 1837

147 ALL CREATURES OF OUR GOD AND KING

Make a joyful noise to God, all the earth.
Psalm 66:1

1. All crea - tures of our God and King, Lift
2. Thou rush - ing wind that art so strong, Ye
3. Dear moth - er earth, who day by day Un -
4. And all ye men of ten - der heart, For -
5. Let all things their Cre - a - tor bless, And
   Praise God, from whom all bless - ings flow, Praise

up your voice and with us sing: Al - le -
clouds that sail in heav'n a - long, O
fold - ed bless - ings on our way, O
giv - ing oth - ers, take your part, O
wor - ship Him in hum - ble - ness— O
Him, all crea - tures here be - low, Al - le -

lu - ia, Al - le - lu - ia! Thou
praise Him! Al - le - lu - ia! Thou
praise Him! Al - le - lu - ia! The
sing ye! Al - le - lu - ia! Ye
praise Him! Al - le - lu - ia! Praise,
lu - ia, Al - le - lu - ia! Praise

burn - ing sun with gold - en beam, Thou
ris - ing morn, in praise re - joice, Ye
flow'rs and fruits that in thee grow, Let
who long pain and sor - row bear, Praise
praise the Fa - ther, praise the Son, And
Him a - bove, ye heav'n - ly host, Praise

sil - ver moon with soft - er gleam: O praise Him,
lights of eve - ning, find a voice: O praise Him,
them His glo - ry al - so show: O praise Him,
God and on Him cast your care: O praise Him,
praise the Spir - it, Three in One: O praise Him,
Fa - ther, Son and Ho - ly Ghost: Al - le - lu - ia,

O praise Him! Al - le - lu - ia, Al - le -
Al - le - lu - ia! Al - le - lu - ia, Al - le -

lu - ia! Al - le - lu - ia!
lu - ia! Al - le - lu - ia!

Text: Francis of Assisi, 1182-1226; tr. by William H. Draper, 1855-1933, © J. Curwen & Sons, Ltd., London.
Tune: LASST UNS ERFREUEN, LM with alleluias; *Geistliche Kirchengesäng,* 1623; arr. by Norman Johnson, © 1968, Singspiration Music

148 How Great Thou Art

Great are the works of the LORD, studied by all who delight in them.
Psalm 111:2

1. O Lord my God, when I in awe-some
2. When thru the woods and for-est glades I
3. And when I think that God, His Son not
4. When Christ shall come with shout of ac-cla-

won-der Con-sid-er all the worlds Thy hands have
wan-der And hear the birds sing sweet-ly in the
spar-ing, Sent Him to die, I scarce can take it
ma-tion And take me home, what joy shall fill my

made, I see the stars, I hear the roll-ing
trees, When I look down from loft-y moun-tain
in That on the cross, my bur-den glad-ly
heart! Then I shall bow in hum-ble ad-o-

thun-der, Thy pow'r thru-out the un-i-verse dis-played!
gran-deur And hear the brook and feel the gen-tle breeze.
bear-ing, He bled and died to take a-way my sin!
ra-tion And there pro-claim, my God, how great Thou art!

Then sings my soul, my Sav-ior God, to Thee; How great Thou art, how great Thou art! Then sings my soul, my Sav-ior God, to Thee; How great Thou art, How great Thou art!

Text: Stuart K. Hine, 1899-1989
Tune: O STORE GUD, 11 10 11 10 with refrain; Stuart K. Hine, 1899-1989
© 1953, S.K. Hine, assigned to Manna Music, Inc.

149 THIS IS MY FATHER'S WORLD

The earth is the LORD's and all that is in it, the world, and those who live in it.
Psalm 24:1

1. This is my Fa-ther's world, And to my list-'ning
2. This is my Fa-ther's world— The birds their car - ols
3. This is my Fa-ther's world— O let me ne'er for -

ears All na - ture sings, and round me rings The
raise; The morn - ing light, sun shin - ing bright, De -
get That tho' the wrong seems oft so strong God

mu - sic of the spheres. This is my Fa-ther's world! I
clares its Mak - er's praise. This is my Fa-ther's world! He
is the Rul - er yet. This is my Fa-ther's world! The

rest me in the thought Of rocks and trees, of
shines in all that's fair; In the rus - tling grass I
bat - tle is not done; Je - sus who died shall be

skies and seas— His hand the won - ders wrought.
hear Him pass— He speaks to me ev - 'ry - where.
sat - is - fied, And earth and heav'n be one.

Text: Maltbie D. Babcock, 1858-1901
Tune: TERRA BEATA, SMD; Franklin L. Sheppard, 1852-1930; harm. by Norman Johnson, © 1966, Singspiration Music (ASCAP)

150 He's Got the Whole World in His Hand

In His hand is the life of every living thing and the breath of every human being.
Job 12:10

1. He's got the whole world
2. He's got the sun and the moon
3. He's got the wind and the rain
4. He's got the lit - tle bit - ty ba - by
5. He's got you and me, broth - er,

in His hand, He's got the whole world
in His hand, He's got the sun and the moon
in His hand, He's got the wind and the rain
in His hand, He's got the lit - tle bit - ty ba - by
in His hand, He's got you and me, sis - ter,

in His hand, He's got the whole world
in His hand, He's got the sun and the moon
in His hand, He's got the wind and the rain
in His hand, He's got the lit - tle bit - ty ba - by
in His hand, He's got ev - 'ry - bod - y here

in His hand, He's got the whole world in His hand.

Text: Traditional
Tune: WHOLE WORLD, Irregular; Negro spiritual; arr. by Hezekiah Brinson, Jr., b.1958, © 1990

GOD IS A GOOD GOD   151

O give thanks to the LORD, for He is good; for His steadfast love endures forever.
1 Chronicles 16:34

God is a good God. He's a great God. He can
do an-y-thing but fail. He has
moved so man-y moun-tains out of my
way. God is a won-der-ful God.

Text: Keith Hunter, ©
Tune: Keith Hunter, ©; arr. by Stephen Key, and Nolan Williams, Jr., b.1969, © 2000, GIA Publications, Inc.
Published by Arrand Publishing Co.

152 GOD HAS SMILED ON ME

May God be gracious to us and bless us and make His face to shine upon us.
Psalm 67:1

Refrain

God has smiled on me, He has set me free.

God has smiled on me, He's been good to me.

1. He is the source of all my joy, He
2. A light un-to my path is He, My

fills me with His love. The grace that I em-ploy,
strength when I would fall. He guides each day for me,

He sends down from a-bove.
God is my all and all.

D.S.

Text: Isaiah Jones, Jr., © 1973, Davike Music Co.
Tune: SMILED ON ME, 8 6 6 6 with refrain; Isaiah Jones, Jr., © 1973, Davike Music Co.; arr. by Nolan Williams, Jr., b.1969, © 2000, GIA
  Publications, Inc.

153 For God So Loved the World

Believe on the Lord Jesus, and you will be saved...
Acts 16:31

For God so loved the world that He gave His on-ly be-got-ten Son, that who-so-ev-er be-liev-eth on Him should not per-ish, should not per-ish, but they shall have, they shall have ev-er-last-ing life.

Text: Lanny Wolfe
Tune: Lanny Wolfe; arr. by Evelyn Simpson-Curenton, b.1953
© 1982, Lanny Wolfe Music

Oh, What He's Done for Me 154

He does great things and unsearchable, marvelous things without number.
Job 5:9

1. Oh, what He's done for me.
Oh, what He's done for me.
Oh, what He's done for me. I
nev-er shall for-get what He's done for me.

2. He took my feet out the miry clay, that's...
3. He feeds me when I'm hungry, that's...
4. He picked me up and turned me around, that's...
5. He gave me a home in glory, that's...

155 It Took a Miracle

Remember the wonderful works He has done, His miracles, and the judgments He uttered.
1 Chronicles 16:14

1. My Father is om - nip - o - tent, And
2. Tho' here His glo - ry has been shown, We
3. The Bi - ble tells us of His pow'r And

that you can't de - ny; A God of might and
still can't ful - ly see The won - ders of His
wis - dom all way thru, And ev - 'ry lit - tle

mir - a - cles— 'Tis writ - ten in the sky.
might, His throne— 'Twill take e - ter - ni - ty.
bird and flow'r Are tes - ti - mo - nies too.

It took a mir-a-cle to put the stars in place, It took a

mir-a-cle to hang the world in space; But when He saved my soul,

Cleansed and made me whole, It took a mir-a-cle of love and grace!

Text: John W. Peterson, b.1921
Tune: IT TOOK A MIRACLE, CM with refrain; John W. Peterson, b.1921
© 1948, 1976, John W. Peterson Music Co.

God Is So Good 156

I believe that I shall see the goodness of the LORD in the land of the living.
Psalm 27:13

1. God is so good, God is so good,
2. He saved my soul, He saved my soul,
3. I'll praise His name, I'll praise His name,

God is so good— O so good to me.
He saved my soul— God's so good to me.
I'll praise His name— God's so good to me.

Text: Traditional
Tune: SO GOOD, 4 4 4 5; Traditional

157 To God Be the Glory

Grace to you and peace from God our Father and the Lord Jesus Christ... to whom be the glory forever and ever.
Galatians 1:3-5

1. To God be the glo - ry— great things He hath
2. O per - fect re - demp - tion, the pur - chase of
3. Great things He hath taught us, great things He hath

done! So loved He the world that He gave us His
blood! To ev - 'ry be - liev - er, the prom - ise of
done, And great our re - joic - ing through Je - sus the

Son, Who yield - ed His life, an a - tone - ment for
God; The vil - est of - fend - er who tru - ly be -
Son; But pur - er and high - er and great - er will

sin, And o - pened the life - gate that all may go in.
lieves, That mo - ment from Je - sus a par - don re - ceives.
be Our won - der, our trans - port, when Je - sus we see.

Praise the Lord, praise the Lord, let the earth hear His voice! Praise the Lord, praise the Lord, let the peo - ple re - joice! O come to the Fa - ther through Je - sus, the Son, and give Him the glo - ry— great things He hath done!

Text: Fanny J. Crosby, 1820-1915
Tune: BE THE GLORY, 11 11 11 11 with refrain; William H. Doane, 1832-1915

158 GREAT IS THY FAITHFULNESS

The steadfast love of the LORD never ceases, His mercies never come to an end... great is Your faithfulness.
Lamentations 3:22-23

1. Great is Thy faith - ful-ness, O God my Fa - ther,
2. Sum - mer and win - ter, and spring-time and har - vest,
3. Par - don for sin and a peace that en - dur-eth,

There is no shad - ow of turn - ing with Thee;
Sun, moon and stars in their cours - es a - bove,
Thine own dear pres - ence to cheer and to guide;

Thou chang - est not, Thy com - pas - sions, they fail not,
Join with all na - ture in man - i - fold wit - ness,
Strength for to - day and bright hope for to - mor-row,

As Thou has been Thou for ev - er wilt be.
To Thy great faith - ful - ness, mer - cy and love.
Bless - ings all mine, with ten thou-sand be - side!

Great is Thy faith-ful-ness! Great is Thy faith-ful-ness!

Morn-ing by morn-ing new mer-cies I see;

All I have need-ed Thy hand hath pro-vid-ed,

Great is Thy faith-ful-ness, Lord un-to me!

Text: Thomas O. Chisholm, 1866-1960
Tune: FAITHFULNESS, 11 10 11 10 with refrain; William M. Runyan, 1870-1957
© 1923, 1951, Hope Publishing Co.

159 GOD NEVER FAILS

Be strong and bold... because it is the LORD your God who goes with you; He will not fail you or forsake you.
Deuteronomy 31:6-8

Refrain

God   nev-er   fails.   God   nev-er   fails.

He a-bides   in   me.   He gives me vic - to - ry.   No,

God   nev-er   fails!   Just keep   the   faith,   and

nev - er cease   to   pray;   just walk   up - right,   call   Him

noon,   day,   or   night.   He'll be there.   He'll be there.   There's

no need to wor - ry, for God nev-er fails!

Verses

1. I nev – er wor - ry, I nev – er fret;
2. No need to wor - ry, no need to cry;

For God Al - might - y has nev - er failed me yet.
I've got my Lord, I know He is on my side.

Though 'buked and scorned, I know that I've been re -
Dai - ly I trust. I nev - er shall doubt

D.C.

born, for God nev - er fails.
Him, for God nev - er fails.

Text: George Jordan, © 1968, Greater Detroit Music and Record Mart
Tune: George Jordan, © 1968, Greater Detroit Music and Record Mart; arr. by Jeffrey P. Radford, © 2000, GIA Publications, Inc.

160 THE LORD IS MY LIGHT

The LORD is my light and my salvation; whom shall I fear?
Psalm 27:1

Verse 1

1. The Lord is my light and my sal - va - tion, the

Lord is my light and my sal - va - tion, the Lord is my light and

my sal - va - tion. Whom shall I fear?

Refrain

Whom shall I fear? Whom shall I fear? The

Last time to Coda

Lord is the strength of my life. Whom shall I fear?

be of good cour - age, wait on the Lord and

be of good cour - age. Whom shall I fear?

Refrain

Whom shall I fear? Whom shall I fear? The

Lord is the strength of my life. Whom shall I fear?

Text: Lillian Bouknight, © 1980, Savgos Music, Inc.
Tune: Lillian Bouknight, © 1980, Savgos Music, Inc.; arr. by Stephen Key, © 2000, GIA Publications, Inc.

OLD TIME RELIGION 161

I am reminded of your sincere faith... first in your grandmother... and your mother... and now, I am sure, lives in you.
2 Timothy 1:5

Refrain: Give me that old time re - lig - ion, Give me that
1. It was good for Paul and Si - las, It was
2. It was good for the He - brew chil - dren, It was
3. It was good for our moth - ers, It was
4. Makes me love ev - 'ry - bod - y, Makes me

old time re - lig - ion, Give me that
good for Paul and Si - las, It was
good for the He - brew chil - dren, It was
good for our moth - ers, It was
love ev - 'ry - bod - y, Makes me

old time re - lig - ion,
good for Paul and Si - las,
good for the He - brew chil - dren, It's good e - nough for me.
good for our moth - ers,
love ev - 'ry bod - y,

Text: Traditional
Tune: OLD TIME RELIGION, Irregular; traditional; arr. by Joseph Joubert, © 2000, GIA Publications, Inc.

162 Yes, God Is Real

...he prays to God, and is accepted by Him, he comes into His presence with joy...
Job 33:26

1. There are some things I may not
2. Some folks may doubt, some folks may
3. I can - not tell just how you

know, There are some plac - es I can - not
scorn, All can de - sert and leave me a -
felt When Je - sus took your sins a -

go, But I am sure of this one
lone, But as for me I'll take God's
way, But since that day, yes, since that

thing,   That God is real for I can feel Him deep with-in.
part,   For God is real and I can feel Him in my heart.
hour,   God has been real for I can feel His ho-ly pow'r.

Solo:

Yes, God is real, He's real in my soul; Yes, God is

Yes, God is yes, God is real, real in my soul;

real for He has washed and made me whole; His love for

real for He has washed and made me whole;

me   is like pure gold.   Yes, God is

His   love for me   is   like pure gold. Yes, God is

Last time

real   for I can feel   Him in my   soul.

Last time

real   for I can feel   Him in my Him   in   my soul.

Last time

Text: Kenneth Morris, 1917-1988
Tune: GOD IS REAL, 8 9 8 12 with refrain; Kenneth Morris, 1917-1988; arr. by Evelyn Simpson-Curenton, b.1953
© 1944, Martin and Morris Inc., admin. by Unichappell Music, Inc.

NEARER, MY GOD, TO THEE   163

But for me it is good to be near God; I have made the Lord GOD my refuge...
Psalm 73:28

1. Near - er, my   God, to   Thee,   Near - er   to   Thee!
2. Though like the   wan - der - er,   The   sun gone   down,
3. There   let the   way ap - pear,   Steps   un - to   heav'n;
4. Then,   with my   wak - ing thoughts   Bright   with Thy   praise,
5. Or   if, on   joy - ful wing   Cleav - ing the   sky,

E'en   though it   be   a cross   That   rais - eth   me,
Dark - ness   be   o - ver me,   My   rest   a   stone;
All   that Thou   send - est me,   In   mer - cy   giv'n;
Out   of   my   ston - y griefs   Beth - el   I'll   raise;
Sun,   moon, and   stars for - got,   Up - ward   I   fly,

Still   all   my   song shall be,   Near - er, my   God, to   Thee;
Yet   in   my   dreams I'd be   Near - er, my   God, to   Thee;
An - gels   to   beck - on me   Near - er, my   God, to   Thee;
So   by   my   woes to   be   Near - er, my   God, to   Thee;
Still   all   my   song shall be,   Near - er, my   God, to   Thee;

Near - er, my   God, to   Thee,   Near - er   to   Thee!

Text: Sarah F. Adams, 1805-1848
Tune: BETHANY, 6 4 6 4 66 6 4; Lowell Mason, 1792-1872

164 SIYAHAMBA

Walk while you have the light, so that the darkness may not overtake you.
John 12:35

Si - ya - hamb'   e - ku - kha - nyen' kwen - khos',
We are   march - ing* in the   light   of   God,

1.

si - ya - hamb' e - ku - kha - nyen' kwen - khos'.
we   are march - ing   in the   light   of   God.

2.

kwen - khos'   si - ya -
of   God   we are

hamb' e - ku - kha - nyen' kwen   kha - nyen' kwen - khos'.   Si - ya -
march - ing   in the   light   of   the   light   of   God,   we are

kwen - khos'
of   God

Alternate text: dancing, singing, praying...

African phonetics:
See-yah-hahmb eh-koo-kah-nyen kwen-kose
See-yah-hahm-bah

Text: South African folksong
Tune: South African folksong
© 1984, Utryck, admin. by Walton Music Corporation

165 THE GLORY OF THE LORD

...the spirit lifted me up, and brought me into the inner court; and the glory of the LORD filled the temple.
Ezekiel 43:5

When the glo-ry of the Lord fills this ho-ly tem-ple, He will lift us high. And on an-gels' wings we'll rise to the pure and ho-ly, when His Spir-it fills this place.

*Alternate text: Let Thy glory... Let Thy glory fill this place...

Text: Gloria Gaither, b.1942, William Gaither, b.1936, and Richard Smallwood
Tune: Gloria Gaither, b.1942, William Gaither, b.1936, and Richard Smallwood; arr. by Nolan Williams, Jr., b.1969
© 1988, Gaither Music Co. and Century Oak /Richwood Music

166 IN HIS PRESENCE

...we know that the One who raised the Lord Jesus will raise us also with Jesus, and will bring us... into His presence.
2 Corinthians 4:14

1. In His pres - ence there is com - fort;
2. In Your pres - ence there is com - fort;

In His pres - ence there is peace.
In Your pres - ence there is peace.

When we seek the Fa - ther's heart we will
When we seek to know Your heart we will

find   such blessed   as - sur - rance   In the
find   such blessed   as - sur - rance   In Your

pres - ence   of   the Lord.
ho - ly   pres - ence, Lord.

Text: Dick Tunney, b.1956 and Melodie Tunney, b.1960
Tune: Dick Tunney, b.1956 and Melodie Tunney, b.1960
© 1988 and arr. © 1990, BMG Songs, Inc., Dick and Mel Music, and Pamela Kay Music

167 IN THE PRESENCE OF JEHOVAH

You show me the path of life. In Your presence there is fullness of joy; in Your right hand are pleasures forevermore.
Psalm 16:11

In the pres - ence of Je - ho - vah,

God Al - might - y Prince of Peace,

Troub-les van - ish, hearts are mend - ed

in the pres - ence of the King!

Text: African-American traditional
Tune: African-American traditional; arr. by Walter Owens, Jr., © 2000, GIA Publications, Inc.

Oh, the Glory of Your Presence 168

...the priests could not stand to minister because of the cloud; for the glory of the LORD filled the house of God.
2 Chronicles 5:14

Oh, the glo - ry of Your pres - ence;

we, Your tem - ple give You rev - 'rence.

Come and rise to Your rest, and be blest by our

praise as we glo - ry in Your em - brace,

as Your pres - ence now fills this place.

Text: Steve Fry, b.1954
Tune: Steve Fry, b.1954
© 1983, BMG Songs/Birdwing Music (ASCAP)

169 OVER MY HEAD

I heard a voice from heaven like the sound of many waters and like the sound of loud thunder...
Revelation 14:2

1. O-ver my head I see trou-ble in the air. O-ver my head I see trou-ble in the air. O-ver my head I see trou-ble in the air;
2. O-ver my head I hear mu-sic in the air. O-ver my head I hear mu-sic in the air. O-ver my head I hear mu-sic in the air;
3. O-ver my head I hear sing-ing in the air. O-ver my head I hear sing-ing in the air. O-ver my head I hear sing-ing in the air;
4. O-ver my head I see glo-ry in the air. O-ver my head I see glo-ry in the air. O-ver my head I see glo-ry in the air;

There must be a God some-where!

Text: Traditional
Tune: OVER MY HEAD, 11 11 11 7; traditional; arr. by Nolan Williams, Jr., b.1969, © 2000, GIA Publications, Inc.

O GOD, OUR HELP IN AGES PAST 170

Lord, You have been our dwelling place in all generations...from everlasting to everlasting You are God.
Psalm 90:1-2

1. O God, our help in a - ges past, Our
2. Un - der the shad - ow of Thy throne Still
3. Be - fore the hills in or - der stood Or
4. Time, like an ev - er - roll - ing stream, Bears
5. O God, our help in a - ges past, Our

hope for years to come, Our shel - ter from the
may we dwell se - cure; Suf - fi - cient is Thine
earth re - ceived her frame, From ev - er - last - ing
all its sons a - way; They fly, for - got - ten,
hope for years to come, Be Thou our guide while

storm - y blast, And our e - ter - nal home!
arm a - lone, And our de - fense is sure.
Thou art God, To end - less years the same.
as a dream Dies at the o - p'ning day.
life shall last, And our e - ter - nal home.

Text: Isaac Watts, 1674-1748
Tune: ST. ANNE, CM; William Croft, 1678-1721

171 MAJESTY, WORSHIP HIS MAJESTY

The LORD is king, He is robed in majesty; the LORD is robed, He is girded with strength.
Psalm 93:1

Maj - es - ty,   wor-ship His maj - es - ty;   un - to
Je - sus   be all glo - ry,   hon - or, and   praise.
Maj - es - ty,   king-dom au - thor - i - ty,   flow from His
throne   un - to His own;   His an-them raise.   So ex -

alt, lift up on high the name of Je - sus. Mag - ni -

fy, come glo - ri - fy Christ Je - sus, the King.

Maj - es - ty, wor-ship His maj - es - ty, Je - sus who

died, now glo - ri - fied, King of all kings.

Text: Jack Hayford
Tune: MAJESTY, Irregular; Jack Hayford; arr. by Eugene Thomas
© 1981, Rocksmith Music

172 PRAISE HIM

Praise the LORD! Praise the LORD, O my soul!
Psalm 146:1

Refrain

Praise Him! Praise Him! Praise Him! Praise Him!
Glo - ry! Glo - ry! In all things give Him glo - ry.

Je - sus, bless-ed Sav - ior He's wor-thy to be praised.

Verse 1

1. From the ris - ing of the sun un - til the go - ing down of the

D.C.

same, He's wor-thy, Je-sus is wor-thy, He's wor-thy to be praised.

Verse 2

2. God is our rock, hope of sal - va - tion; A

strong de - liv-er-er in Him will I al-ways trust.

Text: Donnie Harper
Tune: Donnie Harper; arr. by Stephen Key
© 1986, Bud John Tunes, Inc.

O COME, LET US ADORE HIM 173

Let us rejoice and exult and give Him the glory...
Revelation 19:7

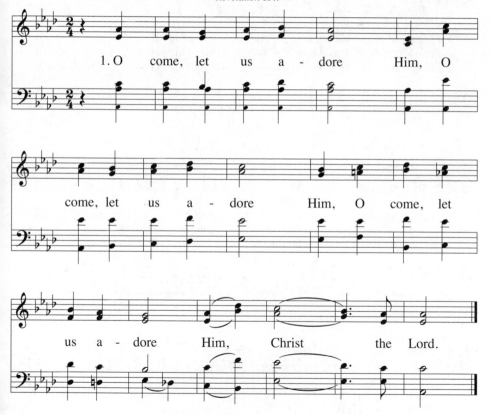

1. O come, let us a - dore Him, O

come, let us a - dore Him, O come, let

us a - dore Him, Christ the Lord.

2. For He alone is worthy,
3. Let's praise His name together,
4. We'll give Him all the glory,

Text: St. 1, John F. Wade, c.1711-1786; tr. by Frederick Oakeley, 1802-1880, alt.
Tune: ADESTE FIDELES, 7 7 7 3; John F. Wade, c.1711-1786; arr. by Stephen Key, © 2000, GIA Publications, Inc.

174 WE HAVE COME INTO THIS HOUSE

Worship the LORD with gladness; come into His presence with singing.
Psalm 100:2

1. We have come in - to this house to
2. So, for - get a - bout your - self,
3. Let us lift up ho - ly hands,

gath - er in His name and wor - ship Him. We have
con - cen-trate on Him and wor - ship Him. So, for -
mag - ni - fy His name and wor - ship Him. Let us

come in - to this house to gath - er in His name and
get a - bout your - self, con - cen-trate on Him and
lift up ho - ly hands, mag - ni - fy His name and

wor - ship Him. We have come in - to this house to
wor - ship Him. So, for - get a - bout your - self,
wor - ship Him. Let us lift up ho - ly hands,

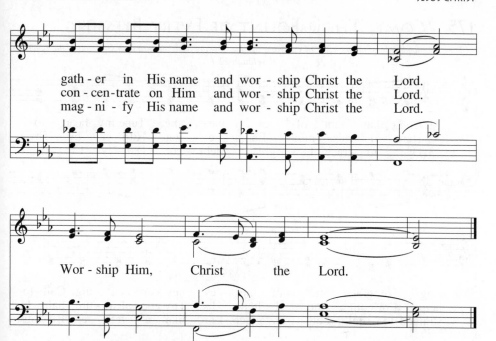

gath - er   in   His name   and wor - ship Christ the   Lord.
con - cen - trate on Him   and wor - ship Christ the   Lord.
mag - ni - fy His name   and wor - ship Christ the   Lord.

Wor - ship Him,   Christ   the   Lord.

Text: Bruce Ballinger, b.1945, alt., © 1976, Sound III
Tune: WORSHIP HIM, 16 16 18 6; Bruce Ballinger, b.1945, © 1976, Sound III; arr. by Stephen Key, © 2000, GIA Publications, Inc.

175 COME, THOU FOUNT OF EVERY BLESSING

Then the angel showed me the river of the water of life... flowing from the throne of God and of the Lamb.
Revelation 22:1

1. Come, thou Fount of ev-'ry bless-ing, Tune my heart to sing Thy grace; Streams of mer - cy, nev-er ceas-ing, Call for songs of loud-est praise: Teach me some me - lo-dious son - net, Sung by flam - ing tongues a-bove; Praise the

2. Here I raise mine *Eb-en - e - zer; Hith-er by Thy help I'm come; And I hope, by Thy good pleas-ure, Safe-ly to ar - rive at home: Je - sus sought me when a stran - ger, Wan-d'ring from the fold of God; He, to

3. O to grace how great a debt - or Dai - ly I'm con-strained to be! Let Thy grace, Lord, like a fet - ter, Bind my wan - d'ring heart to Thee: Prone to wan - der, Lord, I feel it, Prone to leave the God I love; Here's my

* I Samuel 7:12

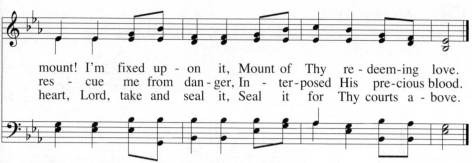

mount! I'm fixed up - on it, Mount of Thy re - deem-ing love.
res - cue me from dan - ger, In - ter-posed His pre-cious blood.
heart, Lord, take and seal it, Seal it for Thy courts a - bove.

Text: Robert Robinson, 1735-1790
Tune: NETTLETON, 8 7 8 7 D; Wyeth's *Repository of Sacred Music, Pt. II,* 1813

JESUS 176

...everyone was awestruck; and the name of the Lord Jesus was praised.
Acts 19:17

1. Je - sus, Je - sus,
2. I wor - ship You, I wor - ship You,
3. I love You, Lord, I love You, Lord,

Je - sus, Je - sus, Je - sus.

Coda

Je - sus, Je - sus.

Text: Anonymous
Tune: Anonymous; arr. by Valeria A. Foster, © 2000, GIA Publications, Inc.

177 WORSHIP HIM

Lord, who will not fear and glorify Your name? For You alone are holy.
Revelation 15:4

Wor - ship Him.　　　　Wor - ship Him.

Je - sus　Christ　our　Lord.

Wor - ship Him.　　　　Wor - ship Him.

Je - sus Christ our Lord.

Text: Leslie Parker Barnes, © 1991
Tune: Leslie Parker Barnes, © 1991; arr. by Bernadette B. Salley

178 PRAISE HIM! PRAISE HIM!

Praise the LORD! Praise, O servants of the LORD; praise the name of the LORD.
Psalm 113:1

1. Praise Him! praise Him! Je - sus, our bless - ed Re - deem - er!
2. Praise Him! praise Him! Je - sus, our bless - ed Re - deem - er!
3. Praise Him! praise Him! Je - sus, our bless - ed Re - deem - er!

Sing, O earth— His won - der - ful love pro - claim!
For our sins He suf - fered and bled and died;
Heav'n - ly por - tals loud with ho - san - nas ring!

Hail Him! hail Him! high - est arch - an - gels in glo - ry,
He our Rock, our hope of e - ter - nal sal - va - tion,
Je - sus, Sav - ior, reign - eth for ev - er and ev - er,

Strength and hon - or give to His ho - ly name!
Hail Him! hail Him! Je - sus the Cru - ci - fied.
Crown Him! crown Him! Proph - et and Priest and King!

Like a shep - herd Je - sus will guard His chil - dren—
Sound His prais - es— Je - sus who bore our sor - rows—
Christ is com - ing, o - ver the world vic - to - rious—

In His arms He car - ries them all day long:
Love un - bound - ed, won - der - ful, deep and strong:
Pow'r and glo - ry un - to the Lord be - long:

Praise Him! praise Him! tell of His ex - cel - lent great - ness!

Praise Him! praise Him! ev - er in joy - ful song!

Text: Fanny J. Crosby, 1820-1915
Tune: JOYFUL SONG, 12 10 12 10 11 10 with refrain; Chester G. Allen, 1838-1878

179 THE LAMB

Clean out the old yeast so that you may be a new batch... For our paschal lamb, Christ, has been sacrificed.
1 Corinthians 5:7

1. Hal-le - lu - jah to the Lamb of God; Hal-le-
2. Ho - ly is the Lamb of God;
3. Wor - thy is the Lamb of God;
4. Je - sus, You're the Lamb of God;

lu - jah to the Lamb of God;
Ho - ly is the Lamb of God;
Wor - thy is the Lamb of God;
Je - sus, You're the Lamb of God; We

bow down be-fore You; we wor-ship and a-dore You. Hal-le-

lu - jah to the Lamb of God.
Ho - ly is the Lamb of God.
Wor - thy is the Lamb of God.
Je - sus, You're the Lamb of God.

The per-fect sac-ri-fice You are. The great-est gift in life by far. In hum-ble grat-i-tude I come. Hal-le-lu-jah to the Lamb of God.

Text: V. Michael McKay
Tune: V. Michael McKay
© Schaff Music Publishing

180 HALLELUYA! PELO TSA RONA

For this I will extol You, O LORD, among the nations, and sing praises to Your name.
2 Samuel 22:50

Refrain

Ha - le - lu - ya! Pe - lo tsa ro - na, di tha -
Hal - le - lu - ya! We sing Your prais - es, all our

bi - le ka - o - fe - la. Ha - le - lu - ya! Pe - lo tsa
hearts are filled with glad - ness. Hal - le - lu - ya! We sing Your

ro - na, di tha - bi - le ka - o - fe - la.
prais - es, all our hearts are filled with glad - ness.

Verses

1. Ke Mo - re - na Je - so, ya re
2. O na na le bo mang? Le ba -
1. Christ the Lord to us said: I am
2. Now he sends us all out, strong in

du - me - let - seng,   ya re du - me - let -
ru - tu - wa ba ha - e,   O na na le bo
wine,   I am bread,   I am wine,   I am
faith,   free of doubt,   strong in faith,   free of

seng   ho   tsa - mai - sa   e - van - ge - di.
mang?   Le   ba - ru - tu - wa   ba   ha - e.
bread,   give   to   all   who thirst and hun - ger.
doubt,   to   pro - claim the   joy - ful Gos - pel.

African phonetics:

Refrain

Hah-lay-loo-yah! Pay-loh tsah roh-nah, dee tah-bil-lay kah-oh-fay-lah. (2x)

Verses

1. Lay Mow-ray-nah Jay-zoh, yah ray doo-may-layt-sang, yah ray doo-may-layt-sang,
   hoh tsah-mah-sah ay-vahn-heh-dee.

2. Oh nah nah lay boh mahng? Lay bah-roo-too-wah bah hah-ay. (2x)

Text: South African spiritual (Sotho)
Tune: South African spiritual
© 1984, Utryck, admin. by Walton Music Corporation

181 HIGH PRAISE

I will praise the LORD as long as I live; I will sing praises to my God all my life long.

Psalm 146:2

Precious, ho - ly bless - ed Sav - ior, You are wor - thy

to be praised. Heav - en and earth bow be - fore You,

You are wor - thy to be praised.

Special Chorus*

Pre-cious, ho - ly bless-ed Sav-ior, You are wor-thy to be praised.

Hal - le - lu - jah, Hal - le - lu - jah,
Pre-cious, ho - ly bless-ed Sav-ior, Hal - le - lu - jah,

Hal - le - lu - jah,

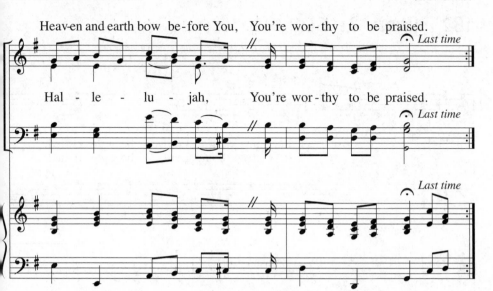

Begin with soprano line, then add each part one at a time.

Text: Margaret Pleasant Douroux, b.1941, © 1989
Tune: Margaret Pleasant Douroux, b.1941, © 1989; arr. by Nolan Williams, Jr., b.1969, © 2000, GIA Publications, Inc.

182 LORD, BE GLORIFIED

Who is this King of glory? The LORD of hosts, he is the King of glory.
Psalm 24:10

Verses 1, 2

1. In my life, Lord, be glo-ri-fied,
2. In my home, Lord, be glo-ri-fied,

be glo-ri-fied; In my life, Lord, be glo-ri-fied to - day.
be glo-ri-fied; In my home, Lord, be glo-ri-fied to -

day.

Verses 3, 4

3. In Your Church, Lord, be glo-ri-fied,
4. In my heart, Lord, be glo-ri-fied,

be glo-ri-fied; In Your Church, Lord, be glo-ri-fied to-day.
be glo-ri-fied; In my heart, Lord, be glo-ri-fied to-day.

Text: Bob Kilpatrick
Tune: Bob Kilpatrick
© 1978, Bob Kilpatrick Music. Assigned 1998 to The Lorenz Corporation.

We Are Standing on Holy Ground 183

"Come no closer! Remove the sandals from your feet, for the place on which you are standing is holy ground."
Exodus 3:5

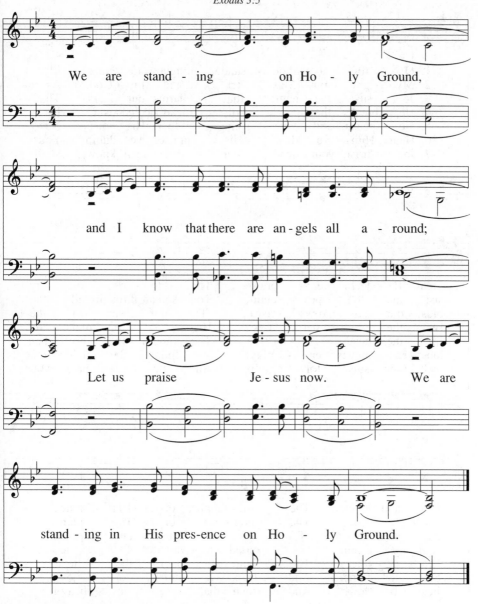

We are stand-ing on Ho-ly Ground,

and I know that there are an-gels all a - round;

Let us praise Je-sus now. We are

stand-ing in His pres-ence on Ho - ly Ground.

Text: Geron Davis, b.1960
Tune: Geron Davis, b.1960; arr. by Nolan Williams, Jr., b.1969
© 1983, Meadowgreen Music Co./Songchannel Music Co.

184 O For a Thousand Tongues to Sing

Then my tongue shall tell of Your righteousness and of Your praise all day long.
Psalm 35:28

1. O for a thou - sand tongues to sing My great Re - deem - er's praise, The glo - ries of my God and King, The tri - umphs of His grace!

2. My gra - cious Mas - ter and my God, As - sist me to pro - claim, To spread through all the earth a - broad The hon - ors of Thy name.

3. Je - sus! the name that charms our fears, That bids our sor - rows cease, 'Tis mu - sic in the sin - ner's ears, 'Tis life, and health, and peace.

4. He breaks the pow'r of can - celed sin, He sets the pris - 'ner free; His blood can make the foul - est clean; His blood a - vailed for me.

5. He speaks, and lis - t'ning to His voice, New life the dead re - ceive; The mourn - ful, bro - ken hearts re - joice; The hum - ble poor, be - lieve.

*6. Hear Him, ye deaf; His praise, ye dumb, Your loos - ened tongues em - ploy; Ye blind, be - hold your Sav - ior come, And leap, ye lame, for joy.

7. In Christ, your head, you then shall know, Shall feel your sins for - giv'n; An - tic - i - pate your heav'n be - low, And own that love is heav'n.

*May be omitted.

Text: Charles Wesley, 1707-1788
Tune: AZMON, CM; Carl G. Glaser, 1784-1829; arr. by Lowell Mason, 1792-1872

LET'S JUST PRAISE THE LORD 185

Let everything that breathes praise the LORD! Praise the LORD!
Psalm 150:6

Let's just praise the Lord! Praise the Lord! Let's just

lift our *hands t'ward heav-en and praise the

Lord; Let's just praise the Lord! praise the Lord,

Let's just lift our *hands t'ward heav-en and praise the Lord.

*Substitute voice, heart, etc.

Text: Gloria Gaither, b.1942, and William J. Gaither, b.1936
Tune: William J. Gaither, b.1936
© 1972, William J. Gaither, Inc.

186 WHEN MORNING GILDS THE SKIES

O LORD, in the morning You hear my voice; in the morning I plead my case to You, and watch.
Psalm 5:3

1. When morn - ing gilds the skies, My heart, a -
2. Does sad - ness fill my mind? A sol - ace
3. In heav'n's e - ter - nal bliss The love - liest
4. Be this, while life is mine, My can - ti -

wak - ing, cries, May Je - sus Christ be praised! A -
here I find: May Je - sus Christ be praised! Or
strain is this: May Je - sus Christ be praised! The
cle di - vine: May Je - sus Christ be praised! Be

like at work and prayer To Je - sus I re -
fades my earth - ly bliss? My com - fort still is
pow'rs of dark - ness fear When this sweet chant they
this the e - ter - nal song, Through all the a - ges

pair: May Je - sus Christ be praised!
this: May Je - sus Christ be praised!
hear: May Je - sus Christ be praised!
long: May Je - sus Christ be praised!

Text: German traditional; trans. Edward Caswall, 1814-1878
Tune: LAUDES DOMINI, 66 6 D; Joseph Barnby, 1838-1896

HAIL TO THE LORD'S ANOINTED 187

The Spirit of the Lord is upon me, because He has anointed me to bring good news to the poor.
Luke 4:18

1. Hail to the Lord's A - noint - ed, Great Da - vid's great - er Son!
2. He comes with suc - cor speed - y To those who suf - fer wrong;
3. He shall come down like show - ers Up - on the fruit - ful earth,
4. To Him shall prayer un - ceas - ing And dai - ly vows as - cend;

Hail in the time ap - point - ed, His reign on earth be - gun!
To help the poor and need - y, And bid the weak be strong;
Love, joy, and hope, like flow - ers, Spring in His path to birth:
His king - dom still in - creas - ing, A king - dom with - out end:

He comes to break op - pres - sion, To set the cap - tive free;
To give them songs for sigh - ing, Their dark - ness turn to light,
Be - fore Him, on the moun - tains, Shall peace, the her - ald, go,
The tide of time shall nev - er His cov - e - nant re - move,

To take a - way trans - gres - sion, And rule in eq - ui - ty.
Whose souls, con - demned and dy - ing, Are pre - cious in His sight.
And right - eous - ness, in foun - tains, From hill to val - ley flow.
His name shall stand for - ev - er; That Name to us is Love.

Text: James Montgomery, 1771-1854
Tune: SHEFFIELD, 7 6 7 6 D; English melody

188 O Come, O Come, Emmanuel

"...the virgin shall conceive and bear a Son, and they shall name Him Emmanuel," which means "God is with us."
Matthew 1:23

Unison

1. O come, O come, Em - man - u - el, And
2. O come, thou Wis - dom from on high, And
3. O come, De - sire of na - tions, bind All
4. O come, thou Day-spring, come and cheer Our

ran - som cap - tive Is - ra - el, That
or - der all things, far and nigh; To
peo - ples in one heart and mind; Bid
spir - its by Thine ad - vent here; Dis -

mourns in lone - ly ex - ile here Un -
us the path of knowl - edge show, And
en - vy, strife, and quar - rels cease; Fill
perse the gloom - y clouds of night, And

til the Son of God ap - pear.
cause us in her ways to go.
the whole world with heav - en's peace.
death's dark shad - ows put to flight.

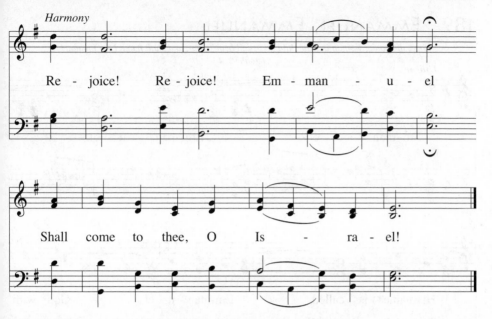

Harmony

Re - joice! Re - joice! Em - man - u - el

Shall come to thee, O Is - ra - el!

Text: Latin 9th C., tr. st. 1, 4, by John Mason Neale, 1818-1866; st. 2, 3, by Henry Sloane Coffin, 1877-1954
Tune: VENI EMMANUEL, LM with refrain; adapt. by Thomas Helmore, 1811-1890

189 EMMANUEL, EMMANUEL

Look, the young woman is with child and shall bear a Son, and shall name Him Immanuel.
Isaiah 7:14

Em-man - u - el,   Em-man - u - el,   His name is called Em-man - u - el.   God with us,   re-vealed in us,   His name is called Em-man - u - el.

Text: Bob McGee, b.1949
Tune: McGEE, Irregular; Bob McGee, b.1949
© 1976, C.A. Music (div. of C. A. Records, Inc.) ASCAP

WHILE WE ARE WAITING, COME 190

The one who testifies to these things says, "Surely I am coming soon." Amen. Come, Lord Jesus!
Revelation 22:20

1. While we are wait - ing, come;
2. With pow'r and glo - ry, come;
3. Come, Sav - ior, quick - ly come;

While we are wait - ing, come.
With pow'r and glo - ry, come.
Come, Sav - ior, quick - ly come.

Je - sus, our Lord, Em - man - u - el,

While we are wait - ing, come.

Text: Claire Cloninger
Tune: Don Cason
© 1986, Word Music

191   WHEN THE ROLL IS CALLED UP YONDER

The Lord Himself... with the sound of God's trumpet, will descend from heaven, and the dead in Christ will rise first.
1 Thessalonians 4:16

1. When the trum - pet of the Lord shall sound and
2. On that bright and cloud - less morn - ing when the
3. Let us la - bor for the Mas - ter from the

time shall be no more, And the morn - ing breaks e -
dead in Christ shall rise And the glo - ry of His
dawn till set - ting sun, Let us talk of all His

ter - nal, bright and fair— When the saved of earth shall
res - ur - rec - tion share— When His cho - sen ones shall
won - drous love and care; Then when all of life is

gath - er o - ver on the oth - er shore, And the
gath - er to their home be - yond the skies, And the
o - ver and our work on earth is done, And the

roll   is called   up yon - der— I'll   be   there!

When the roll   is called up yon   -   der,

When the roll is called up yon - der I'll be there,

When the roll   is called up yon   -   der, When the

When the roll is called up yon - der I'll be there,

roll   is called up yon - der— When the

When   the roll   is

roll   is called up yon - der I'll   be   there!

Text: James M. Black, 1856-1938
Tune: ROLL CALL, 15 11 15 11 with refrain; James M. Black, 1856-1938

192 SIGN ME UP

And I heard a voice from heaven saying, "Write this: Blessed are the dead who from now on die in the Lord."
Revelation 14:13

Sign me up for the Chris-tian ju - bi - lee,

Write my name on the roll.

I've been changed since the Lord has lift-ed me.

I want to be read-y when Je - sus comes.

When Je - sus comes, oh, the trum-pet will sound

loud, When my Sav - ior comes, all the
saints in Christ shall rise, Oh, I've been
changed since the Lord has lift - ed me, I
want to be read - y when Je - sus comes.

Last time

Last time

Text: Kevin Yancy and Jerome Metcalfe
Tune: Kevin Yancy and Jerome Metcalfe; arr. by Jimmie Abbington
© 1979, 2000, GIA Publications, Inc.

193 SOON AND VERY SOON

...for He is Lord of lords and King of kings, and those with Him are called and chosen, and faithful.
Revelation 17:14

1. Soon and ver - y soon   we are goin' to see the King,
2. No   more cry - in' there   we are goin' to see the King,
3. No   more dy - in' there   we are goin' to see the King,
4. Soon and ver - y soon   we are goin' to see the King,

Soon and ver - y soon   we are goin' to see the King,
No   more cry - in' there   we are goin' to see the King,
No   more dy - in' there   we are goin' to see the King,
Soon and ver - y soon   we are goin' to see the King,

Soon and ver - y soon   we are goin' to see the King,
No   more cry - in' there   we are goin' to see the King,
No   more dy - in' there   we are goin' to see the King,
Soon and ver - y soon   we are goin' to see the King,

Hal - le - lu - jah, Hal - le - lu - jah, we're

goin' to see the King! Hal - le - lu - jah,

Hal - le - lu - jah, Hal - le -

lu - jah, Hal - le - lu - jah.

Text: Andraé Crouch, b.1945
Tune: SOON AND VERY SOON, 12 12 12 14; Andraé Crouch, b.1945
© 1976, Bud John Songs, Inc./Crouch Music (ASCAP)

194 COME, YE THANKFUL PEOPLE, COME

Enter His gates with thanksgiving, and His courts with praise. Give thanks to Him, bless His name.
Psalm 100:4

1. Come, ye thank-ful peo-ple, come— Raise the song of har-vest-home: All is safe-ly gath-ered in Ere the win-ter storms be-gin. God, our Mak-er, doth pro-vide For our wants to be sup-plied:

2. All the world is God's own field, Fruit un-to His praise to yield: Wheat and tares to-geth-er sown, Un-to joy or sor-row grown. First the blade and then the ear, Then the full corn shall ap-pear:

3. For the Lord our God shall come And shall take His har-vest home: From His field shall in that day All of-fens-es purge a-way— Give His an-gels charge at last In the fire the tares to cast,

4. E-ven so, Lord, quick-ly come To Thy fi-nal har-vest-home: Gath-er Thou Thy peo-ple in, Free from sor-row, free from sin; There, for-ev-er pu-ri-fied, In Thy pres-ence to a-bide:

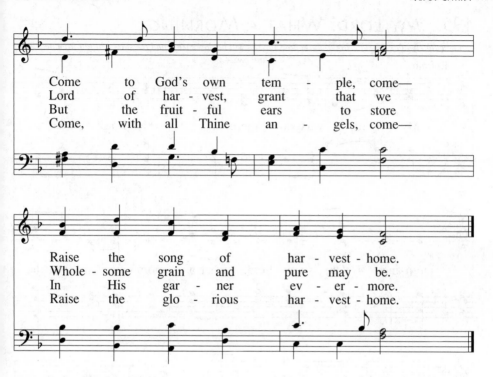

Come to God's own tem - ple, come—
Lord of har - vest, grant that we
But the fruit - ful ears to store
Come, with all Thine an - gels, come—

Raise the song of har - vest - home.
Whole - some grain and pure may be.
In His gar - ner ev - er - more.
Raise the glo - rious har - vest - home.

Text: Henry Alford, 1810-1871
Tune: ST. GEORGE'S WINDSOR, 77 77 D; George J. Elvey, 1816-1893

195   MY LORD! WHAT A MORNING

Immediately after the suffering of those days the sun will be darkened... and the stars will fall from heaven.
Matthew 24:29

Refrain

My   Lord!   what a   morn-ing,   My   Lord!   what a

morn-ing,   Oh,   my Lord!   what a   morn - ing,   When the

stars   be-gin   to   fall.   When the   stars   be-gin   to   fall.

Verses

1. You   will   hear   the trum - pet   sound
2. You   will   hear   the sin - ner   cry   To wake the
3. You   will   hear   the Chris-tian   shout

na - tions un - der - ground,   Look-ing   to   my   God's   right

hand   When the   stars   be - gin   to   fall.

Text: Negro spiritual
Tune: WHAT A MORNING, 7 8 7 7 with refrain; Negro spiritual; arr. by Melva Costen, © 1990

196 WHERE SHALL I BE?

The nations raged, but Your wrath has come, and the time for judging the dead, for rewarding Your servants...
Revelation 11:18

1. When judg-ment day is draw-ing nigh, Where shall I be?
2. When wick-ed men His wrath shall see, Where shall I be?
3. When heav'n and earth as some great scroll, Where shall I be?
4. All trou-ble done, all con-flict past, Where shall I be?

When God the works of men shall try, Where shall I be?
And to the rocks and moun-tains flee, Where shall I be?
Shall from God's an-gry pres-ence roll, Where shall I be?
And old A-pol-yon bound at last, Where shall I be?

When east and west the fire shall roll, Where shall I be?
When hills and moun-tains flee a-way, Where shall I be?
When all the saints re-deemed shall stand, Where shall I be?
When Christ shall reign from shore to shore, Where shall I be?

How will it be with my poor soul; Where shall I be?
When all the works of men de-cay, Where shall I be?
For-ev-er blest at God's right hand, Where shall I be?
And peace a-bide for-ev-er-more, Where shall I be?

O where shall I be when the first trum - pet sounds, O
where shall I be when it sounds so loud? When it sounds so loud as to
wake up the dead? O where shall I be when it sounds?

Text: Charles P. Jones
Tune: JUDGEMENT DAY, 8 4 8 4 with refrain; Charles P. Jones

197 Joy to the World

He will reign over the house of Jacob forever, and of His kingdom there will be no end.
Luke 1:33

1. Joy to the world! the Lord is come: Let earth re-
2. Joy to the world! the Sav-ior reigns: Let us, our
3. He rules the world with truth and grace, And makes the

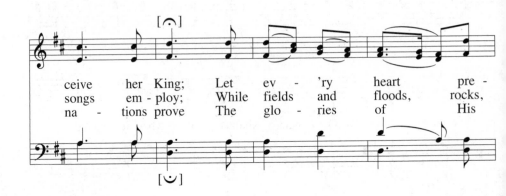

ceive her King; Let ev - 'ry heart pre -
songs em - ploy; While fields and floods, rocks,
na - tions prove The glo - ries of His

pare Him room, And heav'n and na - ture
hills, and plains; Re - peat the sound - ing
right - eous - ness, And won - ders of His

And
Re -
And

sing,   And heav'n and   na - ture sing,   And
joy,   Re - peat the sound-ing joy,   Re -
love,   And won - ders of His love,   And

heav'n and   na - ture   sing,   And heav'n and na - ture
peat   the sound-ing   joy,   Re - peat the sound-ing
won - ders   of His   love,   And won - ders of His

heav'n,   and   heav'n   and   na - ture   sing.
peat,   re - peat   the   sound - ing   joy.
won - ders,   won - ders   of   His   love.

sing,   And heav'n   and   na - ture   sing.
joy,   Re - peat   the   sound - ing   joy.
love,   And won   ders   of   His   love.

Text: Psalm 98; Isaac Watts, 1674-1748
Tune: ANTIOCH, CM; arr. from George F. Handel, 1685-1759, in T. Hawkes' *Collection of Tunes,* 1833

198 A Stable Lamp Is Lighted

They went with haste and found Mary and Joseph, and the child lying in the manger.
Luke 2:16

1. A sta - ble lamp is light - ed Whose glow shall wake the sky; The stars shall bend their voic - es, And ev - 'ry stone shall cry. And
2. Child through Da - vid's cit - y Shall ride in tri - umph by; The palm shall strew its branch - es, And ev - 'ry stone shall cry. And
3. He shall be for - sak - en, And yield - ed up to die; The sky shall groan and dark - en, And ev - 'ry stone shall cry. And
4. now, as at the end - ing, The low is lift - ed high; The stars shall bend their voic - es, And ev - 'ry stone shall cry. And

ev - 'ry stone shall cry, And straw like gold shall shine;
ev - 'ry stone shall cry, Though heav - y, dull, and dumb,
ev - 'ry stone shall cry, For hearts made hard by sin:
ev - 'ry stone shall cry, In prais - es of the child

A barn shall har - bor heav - en, A stall be - come a
And lie with - in the road - way To pave His king - dom
God's blood up - on the spear - head, God's love re - fused a -
By whose de - scent a - mong us The worlds are rec - on -

1.-3.

shrine.
come.
gain.
ciled.

4.

This
Yet
But

Text: Richard Wilbur, b.1921, © 1961, 1989
Tune: ANDUJAR, 7 6 7 6 6 6 7 6; David Hurd, b.1950, © 1984, GIA Publications, Inc.

199 O COME, ALL YE FAITHFUL

"Let us go now to Bethlehem and see this thing that has taken place, which the Lord has made known to us."
Luke 2:15, 20

1. O come, all ye faith-ful, joy-ful and tri-um-phant, O
2. Sing, choirs of an-gels, sing in ex-ul-ta-tion,
3. Yea, Lord, we greet Thee, born this hap-py morn-ing,

come ye, O come ye to Beth - le - hem;
Sing, all ye cit - i - zens of heav'n a - bove!
Je - sus, to Thee be all glo - ry giv'n;

Come and be-hold Him, born the King of an - gels;
Glo - ry to God, all glo-ry in the high - est;
Word of the Fa - ther, now in flesh ap - pear - ing;

O come, let us a - dore Him, O come, let us a - dore Him,

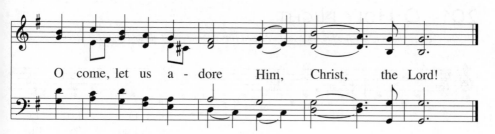

O come, let us a - dore Him, Christ, the Lord!

Text: *Adeste fideles;* John F. Wade, c.1711-1786; tr. by Frederick Oakeley, 1802-1880, alt.
Tune: ADESTE FIDELES, Irregular with refrain; John F. Wade, c.1711-1786

HE CAME DOWN 200

For God so loved the world that He gave His only Son, so that everyone who believes in Him may... have eternal life.
John 3:16

He came down that we may have *love; He

came down that we may have love; He came down that we may

Solo: Why did He come?

have love, Hal-le-lu - jah for ev-er - more.

Substitute peace, joy, hope, life, *etc.*

Text: Cameroon traditional
Tune: Cameroon traditional; tr. and arr. by John L. Bell, b.1949, © 1990, Iona Community, GIA Publications, Inc., agent

201 O Holy Night

And she gave birth to her firstborn son and wrapped Him in bands of cloth, and laid Him in a manger...
Luke 2:7

1. O   ho - ly
2. Led   by   the
3. Tru - ly   He

night!   the stars are bright - ly shin - ing;   It   is   the
light   of faith se - rene - ly beam - ing,   With glow - ing
taught   us   to   love   one an - oth - er;   His   law   is

night   of   the dear   Sav - ior's birth.
hearts   by   His cra - dle   we stand.
love   and   His gos - pel   is peace.

Long   lay   the world   in sin   and er - ror
So   led   by light   of   a   star   sweet - ly
Chains   shall He break,   for   the slave   is   our

pin - ing, Till He ap-peared and the soul felt its
gleam - ing, Here came the Wise Men from O - ri - ent
broth - er, And in His name all op-pres - sion shall

worth.
land.
cease.

A thrill of hope— the
The King of kings lay
Sweet hymns of joy in

wea - ry world re-joic - es, For yon - der breaks a
thus in low - ly man - ger, In all our tri - als
grate - ful cho - rus raise we; Let all with - in us

new and glo - rious morn! Fall on your knees! O
born to be our Friend. He knows our need— to our
praise His ho - ly name. Christ is the Lord! O

hear the an - gel voic - es! O night di -
weak - ness is no stran - ger. Be - hold your
praise His name for-ev - er! His pow'r and

vine, O night when Christ was
King, be - fore Him low - ly
glo - ry ev - er - more pro -

born! O night, O ho - ly
bend! Be - hold your King, be -
claim! *His pow'r and glo - ry

1., 2. **3.**

night, O night di - vine!
fore Him low - ly bend!
ev - er - more pro - claim!

*Optional extended or choral ending

His pow'r and glo - ry

ev - er - more pro - claim!

Text: John S. Dwight
Tune: CANTIQUE DE NOEL, Irregular; Adolphe Adam, 1803-1856

GO TELL IT ON THE MOUNTAIN 202

So they went with haste and found Mary and Joseph, and the child lying in the manger.
Luke 2:16

Refrain

Go tell it on the moun - tain, O-ver the hills and ev - 'ry-where,

Go tell it on the moun - tain that Je - sus Christ is born.

Verses

1. While shep-herds kept their watch-ing O'er si - lent flocks by night,
2. The shep-herds feared and trem-bled When lo! a - bove the earth,
3. Down in a low - ly man - ger The hum - ble Christ was born,

D.C.

Be - hold, through-out the heav-ens There shone a ho - ly light.
Rang out the an - gel cho - rus That hailed our Sav - ior's birth.
And God sent us sal - va - tion That bless - ed Christ-mas morn.

Text: Negro spiritual; adapt. by John W. Work, Jr., 1871-1925, © Mrs. John W. Work, III
Tune: GO TELL IT ON THE MOUNTAIN, 7 6 7 6 with refrain; Negro spiritual; arr. by Valeria A. Foster, © 2000, GIA Publications, Inc.

203 MESSIAH NOW HAS COME

For my eyes have seen Your salvation,... a light for revelation to the Gentiles.
Luke 2:30, 32

1. From His throne a - bove   The   King   of   Love   Came
2. In   His   life we find   New   hope sub - lime,   His
3. In   the   hearts of all,   Sal - va - tion's   call   Is

down to   set   us   free.   With   His   gift   of   life,   He
King-dom   will   ful - fill   God's man - date for peace,   All
an - swered   ev - er   more.   God's   re - demp-tion tale,   Em -

sac - ri - ficed   From   a   man - ger   to   a   tree.
con - flicts   ceased,   On   earth on - ly   good - will.
man - u - el,   We   wor - ship   and   a - dore.

So   we   sing, we   sing,   the   heav - ens   ring,   Hail

God's a-noint-ed One! Now-ell, Now-ell, glad tid-ings tell, Mes - si-ah now has come!

Text: Nolan Williams, Jr., b.1969
Tune: MESSIAH, 54 6 D with refrain; Nolan Williams, Jr., b.1969
© 1996, NEWorks Publishing

204 O Little Town of Bethlehem

O Bethlehem... from you shall come forth for me one who is to rule in Israel, whose origin is from of old...
Micah 5:2

1. O lit - tle town of Beth - le - hem, How
2. For Christ is born of Mar - y, And
3. How si - lent - ly, how si - lent - ly, The
4. O ho - ly Child of Beth - le - hem! De -

still we see thee lie! A - bove thy deep and
gath - ered all a - bove, While mor - tals sleep, the
won - drous gift is giv'n! So God im - parts to
scend to us we pray; Cast out our sin and

dream - less sleep The si - lent stars go by;
an - gels keep Their watch of won - d'ring love.
hu - man hearts The bless - ings of His heav'n.
en - ter in, Be born in us to - day.

Yet in the dark streets shin - eth The ev - er - last - ing
O morn - ing stars, to - geth - er Pro - claim the ho - ly
No ear may hear His com - ing, But in this world of
We hear the Christ - mas an - gels The great glad tid - ings

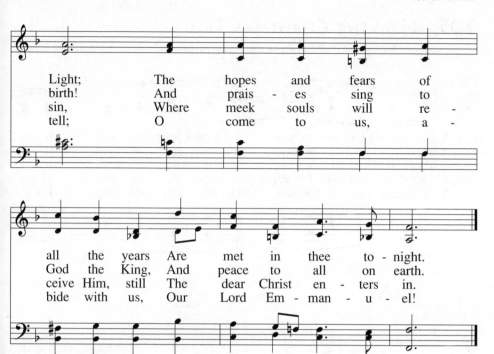

Light; The hopes and fears of
birth! And prais - es sing to
sin, Where meek souls will re -
tell; O come to us, a -

all the years Are met in thee to - night.
God the King, And peace to all on earth.
ceive Him, still The dear Christ en - ters in.
bide with us, Our Lord Em - man - u - el!

Text: Phillips Brooks, 1835-1893
Tune: ST. LOUIS, 8 6 8 6 7 6 8 6; Lewis H. Redner, 1831-1908

205 HEAVEN'S CHRISTMAS TREE

...they are now justified by His grace as a gift, through the redemption that is in Christ Jesus...
Romans 3:24-25

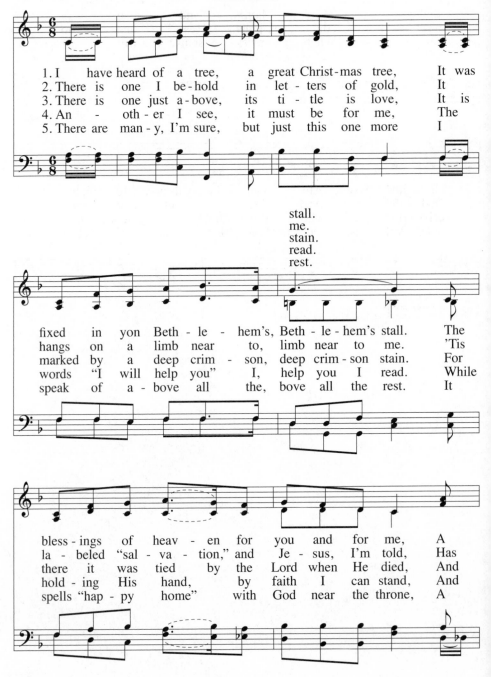

1. I   have heard of a tree,   a   great Christ-mas tree,   It was
2. There is   one   I   be-hold   in   let - ters   of   gold,   It
3. There is   one just a-bove,   its   ti - tle   is   love,   It is
4. An -   oth - er   I see,   it   must   be   for   me,   The
5. There are   man - y, I'm sure,   but   just   this   one   more   I

stall.
me.
stain.
read.
rest.

fixed   in   yon   Beth - le - hem's,   Beth - le - hem's stall.   The
hangs   on   a   limb   near   to,   limb   near   to   me.   'Tis
marked   by   a   deep   crim - son,   deep   crim - son   stain.   For
words   "I   will   help   you"   I,   help   you   I   read.   While
speak   of   a - bove   all   the,   bove   all   the   rest.   It

bless - ings   of   heav - en   for   you   and   for   me,   A
la - beled   "sal - va - tion,"   and   Je - sus,   I'm told,   Has
there   it   was   tied   by   the   Lord   when   He   died,   And
hold - ing   His   hand,   by   faith   I   can   stand,   And
spells "hap - py   home"   with   God   near   the   throne,   A

Christ - mas   pres - ent   for   all.
bought   that   pack - age   for   me.
glo - ry   to   His   dear   name.
this   is   the   pack - age   I   need.
place   where the   wea - ry   shall   rest.

There is   a pack-age for   me on that tree;   A pre - cious

to - ken   that   some-one loves me.   Oh   yes,   I   can see   on

Cal - va - ry's Tree,   That   there is   a pack-age   for   me.

Text: Charles A. Tindley, 1851-1933
Tune: HEAVEN'S CHRISTMAS TREE, 11 9 11 7 with refrain, Charles A. Tindley, 1851-1933; arr. by Charles A. Tindley, Jr.

206 Angels We Have Heard on High

And suddenly there was with the angel a multitude of the heavenly host, praising God...
Luke 2:14

1. An - gels we have heard on high Sweet - ly sing - ing
2. Shep-herds, why this ju - bi - lee? Why your joy - ous
3. Come to Beth - le - hem and see Him whose birth the

o'er the plains, And the moun-tains in re - ply
strains pro - long? What the glad-some tid - ings be,
an - gels sing; Come a - dore, on bend - ed knee,

Ech - o - ing their joy - ous strains.
Which in - spire your heav'n - ly song. Glo -
Christ, the Lord, the new - born King.

ri - a

in ex - cel - sis De - o, Glo - - - - ri - a in ex - cel - sis De - o.

Text: *Les anges dans nos campagnes,* French c.18th C.; tr. from *Crown of Jesus Music,* London, 1862
Tune: GLORIA, 7 7 7 7 with refrain; French traditional

207 ANGELS, FROM THE REALMS OF GLORY

The angel said, "Do not be afraid... to you is born this day in the city of David a Savior, who is the Messiah, the Lord."
Luke 2:10-11

1. An - gels, from the realms of glo - ry, Wing your flight o'er
2. Shep-herds, in the fields a - bid - ing, Watch-ing o'er your
3. Sag - es, leave your con - tem-pla-tions, Bright - er vi - sions
4. Saints be - fore the al - tar bend-ing, Watch-ing long in

all the earth; You who sang cre - a - tion's sto - ry,
flocks by night, God with man is now re - sid - ing,
beam a - far; Seek the great De - sire of na - tions,
hope and fear, Sud - den - ly the Lord, de - scend - ing,

Now pro - claim Mes - si - ah's birth:
Yon - der shines the in - fant Light:
You have seen His na - tal star: Come and wor-ship,
In His tem - ple shall ap - pear:

come and wor - ship, Wor-ship Christ, the new-born King.

Text: James Montgomery, 1771-1854
Tune: REGENT SQUARE, 8 7 8 7 8 7; Henry Smart, 1813-1879

Away in a Manger 208

While they were there, the time came for her to deliver her child.
Luke 2:6

1. A - way in a man - ger, no crib for a bed,
2. The cat - tle are low - ing, the ba - by a - wakes,
3. Be near me, Lord Je - sus! I ask You to stay

The lit - tle Lord Je - sus laid down His sweet head.
But lit - tle Lord Je - sus, no cry - ing He makes.
Close by me for ev - er, and love me, I pray.

The stars in the bright sky looked down where He lay,
I love you, Lord Je - sus! look down from the sky,
Bless all the dear chil - dren in Your ten - der care,

The lit - tle Lord Je - sus, a - sleep on the hay.
And stay by my cra - dle till morn - ing is nigh.
And fit us for heav - en, to live with You there.

Text: St. 1-2, anonymous, st. 3, John T. McFarland 1851-1913
Tune: CRADLE SONG, 11 11 11 11; William J. Kirkpatrick, 1838-1921

209 AWAY IN A MANGER

While they were there, the time came for her to deliver her child.
Luke 2:6

1. A - way in a man - ger, no crib for a bed, The
2. The cat - tle are low - ing, the Ba - by a - wakes, But

lit - tle Lord Je - sus laid down His sweet head; The
lit - tle Lord Je - sus, no cry - ing He makes; I

stars in the sky looked down where He lay,
love Thee, Lord Je - sus! look down from the sky,

The lit - tle Lord Je - sus, a - sleep on the hay.
And stay by my cra - dle till morn - ing is nigh.

3. Be near me, Lord Je - sus, I ask Thee to stay Close

by me for - ev - er, and love me, I pray; Bless

all the dear chil - dren in Thy ten - der care, And

take us to heav - en, to live with Thee there.

Text: St. 1-2, anonymous, st. 3, John T. McFarland, 1851-1913
Tune: MUELLER, 11 11 11 11; James R. Murray, 1841-1905; arr. by Nolan Williams, Jr., b.1969, © 2000, GIA Publications, Inc.

210 WONDERFUL COUNSELOR

For a child has been born for us... authority rests upon His shoulders; and He is named Wonderful Counselor.
Isaiah 9:6

1. Oh, who do you call the won-der-ful coun-sel-or?
2. Oh, I call Je-sus the won-der-ful coun-sel-or.

Oh, glo-ry hal-le-lu-jah! Oh,

glo-ry hal-le-lu-jah! Glo-ry hal-le-lu-jah to the new-born King!

Text: Negro spiritual
Tune: Negro spiritual; arr. by Evelyn Simpson-Curenton, b.1953, © 2000, GIA Publications, Inc.

SILENT NIGHT, HOLY NIGHT 211

For we observed His star at its rising, and have come to pay Him homage.
Matthew 2:2

1. Si - lent night, ho - ly night, All is calm,
2. Si - lent night, ho - ly night, Shep-herds quake
3. Si - lent night, ho - ly night, Son of God,

all is bright Round yon Vir - gin Moth - er and Child,
at the sight; Glo - ries stream from heav - en a - far,
love's pure light Ra - diant beams from Thy ho - ly face,

Ho - ly In - fant so ten - der and mild, Sleep in heav - en - ly
Heav'n - ly hosts sing al - le - lu - ia; Christ, the Sav - ior, is
With the dawn of re - deem - ing grace, Je - sus, Lord, at Thy

peace, Sleep in heav - en - ly peace.
born! Christ, the Sav - ior, is born!
birth, Je - sus, Lord, at Thy birth.

Text: *Stille Nacht, heilige Nacht;* Joseph Mohr, 1792-1849; tr. John F. Young, 1820-1885
Tune: STILLE NACHT, 66 89 66; Franz X. Gruber, 1787-1863

212 RISE UP, SHEPHERD, AND FOLLOW

"Let us go now to Bethlehem and see this thing that has taken place, which the Lord has made known to us."
Luke 2:15

1. There's a star in the East on Christ - mas morn,
2. If you take good heed to the an - gel's words,

Rise up, shep - herd, and fol - low, It will
Rise up, shep - herd, and fol - low, You'll for -

lead to the place where the Christ was born,
get your flocks, you'll for - get your herds,

Rise up, shep - herd, and fol - low.
Rise up, shep - herd, and fol - low.

Fol - low, fol - low, Rise up, shep - herd, and fol - low, Fol - low the Star of Beth - le - hem, Rise up, shep - herd, and fol - low.

Text: Negro spiritual
Tune: Negro spiritual; arr. by Joseph Joubert, © 2000, GIA Publications, Inc.

213 RISE UP, SHEPHERD, AND FOLLOW

"Let us go now to Bethlehem and see this thing that has taken place, which the Lord has made known to us."
Luke 2:15

1. There's a star in the East on Christ-mas morn,
2. If you take good heed to the an-gel's words,

Rise up, shep-herd, and fol - low, It will lead
Rise up, shep-herd, and fol - low, You'll for - get

to the place where the Christ was born,
your flocks, you'll for - get your herds,

Rise up, shep-herd, and fol - low.
Rise up, shep-herd, and fol - low.

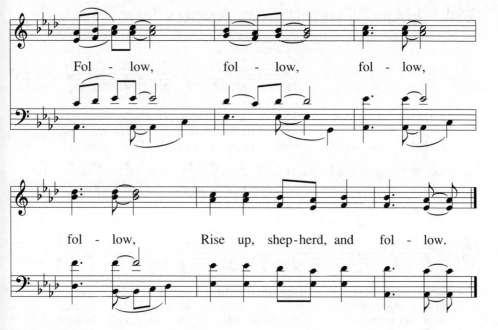

Fol - low, fol - low, fol - low, fol - low, Rise up, shep-herd, and fol - low.

Text: Negro spiritual
Tune: Negro spiritual; arr. by Joseph Joubert, © 2000, GIA Publications, Inc.

214 HARK! THE HERALD ANGELS SING

"Glory to God in the highest heaven, and on earth peace among those whom He favors!"
Luke 2:13-14

1. Hark! the her - ald an - gels sing, "Glo - ry to the
2. Christ, by high - est heav'n a - dored, Christ the ev - er -
3. Hail the heav'n - born Prince of Peace! Hail the Sun of

new - born King; Peace on earth, and mer - cy mild
last - ing Lord: Late in time be - hold Him come,
Right - eous - ness! Light and life to all He brings,

God and sin - ners rec - on - ciled!" Joy - ful, all you
Off - spring of the Vir - gin's womb. Veiled in flesh the
Ris'n with heal - ing in His wings. Mild He lays His

na - tions, rise, Join the tri - umph of the skies;
God - head see: Hail the in - car - nate De - i - ty,
glo - ry by, Born that we no more may die,

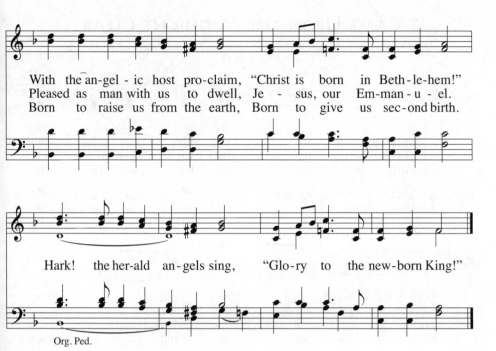

With the an-gel - ic host pro-claim, "Christ is born in Beth-le-hem!"
Pleased as man with us to dwell, Je - sus, our Em-man - u - el.
Born to raise us from the earth, Born to give us sec-ond birth.

Hark! the her-ald an - gels sing, "Glo-ry to the new-born King!"

Org. Ped.

Text: Charles Wesley, 1707-1788, alt.
Tune: MENDELSSOHN, 77 77 D with refrain; Felix Mendelssohn, 1809-1847

215 It Came Upon the Midnight Clear

Bless the Lord, you angels of the Lord; sing praise to Him and highly exalt Him forever.
Azariah 37

1. It came up-on the mid - night clear, That glo - rious song of old, From an - gels bend - ing near the earth To touch their harps of gold: "Peace

2. Still through the clo - ven skies they come, With peace - ful wings un - furled, And still their heav'n - ly mu - sic floats O'er all the wea - ry world: A -

3. Yet with the woes of sin and strife, The world has suf - fered long; Be - neath the heav'n - ly hymn have rolled Two thou - sand years of wrong; And

4. For, lo, the days are has - t'ning on, By proph - ets seen of old, When with the ev - er - cir - cling years Shall come the time fore - told, When

on the earth, good will to all From
bove its sad and low - ly plains They
war - ring hu - man - kind hears not The
peace shall o - ver all the earth Its

heav'n's all gra - cious King"; The
bend on hov - 'ring wing, And
tid - ings which they bring; O
an - cient splen - dors fling, And

world in sol - emn still - ness lay, To
ev - er o'er its Ba - bel sounds The
hush the noise and cease your strife And
all the world give back the song Which

hear the an - gels sing.
bless - ed an - gels sing.
hear the an - gels sing.
now the an - gels sing.

Text: Edmund H. Sears, 1810-1876, alt.
Tune: CAROL, CMD; Richard S. Willis, 1819-1900

216 BEHOLD THE STAR

When they saw that the star had stopped, they were overwhelmed with joy... they saw the child with Mary...
Matthew 2:10-11

Refrain

Be-hold the star! Be-hold the star up yon-der!

Be-hold the star! It is the star of Beth - le - hem.

Verses

1. There was no room found in the inn,
2. The wise men came from the East
3. A song broke forth up - on the night.

Last time

Beth - le - hem. (ooh)

For Him who was born
To wor - ship Him, the
Peace on earth, good -

It is the star of Beth - le - hem. (ooh)

free   from   sin.   Oh,
"Prince of   Peace."
will   to   men.

It   is   the   star   of   Beth - le - hem.

Text: Negro spiritual
Tune: BEHOLD THE STAR, LM with refrain; Negro spritual; arr. by Nolan Williams, Jr., b.1969, © 2000, GIA Publications, Inc.

217 JESUS, THE LIGHT OF THE WORLD

I have come as light into the world, so that everyone who believes in me should not remain in the darkness.
John 12:46

1. Hark the her - ald an - gels sing.
2. Joy - ful, all ye na - tions, rise.
3. Christ, by high - est heav'n a - dored.
4. Hail, the heav'n - born Prince of Peace.

Je - sus, the light of the world.

Glo - ry to the new - born King,
Join the tri - umph of the skies.
Christ, the ev - er - last - ing Lord,
Hail, the Sun of right - eous - ness!

Je - sus, the light of the world.

We'll walk in the light, beau - ti - ful light.

Come where the dew-drops of mer - cy shine right. Oh,

shine all a - round us by day and by night.

Je - sus, the light of the world.

Text: George D. Elderkin; verses by Charles Wesley, 1707-1788
Tune: WE'LL WALK IN THE LIGHT, 7 7 7 7 with refrain; George D. Elderkin; arr. by Evelyn Simpson-Curenton, b.1953, © 2000, GIA
    Publications, Inc.

218 WE THREE KINGS OF ORIENT ARE

...they saw the child with Mary His mother; and they knelt down and paid Him homage.
Matthew 2:11

1. We three kings of O - ri - ent are, Bear - ing gifts we
2. Born a babe on Beth - le - hem's plain, Gold we bring to
3. Frank - in - cense to of - fer have I; In - cense owns a
4. Myrrh is mine: its bit - ter per - fume Breathes a life of
5. Glo - rious now be - hold Him rise, King and God and

tra - verse a - far Field and foun - tain, Moor and
crown Him a - gain; King for ev - er, Ceas - ing
De - i - ty nigh, Prayer and prais - ing Glad - ly
gath - 'ring gloom; Sor - rowing, sigh - ing, Bleed - ing,
sac - ri - fice: Heav'n sings, "Hal - le - lu - jah!"

moun - tain, Fol - low - ing yon - der star.
nev - er, O - ver us all to reign.
rais - ing, Wor - ship - ing God on high. O star of
dy - ing, Sealed in the stone cold tomb.
"Hal - le - lu - jah!" earth re - plies.

won - der, star of night, Star with roy - al beau - ty bright, West - ward

lead - ing, still pro - ceed - ing, Guide us to Thy per - fect Light.

Text: Matthew 2:1-11; John H. Hopkins, Jr., 1820-1891
Tune: KINGS OF ORIENT, 88 44 6 with refrain; John H. Hopkins, Jr., 1820-1891

BRIGHTEST AND BEST 219

...there went the star that they had seen at its rising, until it stopped over the place where the child was.
Matthew 2:9

1. Bright - est and best of the sons of the morn - ing,
2. Say, shall we yield Him in cost - ly de - vo - tion,
3. Vain - ly we of - fer each am - ple ob - la - tion,
4. Cold on His cra - dle the dew - drops are shin - ing,

Dawn on our dark - ness and lend us Thine aid,
O - dors of E - dom and of - f'rings di - vine,
Vain - ly with gifts would His fa - vor se - cure;
Low lies His head with the beasts of the stall;

Star of the east, the ho - ri - zon a - dorn - ing,
Gems of the moun - tain and pearls of the o - cean,
Rich - er by far is the heart's ad - o - ra - tion,
An - gels a - dore Him in slum - ber re - clin - ing,

Guide where our in - fant Re - deem - er is laid.
Myrrh from the for - est, or gold from the mine?
Dear - er to God are the prayers of the poor.
Mak - er and Mon - arch and Sav - ior of all.

Text: Reginald Heber, 1783-1826
Tune: MORNING STAR, 11 10 11 10; John P. Harding

220 What Child Is This

This child is destined for the falling and the rising of many in Israel...
Luke 2:34

1. What Child is this, who, laid to rest, On
2. Why lies He in such low es-tate Where
3. So bring Him in-cense, gold and myrrh, Come

Mar - y's lap is sleep - ing? Whom an - gels greet with
ox and ass are feed - ing? Good Chris - tian, fear; for
peas - ant, king to own Him; The King of kings sal -

an - thems sweet, While shep - herds watch are keep-ing?
sin - ners here The si - lent Word is plead-ing.
va - tion brings, Let lov - ing hearts en - throne Him.

This, this is Christ the King, Whom shep-herds guard and an-gels sing;

Haste, haste to bring Him laud, The Babe, the Son of Mar - y.

Text: William C. Dix, 1827-1898
Tune: GREENSLEEVES, 8 7 8 7 with refrain; English melody, 16th C.; harm. by John Stainer, 1840-1901

PEACE! BE STILL! 221

He said to the sea, "Peace! Be still!" Then the wind ceased, and there was a dead calm.
Mark 4:39

Mas - ter, the tem - pest is rag - ing! The

bil - lows are toss - ing high! The

sky is o'er-shad - owed with black-ness, No

shel - ter or help is nigh: "Car - est Thou

not that we per - ish?" How canst Thou lie a -

sleep,   When each mo - ment   so mad - ly   is

threat-'ning   A   grave in the   an - gry   deep?

The winds   and   the waves shall   o - bey   Thy

will.   Peace, be still!   Peace, be still!

Peace, be still!   Peace, be still!   Wheth-er   the wrath of   the

storm - tossed sea, Or de - mons, or men, or what-

ev - er it be, No wa - ter can swal - low the

ship where lies the Mas - ter of o - cean and

earth and skies; They all shall sweet-ly o-bey Thy

will! Peace! Peace, be still!

Text: Mary A. Baker
Tune: H. R. Palmer; arr. by Nolan Williams, Jr., b.1969, from a version by Rev. James Cleveland, © 2000, GIA Publications, Inc.

222 JESUS IS A ROCK IN A WEARY LAND

The stone that the builders rejected has become the very head of the corner.
1 Peter 2:7

Refrain

Je-sus is a rock in a wea-ry land, a wea-ry land, a

wea-ry land; My Je - sus is a rock in a

wea-ry land, a shel-ter in the time of storm.

Verses

1. No man can do like Je - sus, Not a
2. When Je - sus was on earth, The
3. ξ Yon - der comes my Sav - ior, Him

mum - bling word He said; He went
flesh was ver - y weak; He
whom I love so well; He

walk - ing down to La - za-rus' grave, And He
gir - dled Him - self with a tow'l, And
has the palm of vic - to - ry, And the

D.C.

raised him from the dead.
washed His dis - ci - ples feet.
keys of death and Hell.

Text: Traditional
Tune: WEARY LAND, 6 6 8 6 with refrain; traditional; arr. by Wyatt Tee Walker, ©; administered by GIA Publications, Inc.

223 HE CALMED THE OCEAN

...He made the storm be still, and the waves of the sea were hushed.
Psalm 107:29

Solo:

said He would. 1. Down by the sea of Gal - li - lee,
2. If you don't be - lieve I've been re-deemed

All:

Said He would calm the rag-ing sea, Said He would,

Solo:

said He would, Drop your nets and fol - low me
Fol-low me down to the Jor - dan's stream

All:

Said He would calm the rag - ing sea,

Said He would, said He would.

Text: Prof. L. S. Boswell
Tune: Kenneth Morris, 1917-1988
© 1937, First Church of Deliverance

224 HOSANNA

...those who followed were shouting, "Hosanna! Blessed is the one who comes in the name of the Lord!"
Mark 11:9

san - na Bless - ed is He who

comes in the name of the Lord.

Bless-ed is He who comes in the name of the Lord.

Text: Mark 11:9
Tune: Patrick Roaché, ©; administered by GIA Publications, Inc.; arr. by Evelyn Simpson-Curenton, b.1953, © 2000, GIA Publications, Inc.

225 RIDE ON, KING JESUS

In Your majesty ride on victoriously for the cause of truth and to defend the right.
Psalm 45:4

great get-tin' up morn-ing, fare ye well, fare ye well. In that

Repeat ad lib.

Last time

well, fare ye well. No man can a-hin-der me, no

man can a-hin-der me, no man can a-hin-der me, no

man can a-hin-der me. Ride on, King Je-sus.

Text: Traditional
Tune: Negro spiritual; arr. by Stephen Key, from a version by Ernest Davis, © 2000, GIA Publications, Inc.

226 ALL GLORY, LAUD, AND HONOR

To the King of the ages, immortal, invisible, the only God, be honor and glory forever and ever. Amen.
1 Timothy 1:17

All glo - ry, laud, and hon - or To

You, Re - deem - er, King! To whom the lips of

chil - dren Made sweet ho - san - nas ring.

1. You are the King of Is - ra - el, And
2. The com - pa - ny of an - gels Are
3. The peo - ple of the He - brews With
4. To You be - fore Your pas - sion They
5. Their prais - es You ac - cept - ed, Ac -

Da - vid's roy - al Son, Now in the Lord's Name
prais - ing You on high; And mor - tals, joined with
palms be - fore You went: Our praise and prayers and
sang their hymns of praise: To You, now high ex -
cept the prayers we bring, Great source of love and

D.C.

com - ing, Our King and Bless - ed One.
all things Cre - a - ted, make re - ply.
an - thems Be - fore You we pre - sent.
alt - ed, Our mel - o - dy we raise.
good - ness, Our Sav - ior and our King.

Text: *Gloria, laus et honor;* Theodulph of Orleans, c.760-821; tr. by John M. Neale, 1818-1866, alt.
Tune: ST. THEODULPH, 7 6 7 6 D; Melchior Teschner, 1584-1635

227 ALL HAIL, KING JESUS

"Hosanna! Blessed is the one who comes in the name of the Lord—the King of Israel!"
John 12:13

All hail, King Je - sus, All hail, Em - man - u - el:

King of kings, Lord of lords, Bright Morn - ing

Star. And through - out e - ter - ni -

ty I'm goin' to praise Him, And for -

ev - er - more I will reign with Him.

O, HOW HE LOVES YOU AND ME   228

God proves His love for us in that while we still were sinners Christ died for us.
Romans 5:8

1. O, how He loves you and me, O, how He
   loves you and me, He gave His life, what
   more could He give; O, how He loves me, O, how He
   loves me, O, how He loves you and me.

2. Je-sus to Cal-v'ry did go, His love for
   all He did show; What He did there brought
   hope from de-spair: O, how He loves me, O, how He
   loves me, O, how He loves you and me.

Text: Kurt Kaiser, b.1934
Tune: PATRICIA, 77 4 5 5 5 7; Kurt Kaiser, b.1934; arr. by Nolan Williams, Jr., b.1969, Evelyn Simpson-Curenton, b.1953, and Robert J. Fryson
© 1975, Word Music, Inc. (ASCAP)

229 A Perfect Sacrifice

He has appeared once for all at the end of the age to remove sin by the sacrifice of Himself.
Hebrews 9:26

1. Ho - ly One,   Je - sus Christ,   the on - ly One

2. Lord, I yield,   yes, I give   this my song,

wor-thy to give His   life,   for the sins

my praise   of sac - ri - fice.   I give you my life,

of all man - kind: such a per-

you've al-read-y paid the price: such a per-

fect sac - ri - fice, Je - sus Christ!

fect sac - ri - fice, Je - sus Christ!

230 JESUS, REMEMBER ME

Then he said, "Jesus, remember me when You come into Your kingdom."
Luke 23:42

Ostinato Refrain

Je - sus,   re - mem - ber me   when you come in - to Your King - dom.

Je - sus,   re - mem - ber me   when you come in - to Your King - dom.

Flute

(Je - sus,   re - mem - ber me)

Text: Luke 23:42; Taizé Community, 1981
Tune: Jacques Berthier, 1923-1994

© 1981, Les Presses de Taizé, GIA Publications, Inc., agent

231 JUST FOR ME

For this is My blood of the covenant, which is poured out for many for the forgiveness of sins.
Matthew 26:28

Optional Solo:

Oh, what a shame to kill Him, as He hung on that rug - ged cross. His death was sure - ly need - ed to save this world from be - ing lost. My blind - ed eyes were o - pen so that I might see. *Choir:* He did all that just for me.

Text: Kenneth W. Louis
Tune: Kenneth W. Louis
© 1986, Kenneth W. Louis

232 HE LIFTED ME

I will extol You, O LORD, for You have drawn me up, and did not let my foes rejoice over me.
Psalm 30:1

1. In lov - ing - kind - ness Je - sus came, My
2. He called me long be - fore I heard, Be -
3. His brow was pierced with man - y a thorn, His
4. Now on a high - er plane I dwell, And

soul in mer - cy to re - claim, And from the depths of
fore my sin - ful heart was stirred, But when I took Him
hands by cru - el nails were torn, When from my guilt and
with my soul I know 'tis well; Yet how or why, I

me.

sin and shame Thru grace He lift - ed me.
at His word, For - giv'n He lift - ed me.
grief, for - lorn, In love He lift - ed me. He lift - ed me.
can - not tell, He should have lift - ed me.

me.

From sink - ing sand He lift - ed me, With

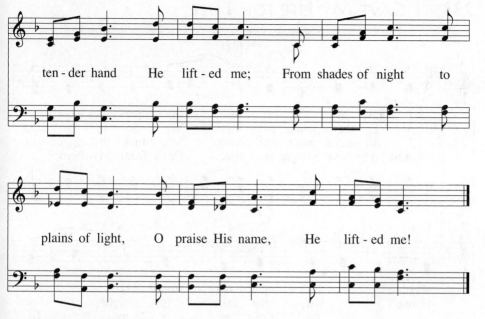

ten - der hand   He   lift - ed   me;   From shades of night   to

plains of light,   O   praise His name,   He   lift - ed me!

Text: Charles H. Gabriel, 1856-1932
Tune: HE LIFTED ME, 888 6 with refrain; Charles H. Gabriel, 1856-1932

233 I Gave My Life for Thee

I am the good shepherd. The good shepherd lays down His life for the sheep.
John 10:11

1. I gave My life for thee, My pre-cious blood I
2. My Fa-ther's house of light, My glo-ry-cir-cled
3. I suf-fered much for thee, More than thy tongue can
4. And I have brought to thee, Down from My home a-

shed, That thou might'st ran-somed be, And
throne I left, for earth-ly night, For
tell, Of bit-t'rest ag-o-ny, To
bove, Sal-va-tion full and free, My

quick-ened from the dead; I gave, I gave My
wan-d'rings sad and lone; I left, I left it
res-cue thee from hell; I've borne, I've borne it
par-don and My love; I bring, I bring rich

life for thee— What hast thou giv'n for Me?
all for thee— Hast thou left aught for Me?
all for thee— What hast thou borne for Me?
gifts to thee— What hast thou brought to Me?

Text: Frances R. Havergal, 1836-1879
Tune: KENOSIS, 6 6 6 6 8 6; Philip P. Bliss, 1838-1876

THE WINDOWS OF HEAVEN 234

If you conquer, you will be clothed like them in white robes, and I will not blot your name out of the book of life...
Revelation 3:5

The win - dows of heav - en are o - pen,

The fi - re is fall - ing to - night. I've got

joy, joy, joy in my heart, Since Je - sus made

ev - 'ry - thing right. I gave Him my

old dirt - y gar - ment, He gave me a

robe of pure white, And now I'm feast - ing on

man - na from heav - en, and that's why I'm

hap - py to - night.

1.   2.

1.   2.   Optional ending

Optional seque to "One Day"

Text: Traditional
Tune: Traditional; arr. by Evelyn Simpson-Curenton, b.1953, © 2000, GIA Publications, Inc.

235 ONE DAY

The sun shall be turned to darkness and the moon to blood, before the coming of the Lord's great and glorious day.
Acts 2:20

Living He loved me, dying He saved me, buried He carried my sins far away. Rising He justified, freed me for heaven.

One day He's com-ing back, glo - ri-ous day.

Text: J. Wilbur Chapman
Tune: Charles H. Marsh; arr. by Evelyn Simpson-Curenton, b.1953, © 2000, GIA Publications, Inc.

I LOVE HIM 236

Rejoice in the Lord always; again I will say, Rejoice.
Philippians 4:4

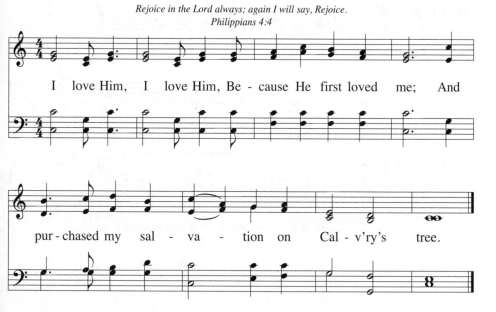

I love Him, I love Him, Be - cause He first loved me; And

pur - chased my sal - va - tion on Cal - v'ry's tree.

Text: African-American folk song
Tune: African-American folk song

237 He's So Real

Many Samaritans from that city believed in Him because of the woman's testimony.
John 4:39

He's so real, real in my soul to-day.

He has washed all of my sins a-way.

Je - sus' love just bub - bles o - ver

in my soul.

I'M SO GLAD 238

If my father and mother forsake me, the LORD will take me up.
Psalm 27:10

1. I'm so glad Je-sus lift-ed me. I'm so glad Je-sus lift-ed me. I'm so glad Je-sus lift-ed me, I'm glad that sing-in' Glo-ry, Hal-le-lu-jah, Je-sus lift-ed me!

2. Satan had me bound; Jesus lifted me...
3. When I was in trouble, Jesus lifted me...

Text: African-American traditional
Tune: African-American traditional; arr. by Evelyn Simpson-Curenton, b.1953, © 2000, GIA Publications, Inc.

239 CALVARY

... they crucified Jesus there with the criminals, one on His right and one on His left.
Luke 23:33

Refrain

Cal - va - ry, Cal - va - ry, Cal - va -

ry, Cal - va - ry, Cal - va - ry,

Cal - va - ry, Sure - ly He died on Cal - va - ry.

Verses

1. Ev - 'ry time I think a - bout Je - sus, Ev - 'ry
2. Sin - ner, do you love my Je - sus? Sin - ner,
3. We are climb - ing Ja - cob's lad - der, We are
4. Ev - 'ry round goes high - er and high - er, Ev - 'ry

time I think a - bout Je - sus, Ev - 'ry time I
do you love my Je - sus? Sin - ner, do you
climb - ing Ja - cob's lad - der, We are climb - ing
round goes high - er and high - er, Ev - 'ry round goes

D.C.

think a - bout Je - sus,
love my Je - sus?
Ja - cob's lad - der,
high-er and high - er,

Sure - ly He died on Cal - va - ry.

May be sung as a unison a cappella piece.

Text: Negro spiritual
Tune: CALVARY, LM with refrain; Negro spiritual

240 He Will Remember Me

Then an angel from heaven appeared to Him and gave Him strength.
Luke 22:43

1. When on the cross of Cal - v'ry The Lord was cru - ci - fied;
2. O, what a shame to kill Him There on that rug - ged cross;
3. At His dear feet I'm kneel-ing, My sins I now con - fess;

The mob stood 'round a - bout Him And mocked un - til He died.
But such a death was need - ed To res - cue all the lost.
I bow in deep re - pen-tance, My soul He'll sure - ly bless.

Two thieves were nailed be - side Him To share the ag - o - ny,
His blood was made a ran - som To set the cap-tives free,
My blind - ed eyes He o - pens So that the light I see,

But one of them cried out to Him, "O Lord re - mem - ber me."
I know that I'm in - clud - ed, and He will re - mem - ber me.
And when I reach the pearl - y gates, He will re - mem - ber me.

Text: Eugene M. Bartlett, 1885-1941
Tune: REMEMBER ME, 7 6 7 6 7 6 8 6 with refrain; Eugene M. Bartlett, 1885-1941; arr. by Nolan Williams, Jr., b.1969
© 1976, Albert E. Brumley & Sons

241 KNEEL AT THE CROSS

...the cross is foolishness to those who are perishing, but to us who are being saved it is the power of God.
1 Corinthians 1:18

1. Kneel at the cross, Christ will meet you there,
2. Kneel at the cross, There is room for all
3. Kneel at the cross, Give your i - dols up,

Come while He waits for you; List to His voice,
Who would His glo - ry share; Bliss there a - waits,
Look un - to realms a - bove; Turn not a - way

Leave with Him your care And be - gin life a - new.
Harm can ne'er be - fall Those who are an - chored there.
To life's spark - ling cup; Trust on - ly in His love.

Kneel at the cross, Leave ev - 'ry

Kneel at the cross, Kneel at the cross, Leave ev-'ry care,

care;　　　Kneel　　　　at　the　cross,

Leave ev-'ry care;　Kneel　at the cross,　　　Kneel　at the cross,

there.

Je - sus　will meet　you　there,　meet　you there.

there.

Text: Charles E. Moody, fl.1924
Tune: KNEEL AT THE CROSS, 4 5 6 D with refrain; Charles E. Moody, fl.1924
© 1924, Stamps-Baxter Music (BMI)

242 LIFT HIGH THE CROSS

...so must the Son of Man be lifted up, that whoever believes in Him may have eternal life.
John 3:14-15

Refrain
Unison

Lift high the cross, the love of Christ pro-claim till

all the world a-dore His sa-cred name.

Verses
Harmony

1. Come, Chris-tians, fol-low where the Mas-ter trod, Our
2. Led on their way by this tri-um-phant sign, The
3. Each new-born fol-l'wer of the Cru-ci-fied Bears
4. O Lord, once lift-ed on the glo-rious tree, Your
5. So shall our song of tri-umph ev-er be: Praise

D.C.

King vic-to-rious, Christ, the Son of God.
hosts of God in con-quering ranks com-bine.
on the brow the seal of Him who died.
death has bought us life e-ter-nal-ly.
to the Cru-ci-fied for vic-to-ry!

Text: 1 Corinthians 1:18; George W. Kitchin, 1827-1912, and Michael R. Newbolt, 1874-1956, alt.
Tune: CRUCIFER, 10 10 with refrain; Sydney H. Nicholson, 1875-1947
© 1974, Hope Publishing Co.

WHEN I SURVEY THE WONDROUS CROSS   243

May I never boast of anything except the cross of our Lord Jesus Christ...
Galatians 6:14

1. When I sur - vey the won - drous cross
2. For - bid it, Lord, that I should boast,
3. See, from His head, His hands, His feet,
4. Were the whole realm of na - ture mine,

On which the Prince of glo - ry died,
Save in the death of Christ, my God;
Sor - row and love flow min - gled down;
That were a pres - ent far too small:

My rich - est gain I count but loss,
All the vain things that charm me most—
Did e'er such love and sor - row meet,
Love so a - maz - ing, so di - vine,

And pour con - tempt on all my pride.
I sac - ri - fice them to His blood.
Or thorns com - pose so rich a crown?
De - mands my soul, my life, my all.

Text: Isaac Watts, 1674-1748
Tune: HAMBURG, LM; Gregorian Chant; arr. by Lowell Mason, 1792-1872

244 THE OLD RUGGED CROSS

For many live as enemies of the cross of Christ...
Philippians 3:18

1. On a hill far a - way stood an old rug - ged cross,
2. O that old rug - ged cross, so de - spised by the world,
3. In the old rug - ged cross, stained with blood so di - vine,
4. To the old rug - ged cross I will ev - er be true,

The em - blem of suf - f'ring and shame;
Has a won - drous at - trac - tion for me;
A won - drous beau - ty I see;
Its shame and re - proach glad - ly bear;

And I love that old cross where the dear - est and best
For the dear Lamb of God left His glo - ry a - bove
For 'twas on that old cross Je - sus suf - fered and died
Then He'll call me some day to my home far a - way,

For a world of lost sin - ners was slain.
To bear it to dark Cal - va - ry.
To par - don and sanc - ti - fy me.
Where His glo - ry for ev - er I'll share.

old rug-ged cross,

So I'll cher-ish the cross, the old rug-ged cross, Till my

old rug-ged

tro-phies at last I lay down; I will cling to the cross, the

cross,

old rug-ged cross, And ex-change it some day for a crown.

Text: George Bennard, 1873-1960
Tune: OLD RUGGED CROSS, 12 8 12 8 with refrain; George Bennard, 1873-1960

245 THERE'S ROOM AT THE CROSS FOR YOU

Everything that the Father gives me will come to me, and anyone who comes to me I will never drive away.
John 6:37

1. The cross up-on which Je-sus died Is a shel-ter in which we can hide; And its grace so free Is suf-fi-cient for me, And deep is its foun-tain— as wide as the sea.

2. Tho mil-lions have found Him a friend And have turned from the sins they have sinned, The Sav-ior still waits To o-pen the gates And wel-come a sin-ner be-fore it's too late.

3. The hand of my Sav-ior is strong, And the love of my Sav-ior is long; Through sun-shine or rain, Through loss or in gain, The blood flows from Cal-v'ry to cleanse ev-'ry stain.

There's room   at the cross   for   you,   There's room at the cross for

you;   Tho'   mil-lions have come, There's still room for   one—

Yes, there's room   at   the cross   for   you.

Text: Ira Stamphill, b.1914
Tune: STAMPHILL, 88 45 11 with refrain; Ira Stamphill, b.1914
© 1946, Singspiration Music (ASCAP)

246   AT CALVARY

When they came to the place that is called The Skull, they crucified Jesus there with the criminals.
Luke 23:33

1. Years I spent in van - i - ty and pride,
2. By God's Word at last my sin I learned—
3. Now I've giv'n to Je - sus ev - 'ry - thing,
4. O the love that drew sal - va - tion's plan!

Car - ing not my Lord was cru - ci - fied, Know - ing
Then I trem - bled at the Law I'd spurned, Till my
Now I glad - ly own Him as my King, Now my
O the grace that brought it down to man! O the

not it was for me He died on Cal - va - ry.
guilt - y soul im - plor - ing turned to Cal - va - ry.
rap - tured soul can on - ly sing of Cal - va - ry.
might - y gulf that God did span at Cal - va - ry.

Mer - cy there was great and grace was free, Par - don

there was mul - ti -plied   to   me,   There   my bur-dened soul found

lib - er - ty—   At   Cal - va - ry.

Text: William R. Newell, 1868-1956
Tune: AT CALVARY, 99 13 with refrain; Daniel B. Towner, 1850-1919; arr. by Evelyn Simpson-Curenton, b.1953, © 2000, GIA Publications,
    Inc.

247 BENEATH THE CROSS OF JESUS

When the centurion saw what had taken place, he praised God and said, "Certainly this man was innocent."
Luke 23:47

1. Be - neath the cross of Je - sus I glad - ly take my
2. Up - on that cross of Je - sus My eyes at times can
3. I take, O cross, thy shad - ow For my a - bid - ing

stand: The shad - ow of a might - y rock With -
see The ver - y dy - ing form of One Who
place; I ask no oth - er sun - shine than The

in a wea - ry land, A home with - in the
suf - fered there for me; And from my smit - ten
sun - shine of His face, Con - tent to let the

wil - der - ness, A rest up - on the way, From the
heart, with tears, Two won - ders I con - fess— The
world go by, To know no gain or loss, My

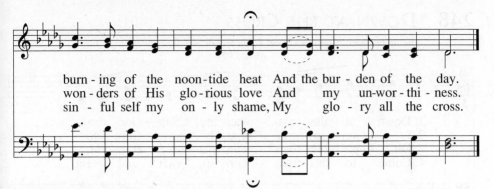

burn - ing of the noon-tide heat And the bur - den of the day.
won - ders of His glo-rious love And my un-wor - thi - ness.
sin - ful self my on - ly shame, My glo - ry all the cross.

Text: Elizabeth C. Clephane, 1830-1869
Tune: ST. CHRISTOPHER, 7 6 8 6 8 6 8 6; Frederick C. Maker, 1844-1927

248 Down at the Cross

He said to them, "This is my blood of the covenant, which is poured out for many."
Mark 14:24

1. Down at the cross where my Sav - ior died,
2. I am so won - drous-ly saved from sin,
3. Oh, pre - cious foun - tain that saves from sin,
4. Come to this foun - tain so rich and sweet,

Down where for cleans - ing from sin I cried,
Je - sus so sweet - ly a - bides with - in;
I am so glad I have en - tered in;
Cast thy poor soul at the Sav - ior's feet;

There to my heart was the blood ap - plied; Sing-in',
There at the cross where He took me in; Sing-in',
There Je-sus saves me and keeps me clean; Sing-in',
Plunge in to - day, and be made com - plete; Sing-in',

name!   I'm sing-in'

Glo - ry to His name, His name!

name!   I'm sing-in'

Glo - ry to His name, Pre-cious name.

I'm sing-in'

Glo - ry to His name, Pre-cious name.

His name.

There to my heart was the blood ap - plied; sing-in'

name.

Glo - ry to His name, His name.

name.

Text: Elisha A. Hoffman, 1839-1929
Tune: GLORY TO HIS NAME, 999 7 with refrain; John H. Stockton, 1813-1877; arr. by Evelyn Simpson-Curenton, b.1953, © 2000, GIA
   Publications, Inc.

249 He Looked beyond My Fault

When He went ashore, He saw a great crowd; and He had compassion for them and cured their sick.
Matthew 14:14

A - maz-ing grace   shall al-ways be my song of   praise,

For it was grace   that bought my lib - er - ty;

I do not know   just why Christ came to   love me so,

He looked be - yond   my fault and saw my   need.

I shall for - ev - er lift mine eyes to   Cal - va - ry,

To view the cross where Je - sus died for me;

How mar - vel - ous the grace that caught my fall - ing soul,

He looked be - yond my fault and saw my need.

Text: Dottie Rambo, b.1934, © 1968, John T. Benson Publishing Co. (ASCAP)
Tune: LONDONDERRY AIRE, 11 10 11 10 D; traditional

250 O Sacred Head, Sore Wounded

...then they will hand Him over to the Gentiles to be mocked and flogged and crucified...
Matthew 20:19

1. O sa - cred head, sore wound - ed,
2. Thy beau - ty, long de - sir - ed,
3. In Thy most bit - ter pas - sion
4. What lan - guage shall I bor - row
5. My days are few, O fail not,

De - filed and put to scorn;
Hath van - ished from our sight;
My heart to share doth cry,
To thank Thee, dear - est friend,
With Thine im - mor - tal pow'r,

O king - ly head, sur - round - ed
Thy pow'r is all ex - pir - ed,
With Thee for my sal - va - tion
For this Thy dy - ing sor - row,
To hold me that I quail not

With mock - ing crown of thorn;
And quenched the light of light.
Up - on the cross to die.
Thy pit - y with - out end?
In death's most fear - ful hour:

What sor - row mars Thy grand - eur?
Ah me! for whom Thou di - est,
Ah, keep my heart thus mov - ed
Oh, make me Thine for - ev - er!
That I may fight be - friend - ed,

Can death Thy bloom de - flow'r?
Hide not so far Thy grace:
To stand Thy cross be - neath,
And should I faint - ing be,
And see in my last strife

O coun - te - nance whose splen - dor
Show me, O Love most high - est,
To mourn Thee, well - be - lov - ed,
Lord, let me nev - er, nev - er
To me Thine arms ex - tend - ed

The hosts of heav'n a - dore!
The bright - ness of Thy face.
Yet thank Thee for Thy death.
Out - live my love for Thee.
Up - on the cross of life.

Text: Paulus Gerhardt, 1607-1676, sts. 1-3, 5, tr. Robert S. Bridges, 1844-1930, st. 4, tr. James W. Alexander, 1804-1859, alt.
Tune: REDDING, 7 6 7 6 D; David Hurd, b.1950, © 1983, GIA Publications, Inc.

251 O Sacred Head Surrounded

There they crucified Him, and with Him two others, one on either side, with Jesus between them.
John 19:18

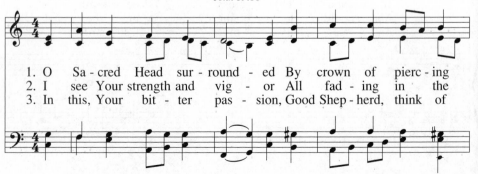

1. O Sa - cred Head sur - round - ed By crown of pierc - ing
2. I see Your strength and vig - or All fad - ing in the
3. In this, Your bit - ter pas - sion, Good Shep - herd, think of

thorn! O bleed - ing Head, so wound - ed, Re -
strife, And death with cru - el rig - or, Be -
me With Your most sweet com - pas - sion, Un -

viled and put to scorn! The pow'r of death comes
reav - ing You of life; O ag - o - ny and
worth - y though I be: Be - neath Your cross a -

o'er You, The glow of life de - cays, Yet
dy - ing! O love to sin - ners free! Je -
bid - ing For ev - er would I rest, In

an - gel hosts a - dore You, And trem - ble as they gaze.
sus, all grace sup - ply - ing, O turn Your face on me.
Your dear love con - fid - ing, And with Your pres - ence blest.

Text: *Salve caput cruentatum;* ascr. to Bernard of Clairvaux, 1091-1153; tr. by Henry Baker, 1821-1877
Tune: PASSION CHORALE, 7 6 7 6 D; Hans Leo Hassler, 1564-1612; harm. by J. S. Bach, 1685-1750

252 Jesus, Keep Me Near the Cross

And I, when I am lifted up from the earth, will draw all people to myself.
John 12:32

1. Je - sus, keep me near the cross; There's a pre - cious foun - tain, Free to all, a heal - ing stream, Flows from Cal - v'ry's moun - tain.
2. Near the cross, a trem - bling soul, Love and mer - cy found me; There the bright and morn-ing star Sheds its beams a - round me.
3. Near the cross! O Lamb of God, Bring its scenes be - fore me; Help me walk from day to day With its shad - ows o'er me.
4. Near the cross I'll watch and wait, Hop - ing, trust - ing ev - er, Till I reach the gold - en strand Just be - yond the riv - er.

In the cross, in the cross, Be my glo - ry ev - er, Till my rap - tured soul shall find Rest be - yond the riv - er.

Text: Fanny J. Crosby, 1820-1915
Tune: NEAR THE CROSS, 7 6 7 6 with refrain; William H. Doane, 1832-1915; harm. by J. Jefferson Cleveland, 1937-1988, and
   Verolga Nix-Allen, b.1933, © 1981, Abingdon Press

LEAD ME TO CALVARY 253

Then they brought Jesus to the place called Golgotha (which means the place of a skull).
Mark 15:22

1. King of my life I crown Thee now— Thine shall the
2. Show me the tomb where Thou wast laid, Ten - der - ly
3. Let me like Mar - y, thru the gloom, Come with a
4. May I be will - ing, Lord, to bear Dai - ly my

glo - ry be; Lest I for - get Thy thorn-crowned brow,
mourned and wept; An - gels in robes of light ar - rayed
gift to Thee; Show to me now the emp - ty tomb—
cross for Thee; E - ven Thy cup of grief to share—

Lead me to Cal - va - ry.
Guard - ed Thee whilst Thou slept.
Lead me to Cal - va - ry.
Thou hast borne all for me.

Lest I for - get Geth -

sem - a - ne, Lest I for - get Thine ag - o - ny,

Lest I for - get Thy love for me, Lead me to Cal - va - ry.

Text: Jennie E. Hussey, 1874-1958
Tune: DUNCANNON, CM with refrain; William J. Kirkpatrick, 1838-1921

254 WERE YOU THERE?

...God raised Him up, having freed Him from death, because it was impossible for Him to be held in its power.
Acts 2:23-24

1. Were you there when they cru - ci - fied my
2. Were you there when they nailed Him to the
3. Were you there when they pierced Him in the
4. Were you there when the sun re - fused to
5. Were you there when they laid Him in the

Lord? (were you there?) Were you there when they
tree? (to the tree?) Were you there when they
side? (in the side?) Were you there when they
shine? (were you there?) Were you there when the
tomb? (in the tomb?) Were you there when they

cru - ci - fied my Lord?
nailed Him to the tree?
pierced Him in the side?   Oh!   Some-times it
sun re - fused to shine?
laid Him in the tomb?

caus - es me to trem - ble, trem - ble, trem - ble,

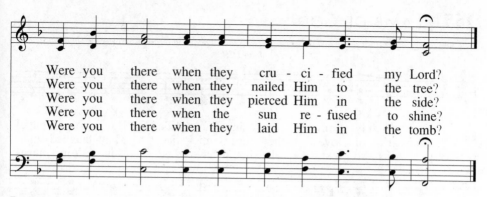

Were you   there when they   cru - ci - fied   my Lord?
Were you   there when they   nailed Him to   the tree?
Were you   there when they   pierced Him in   the side?
Were you   there when the   sun   re - fused to shine?
Were you   there when they   laid Him   in   the tomb?

Text: Negro spiritual
Tune: WERE YOU THERE, 10 10 with refrain; Negro spiritual; arr. by John Work and Frederick Work

255 LAMB OF GOD

...he saw Jesus coming toward him and declared, "Here is the Lamb of God who takes away the sin of the world!"
John 1:29

1. Your on-ly Son, no sin to hide, But You have
2. Your gift of love they cru-ci-fied, They laughed and
3. I was so lost, I should have died, But You have

sent Him from Your side To walk up-on this guilt-y
scorned Him as He died: The hum-ble King they named a
brought me to Your side To be led by Your staff and

sod, And to be-come the Lamb of God. *(To verse 2)*
fraud, And sac-ri-ficed the Lamb of God. *(To refrain)*
rod, And to be called a lamb of God. *(To refrain)*

O Lamb of God, sweet Lamb of God, I love the

ho - ly Lamb of God! O wash me in His pre-cious

blood, My Je-sus Christ, the Lamb of God. God.

Text: Twila Paris, b.1958
Tune: LAMB OF GOD, LM with refrain; Twila Paris, b.1958
© 1985, Straightway Music/Mountain Spring Music (ASCAP)

256 THE BLOOD WILL NEVER LOSE ITS POWER

...now that we have been justified by His blood, will we be saved through Him from the wrath of God.
Romans 5:9

1. The blood that Je - sus shed for me,
2. It soothes my doubts and calms my fears,

Way back on Cal - va - ry, The
And it dries all my tears; The

blood that gives me strength from day to

day, It will nev - er lose its pow'r.

It reach-es from the high - est moun-tain.

(moun - tain) And it flows to the low - est val - ley.

(val - ley) The blood that gives me strength from day to

day, It will nev - er lose its pow'r.

Text: Andraé Crouch, b.1945, © 1966, 1994, Manna Music, Inc.
Tune: THE BLOOD, 86 10 7 with refrain; Andraé Crouch, b.1945, © 1966, 1994, Manna Music, Inc.; arr. by Nolan Williams, Jr., b.1969, © 2000,
   GIA Publications, Inc.

257 THERE IS A FOUNTAIN

...for this is my blood of the covenant, which is poured out for many for the forgiveness of sin.
Matthew 26:28

1. There is a foun - tain filled with blood Drawn from Im-
2. The dy - ing thief re - joiced to see That foun - tain
3. Dear dy - ing Lamb, Thy pre - cious blood Shall nev - er
4. E'er since by faith I saw the stream Thy flow - ing

man - uel's veins, And sin - ners plunged be - neath that flood
in his day, And there may I, though vile as he,
lose its pow'r, Till all the ran - somed Church of God
wounds sup - ply, Re - deem - ing love has been my theme

Lose all their guilt-y stains: Lose all their guilt-y stains,
Wash all my sins a - way: Wash all my sins a - way,
Be saved to sin no more: Be saved to sin no more,
And shall be till I die: And shall be till I die,

Lose all their guilt - y stains; And sin - ners plunged be -
Wash all my sins a - way; And there may I, though
Be saved to sin no more; Till all the ran - somed
And shall be till I die; Re - deem - ing love has

neath	that flood	Lose	all	their guilt - y	stains.
vile	as he,	Wash	all	my sins a -	way.
Church	of God	Be	saved	to sin no	more.
been	my theme	And	shall	be till I	die.

Text: William Cowper, 1731-1800
Tune: CLEANSING FOUNTAIN, 8 6 8 66 6 8 6; Early American melody

258 THERE IS POWER IN THE BLOOD

In Him we have redemption through His blood... according to the riches of His grace.
Ephesians 1:7

1. Would you be free from the bur - den of sin? There's
2. Would you be free from your pas - sion and pride? There's
3. Would you be whit - er, yes bright - er than snow? There's
4. Would you do serv - ice for Je - sus, your King? There's

pow'r in the blood,   pow'r in the blood;
pow'r in the blood,   pow'r in the blood;
pow'r in the blood,   pow'r in the blood;
pow'r in the blood,   pow'r in the blood;

Would you o'er e - vil a vic - to - ry win? There's
Come for a cleans - ing to Cal - va - ry's tide— There's
Sin - stains are lost in its life - giv - ing flow— There's
Would you live dai - ly His prais - es to sing? There's

won - der - ful pow'r in the blood.

There is pow'r, pow'r, won-der-work-ing pow'r In the
there is pow'r,

blood of the Lamb; There is
In the blood of the Lamb; There is

pow'r, pow'r, won-der-work-ing pow'r In the
pow'r, there is pow'r,

pre - cious blood of the Lamb.

Text: Lewis E. Jones, 1865-1936
Tune: POWER IN THE BLOOD, 10 9 10 8 with refrain; Lewis E. Jones, 1865-1936

259 THROUGH THE BLOOD

He has rescued us from the power of darkness and transferred us into the kingdom of His beloved Son...
Colossians 1:13-14

1. Blood of Je - sus, shed for me;
2. If all sin were mine a - lone,
3. By the Fa - ther's plan di - vine,
4. I shall see Him face to face,

Pre - cious blood, my cov - 'ring be. The
Je - sus' blood would still a - tone.
There's a prom - ise He's de - signed:
Prais - ing God; For by His grace,

Last time to Coda

on - ly view God has of me is
I've been made God's ver - y own
That His life is one with mine,
All my sin has been e - rased

rit. last time   [1.]   [2., 3.]

Through the blood of Je - sus. sus.

Coda

Through the blood of Je - sus.

Text: Ed Kee and Dale Mathews
Tune: THROUGH THE BLOOD, 777 7; Ed Kee and Dale Mathews
© 1987, New Spring Publishing, Inc. (ASCAP)

OH, IT IS JESUS 260

"If I but touch His clothes, I will be made well."
Mark 5:27-28

Chorus

Oh, it is Je - sus. Yes, it is Je - sus. It's

Je - sus in my soul. For I have touched the hem of His

gar - ment and His blood has made me whole.

Text: Andraé Crouch, b.1945
Tune: Andraé Crouch, b.1945; arr. by Stephen Key
© Crouch Music (ASCAP)

261 VICTORY IN JESUS

But thanks be to God, who gives us the victory through our Lord Jesus Christ.
1 Corinthians 15:57

1. I heard an old, old sto - ry, how a Sav - ior came from
2. I heard a - bout His heal - ing, of His cleans - ing pow'r re -
3. I heard a - bout a man - sion He has built for me in

glo - ry, How He gave His life on Cal - va - ry to
veal - ing, How He made the lame to walk a - gain and
glo - ry, And I heard a - bout the streets of gold be -

save a wretch like me; I heard a - bout His
caused the blind to see; And then I cried, "Dear
yond the crys - tal sea; A - bout the an - gels

groan - ing, of His pre - cious blood's a - ton - ing, Then
Je - sus, come and heal my bro - ken spir - it," And
sing - ing and the old re - demp - tion sto - ry, And

I re-pent-ed of my sins and won the vic-to-ry.
some-how Je-sus came and brought to me the vic-to-ry.
some sweet day I'll sing up there the song of vic-to-ry.

O vic-to-ry in Je-sus, my Sav-ior, for-ev-er! He

sought me and bought me with His re-deem-ing blood; He

loved me ere I knew Him, and all my love is due Him— He

plunged me to vic-to-ry be-neath the cleans-ing flood.

Text: Eugene M. Bartlett, 1885-1941
Tune: HARTFORD, 15 15 15 14 with refrain; Eugene M. Bartlett, 1885-1941
© 1939, E.M. Bartlett, renewed 1967 by Mrs. E.M. Bartlett. Assigned to Albert E. Brumley & Sons/SESAC

262 NOTHING BUT THE BLOOD OF JESUS

...without the shedding of blood there is no forgiveness of sins.
Hebrews 9:22

1. What can wash a - way my sin? Noth-ing but the blood of Je - sus;
2. For my par-don this I see— Noth-ing but the blood of Je - sus;
3. Noth - ing can for sin a - tone— Noth-ing but the blood of Je - sus;
4. This is all my hope and peace— Noth-ing but the blood of Je - sus;

What can make me whole a - gain? Noth-ing but the blood of Je - sus.
For my cleans-ing, this my plea— Noth-ing but the blood of Je - sus.
Naught of good that I have done— Noth-ing but the blood of Je - sus.
This is all my right-eous-ness— Noth-ing but the blood of Je - sus.

Oh! pre-cious is the flow That makes me white as snow;

No oth-er fount I know, Noth-ing but the blood of Je - sus.

Text: Robert Lowry, 1826-1899
Tune: PLAINFIELD, 7 8 7 8 with refrain; Robert Lowry, 1826-1899; arr. by Nolan Williams, Jr., b.1969, © 2000, GIA Publications, Inc.

ALAS! AND DID MY SAVIOR BLEED 263

...God proves his love for us in that while we still were sinners Christ died for us.
Romans 5:8

1. A - las! and did my Sav - ior bleed,
2. Was it for crimes that I have done,
3. Well might the sun in dark - ness hide,
4. But drops of grief can ne'er re - pay

And did my Sov - 'reign die?
He groaned up - on the tree?
And shut His glo - ries in,
The debt of love I owe;

Would He de - vote that sa - cred head
A - maz - ing pit - y! Grace un - known!
When God, the might - y ma - ker, died
Here, Lord, I give my - self a - way;

For sin - ners such as I?
And love be - yond de - gree!
For man the crea - ture's sin.
'Tis all that I can do.

Text: Isaac Watts, 1674-1748
Tune: MARTYRDOM, CM; Hugh Wilson, 1766-1824; arr. by Nolan Williams, Jr., b.1969, © 2000, GIA Publications, Inc.

264   AT THE CROSS

...the cross is foolishness to those who are perishing, but to us who are being saved it is the power of God.
1 Corinthians 1:18

1. A - las! and did my Sav - ior bleed? And
2. Was it for crimes that I have done He
3. Well might the sun in dark - ness hide And
4. But drops of grief can ne'er re - pay The

did my Sov - 'reign die? Would He de - vote that
groaned up - on the tree? A - maz - ing pit - y!
shut His glo - ries in, When Christ, the might - y
debt of love I owe: Here, Lord, I give my -

sa - cred head For such a one as I?
grace un - known! And love be - yond de - gree!
Mak - er, died For man the crea - ture's sin.
self a - way— 'Tis all that I can do!

At the cross, at the cross where I first saw the light, And the

bur - den of my heart rolled a - way— It was

rolled a - way—

there by faith I re - ceived my sight, And

now I am hap - py all the day!

Text: Verses, Isaac Watts, 1674-1748; refrain, Ralph E. Hudson, 1843-1901
Tune: HUDSON, CM with refrain; Ralph E. Hudson, 1843-1901

265 OH, THE BLOOD OF JESUS

You know that you were ransomed from the futile ways... with the precious blood of Christ...
1 Peter 1:18-19

1. Oh, the blood of Je - sus,   Oh, the blood of
2. Oh, the word of Je - sus,   Oh, the word of
3. Oh, the love of Je - sus,   Oh, the love of

Je - sus,   Oh, the blood of Je - sus, it must not suf - fer
Je - sus,   Oh, the word of Je - sus, it cleans - es white as
Je - sus,   Oh, the love of Je - sus, it makes His bod - y

Text: Anonymous
Tune: Anonymous; arr. by Jimmie Abbington, © 2000, GIA Publications, Inc.

266 How Can You Recognize a Child of God

It is that very Spirit bearing witness with our spirit that we are children of God.
Romans 8:16

How can you rec - og - nize a child of God?

How can you rec - og - nize a child of God?

How can you rec - og - nize a child of God? He's been

washed in the blood of the Lamb. Oh,

oh, hal - le - lu - jah, hal - le - lu - jah! I've been

washed in the blood of the Lamb. Oh,

oh, hal - le - lu - jah, hal - le - lu - jah! A

child of God I am. How can you rec - og - nize a

child of God? I've been washed in the blood of the Lamb.

Text: Margaret Pleasant Douroux, b.1941
Tune: Margaret Pleasant Douroux, b.1941
© 1988, Margaret Pleasant Douroux

267 I Know It Was the Blood

...we have redemption through His blood, the forgiveness of our trespasses, according to the riches of His grace...
Ephesians 1:7-8

1. I know it was the blood,
2. They whipped Him all night long,
3. They pierced Him in His side,
4. He nev-er said a mum - blin' word,
5. He hung His head and died,
6. He's com - ing back a - gain,

I know it was the blood,
They whipped Him all night long,
They pierced Him in His side,
He nev-er said a mum - blin' word,
He hung His head and died,
He's com - ing back a - gain,

I know it was the blood for me.
They whipped Him all night long for me.
They pierced Him in His side for me.
He nev-er said a mum - blin' word for me.
He hung His head and died for me.
He's com - ing back a - gain for me.

One day when I was lost He died up-on the cross.

I know it was the blood for me.

Text: African-American traditional
Tune: IT WAS THE BLOOD, 66 8 with refrain; African-American traditional; arr. by Evelyn Simpson-Curenton, b.1953, © 2000, GIA
    Publications, Inc.

268   I See a Crimson Stream

He said to them, "This is my blood of the covenant, which is poured out for many."
Mark 14:24

1. On Cal-v'ry's hill of sor-row Where sin's de-mands were paid, And rays of hope for to-mor-row A-cross our path were laid.
2. To-day no con-dem-na-tion A-bides to turn a-way My soul from His sal-va-tion, He's in my heart to stay.
3. When gloom and sad-ness whis-per You've sinned, no use to pray, I look a-way to Je-sus, And He tells me to say:
4. And when we reach the por-tal Where life for-ev-er reigns, The ran-somed hosts grand fi-nal, Will be this glad re-frain.

blood.

I see a crim-son stream of blood, stream of blood. It

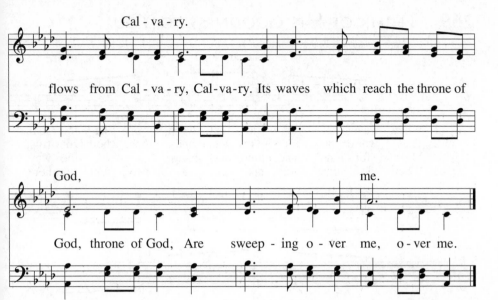

Cal - va - ry.

flows   from   Cal - va - ry,   Cal-va-ry.   Its   waves   which   reach   the   throne   of

God,   me.

God,   throne   of   God,   Are   sweep - ing   o - ver   me,   o - ver   me.

Text: G.T. Haywood
Tune: CRIMSON STREAM, 7 6 7 6 with refrain; G.T. Haywood

269 THINK OF HIS GOODNESS TO YOU

O how abundant is Your goodness that You have laid up for those who fear You...
Psalm 31:19

1. When waves of af - flic - tion sweep o - ver the soul,
2. The world may for - sake you, and those whom you trust
3. Mis - for - tune's dark cloud may hang o - ver the way,
4. When dear ones are tak - en a - way from you here,

And sun - light is hid - den from view,
May prove to be false and un - true;
De - spite your best ef - forts to do;
You loved with af - fec - tion so true,

If ev - er you're tempt - ed to fret or com - plain,
There's One you can trust e - ven un - to the end;
The Sav - ior is guard - ing your treas - ures up there;
Look un - to the Sav - ior for strength to en - dure,

Just think of His good - ness to you.
Just think of His good - ness to you.
Just think of His good - ness to you.
And think of His good - ness to you.

Just think of His good-ness to you; Yes,
His good-ness to you;
think of His good - ness to you; Though
His good-ness to you;
storms o'er thee sweep, He is a - ble to keep; Just
think of His good - ness to you.

Text: R. C. Ward
Tune: GOODNESS, 11 8 11 8 with refrain; R. C. Ward

270   YOUR GRACE AND MERCY

"...My grace is sufficient for you, for power is made perfect in weakness."
2 Corinthians 12:9

Your grace and mer - cy brought me through, I'm liv-ing this mo - ment be - cause of You; I want to thank You,

and praise You too: Your grace and mer - cy brought me through.

mer - cy, Your grace and mer - cy brought me through.

Text: Franklin D. Williams
Tune: Franklin D. Williams; arr. by Nolan Williams, Jr., b.1969

271 AMAZING GRACE

For by grace you have been saved through faith, and this is not your own doing; it is the gift of God.
Ephesians 2:8

1. A - maz - ing grace! how sweet the sound That saved a wretch like me! I once was lost but now I'm found, Was blind but now I see.
2. 'Twas grace that taught my heart to fear, And grace my fears re - lieved; How pre - cious did that grace ap - pear The hour I first be - lieved.
3. The Lord has prom - ised good to me, His word my hope se - cures; He will my shield and por - tion be As long as life en - dures.
4. Through man - y dan - gers, toils and snares, I have al - read - y come; 'Twas grace hath brought me safe thus far, And grace will lead me home.
5. When we've been there ten thou - sand years, Bright shin - ing as the sun, We've no less days to sing God's praise Than when we'd first be - gun.

Text: St. 1-3, John Newton, 1725-1807, st. 4, attr. to John Rees, fl.1859
Tune: NEW BRITAIN, CM; Virginia Harmony, 1831; arr. by Evelyn Simpson-Curenton, b.1953, © 2000, GIA Publications, Inc.

Amazing Grace 272

Grace be with all who have an undying love for our Lord Jesus Christ.
Ephesians 6:23-24

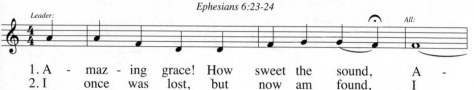

Leader: All:

1. A - maz - ing grace! How sweet the sound, A -
2. I once was lost, but now am found, I
3. (hum throughout)

maz -   ing   grace!
once   was   lost,

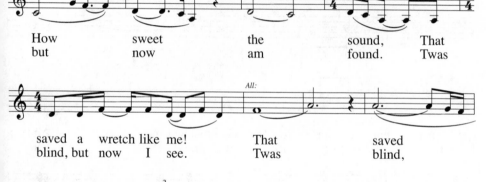

Leader:

How   sweet   the   sound,   That
but   now   am   found.   Twas

All:

saved a wretch like me!   That   saved
blind, but now I see.   Twas   blind,

a   wretch   like   me!
but   now   I   see.

Text: John Newton, 1725-1807
Tune: Meter hymn; arr. by Evelyn Simpson-Curenton, b.1953, © 2000, GIA Publications, Inc.

273 HE TOUCHED ME

He stretched out His hand and touched him, saying, "I do choose. Be made clean!"
Matthew 8:3

1. Shack - led by a heav - y bur - den,
2. Since I met this bless - ed Sav - ior,

'Neath a load of guilt and shame;
Since He cleansed and made me whole;

Then the hand of Je - sus touched me, And
I will nev - er cease to praise Him, I'll

now I am no long - er the same.
shout it while e - ter - ni - ty rolls.

He touched me, O, He touched me, and O, the joy that floods my soul; Some-thing hap-pened, and now I know, He touched me and made me whole.

Text: William J. Gaither, b.1936
Tune: HE TOUCHED ME, 8 7 8 9 with refrain; William J. Gaither, b.1936

274 Touch Me, Lord Jesus

I will not leave you orphaned; I am coming to you.
John 14:18

1. Touch, touch me, Lord Je - sus,
2. Mold, mold me, dear Sav - ior;
3. Feed, feed me, dear Je - sus,
4. Guide, guide me, Je - ho - vah,

With Thy hand of mer - cy,
As I bow be - fore Thee,
From Thy ho - ly ta - ble,
Thro' this vale of sor - row,

Make each throb - bing heart - beat
Pros - trate, pros - trate and help - less,
Rain, rain bread from heav - en,
I am safe for - ev - er,

Feel Thy pow'r di - vine. O
Make my heart Thy throne. O
Let my cup o'er - flow. O
Trust - ing in Thy love. O

take my will for - ev - er,
purge my dross with his - sop;
na - ked, sick and hun - gry;
bear me thro' the cur - rent;

I will doubt Thee nev - er, O Lord, please
Burn me with Thy fire; O Lord, please
Poor and weak and lone - ly, O Lord, please
O'er the chil - ly Jor - dan, O Lord, please

cleanse me, my dear Sav - ior,
make, make me and use me;
feed feed me, Lord Je - sus
lead me, my dear Sav - ior

Make me whol - ly Thine.
Ev - er all Thine own.
Till I want no more.
To my home a - bove.

Text: Lucie E. Campbell, 1885-1963
Tune: TOUCH ME, 6 6 6 5 D; Lucie E. Campbell, 1885-1963; arr. Evelyn Simpson-Curenton, b.1953, © 2000, GIA Publications, Inc.

275 He Lives

The women were terrified... but the men said to them, "Why do you look for the living among the dead?"
Luke 24:5

1. I serve a ris - en Sav - ior, He's in the world to -
2. In all the world a - round me I see His lov - ing
3. Re - joice, re - joice, O Chris - tian, lift up your voice and

day; I know that He is liv - ing, what -
care, And though my heart grows wea - ry I
sing E - ter - nal hal - le - lu - jahs to

ev - er oth - ers say; I see His hand of
nev - er will de - spair; I know that He is
Je - sus Christ, the King! The hope of all who

mer - cy, I hear His voice of cheer, And
lead - ing through all the storm - y blast, The
seek Him, the help of all who find, None

just the time I need Him He's al - ways near.
day of His ap - pear - ing will come at last.
oth - er is so lov - ing, so good and kind.

He lives, He lives, Christ Je - sus lives to -
He lives, He lives,

day! He walks with me and talks with me a -

long life's nar - row way. He lives, He
He lives,

lives, sal - va - tion to im - part! You
He lives,

ask me how I know He lives? He lives with-in my heart.

Text: Alfred H. Ackley, 1887-1960
Tune: ACKLEY, 13 13 13 11 with refrain; Alfred H. Ackley, 1887-1960

276 I Know That My Redeemer Lives

...the Son of Man must be handed over to sinners, and be crucified, and on the third day rise again.
Luke 24:6-7

1. I know that my Re - deem - er lives;
2. He lives, to bless me with His love;
3. He lives, and grants me dai - ly breath;
4. He lives, all glo - ry to His name;

What joy the blest as - sur - ance gives!
He lives, to plead for me a - bove;
He lives, and I shall con - quer death;
He lives, my Sav - ior still the same;

He lives, He lives, who once was dead;
He lives, my hun - gry soul to feed;
He lives, my man - sion to pre - pare;
What joy the blest as - sur - ance gives;

He lives, my ev - er - last - ing Head!
He lives, to help in time of need.
He lives, to bring me safe - ly there.
I know that my Re - deem - er lives!

Text: Samuel Medley, 1738-1799
Tune: DUKE STREET, LM; John Hatton, c.1710-1793

For lower key, see no. 289.

The Strife Is O'er   277

Jesus said to her, "I am the resurrection and the life. Those who believe in me, even though they die, will live...
John 11:25

Refrain

Al - le - lu - ia! Al - le - lu - ia! Al - le - lu - ia!

Verses

1. The strife is o'er, the bat - tle done; Now is the
2. Death's might - iest pow'rs have done their worst, And Je - sus
3. He closed the yawn - ing gates of hell; The bars from
4. On the third morn He rose a - gain, Glo - rious in

Vic - tor's tri - umph won; Now be the song of
has His foes dis - persed; Let shouts of praise and
heav'n's high por - tals fell; Let hymns of praise His
maj - es - ty to reign; O let us swell the

praise be - gun: Al - le - lu - ia!
joy out - burst: Al - le - lu - ia!
tri - umph tell: Al - le - lu - ia!
joy - ful strain: Al - le - lu - ia!

D.C.

Text: *Finita iam sunt praelia;* Latin, 12th C.; tr. by Francis Pott, 1832-1909, alt.
Tune: VICTORY, 888 with alleluias; Giovanni da Palestrina, 1525-1594; adapt. by William H. Monk, 1823-1889

278 Hallelujah to the Risen Lamb

I heard the voice of a great multitude... crying out, Hallelujah! For the Lord our God the Almighty reigns.
Revelation 19:6

Verses

1. Je - sus hung on the cru - el tree; Hal - le -
2. Wom - en came at the break of day; Hal - le -

lu - jah to the ris - en Lamb! And He
Oh, the

gave His life for the likes of me; Hal - le -
an - gel rolled the stone a - way; Hal - le -

lu - jah to the ris - en Lamb!

D.S.

Text: Traditional
Tune: RISEN LAMB, 8 9 10 8 with refrain; traditional; arr. by Charlene Moore Cooper, © 2000, GIA Publications, Inc.

279 THE ANGEL ROLLED THE STONE AWAY

And suddenly there was a great earthquake; for an angel of the Lord... came and rolled back the stone and sat on it.
Matthew 28:2

1. The an-gel rolled the
2. My Je-sus spurned that
3. My Lord will come a-

stone a-way! The an-gel rolled the
dread - ful tomb! My Je-sus spurned that
gain for me! My Lord will come a-

stone a-way! 'Twas on a bright and shin-y
dread - ful tomb! 'Twas on a bright and shin-y
gain for me! And on a bright and shin-y

day,   When the   trum - pet be - gan   to   play, The   an - gel
day,   When the   trum - pet be - gan   to   play, My   Je - sus
day,   When the   trum - pet be - gins to   play, My   Lord will

rolled   the   stone   a -   way!
spurned   that   dread   -   ful   tomb!
come   a - gain   for   me!

Text: Negro spiritual
Tune: ROLLED THE STONE, 8 8 8 8 8; Negro spiritual; arr. by Charlene Moore Cooper, © 2000, GIA Publications, Inc.

280 HE AROSE

Do not be alarmed; you are looking for Jesus of Nazareth who was crucified. He has been raised; He is not here.
Mark 16:6

1. They cru - ci - fied my Sav - ior And nailed Him to the cross. They
2. ⁊ Jo - seph begged His bod - y And laid it in the tomb. ⁊
3. ⁊ Mar - y, she came run - ning, A - look - ing for my Lord. ⁊
4. An an - gel came from heav - en And rolled the stone a - way. An

cru - ci - fied my Sav - ior And nailed Him to the cross. They
Jo - seph begged His bod - y And laid it in the tomb. ⁊
Mar - y, she came run - ning, A - look - ing for my Lord. ⁊
an - gel came from heav - en And rolled the stone a - way. An

cru - ci - fied my Sav - ior And nailed Him to the cross.
Jo - seph begged His bod - y And laid it in the tomb.
Mar - y, she came run - ning, A - look - ing for my Lord.
an - gel came from heav - en And rolled the stone a - way.

And the Lord will bear my spir - it home.

He 'rose, He 'rose, He 'rose from the dead, He

He 'rose, He 'rose, He

'rose, He 'rose, He 'rose from the dead. He

He 'rose, He 'rose, He

'rose, He 'rose, He 'rose from the dead, And the

He 'rose, He 'rose, He

Lord will bear my spir - it home.

Text: Negro spiritual
Tune: HE AROSE, 7 6 7 6 7 6 9 with refrain; Negro spiritual; arr. by Valeria A. Foster, © 2000, GIA Publications, Inc.

281 BECAUSE HE LIVES

In a little while the world will no longer see me, but you will see me; because I live, you also will live.
John 14:19

1. God sent His Son, they called Him Je - sus,
2. How sweet to hold a new - born ba - by,
3. And then one day I'll cross the riv - er,

He came to love, heal, and for - give;
And feel the pride, and joy He gives;
I'll fight life's fi - nal war with pain;

He lived and died to buy my par - don, An
But great - er still the calm as - sur - ance, This
And then as death gives way to vic - t'ry, I'll

emp - ty grave is there to prove my Sav - ior lives.
child can face un - cer - tain days be - cause He lives.
see the lights of glo - ry and I'll know He lives.

Be - cause He lives I can face to - mor - row,

Be - cause He lives all fear is gone;

Be - cause I know He holds the fu - ture.

Last time to Coda 𝄌   D.C.

And life is worth the liv-ing just be-cause He lives.

Coda (Optional Chorus)

know   He holds the fu - ture;   And life is

worth   the liv - ing   just be-cause He lives!

A - men!

Text: Gloria Gaither, b.1942, and William J. Gaither, b.1936
Tune: RESURRECTION, 9 8 9 12 with refrain; William J. Gaither, b.1936; arr. by Nolan Williams, Jr., b.1969

282 CHRIST THE LORD IS RISEN TODAY

He has been raised from the dead, and indeed He is going ahead of you to Galilee; there you will see Him.
Matthew 28:7

4. Sing we to our God a - bove, Al - le - lu - ia!

1. Christ the Lord is ris'n to - day, Al - le - lu - ia!
2. Lives a - gain our glo - rious King, Al - le - lu - ia!
3. Love's re - deem - ing work is done, Al - le - lu - ia!
4. Sing we to our God a - bove, Al - le - lu - ia!

Praise e - ter - nal as His love; Al - le - lu - ia!

Sons of men and an - gels say: Al - le - lu - ia!
Where, O death, is now thy sting? Al - le - lu - ia!
Fought the fight, the bat - tle won, Al - le - lu - ia!
Praise e - ter - nal as His love; Al - le - lu - ia!

Praise, ye heav'n - ly host, Al - le - lu - ia!

Raise your joys and tri-umphs high, Al - le - lu - ia!
Dy - ing once, He all doth save, Al - le - lu - ia!
Death in vain for - bids Him rise, Al - le - lu - ia!
Praise Him, all ye heav'n - ly host, Al - le - lu - ia!

Fa - ther, Son, and Ho - ly Ghost. Al - le - lu - ia!

Sing, ye heav'ns, and earth re - ply: Al - le - lu - ia!
Where thy vic - to - ry, O grave? Al - le - lu - ia!
Christ has o - pened par - a - dise, Al - le - lu - ia!
Fa - ther, Son, and Ho - ly Ghost. Al - le - lu - ia!

Text: Charles Wesley, 1707-1788
Tune: EASTER HYMN, 77 77 with alleluias, *Lyra Davidica*, 1708; descant by Nolan Williams, Jr., b.1969, © 2000, GIA Publications, Inc.

283 CHRIST AROSE

Do not be alarmed; you are looking for Jesus of Nazareth, who was crucified. He has been raised...
Mark 16:6

1. Low   in   the   grave He   lay,   Je - sus, my   Sav - ior!
2. Vain - ly   they watched His   bed,   Je - sus, my   Sav - ior!
3. Death could not   keep   his prey,   Je - sus, my   Sav - ior!

Wait - ing   the   com - ing day,   Je - sus, my   Lord!
Vain - ly   they sealed the   dead,   Je - sus, my   Lord!
He   tore the   bars   a - way,   Je - sus, my   Lord!

Up from the grave He   a-rose,   With a might - y   tri-umph o'er His

He a-rose,

foes;   He a-rose a   vic-tor from the dark   do-main, And He

He a-rose;

lives for - ev - er with His saints to reign; He a-rose! He a-

He a-rose!

rose! Hal - le - lu - jah! Christ a - rose!

He a-rose!

Text: Robert Lowry, 1826-1899
Tune: CHRIST AROSE, 6 5 6 4 with refrain; Robert Lowry, 1826-1899

284 GO AND TELL MARY AND MARTHA

Thus the word of the Lord spread throughout the region.
Acts 13:49

1. Go and tell Mar-y and Mar-tha, Go and
(2.) tell John and Pe-ter, Go and
(3.) tell all the a - pos-tles, Go and
(4.) tell ev - 'ry bod - y, Go and

tell Mar - y and Mar - tha, Go and
tell John and Pe - ter, Go and
tell all the a - pos - tles, Go and
tell ev - 'ry bod - y, Go and

tell Mar - y and Mar - tha:
tell John and Pe - ter: "Yes,
tell all the a - pos - tles:
tell ev - 'ry bod - y:

1.-3.   4.

Je-sus is ris - en from the dead!" 3. Go from the dead!"
2. Go
4. Go

Text: Negro spiritual
Tune: Negro spiritual; arr. by Charlene Moore Cooper, © 2000, GIA Publications, Inc.

HE IS LORD 285

And every tongue should confess that Jesus Christ is Lord, to the glory of God the Father.
Philippians 2:11

He is Lord, He is Lord! He is ris - en from the

dead and He is Lord! Ev - 'ry knee shall bow, ev - 'ry

tongue con - fess That Je - sus Christ is Lord.

Text: Based on Philippians 2:11
Tune: HE IS LORD, 6 11 10 6; traditional

286 WE WILL GLORIFY

They cried out... "Salvation belongs to our God who is seated on the throne, and to the Lamb!"
Revelation 7:10

1. We will glo - ri - fy the King of kings, We will glo - ri - fy the Lamb; We will glo - ri - fy the Lord of lords, Who is the great I Am.
2. Lord Je - ho - vah reigns in maj - es - ty, We will bow be - fore His throne; We will wor - ship Him in right - eous - ness, We will wor - ship Him a - lone.
3. He is Lord of heav - en, Lord of earth, He is Lord of all who live; He is Lord a - bove the u - ni - verse— All praise to Him we give.
4. Hal - le - lu - jah to the King of kings, Hal - le - lu - jah to the Lamb; Hal - le - lu - jah to the Lord of lords, Who is the great I Am.

Last time

Text: Twila Paris, b.1958
Tune: WE WILL GLORIFY, 9 7 9 6; Twila Paris, b.1958
© 1982, Singspiration Music (ASCAP)

GET ALL EXCITED 287

And they went out and proclaimed the good news everywhere, while the Lord worked with them...
Mark 16:20

Get all ex - cit - ed, go tell ev -'ry - bod - y that Je - sus

Christ is King! Get all ex - cit - ed, go tell ev -'ry - bod - y that

Je - sus Christ is King! Get all ex - cit - ed, go tell

ev - 'ry - bod - y that Je - sus Christ is King!

Je - sus Christ is still the King of kings, King of kings!

288 CROWN HIM WITH MANY CROWNS

...there was a white cloud, and seated on the cloud was one like the Son of Man, with a golden crown on his head...
Revelation 14:14

1. Crown Him with man - y crowns, The Lamb up - on His
2. Crown Him the Lord of life, Who tri - umphed o'er the
3. Crown Him the Lord of love, Be - hold His hands and
4. Crown Him the Lord of peace, Whose pow'r a scep - ter
5. Crown Him the Lord of years, The ris - en Lord sub -

throne; Hark! how the heav'n - ly an - them drowns All
grave, And rose vic - to - rious in the strife For
side, Rich wounds yet vis - i - ble a - bove In
sways From pole to pole, that wars may cease, Ab -
lime, Cre - a - tor of the roll - ing spheres, The

mu - sic but its own. A - wake, my soul, and sing Of
those He came to save. His glo - ries now we sing, Who
beau - ty glo - ri - fied. No an - gel in the sky Can
sorbed in prayer and praise. His reign shall know no end, And
Mas - ter of all time. All hail, Re - deem - er, hail! For

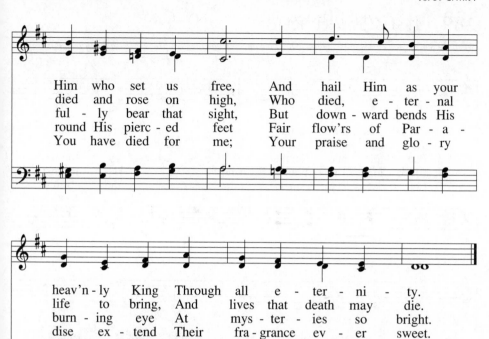

Him who set us free, And hail Him as your
died and rose on high, Who died, e - ter - nal
ful - ly bear that sight, But down - ward bends His
round His pierc - ed feet Fair flow'rs of Par - a -
You have died for me; Your praise and glo - ry

heav'n - ly King Through all e - ter - ni - ty.
life to bring, And lives that death may die.
burn - ing eye At mys - ter - ies so bright.
dise ex - tend Their fra - grance ev - er sweet.
shall not fail Through - out e - ter - ni - ty.

Text: Revelation 19:12; St. 1, 3-5, Matthew Bridges, 1800-1894; St. 2, Godfrey Thring, 1823-1903
Tune: DIADEMATA, SMD; George J. Elvey, 1816-1893

289 JESUS SHALL REIGN

When the Son of Man comes in His glory, and all the angels with Him, then He will sit on the throne of His glory.
Matthew 25:31

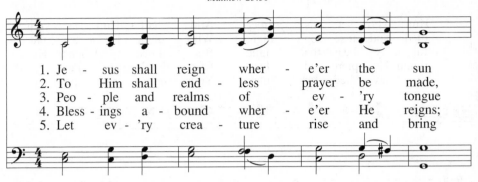

1. Je - sus shall reign wher - e'er the sun
2. To Him shall end - less prayer be made,
3. Peo - ple and realms of ev - 'ry tongue
4. Bless - ings a - bound wher - e'er He reigns;
5. Let ev - 'ry crea - ture rise and bring

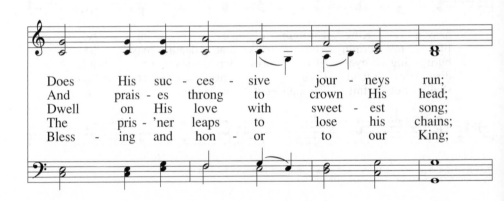

Does His suc - ces - sive jour - neys run;
And prais - es throng to crown His head;
Dwell on His love with sweet - est song;
The pris - 'ner leaps to lose his chains;
Bless - ing and hon - or to our King;

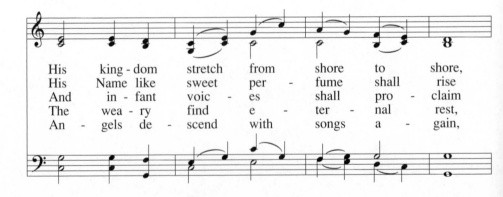

His king - dom stretch from shore to shore,
His Name like sweet per - fume shall rise
And in - fant voic - es shall pro - claim
The wea - ry find e - ter - nal rest,
An - gels de - scend with songs a - gain,

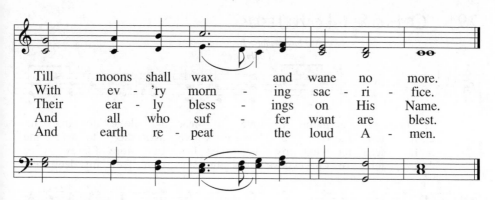

Till moons shall wax and wane no more.
With ev - 'ry morn - ing sac - ri - fice.
Their ear - ly bless - ings on His Name.
And all who suf - fer want are blest.
And earth re - peat the loud A - men.

Text: Isaac Watts, 1674-1748, alt.
Tune: DUKE STREET, LM; John Hatton, c.1710-1793

For higher key, see no. 276.

PSALM 8: O LORD, HOW EXCELLENT 290

O LORD, our Sovereign, how majestic is Your name in all the earth! You have set Your glory above the heavens.
Psalm 8:1

Chorus

O Lord, our Lord, how ex-cel-lent is Thy name.

O Lord, our Lord, how ex-cel-lent is Thy name.

Text: Psalm 8:1
Tune: Richard Smallwood, © Century Oak/Richwood Music; arr. by Stephen Key, © 2000, GIA Publications, Inc.

291 O How I Love Jesus

We love because He first loved us.
1 John 4:19

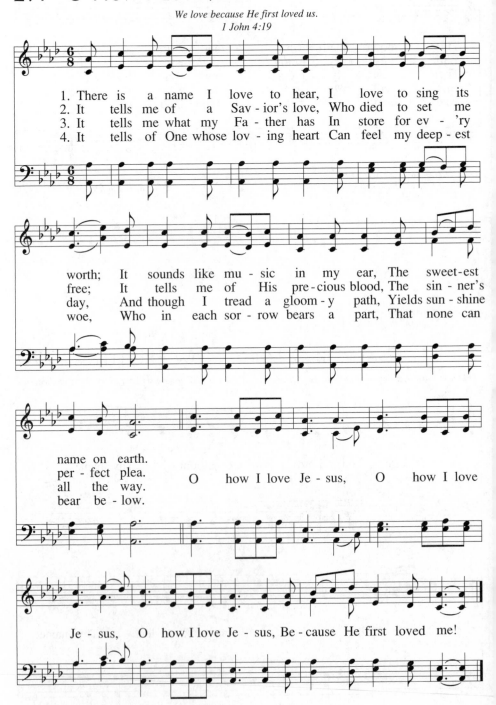

1. There is a name I love to hear, I love to sing its
2. It tells me of a Sav - ior's love, Who died to set me
3. It tells me what my Fa - ther has In store for ev - 'ry
4. It tells of One whose lov - ing heart Can feel my deep - est

worth; It sounds like mu - sic in my ear, The sweet-est
free; It tells me of His pre - cious blood, The sin - ner's
day, And though I tread a gloom - y path, Yields sun - shine
woe, Who in each sor - row bears a part, That none can

name on earth.
per - fect plea.
all the way.
bear be - low.

O how I love Je - sus, O how I love

Je - sus, O how I love Je - sus, Be - cause He first loved me!

Text: Frederick Whitfield, 1829-1904
Tune: HOW I LOVE JESUS, CM with refrain; American melody

ALL HAIL THE POWER OF JESUS' NAME 292

Worthy is the Lamb that was slaughtered to receive... wisdom and might and honor and glory and blessing!
Revelation 5:12

1. All hail the pow'r of Je-sus' name! Let an-gels pros-trate
2. Ye cho-sen seed of Is-rael's race, Ye ran-somed from the
3. Let ev-'ry kin-dred, ev-'ry tribe, On this ter-res-trial
*4. O that with yon-der sa-cred throng, We at His feet may

fall. Bring forth the roy-al di-a-dem, And crown Him
fall, Hail Him who saves you by His grace, And crown Him
ball, To Him all maj-es-ty as-cribe, And crown Him
fall! We'll join the ev-er-last-ing song, And crown Him

Lord of all; Bring forth the roy-al di-a-dem,
Lord of all; Hail Him who saves you by His grace,
Lord of all; To Him all maj-es-ty as-cribe,
Lord of all; We'll join the ev-er-last-ing song,

And crown Him Lord of all!
And crown Him Lord of all!
And crown Him Lord of all!
And crown Him Lord of all!

*Sing this 4th verse if no key change is desired.

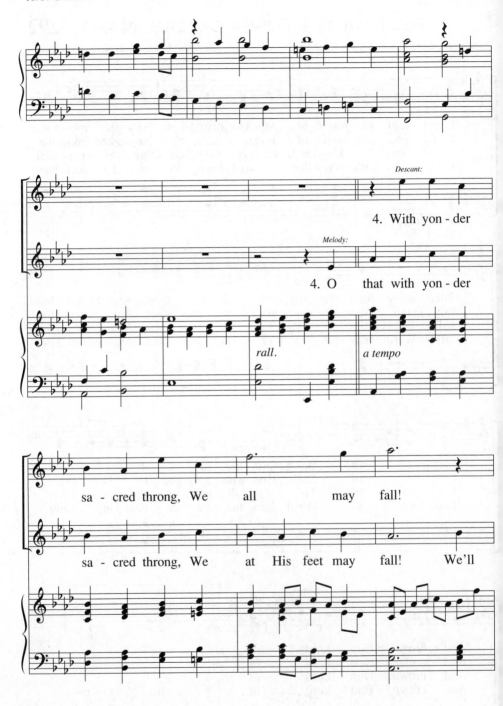

Descant:

4. With yon - der sa - cred throng, We all may fall!

Melody:

4. O that with yon - der sa - cred throng, We at His feet may fall! We'll

rall.   a tempo

Crown Him Lord of

join the ev - er - last-ing song, And crown Him Lord of

all! We'll join the ev-er-last-ing song! And crown Him

all; We'll join the ev-er-last-ing song, And crown Him

rit.

Lord of all! A - men.

Text: Edward Perronet, 1726-1792, alt. by John Rippon, 1751-1836
Tune: CORONATION, 8 6 8 6 8 6; Oliver Holden, 1765-1844; arr. by Nolan Williams, Jr., b.1969, © 2000, GIA Publications, Inc.

293 ALL HAIL THE POWER OF JESUS' NAME

...may those who love Your salvation say continually, "Great is the LORD!"
Psalm 40:16

1. All hail the pow'r of Je - sus' name!
2. Ye cho - sen seed of Is - rael's race,
3. Let ev - 'ry kin - dred, ev - 'ry tribe,
4. Oh, that with yon - der sa - cred throng

Let an - gels pros - trate fall, Let an - gels pros - trate
Ye ran - somed from the fall, Ye ran - somed from the
On this ter - res - trial ball, On this ter - res - trial
We at His feet may fall, We at His feet may

fall. Bring forth the roy - al di - a - dem,
fall, Hail Him who saves you by His grace,
ball, To Him all maj - es - ty as - cribe,
fall! We'll join the ev - er - last - ing song,

Text: Edward Perronet, 1726-1792
Tune: DIADEM, CM with refrain; James Ellor, 1819-1899

294 All Hail the Power of Jesus' Name

...there was a white cloud, and seated on the cloud was one like the Son of Man, with a golden crown on His head...
Revelation 14:14

1. All hail the pow'r of Je - sus' name! Let an - gels pros - trate fall; Bring forth the roy - al di - a - dem,
2. Ye cho - sen seed of Is - rael's race, Ye ran - somed from the fall, Hail Him who saves you by His grace,
3. Let ev - 'ry kin - dred, ev - 'ry tribe, On this ter - res - trial ball, To Him all maj - es - ty as - cribe,
4. O that with yon - der sa - cred throng We at His feet may fall! We'll join the ev - er - last - ing song,

And crown Him, crown Him, crown Him, crown Him Lord of all!

Text: Edward Perronet, 1726-1792, alt. by John Rippon, 1751-1836
Tune: MILES LANE, 8 6 8 with refrain; William Shrubsole, 1760-1806

BLESS THAT WONDERFUL NAME OF JESUS 295

Therefore God also highly exalted Him and gave Him the name that is above every name.
Philippians 2:9

Refrain: Bless that won-der-ful name of Je - sus.
1. There's pow - er in the name of Je - sus.
2. There's heal - ing in the name of Je - sus.

Bless that won-der-ful name of Je - sus.
Pow - er in the name of Je - sus.
Heal - ing in the name of Je - sus.

Bless that won - der - ful name of Je - sus,
Pow - er in the name of Je - sus,
Heal - ing in the name of Je - sus,

no oth - er name I know.

Text: Congregational Praise Song
Tune: Congregational Praise Song; arr. by Stephen Key, © 2000, GIA Publications, Inc.

296 PERFECT PRAISE

O LORD, our Sovereign, how majestic is Your name in all the earth!
Psalm 8:9

*Special Chorus

*Begin with tenor line, repeat adding alto, soprano and bass lines respectively.

Text: Brenda Joyce Moore, © 1989
Tune: Brenda Joyce Moore, © 1989; arr. by Nolan Williams, Jr., b.1969, © 2000, GIA Publications, Inc.

297 TAKE THE NAME OF JESUS WITH YOU

And whatever you do, in word or deed, do everything in the name of the Lord Jesus.
Colossians 3:17

1. Take the name of Je - sus with you, Child of
2. Take the name of Je - sus ev - er As pro -
3. At the name of Je - sus bow - ing, When in

sor - row and of woe. It will joy and com - fort
tec - tion ev - 'ry - where. If temp - ta - tions 'round you
heav - en we shall meet, King of kings, we'll glad - ly

give you, Take it then wher - e'er you go.
gath - er, Breathe that ho - ly name in prayer.
crown Him When our jour - ney is com - plete.

Pre - cious name, O how sweet! Hope of

pre - cious name, O how sweet!

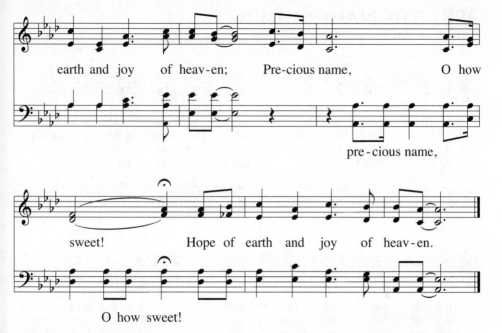

earth and joy   of heav-en;   Pre-cious name,   O how

pre-cious name,

sweet!   Hope of earth   and   joy   of heav-en.

O how sweet!

Text: Lydia Baxter, 1809-1874
Tune: PRECIOUS NAME, 8 7 8 7 with refrain; William H. Doane, 1832-1915

298 THE NAME OF JESUS

Jesus Christ is the same yesterday and today and forever.
Hebrews 13:8

1. The name of Je - sus is so sweet, I
2. I love the name of Him whose heart Knows
3. That name I fond - ly love to hear, It
4. No word of man can ev - er tell How

love its mu - sic to re - peat; It makes my joys full
all my griefs, and bears a part; Who bids all anx - ious
nev - er fails my heart to cheer; Its mu - sic dries the
sweet the name I love so well; Oh, let its prais - es

and com - plete, The pre - cious name of Je - sus.
fears de - part— I love the name of Je - sus.
fall - en tear: Ex - alt the name of Je - sus.
ev - er swell, Oh, praise the name of Je - sus.

1. The pre - cious name

rubato

"Je - sus," O how sweet the name! "Je - sus," ev - 'ry day the same;

"Je-sus," let all saints pro-claim   Its   wor-thy praise for - ev - er.

Text: W. C. Martin, b.1901
Tune: THE NAME OF JESUS, 8 8 8 7 with refrain; Edmund S. Lorenz, 1854-1942

299 BLESSED BE THE NAME

So that at the name of Jesus every knee should bend in heaven and on earth and under the earth.
Philippians 2:10

1. All praise to God who reigns a - bove In
2. His name a - bove all names shall stand, Ex -
3. Re - deem - er, Sav - ior, friend of all, Once
4. His name shall be the Coun - sel - or, The

maj - es - ty su - preme, Who gave His Son for
alt - ed more and more, He's seat - ed at God's
ru - ined by the fall, Thou hast de - vised sal -
might - y Prince of Peace, Of all earth's king - doms

all to die, That He might all re - deem!
own right hand, Where an - gel hosts a - dore.
va - tion's call, For Thou hast died for all.
con - quer - or, Whose reign shall nev - er cease!

Bless - ed be the name! Bless - ed be the name!

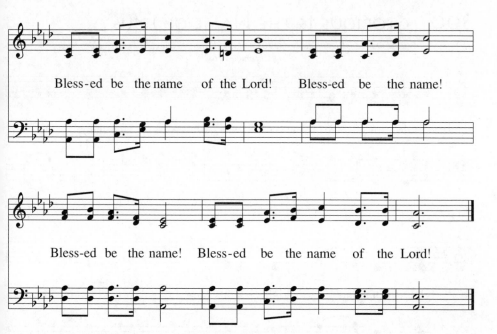

Bless-ed be the name of the Lord! Bless-ed be the name!

Bless-ed be the name! Bless-ed be the name of the Lord!

Text: Verses, William H. Clark, 1854-1925; refrain, Ralph E. Hudson, 1843-1901
Tune: BLESSED NAME, LM with refrain; Ralph E. Hudson, 1843-1901; arr. by Nolan Williams, Jr., b.1969, © 2000, GIA Publications, Inc.

300 Glorious Is the Name of Jesus

Ascribe to the LORD the glory due His name; bring an offering, and come before Him.
1 Chronicles 16:29

Glo-rious is the name of Je-sus, prais - es to His name. Oh,

glo - rious and right - eous and ho - ly is His

name, Oh, glo - ri - ous is His name.

I feel His pres-ence in this place, His Spir - it has con -

trol. Can't you feel His warm em - brace and all the

joy with-in your soul, Oh, glo - ri-ous is His

name, Oh, glo - ri-ous is His name.

Text: Dr. Robert J. Fryson
Tune: Dr. Robert J. Fryson
© 1982, Bob Jay Music Co.

301 There's Something About That Name

...through believing you may have life in His name.
John 20:31

Je - sus, Je - sus, Je - sus! There's just

some-thing a - bout that name!

Mas - ter, Sav - ior, Je - sus! Like the

fra - grance af - ter the rain;

Je - sus, Je - sus, Je - sus! Let all

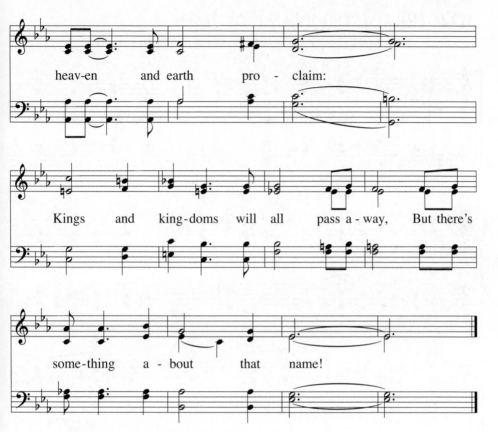

heav-en and earth pro - claim:

Kings and king-doms will all pass a - way, But there's

some-thing a - bout that name!

Text: William J. Gaither, b.1936 and Gloria Gaither, b.1942
Tune: THAT NAME, 6 8 6 8 6 8 9 8; William J. Gaither, b.1936

302 PRAISE THE NAME OF JESUS

From the rising of the sun to its setting the name of the LORD is to be praised.
Psalm 113:3

Praise the name of Je - sus; Praise the name of Je - sus. He's my Rock, He's my For - tress,

He's my De-liv-er - er, in Him will I trust.

Praise the name of Je - sus.

Last time

Text: Psalm 18:1; Roy Hicks, Jr., b.1943
Tune: Roy Hicks, Jr., b.1943; arr. by Joseph Joubert
© 1976, Latter Rain Music

303 IN THE NAME OF JESUS

...there is no other name under heaven given among mortals by which we must be saved.
Acts 4:12

In the name of Je - sus, in the name of Je - sus,

we have the vic - to - ry. In the name of Je - sus,

in the name of Je - sus, Sa - tan, you have to flee.

Oh, what can ev - er stand be - fore us
(Tell me who can)

when we call on that great name? Je - sus, Je - sus,

Text: Congregational Praise Song
Tune: Congregational Praise Song, arr. by Walter Owens, Jr., © 2000, GIA Publications, Inc.

304 So Glad I'm Here

And now, our God, we give thanks to You and praise Your glorious name.
1 Chronicles 29:13

1. So glad I'm here in Je-sus' name;
2. Pray* while I'm here in Je-sus' name;

Oh Lord, I'm
Oh Lord, I'll

So glad I'm here in Je-sus' name!
Pray while I'm here in Je-sus' name!

I don't know what you've come to do,

I've come to praise His name,

I've come to praise His name!

*3. Sing while..., 4. Shout while....

Text: Praise and Worship Song
Tune: Praise and Worship Song; arr. by Nolan Williams, Jr., b.1969, © 2000, GIA Publications, Inc.

So Glad I'm Here 305

And now, our God, we give thanks to You and praise Your glorious name.
1 Chronicles 29:13

*3. Sing while..., 4. Shout while...

Text: Negro spiritual
Tune: Negro spiritual; arr. by Evelyn Simpson-Curenton, b.1953, © 2000, GIA Publications, Inc.

306 HOW MAJESTIC IS YOUR NAME

O LORD, our Sovereign, how majestic is Your name in all the earth!
Psalm 8:9

O Lord, our Lord, how ma - jes - tic is Your name in all the earth. O earth. O Lord,

we praise Your name. O Lord, we

mag - ni - fy Your name: Prince of Peace, Might - y God; O

Lord God Al - might - y. O y.

Text: Michael W. Smith, b.1957
Tune: HOW MAJESTIC, Irregular; Michael W. Smith, b.1957
© 1981, Meadowgreen Music Co. (ASCAP)

His Name Is Wonderful 307

...He is named Wonderful Counselor, Mighty God, Everlasting Father, Prince of Peace.
Isaiah 9:6

1. His name is Won-der-ful, His name is Won-der-ful,
2. He is the might-y King, Mas-ter of ev-'ry-thing,

His name is Won-der-ful, Je-sus, my Lord;

1.

Je-sus, my Lord. He's the great Shep-herd, the Rock of all

2.

a-ges, Al-might-y God is He; Bow down be-fore Him,

Love and a-dore Him, His name is Won-der-ful, Je-sus my Lord.

Text: Audrey Mieir, b.1916
Tune: Audrey Mieir, b.1916
© 1959, 1987, Manna Music, Inc.

308 NO, NOT ONE

...I have called you friends, because I have made known to you everything that I have heard from my Father.
John 15:15

1. There's not a friend like the low - ly Je - sus—
2. No friend like Him is so high and ho - ly—
3. There's not an hour that He is not near us—
4. Was e'er a gift like the Sav - ior giv - en?

No, not one! no, not one! None else could heal all our
No, not one! no, not one! And yet no friend is so
No, not one! no, not one! No night so dark but His
No, not one! no, not one! Will He re - fuse us a

soul's dis - eas - es— No, not one! no, not one!
meek and low - ly— No, not one! no, not one!
love can cheer us— No, not one! no, not one!
home in heav - en? No, not one! no, not one!

Je - sus knows all a - bout our strug-gles, He will guide till the

day is done; There's not a friend like the

low - ly Je - sus— No, not one! no, not one!

Text: Johnson Oatman, Jr., 1856-1922
Tune: HARPER MEMORIAL, 10 6 10 6 with refrain; George C. Hugg, 1848-1907

309   IN TIMES LIKE THESE

We have this hope, a sure and steadfast anchor of the soul.
Hebrews 6:19

1. In times like these you need a Sav - ior, In times like
2. In times like these you need the Bi - ble, In times like
3. In times like these I have a Sav - ior, In times like

these you need an an - chor; Be ver - y sure, be ver - y
these O be not i - dle; Be ver - y sure, be ver - y
these I have an an - chor, I'm ver - y sure, I'm ver - y

sure Your an-chor holds and grips the Sol-id Rock!
sure Your an-chor holds and grips the Sol-id Rock!
sure My an-chor holds and grips the Sol-id Rock!

This Rock is Je - sus, yes, He's the One; This Rock is
This Rock is Je - sus, yes, He's the One; This Rock is
This Rock is Je - sus, yes, He's the One; This Rock is

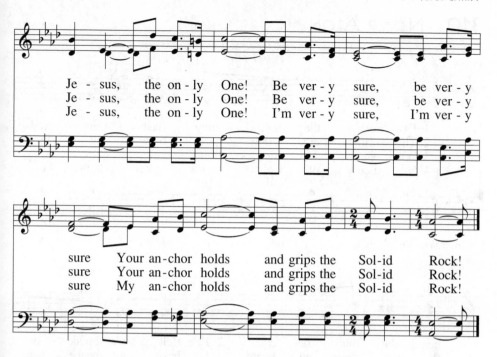

Je - sus, the on - ly One! Be ver - y sure, be ver - y
Je - sus, the on - ly One! Be ver - y sure, be ver - y
Je - sus, the on - ly One! I'm ver - y sure, I'm ver - y

sure Your an - chor holds and grips the Sol - id Rock!
sure Your an - chor holds and grips the Sol - id Rock!
sure My an - chor holds and grips the Sol - id Rock!

Text: Ruth Caye Jones, 1902-1972
Tune: IN TIMES LIKE THESE, 9 9 8 10 D; Ruth Caye Jones, 1902-1972
© 1944, Singspiration Music (ASCAP)

310 NEVER ALONE

I will not leave you orphaned; I am coming to you.
John 14:18

1. I've seen the light - ning flash - ing And
2. The world's fierce winds are blow - ing— Temp-
3. When in af - flic - tion's val - ley I
4. He died on Cal - v'ry's moun - tain, For

Refrain: No, nev - er a - lone,

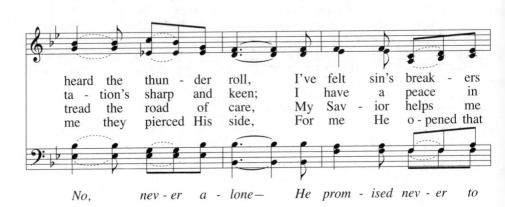

heard the thun - der roll, I've felt sin's break - ers
ta - tion's sharp and keen; I have a peace in
tread the road of care, My Sav - ior helps me
me they pierced His side, For me He o - pened that

No, nev - er a - lone— He prom - ised nev - er to

dash - ing, Try - ing to con - quer my soul;
know - ing My Sav - ior stands be - tween;
car - ry The cross so heav - y to bear;
foun - tain, The crim - son, cleans - ing tide;

leave me, Nev - er to leave me a - lone;

I've heard the voice of Je - sus
He stands to shield me from dan - ger When
Though all a - round me is dark - ness And
For me He's wait - ing in glo - ry Up -

No, nev - er a - lone,

Tell-ing me still to fight on: He prom - ised nev - er to
all my friends are gone: He prom - ised nev - er to
earth - ly joys are flown, My Sav - ior whis-pers His
on His heav-en - ly throne: He prom - ised nev - er to

No, nev - er a - lone; He prom - ised nev - er to

leave me, Nev - er to leave me a - lone.
leave me, Nev - er to leave me a - lone.
prom - ise: Nev - er to leave me a - lone.
leave me, Nev - er to leave me a - lone.

leave me, Nev - er to leave me a - lone.

Text: Anonymous
Tune: NEVER ALONE, 7 6 7 6 7 6 8 7; anonymous; arr. by Nolan Williams, Jr., b.1969, © 2000, GIA Publications, Inc.

311 I Feel Jesus in This Place

...in Christ we speak as persons of sincerity, as persons sent from God and standing in His presence.
2 Corinthians 2:17

I feel Je - sus, I feel Je - sus,

I feel Je - sus in this place.

Yes, my soul does burn with - in me,

I feel Je - sus in this place.

Text: Carman, b.1956, © 1986, Lehsem Music, LLC
Tune: Carman, b.1956, © 1986, Lehsem Music, LLC; arr. by Nolan Williams, Jr., b.1969, © 2000, GIA Publications, Inc.

SPIRIT OF GOD, DESCEND UPON MY HEART 312

Do not cast me away from Your presence, and do not take Your holy spirit from me.
Psalm 51:11

1. Spir - it of God, de - scend up - on my heart;
2. I ask no dream, no proph - et ec - sta - sies,
3. Teach me to feel that Thou art al - ways nigh;
4. Teach me to love Thee as Thine an - gels love,

Wean it from earth; through all its puls - es move;
No sud - den rend - ing of the veil of clay,
Teach me the strug - gles of the soul to bear,
One ho - ly pas - sion fill - ing all my frame;

Stoop to my weak - ness, might - y as Thou art,
No an - gel vis - i - tant, no o - p'ning skies;
To check the ris - ing doubt, the reb - el sigh;
The kin - dling of the heav'n - de - scend - ed Dove,

And make me love Thee as I ought to love.
But take the dim - ness of my soul a - way.
Teach me the pa - tience of un - an - swered prayer.
My heart an al - tar, and Thy love the flame.

Text: George Croly, 1780-1860
Tune: MORECAMBE, 10 10 10 10; Frederick C. Atkinson, 1841-1897

313 I'VE GOT A FEELIN'

...do not worry about your life, what you will eat or what you will drink, or about your body, what you will wear.
Matthew 6:25

The Ho-ly Ghost done told me ev-'ry-

Oh,

thing's gon-na be al - right. The Ho-ly Ghost done

told me ev-'ry-thing's gon-na be al - right, be al - right,

be al - right, be al - right.

Text: Congregational Praise Song
Tune: Congregational Praise Song; arr. by Kenneth Louis and Nolan Williams, Jr., b.1969, © 2000, GIA Publications, Inc.

314 COME, HOLY SPIRIT, HEAVENLY DOVE

But the Advocate, the Holy Spirit, whom the Father will send in my name, will teach you everything...
John 14:26

1. Come, Ho - ly Spir - it, Heav'n - ly Dove, With all Thy quick - 'ning pow'rs; Kin - dle a flame of sa - cred love In these cold hearts of ours.
2. Look, how we grov - el here be - low, Fond of these earth - ly toys; Our souls, how heav - i - ly they go, To reach e - ter - nal joys.
3. In vain we tune our for - mal songs, In vain we strive to rise; Ho - san - nas lan - guish on our tongues, And our de - vo - tion dies.
4. Fa - ther, and shall we ev - er live At this poor dy - ing rate, Our love so faint, so cold to Thee, And Thine to us so great?
5. Come, Ho - ly Spir - it, Heav'n - ly Dove, With all Thy quick - 'ning pow'rs; Come, shed a - broad a Sav - ior's love, And that shall kin - dle ours.

Text: Isaac Watts, 1674-1748
Tune: ST. MARTIN'S, CM; William Tansur, 1700-1783

Holy Ghost, with Light Divine 315

...how much more will the heavenly Father give the Holy Spirit to those who ask Him!
Luke 11:13

1. Ho - ly Ghost, with light di - vine,
2. Ho - ly Ghost, with pow'r di - vine,
3. Ho - ly Ghost, with joy di - vine,
4. Ho - ly Spir - it, all di - vine,

Shine up - on this heart of mine;
Cleanse this guilt - y heart of mine;
Cheer this sad - dened heart of mine;
Dwell with - in this heart of mine;

Chase the shades of night a - way,
Long hath sin with - out con - trol,
Bid my man - y woes de - part,
Cast down ev - 'ry i - dol throne,

Turn my dark - ness in - to day.
Held do - min - ion o'er my soul.
Heal my wound - ed, bleed - ing heart.
Reign su - preme, and reign a - lone.

Text: Andrew Reed, 1787-1862
Tune: MERCY, 77 77; Louis M. Gottschalk, 1829-1869

316 LET IT BREATHE ON ME

...He breathed on them and said to them, "Receive the Holy Spirit."
John 20:22

Refrain

Let it breathe on me, Let it breathe on me, Let the

breath of the Lord, now, breathe on me, Let it

breathe on me, Let it breathe on me, Let the

breath of the Lord, now, breathe on me.

1. While I'm work - ing Lord, in Your vine - yard
2. When the path - way Lord, I can not

here, I can do naught if Thou aren't
see, When the way is dark, Lord, breathe on

near, Oh, come, bless-ed Lord, just so close to
me, Give me grace to know when Thou art

me That I may feel You breathe on me.
near Oh, I pray Thee, Lord, please breathe on me.

D.C.

Text: Magnolia Lewis-Butts
Tune: Magnolia Lewis-Butts; arr. by Joseph Joubert
© Benson Music Group

317 BREATHE ON ME, BREATH OF GOD

...He Himself gives to all mortals life and breath and all things.
Acts 17:25

1. Breathe on me, Breath of God, Fill me with
2. Breathe on me, Breath of God, Un - til my
3. Breathe on me, Breath of God, Till I am
4. Breathe on me, Breath of God, So shall I

life a - new, That I may love what
heart is pure, Un - til with Thee I
whol - ly Thine, Till all this earth - ly
nev - er die, But live with Thee the

Thou dost love And do what Thou wouldst do.
will one will, To do and to en - dure.
part of me Glows with Thy fire di - vine.
per - fect life Of Thine e - ter - ni - ty.

Text: Edwin Hatch, 1835-1889
Tune: TRENTHAM, SM; Robert Jackson, 1840-1914

ANOINTING 318

...the anointing that you received from Him abides in you, and so you do not need anyone to teach you.
1 John 2:27

Text: Donn C. Thomas, © Paragon Music Corp.
Tune: Donn C. Thomas, © Paragon Music Corp.; arr. by Evelyn Simpson-Curenton, b.1953, © 2000, GIA Publications, Inc.

319 HOLY SPIRIT

May God fill you with all joy and hope... so that you may abound in hope by the power of the Holy Spirit.
Romans 15:13

Chorus

We need the pow-er of the Ho-ly Spir-it,

Ho-ly Spir-it. Send Your a-noint-ing. Let it

fall down, fall down,

1. fall down, down on me! 2.

SPIRIT OF THE LIVING GOD 320

And John testified, "I saw the Spirit descending from heaven like a dove, and it remained on Him."
John 1:32

Text: Daniel Iverson, 1890-1977
Tune: IVERSON, Irregular; Daniel Iverson, 1890-1977
© 1935, Birdwing Music (ASCAP)

321 SPIRIT SONG

Now may our Lord Jesus Christ Himself... comfort your hearts and strengthen them in every good work...
2 Thessalonians 2:16, 17

1. Oh, let the Son of God en - fold you, with His
2. Oh, come and sing this song with glad - ness, as your

Spir - it and His love, Let Him fill your heart and
hearts are filled with joy, Lift your hands in sweet sur -

sat - is - fy your soul.
ren - der to His name.
Oh, let Him
Oh, give Him

have the things that hold you, and His Spir - it like a
all your tears and sad - ness, give Him all your years of

dove,   Will de - scend up-on your life, and make you
pain,   And you'll en - ter in - to life in Je - sus'

whole.
name.   Je - sus.   Oh,

Je - sus,   come and fill   your lambs.

Je - sus,   Oh, Je - sus,

come   and   fill   your   lambs.

Text: John Wimber
Tune: John Wimber; arr. by James Abbington
© 1979, Mercy/Vineyard Publishing; admin. by Music Services

322 WITH THY SPIRIT FILL ME

...you will receive power when the Holy Spirit has come upon you.
Acts 1:8

1. Lord, pos - sess me now, I pray, Make me whol - ly
2. Lord, I yield my - self to Thee, All I am or
3. Lord, com - mis - sion me, I pray! Souls are dy - ing

Thine to - day; Glad - ly do I own Thy sway,
hope to be Now and thro' e - ter - ni - ty,
ev - 'ry day; Help me lead them in Thy way,

With Thy spir - it fill me.
With Thy spir - it fill me. With Thy spir - it fill me,
With Thy spir - it fill me.

With Thy spir - it fill me; Make me whol - ly

Thine, I pray, With Thy spir - it fill me.

Text: Oswald J. Smith
Tune: FILL ME, 777 7 with refrain; B.D. Ackley
© 1940, renewed 1969, Word Music, Inc. (ASCAP)

WE ARE ONE 323

...maintain the unity of the Spirit in the bond of peace.
Ephesians 4:3

We are one, we are one. We are one in the

Spir - it, we are one. Hal - le - lu - jah, Hal - le -

lu - jah, we are one in the Spir - it, we are one.

Text: Timothy Wright, ©
Tune: Congregational Praise Song, arr. Valeria A. Foster, © 2000, GIA Publications, Inc.

324 SPIRIT HOLY

Do not cast me away from Your presence, and do not take Your Holy Spirit from me.
Psalm 51:11

1. Spir - it ho - ly in me dwell - ing, Ev - er
2. O how sweet is Thy a - bid - ing! O how
3. Thou hast cleansed me for Thy tem - ple, Gar - nished
4. In me now re - veal Thy glo - ry, Let Thy

work as Thou shalt choose; All my ran - somed pow'rs and
ten - der is the love Thou dost shed a - broad with -
with Thy grac - es rare; All my soul Thou art en -
might be ev - er shown; Keep me from the world's de -

tal - ents For Thy pur - pose Thou shalt use.
in me From the Fa - ther - heart a - bove!
rich - ing By Thy full - ness dwell - ing there.
file - ment, Sa - cred for Thy - self a - lone.

All my

Spir - it ho - ly, Spir - it ho - ly,

Spir - it ho - ly, Spir - it ho - ly,

be - ing

All my be - ing now pos - sess; Lead me,

rule me, work with - in me, Through my

Lead me, rule me, work with - in me,

life Thy will ex - press.

Through my life

Text: Charles W. Naylor
Tune: SPIRIT HOLY, 8 7 8 7 with refrain; Andrew L. Byers

325 EVERY TIME I FEEL THE SPIRIT

God is spirit, and those who worship Him must worship in spirit and truth.
John 4:24

Refrain

Ev - 'ry time I feel the Spir - it mov - ing
in my heart, I will pray. Ev - 'ry time I feel the
Spir - it mov - ing in my heart, I will pray.

Verses

1. Up - on the moun - tain when my God spoke, it looked so
   All a - round me,
2. 'Ol Jor - dan Riv - er, chill - y and cold,
   There ain't but one train that's on this track, shine,

Out of God's mouth came   fire and smoke.
I   asked my   Lord if   all was mine.
It   chills the   bod - y,   but not the soul.
It   runs to   heav - en   and runs right back.

Text: Negro spiritual
Tune: FEEL THE SPIRIT, 98 98 with refrain; Negro spiritual; arr. by Nolan Williams, Jr., b.1969, © 2000, GIA Publications, Inc.

326 Sweet, Sweet Spirit

... agree with one another, live in peace; and the God of love and peace will be with you.
2 Corinthians 13:11

There's a sweet, sweet spir - it in this place,
sweet ex - pres-sions on each face,

And I know that it's the spir - it of the
And I know that it's the pres - ence of the

1. Lord. There are
2. Lord.

Sweet Ho - ly Spir-it,

Sweet Heav'n-ly Dove, Stay right here with us

Fill-ing us with Your love. And for those bless-ings We lift our hearts with praise; With-out a doubt we'll know that we have been re-vived, when we shall leave this place.

Text: Doris Akers, b.1922
Tune: MANNA, Irregular; Doris Akers, b.1922
© 1962, 1990, Manna Music, Inc.

327 Come, Thou Almighty King

Moses and Aaron... came out and blessed the people; and the glory of the LORD appeared to all the people.
Leviticus 9:23

1. Come, Thou Al - might - y King,
2. Come, Thou In - car - nate Word,
3. Come, Ho - ly Com - fort - er,
4. To the great One - in - Three

Help us Thy
Gird on Thy
Thy sa - cred
E - ter - nal

name to sing,
might - y sword,
wit - ness bear
prais - es be,

Help us to praise:
Our prayer at - tend:
In this glad hour:
Hence ev - er - more:

Fa - ther, all - glo - ri - ous, O'er all vic - to - ri - ous,
Come and Thy peo - ple bless, And give Thy word suc - cess—
Thou who al - might - y art, Now rule in ev - 'ry heart,
His sov - 'reign maj - es - ty May we in glo - ry see,

Come and reign o - ver us, An - cient of Days.
Spir - it of ho - li - ness, On us de - scend.
And ne'er from us de - part, Spir - it of pow'r.
And to e - ter - ni - ty Love and a - dore.

Text: Anonymous, c.1757
Tune: ITALIAN HYMN, 66 4 666 4; Felice de Giardini, 1716-1796

HOLY, HOLY 328

...without ceasing they sing, "Holy, holy, holy, the Lord God the Almighty, who was and is and is to come."
Revelation 4:8

Unison

1. Ho - ly, ho - ly, ho - ly, ho - ly, Ho - ly,
2. Gra - cious Fa - ther, gra - cious Fa - ther, We're so
3. Pre - cious Je - sus, pre - cious Je - sus, We're so
4. Ho - ly Spir - it, Ho - ly Spir - it, Come and
5. Hal - le - lu - jah, hal - le - lu - jah, Hal - le -

ho - ly, Lord God Al - might - y:
blest to be Your chil - dren, gra - cious Fa - ther;
glad that You've re - deemed us, pre - cious Je - sus;
fill our hearts a - new, Ho - ly Spir - it;
lu - jah, hal - le - lu - jah;

And we lift our hands be - fore You as a to - ken of our love,

Ho - ly, ho - ly, ho - ly, ho - ly.
Gra - cious Fa - ther, gra - cious Fa - ther.
Pre - cious Je - sus, pre - cious Je - sus.
Ho - ly Spir - it, Ho - ly Spir - it.
Hal - le - lu - jah, hal - le - lu - jah.

Text: Jimmy Owens, b.1930
Tune: HOLY, Irregular; Jimmy Owens, b.1930

329 HOLY, HOLY, HOLY! LORD GOD ALMIGHTY

Let the heavens praise Your wonders, O LORD, Your faithfulness in the assembly of the holy ones.
Psalm 89:5

1. Ho - ly, Ho - ly, Ho - ly! Lord God Al - might - y!
2. Ho - ly, Ho - ly, Ho - ly! all the saints a - dore Thee,
3. Ho - ly, Ho - ly, Ho - ly! though the dark - ness hide Thee,

Ear - ly in the morn - ing our song shall rise to Thee:
Cast - ing down their gold - en crowns a - round the glass - y sea;
Though the eye made blind by sin Thy glo - ry may not see,

Ho - ly, Ho - ly, Ho - ly! mer - ci - ful and might - y,
Cher - u - bim and ser - a - phim fall - ing down be - fore Thee,
On - ly Thou art ho - ly; there is none be - side Thee,

God in three Per - sons, bless - ed Trin - i - ty.
God ev - er - last - ing through e - ter - ni - ty.
Per - fect in pow'r, in love, and pu - ri - ty.

Descant:

4. Ho - ly, Ho - ly! Lord, God Al - might - y!

4. Ho - ly, Ho - ly, Ho - ly! Lord God Al - might - y!

All Thy works shall praise Thy Name in earth, and sky, and sea;

All Thy works shall praise Thy Name in earth, and sky, and sea;

Ho - ly, Ho - ly, mer - ci - ful and might - y,

Ho - ly, Ho - ly, Ho - ly! mer - ci - ful and might - y,

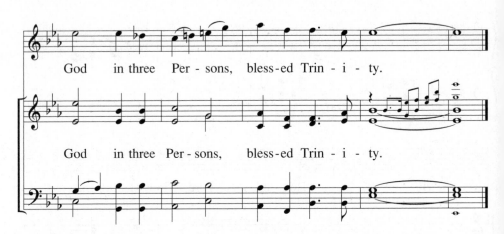

God   in three   Per - sons,   bless-ed Trin - i - ty.

God   in three   Per - sons,   bless-ed Trin - i - ty.

Text: Reginald Heber, 1783-1826, alt.
Tune: NICAEA, 11 12 12 10; John Bacchus Dykes, 1823-1876; arr. by Nolan Williams, Jr., b.1969, © 2000, GIA Publications, Inc.

330   FATHER, I ADORE YOU

Because Your steadfast love is better than life, my lips will praise You.
Psalm 63:2-3

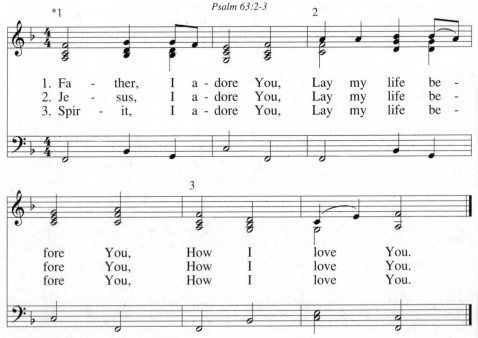

1. Fa - ther, I a - dore You, Lay my life be -
2. Je - sus, I a - dore You, Lay my life be -
3. Spir - it, I a - dore You, Lay my life be -

fore You, How I love You.
fore You, How I love You.
fore You, How I love You.

May be sung as a 3-part round.

Text: Terrye Coelho
Tune: MARANATHA, 6 6 4; Terrye Coelho
© 1972, Maranatha! Music

TELL ME THE STORIES OF JESUS 331

Then Philip began to speak, and starting with this scripture, he proclaimed to him the good news about Jesus.
Acts 8:35

1. Tell me the sto-ries of Je-sus I love to hear;
2. First let me hear how the chil-dren Stood 'round His knee,
3. In-to the cit-y I'd fol-low The chil-dren's band,

Things I would ask Him to tell me If He were here:
And I shall fan-cy His bless-ing Rest-ing on me;
Wav-ing a branch of the palm tree High in my hand;

Scenes by the way-side, Tales of the sea,
Words full of kind-ness, Deeds full of grace,
One of His her-alds, Yes, I would sing

Sto-ries of Je-sus, Tell them to me.
All in the love-light Of Je-sus' face.
Loud-est ho-san-nas, "Je-sus is King!"

Text: William H. Parker, 1845-1929
Tune: STORIES OF JESUS, 84 84 54 54; Frederic A. Challinor, 1866-1952

332 WONDERFUL WORDS OF LIFE

How sweet are Your words to my taste, sweeter than honey to my mouth!
Psalm 119:103

1. Sing them o-ver a-gain to me— Won-der-ful words of
2. Christ, the bless-ed One, gives to all Won-der-ful words of
3. Sweet-ly ech-o the gos-pel call— Won-der-ful words of

Life; Let me more of their beau-ty see—
Life; Lis-ten well to the lov-ing call—
Life; Of-fer par-don and peace to all—

Won-der-ful words of Life. Words of life and
Won-der-ful words of Life. All the won-drous
Won-der-ful words of Life. Je-sus, on-ly

beau-ty, Teach me faith and du-ty:
sto-ry, Show-ing us His glo-ry:
Sav-ior, Sanc-ti-fy for-ev-er:

Beau - ti - ful words, wonder - ful words,

Won - der - ful words of Life; Life.

1.

2.

Text: Philip P. Bliss, 1838-1876
Tune: WORDS OF LIFE, 8 6 8 6 66 with refrain; Philip P. Bliss, 1838-1876

333 ORDER MY STEPS

Our steps are made firm by the LORD, when He delights in our way.
Psalm 37:23

1. Or - der my steps in Your word, dear Lord,
2. Hum - bly I ask Thee, teach me Your will.
3. Bri - dle my tongue, let my words ed - i - fy, Let the

Lead me, guide me, ev - er - y day.
While You are work - ing, help me be still. Though
words of my mouth be ac - cept - a - ble in Thy sight. Take

Send Your a - noint - ing, Fa - ther, I pray.
Sa - tan is bus - y, God is real!
charge of my thoughts, both day and night.

Or - der my steps in Your word. Please,

1. 2.
or-der my steps in Your word. word. I want to walk

1. 2. *piano, ad lib.*

wor - thy. My call - ing to ful - fill.

Please or - der my steps, Lord, And I'll

do Your bless - ed will, The world is ev - er

chang - ing, but You are still the same.

If You or-der my steps, I'll praise Your

name. I want to walk

Text: Psalm 119:133, Glenn Burleigh
Tune: IN YOUR WORD, Irregular; Glenn Burleigh
© 1991, Glenn Burleigh (Burleigh Inspirations Music)

334 BREAK THOU THE BREAD OF LIFE

But He said, "Blessed rather are those who hear the word of God and obey it!"
Luke 11:28

1. Break Thou the bread of life, Dear Lord, to me,
2. Bless Thou the truth, dear Lord, To me, to me,
3. Teach me to live, dear Lord, On - ly for Thee,

As Thou did break the loaves Be - side the sea;
As Thou did bless the bread By Gal - i - lee;
As Thy dis - ci - ples lived In Gal - i - lee;

Be - yond the sa - cred page I seek Thee, Lord;
Then shall all bond - age cease, All fet - ters fall,
Then, all my strug - gles o'er, Then, vic - t'ry won,

My spir - it pants for Thee, O liv - ing word!
And I shall find my peace, My all in all.
I shall be - hold Thee, Lord, The liv - ing One.

Text: Mary A. Lathbury, 1841-1913
Tune: BREAD OF LIFE, 6 4 6 4 D; William F. Sherwin, 1826-1888

Jesus Loves Me 335

As the Father has loved me, so I have loved you; abide in my love.
John 15:9

1. Je - sus loves me! this I know, For the Bi - ble
2. Je - sus loves me! He who died Heav-en's gates to
3. Je - sus loves me! loves me still, Tho' I'm ver - y
4. Je - sus loves me! He will stay Close be - side me

tells me so; Lit - tle ones to Him be - long,
o - pen wide! He will wash a - way my sin,
weak and ill; From His shin - ing throne on high,
all the way; If I love Him when I die,

They are weak, but He is strong.
Let His lit - tle child come in.
Comes to watch me where I lie. Yes, Je-sus loves me.
He will take me home on high.

Yes, Je-sus loves me. Yes, Je-sus loves me, for the Bi-ble tells me so.

Text: Anna B. Warner, 1820-1915
Tune: CHINA, 77 77 with refrain; William B. Bradbury, 1816-1868

336 DEEPER, DEEPER

I pray that you may have the power to comprehend... what is the breadth and length and height and depth...
Ephesians 3:18-19

1. Deep - er, deep - er in the love of Je - sus Dai - ly let me
2. Deep - er, deep - er! bless - ed Ho - ly Spir - it, Take me deep - er
3. Deep - er, deep - er! tho' it cost hard tri - als, Deep-er let me
4. Deep - er, high - er, ev - 'ry day in Je - sus, Till all con - flict

go; High - er, high - er in the school of wis - dom,
still, Till my life is whol - ly lost in Je - sus,
go! Root - ed in the ho - ly love of Je - sus,
past, Finds me con-qu'ror, and in His own im - age

O deep - er yet, I

More of grace to know.
And His per - fect will.
Let me fruit - ful grow.
Per - fect - ed at last.

O deep - er yet, I pray,

pray, And high - er ev - 'ry

deep - er yet, I pray, And high - er ev - 'ry day,

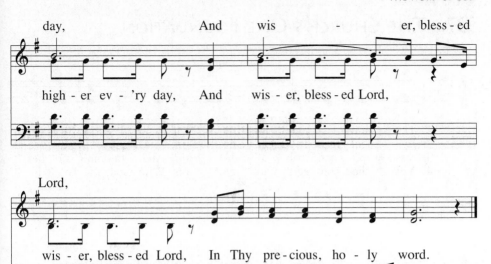

day,   And   wis -   er, bless - ed
high - er ev - 'ry day,   And   wis - er, bless - ed Lord,

Lord,
wis - er, bless - ed Lord,   In Thy pre - cious, ho - ly   word.

Text: Charles P. Jones
Tune: DEEPER, 10 5 10 5 with refrain; Charles P. Jones

337 THE CHURCH'S ONE FOUNDATION

...you are Peter, and on this rock I will build my church, and the gates of Hades will not prevail against it.
Matthew 16:18

1. The Church-'s one foun - da - tion Is Je - sus Christ her
2. E - lect from ev - 'ry na - tion, Yet one o'er all the
3. 'Mid toil and trib - u - la - tion, And tu - mult of her
4. Yet she on earth hath un - ion With God, the Three in

Lord, She is His new cre - a - tion By wa - ter and the
earth, Her char - ter of sal - va - tion, One Lord, one faith, one
war, She waits the con - sum - ma - tion Of peace for ev - er -
One, And mys - tic sweet com - mun - ion With those whose rest is

word; From heav'n He came and sought her To
birth; One ho - ly name she bless - es, Par -
more; Till with the vi - sion glo - rious, Her
won; O hap - py ones and ho - ly! Lord,

be His ho - ly bride; With His own blood He
takes one ho - ly food, And to one hope she
long - ing eyes are blest, And the great Church vic -
give us grace that we Like them, the meek and

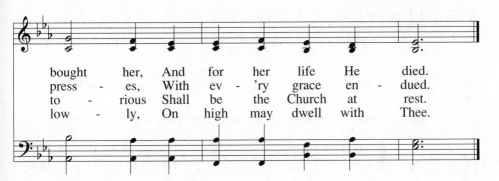

bought	her,	And	for	her	life	He	died.
press -	es,	With	ev - 'ry	grace	en -	dued.
to -	rious	Shall	be	the	Church	at	rest.
low -	ly,	On	high	may	dwell	with	Thee.

Text: Samuel J. Stone, 1839-1900
Tune: AURELIA, 7 6 7 6 D; Samuel S. Wesley, 1810-1876

Alternate text:

1. The Church's one foundation is Christ, God's own true Child
   In whom the whole creation is freed and reconciled
   To bring the Church together, Christ lived and freely died;
   Raised up by God, forever, Christ lives to be our Guide.

2. The world and all the nations, created to be one
   Can live in sweet communion with God and God's own Son
   When we who say we love Him begin to live and BE
   A people with great freedom to gain through harmony.

3. Where are the gifts we're seeking if not in our own hearts?
   To share, to offer others so they may know their parts
   In working as the chosen, whose heritage and hopes
   Are in the great Creator, our Christ, our Lord who knows.

4. Let's offer all our talents and wants for setting free
   The homeless and the hungry, the hurting you and me
   Remembering tomorrow, the Son will rise and shine
   To give us Light and helpers to serve Him while there's time.

Text: Reverend Pamela June Anderson, D.Min., © 1991

338 UNITY

How very good and pleasant it is when kindred live together in unity!
Psalm 133:1

Be - hold how good and how pleas - ant it is for

kin - dred to dwell to - geth - er in u - ni - ty. Be -

hold how good and how pleas - ant it is for kin - dred to

dwell to-geth-er in u - ni-ty.   u - ni-ty.

U - ni-ty,   u - ni-ty,   Lord,   we pray for

u - ni - ty.   U - ni - ty,

u - ni-ty,   Lord,   we pray for   u - ni-ty.

Text: Psalm 133:1, Glorraine Moone, © 1989. Published by Professionals for Christ Publications (BMI)
Tune: Glorraine Moone, © 1989; arr. by Dr. Daniel Mario Cason II. Published by Professionals for Christ Publications (BMI);
    adapt. Valeria Foster, © 2000, GIA Publications, Inc.

339 For All the Saints

Remember your leaders,... consider the outcome of their way of life, and imitate their faith.
Hebrews 13:7

1. For all the saints who from their la - bors
2. You were their rock, their for - tress and their
3. O may Your sol - diers, faith - ful, true and
7. But then there breaks a yet more glo - rious
8. From earth's wide bounds, from o - cean's far - thest

rest, All who by faith be - fore the world con -
might; You, Lord, their Cap - tain in the well - fought
bold, Fight as the saints who no - bly fought of
day: The saints tri - um - phant rise in bright ar -
coast, Through gates of pearl streams in the count - less

fessed, Your name, O Je - sus, be for ev - er blest.
fight; You in the dark - ness drear, their one true light.
old, And win with them, the vic - tor's crown of gold.
ray; The King of glo - ry pass - es on His way.
host, Sing - ing to Fa - ther, Son, and Ho - ly Ghost:

Al - le - lu - ia! Al - le - lu - ia!

Harmony:

4. O blest com - mun - ion, fam - i - ly di - vine!
5. And when the strife is fierce, the war - fare long,
6. The gold - en eve - ning bright-ens in the west;

We fee - bly strug - gle, they in glo - ry shine;
Steals on the ear the dis - tant tri - umph song,
Soon, soon to faith - ful war - riors comes their rest;

Yet all are one with - in Your great de - sign.
And hearts are brave a - gain, and arms are strong.
Sweet is the calm of par - a - dise the blest.

Al - le - lu - ia! Al - le - lu - ia!

Text: William W. How, 1823-1897
Tune: SINE NOMINE, 10 10 10 with alleluias; Ralph Vaughan Williams, 1872-1958, © Oxford University Press

340 WELCOME TO MY FATHER'S HOUSE

My house shall be called a house of prayer for all the nations.
Mark 11:17

Wel-come to my Fa - ther's house.
You are in my Fa - ther's house.

Oh, what a bless - ed priv - i - lege!
It is writ - ten, it's a house of prayer.

Take the time to talk to, God; Tell Him just what's on your heart.
When you pray in Je - sus'name, You'll ex - pe - ri - ence a change

Wel-come to my Fa - ther's house! Tell Him

just what you're go - ing through; Lis - ten,

He's got a word for you. Ask Him, let Him

show you what to do. Wel-come to my Fa - ther's house.

Text: V. Michael McKay
Tune: V. Michael McKay
© Schaff Music Publishing

341 BLEST BE THE TIE THAT BINDS

Above all, clothe yourselves with love, which binds everything together in perfect harmony.
Colossians 3:14

1. Blest be the tie that binds Our hearts in
2. Be - fore our Fa - ther's throne We pour our
3. We share each oth - er's woes, Each oth - er's
4. From sor - row, toil, and pain, And sin we

Chris - tian love; The fel - low - ship of
ar - dent prayers; Our fears, our hopes, our
bur - dens bear; And of - ten for each
shall be free; And per - fect love and

kin - dred minds Is like to that a - bove.
aims are one, Our com - forts and our cares.
oth - er flows The sym - pa - thiz - ing tear.
joy shall reign Through all e - ter - ni - ty.

Text: John Fawcett, 1740-1817
Tune: DENNIS, SM; John G. Nägeli, 1773-1836; arr. by Lowell Mason, 1792-1872

WE GATHER TOGETHER 342

We your people...will give thanks to You forever; from generation to generation we will recount Your praise.
Psalm 79:13

1. We gath - er to - geth - er to ask the Lord's bless - ing;
2. Be - side us to guide us, our God with us join - ing,
3. We all do ex - tol You our lead - er tri - um - phant,

He chas - tens and has - tens His will to make known;
Whose king - dom calls all to the love which en - dures.
And pray that You still our de - fend - er will be.

The wick - ed op - press - ing now cease from dis - tress - ing:
So from the be - gin - ning the fight we were win - ning:
Let Your con - gre - ga - tion es - cape trib - u - la - tion:

Sing prais - es to His name; He for - gets not His own.
You, Lord, were at our side; all glo - ry be Yours!
Your name be ev - er praised! O Lord, make us free!

Text: *Wilt heden nu treden*, Netherlands folk hymn; tr. by Theodore Baker, 1851-1934, alt.
Tune: KREMSER, 12 11 12 11; *Neder-landtsch Gedenckclanck*, 1626; harm. by Edward Kremser, 1838-1914

343 RENEW THY CHURCH, HER MINISTRIES RESTORE

No one after lighting a lamp puts it under the bushel basket, but on the lampstand, and it gives light to all in the house.
Matthew 5:15

1. Re - new Thy church, her min - is - tries re - store:
2. Teach us Thy Word, re - veal its truth di - vine;
3. Teach us to pray, for Thou art ev - er near;
4. Teach us to love, with strength of heart and mind,

Both to serve and a - dore. Make her a - gain as
On our path let it shine. Tell of Thy works, Thy
Thy still voice let us hear. Our souls are rest - less
Ev - 'ry - one, all man - kind. Break down old walls of

salt through-out the land, And as light from a stand.
might - y acts of grace; From each page show Thy face.
till they rest in Thee: This our glad des - ti - ny.
prej - u - dice and hate; Leave us not to our fate.

'Mid som - ber shad - ows of the night Where
As Thou hast loved us, sent Thy Son, And
Be - fore Thy pres - ence keep us still, That
As Thou hast loved and giv'n Thy life To

greed and ha - tred spread their blight, O send us forth with
our sal - va - tion now is won, O let our hearts with
we may find for us Thy will And seek Thy guid - ance
end hos - til - i - ty and strife, O share Thy grace from

pow'r en - dued: Help us, Lord, be re - newed!
love be stirred: Help us, Lord, know Thy Word!
ev - 'ry day: Teach us, Lord, how to pray!
heav'n a - bove: Teach us, Lord, how to love!

Text: Kenneth L. Cober, b.1902; © 1960, Kenneth Cober, renewed 1985, Judson Press
Tune: ALL IS WELL, 10 6 10 6 88 86; J. T. White's *Sacred Harp*

344 JUST AS I AM

He cried out, "Let anyone who is thirsty come to me, and let the one who believes in me drink."
John 7:37-38

1. Just as I am, with-out one plea,
2. Just as I am, and wait-ing not
3. Just as I am, though tossed a-bout,
4. Just as I am, Thou wilt re-ceive,

But that Thy blood was shed for me,
To rid my soul of one dark blot;
With man-y a con-flict, man-y a doubt,
Wilt wel-come, par-don, cleanse, re-lieve;

And that Thou bidst me come to Thee, O
To Thee, whose blood can cleanse each spot, O
Fight-ings with-in and fears with-out, O
Be-cause Thy prom-ise I be-lieve, O

Lamb of God, I come.

Just as I am, Just as I am,
Just as I am, Just as I

Just as I am, Just as I am,

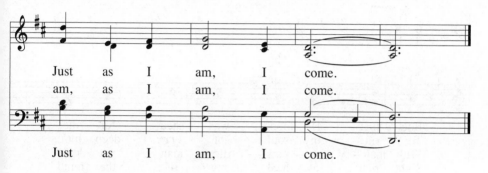

Just as I am, I come.
am, as I am, I come.

Just as I am, I come.

Text: Charlotte Elliott, 1789-1871
Tune: JUST AS I AM, 888 6 with refrain; adapt. from Gaul's, *The Holy City*, by Evelyn Simpson-Curenton, b.1953, © 2000, GIA Publications, Inc.

345 JUST AS I AM

He cried out, "Let anyone who is thirsty come to me, and let the one who believes in me drink."
John 7:37-38

1. Just as I am, with - out one plea,
2. Just as I am, and wait - ing not
3. Just as I am, though tossed a - bout
4. Just as I am— poor, wretch - ed, blind;
5. Just as I am— Thou wilt re - ceive,

But that Thy blood was shed for me,
To rid my soul of one deep blot,
With man - y a con - flict, man - y a doubt,
Sight, rich - es, heal - ing of the mind,
Wilt wel - come, par - don, cleanse, re - lieve,

And that Thou bidd'st me come to Thee,
To Thee whose blood can cleanse each spot,
Fight - ings and fears with - in, with - out,
Yea, all I need in Thee to find,
Be - cause Thy prom - ise I be - lieve,

O Lamb of God, I come! I come!

Text: Charlotte Elliott, 1789-1871
Tune: WOODWORTH, LM; William B. Bradbury, 1816-1868

GIVE YOUR LIFE TO CHRIST 346

For you have died, and your life is hidden with Christ in God.
Colossians 3:3

1. Come to - day, don't de - lay. Make Him your choice.
2. If you come to Him right now, He'll see you through.
3. Cast your cares up - on the Lord. He'll bear them all.

Je - sus wants to save you. Give your life to Christ.
He will nev - er fail you. Give your life to Christ.
Je - sus will pro - tect you. Give your life to Christ.

Give Him all your bur - dens. Give them all to Je - sus.

Je - sus wants to save you; you should give your life to Christ.

Text: Michael Kenneth Ross
Tune: GIVE YOUR LIFE, 6 4 6 5 with refrain; Michael Kenneth Ross
© 1995, MKR Music

347 SOFTLY AND TENDERLY JESUS IS CALLING

Come to me, all you that are weary and are carrying heavy burdens, and I will give you rest.
Matthew 11:28

1. Soft - ly and ten - der - ly Je - sus is call - ing,
2. Why should we tar - ry when Je - sus is plead - ing,
3. Time is now fleet - ing, the mo - ments are pass - ing,
4. O for the won - der - ful love He has prom - ised,

Call - ing for you and for me;
Plead - ing for you and for me?
Pass - ing from you and from me;
Prom - ised for you and for me;

See, on the por - tals He's wait - ing and watch - ing,
Why should we lin - ger and heed not His mer - cies,
Shad - ows are gath - er - ing, death-beds are com - ing,
Though we have sinned He has mer - cy and par - don,

Watch - ing for you and for me.
Mer - cies for you and for me?
Com - ing for you and for me.
Par - don for you and for me.

Come home, come home,
come home, come home,
come home, Ye who are
come home, come home,
wea - ry, come home; Ear - nest-ly, ten - der - ly,
Je - sus is call-ing— Call-ing, "O sin-ner, come home!"

Text: Will L. Thompson, 1847-1909
Tune: THOMPSON, 11 7 11 7 with refrain; Will L. Thompson, 1847-1909

348 Somebody's Knockin'

Listen! I am standing at the door, knocking...
Revelation 3:20

Some-bod - y's knock-in' at your door; Some-bod - y's

knock-in' at your door; O sin - ner, why don't you

an - swer? Some-bod - y's knock-in' at your door.

Solo:
All:

1. Knocks like Je - sus,
2. Can't you hear Him?
3. Je - sus calls you,
4. Can't you trust Him?

Some-bod - y's knock-in' at your

Text: Negro spiritual
Tune: SOMEBODY'S KNOCKIN', Irregular; Negro spiritual; harm. by Richard Proulx, b.1937, alt., © 1986, GIA Publications, Inc.

349 'TIS THE OL' SHIP OF ZION

Walk about Zion, go all around it... that you may tell the next generation that this is God, our God forever and ever.
Psalm 48:12-14

Verse 1
rubato

1. 'Tis the ol' ship of Zi - on, 'Tis the
ol' ship of Zi - on, 'Tis the ol' ship of
Zi - on; Get on board, get on board!

Verses 2-4

2. It has land-ed man-y a thou-sand, It has
3. King Je - sus is the cap - tain, King
4. Hum

land-ed man-y a thou-sand, It has land-ed man-y a
Je - sus is the cap-tain, King Je - sus is the
(hum)

thou - sand; Get on board, get on board!
cap - tain; Get on board, get on board!
Get on board, get on board!

Text: Negro spiritual
Tune: OL' SHIP OF ZION, 7 7 7 6; Negro spiritual; arr. by Stanley Thurston, © 2000, GIA Publications, Inc.

350 I Am Praying For You

I am asking... on behalf of those whom you gave me, because they are Yours.
John 17:9

1. I have a Sav - ior, He's plead - ing in glo - ry, A
2. I have a Fa - ther; to me He has giv - en A
3. I have a robe: 'tis re - splen - dent in white - ness, A -
4. When Je - sus has found you, tell oth - ers the sto - ry, That

dear, lov - ing Sav - ior, though earth - friends be few; And
hope for e - ter - ni - ty, bless - ed and true; And
wait - ing in glo - ry my won - der - ing view; Oh,
my lov - ing Sav - ior is your Sav - ior, too; Then

now He is watch - ing in ten - der - ness o'er me, But,
soon will He call me to meet Him in heav - en, But,
when I re - ceive it all shin - ing in bright - ness, Dear
pray that your Sav - ior may bring them to glo - ry And

oh, that my Sav - ior were your Sav - ior, too.
oh, that He'd let me bring you with me, too!
friend, could I see you re - ceiv - ing one, too!
prayer will be an - swered—'twas an - swered for you!

For you I am pray - ing, For you I am pray - ing, For you I am pray - ing, I'm pray - ing for you.

Text: S. O'Malley Cluff
Tune: I AM PRAYING FOR YOU, 11 11 12 11 with refrain; Ira D. Sankey, 1840-1908; arr. by Valeria A. Foster, © 2000, GIA Publications, Inc.

351 JESUS IS CALLING

The Teacher is here and is calling for you.
John 11:28

1. Je - sus is ten - der - ly call - ing thee home—
2. Je - sus is call - ing the wea - ry to rest—
3. Je - sus is wait - ing, O come to Him now—
4. Je - sus is plead - ing, O list to His voice—

Call - ing to - day, call - ing to - day;
Call - ing to - day, call - ing to - day;
Wait - ing to - day, wait - ing to - day;
Hear Him to - day, hear Him to - day;

Why from the sun - shine of love wilt thou roam
Bring Him thy bur - den and thou shalt be blest—
Come with thy sins, at His feet low - ly bow—
They who be - lieve on His name shall re - joice—

Far - ther and far - ther a - way?
He will not turn thee a - way.
Come, and no long - er de - lay.
Quick - ly a - rise and a - way.

Call - ing to - day, Call - ing to -

Call - ing, call-ing to - day, to - day, Call - ing, call - ing to -

day, Je - sus is call - ing, Is

day, to - day; Je - sus is ten-der-ly call-ing to-day, Is

ten - der - ly call - ing to - day.

Text: Fanny J. Crosby, 1820-1915
Tune: CALLING TODAY, 10 8 10 7 with refrain; George C. Stebbins, 1846-1945

352 PLENTY GOOD ROOM

In my Father's house there are many dwelling places.
John 14:2

Plen - ty good room, plen - ty good room, plen - ty good room in my Fa - ther's king - dom, Plen - ty good room, plen - ty good room, just choose your seat and sit down.

1. I would not be a sin - ner,
2. I would not be a li - ar, I'll
3. I would not be a back - slid - er,

tell you the rea - son why; cause

if my Lord should call on me I

would - n't be read - y to die.

Text: Negro spiritual
Tune: Negro spiritual; arr. by Joseph Joubert, © 2000, GIA Publications, Inc.

353 IS THERE ANY ROOM IN YOUR HEART FOR JESUS?

Store up for yourselves treasures in heaven... For where your treasure is, there your heart will be also.
Matthew 6:20-21

Refrain

Is there an-y room in your heart for Je - sus?

Him?
Is there an-y room for Him, room for Him?

Is there an - y room for the King of kings?

Last time to Coda

Is there an - y room for Him?

Verses

1. He was born just a babe in Beth - le - hem,
   an - gels de - clared His com - ing,

Born in a man - ger stall. If you let Him
Glo - ry to God on high. If you let Him

Last time **D.C.**

en - ter your heart, He will be your all in all. 2. The
en - ter your heart, His Spir - it will stay close by.

Coda   There is room,   there is room,

Him?   There is room,   there is room, there is

room in my heart for the King of kings. There is room for Him.

354 COME TO JESUS

The Lord is... patient with you, not wanting any to perish, but all to come to repentance.
2 Peter 3:9

1. Come to Je - sus, Come to Je - sus, Come to

Je - sus just now, just now. Come to

Je - sus, Come to Je - sus just now!

2. Only trust Him,...
3. He is able,...
4. He will save you,...

Text: Traditional
Tune: COME TO JESUS, 4 4 8 4 6; traditional; arr. by Evelyn Simpson-Curenton, b.1953, © 2000, GIA Publications, Inc.

We Offer Christ 355

...we are slaves not under the old written code but in the new life of the Spirit.
Romans 7:6

We of-fer Christ to you, oh, my broth-er, We of-fer Christ to you, oh, my sis-ter. He will give you brand new life Through life a-bun-dant-ly; Oh come, come on to Christ.

356 FOLLOW JESUS

If any want to become my followers, let them deny themselves and take up their cross daily and follow me.
Luke 9:23

1. This old, sin - ful world a - round me Is not
2. We must walk right, we must talk right, Seek the
3. Sa - tan's bus - y, try'n to block us, Trap us

what I'm long - ing for. There's a bet - ter place called
way which Christ has shown. Just o - bey the law that's
in the way of sin. But re - buke him and de -

heav - en; Our e - ter - nal life's re - ward.
writ - ten; Bring - ing oth - ers to the fold.
nounce him; Hide the Word of Christ with - in.

Fol - low Je - sus, fol - low Je - sus, won't you

make that choice to - day? He will give you joy and

com - fort. He is just a prayer a - way.

Text: Waymon L. Burwell, Sr., © 1993, alt.
Tune: FOLLOW JESUS, 8 7 8 7 with refrain; Waymon L. Burwell, Sr., © 1993; arr. by Nolan Williams, Jr., b.1969, © 2000, GIA Publications, Inc.
Administered by GIA Publications, Inc.

357　JESUS PAID IT ALL

For the Son of Man came…to give His life a ransom for many.
Mark 10:45

1. I hear the Sav - ior say, "Your strength in -
2. Lord, now in - deed I find Your pow'r, and
3. For noth - ing good have I Where - by Your
4. And when be - fore the throne I stand in

deed is small! Child of weak - ness, watch and pray,
Yours a - lone, Can change the lep - er's spots
grace to claim— I'll wash my gar - ments white
Him com - plete, "Je - sus died my soul to save,"

Find in Me your all in all."
And melt the heart of stone.
In the blood of Cal - v'ry's Lamb.　　Je - sus paid it
My lips shall still re - peat.

all, All to Him I owe; Sin had left a crim - son

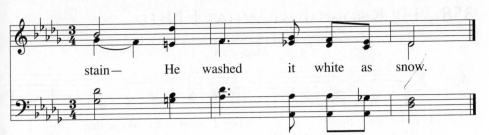

stain— He washed it white as snow.

Text: Elvina M. Hall, 1820-1889
Tune: ALL TO CHRIST, 6 6 7 7 with refrain; John T. Grape, 1835-1915

358 HE KNOWS JUST WHAT I NEED

...your Father knows what you need before you ask Him.
Matthew 6:8

1. There are times when I want to do wrong, so I
2. Some - times in His per - mis - sive will He

go to God in prayer. He com - forts me and He
lets me have my way. When I've fouled up and

guides me a - long. He knows just what I need.
can't re - treat He's there to guard my stay.

He knows just what I need, He a - lone de - cides for

me. Tho' temp-ta - tions come, He is al - ways there, He knows

just what I need. He knows just what I

need, He knows just what I need.

Text: Dr. Robert J. Fryson
Tune: HE KNOWS, Irregular with refrain; Dr. Robert J. Fryson
© 1984, Bob Jay Music Co.

359 O Happy Day

Rejoice in the Lord always; again I will say, Rejoice.
Philippians 4:4

1. O hap - py day that fixed my choice On Thee, my
2. O hap - py bond that seals my vows To Him who
3. 'Tis done, the great trans - ac - tion's done— I am my
4. Now rest, my long - di - vid - ed heart, Fixed on this

Sav - ior and my God! Well may this glow - ing heart re -
mer - its all my love! Let cheer - ful an - thems fill His
Lord's and He is mine; He drew me, and I fol - lowed
bliss - ful cen - ter, rest; Nor ev - er from my Lord de -

joice And tell its rap - tures all a - broad.
house, While to that sa - cred shrine I move.
on, Charmed to con - fess the voice di - vine.
part, With Him of ev - 'ry good pos - sessed.

Hap - py day, hap - py day, When Je - sus

washed my sins a - way! He taught me how to watch and

pray And live re - joic - ing ev - 'ry day; Hap - py

day, hap - py day, When Je - sus washed my sins a - way!

Text: Philip Doddridge, 1702-1751
Tune: HAPPY DAY, LM with refrain; Edward F. Rimbault, 1816-1876

360 I Know the Lord Has Laid His Hands on Me

You hem me in, behind and before, and lay Your hand upon me.
Psalm 139:5

Oh, I know the Lord, I know the Lord, I know the Lord has laid His hands on me. Oh, I know the Lord, I know the Lord, I know the Lord has laid His hands on me.

Verses

1. Did ev - er you see the like be - fore?
   Je - sus preach - ing to the poor.
2. Oh, was - n't that a hap - py day
   Je - sus washed my sins a - way?

1.

2.

D.C.

I know the Lord has laid His hands on me, King
I know the Lord has laid His   hands on me.
I know the Lord has laid His hands on me, When
I know the Lord has laid His   hands on me.

Text: Negro spiritual
Tune: HANDS ON ME, Irregular with refrain; Negro spiritual; arr. by Valeria A. Foster, © 2000, GIA Publications, Inc.

361 I Will Arise

Whoever follows me will never walk in darkness but will have the light of life.
John 8:12

1. Come, ye sin - ners, poor and need - y,
2. Come, ye thirst - y, come, and wel - come,
3. Come, ye wea - ry, heav - y - lad - en,

Weak and wound - ed, sick and sore; Je - sus read - y
God's free boun - ty glo - ri - fy; True be - lief and
Lost and ru - ined by the fall; If you tar - ry

stands to save you, Full of pit - y, love, and pow'r.
true re - pen - tance, Ev - 'ry grace that brings you nigh.
till you're bet - ter, You will nev - er come at all.

I will a - rise and go to Je - sus, He will em - brace me

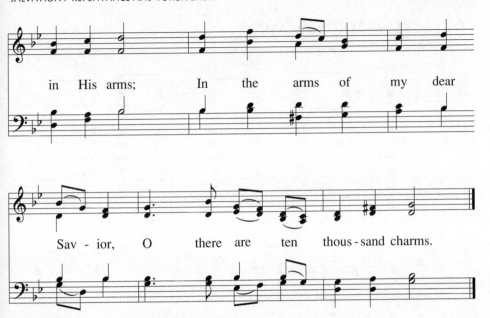

in His arms; In the arms of my dear

Sav - ior, O there are ten thous - sand charms.

Text: Joseph Hart
Tune: RESTORATION, 8 7 8 7 with refrain; Walker's *Southern Harmony*, 1835

This tune can also be used for
What a Friend We Have in Jesus *and*
Guide Me, O Thou Great Jehovah.

362 NEW BORN AGAIN

Very truly, I tell you, no one can see the kingdom of God without being born from above.
John 3:3

1. I found free grace and dy - ing love,
2. I know my Lord has set me free, I'm
3. My Sav - ior died for you and me,

new-born a - gain. Been long time talk - ing 'bout my

tri-als here be-low. free grace, free grace,

Oh, there's free grace, free grace,

free grace, sin - ner. free grace,

free grace, sin - ner. Oh, there's free grace,

free grace, I'm new-born a - gain.

yes, I'm

Oh, I'm

so glad, so glad I'm new-born a - gain. Been

long time talk - ing 'bout my tri - als here be - low.

Text: Negro spiritual
Tune: Negro spiritual; arr. by Roland M. Carter, b. 1942, © 1999, Mar-Vel

363 CHRIST IS ALL

In that renewal there is no longer Greek and Jew,... slave and free; but Christ is all and in all!
Colossians 3:11

1. I don't pos - sess hous - es or lands, fine clothes or jew'l-ry,
2. There are some folk who look and long for this world's rich - es,
3. Yes Christ is all, means more to me than this world's rich - es,

Sor - rows and cares in this old world my lot seems to
There are some folk who look for pow'r, po - si - tion
He is my sight, my guid-ing light thro' path - less

be, But I have a Christ who paid the price way back on
too, But I have a Christ all in my life, this makes me
seas, Yes it's might - y nice to own a Christ who will my

Cal - v'ry, And Christ is all, all and all this world to
hap - py, For Christ is all, all and all this world to
friend be, Yes Christ is all, all and all this world to

Text: Kenneth Morris
Tune: CHRIST IS ALL, 13 13 14 11 with refrain; Kenneth Morris; arr. by Evelyn Simpson-Curenton
© 1946, Unichappell Music, Inc.

364 KING JESUS IS A-LISTENIN'

But truly God has listened; He has given heed to the words of my prayer.
Psalm 66:19

Refrain

King Je-sus is a-lis-ten-in' all day long, King

Je-sus is a-lis-ten-in' all day long, King Je-sus is a lis-ten-in'

all day long, To hear some sin-ner pray.

Verses

1. That Gos-pel train is com-in', A-rum-blin' through the
2. I know I been con-vert-ed, I ain't gon' make no a -

lan',   I   hear them wheels a - hum-min',   Get
larm, For my soul   is bound for   glo - ry,   And the

D.C.

read -   y   for   that   train!
dev - il can't   do me no   harm.

Text: Traditional
Tune: KING JESUS, 7 6 7 7 with refrain; Negro spiritual; arr. by Carl Haywood, b.1949, from *The Haywood Collection of Negro Spirituals,*
  © 1992

365 JUST LET HIM IN

Listen! I am standing at the door, knocking; if you hear my voice and open the door, I will come in to you...
Revelation 3:20

He'll take a - way all of your heart-aches, He'll take a -

way all of your sins, He'll help you to bear all of your

bur-dens if you will on-ly let Him in. When sin and

grief have filled your soul, just tell my Je - sus, He'll make you

whole. He'll take a - way all, all of your bur-dens, just let Him in.

Text: S. Boddie, ©
Tune: S. Boddie, ©; arr. by Bill Cummings, © 2000, GIA Publications, Inc.

AN EVENING PRAYER 366

Have mercy on me, O God... Wash me thoroughly from my iniquity, and cleanse me from my sin.
Psalm 51:1-2

1. If I have wound-ed an-y soul to-day,
2. If I have ut-tered i-dle words or vain,
3. If I have been per-verse, or hard, or cold,
4. For-give the sins I have con-fessed to Thee;

If I have caused one foot to go a-stray,
If I have turned a-side from want or pain,
If I have longed for shel-ter in the fold,
For-give the se-cret sins I do not see;

If I have walked in my own will-ful way,
Lest I of-fend some oth-er through the strain,
When Thou hast giv-en me some fort to hold,
O guide me, love me, and my keep-er be.

1.-3. Dear Lord, for-give! (for-give!)

4. A-men. (A-men.)

Text: C. M. Battersby
Tune: EVENING, 10 10 10 4; Charles Gabriel, 1856-1932

367 Come Out the Wilderness

He went into all the region around the Jordan, proclaiming a baptism of repentance for the forgiveness of sins.
Luke 3:3

Solo:
1. Tell me, how did you feel when you
2. Did you get bap - tized when you come out the wil-der-ness,
3. Did your soul feel hap-py when you

come out the wil-der-ness, come out the wil-der-ness. Did you

Solo:
Tell me,
Did your

how did you feel when you
get bap - tized when you come out the wil-der-ness,
soul feel hap-py when you

lean-ing on the Lord. I am lean-ing on the

Lord, I am lean - ing on the Lord. I am

lean - ing on the Lord who died on Cal - va - ry.

Text: Negro spiritual
Tune: Negro spiritual; arr. by Evelyn Simpson-Curenton, b.1953, © 2000, GIA Publications, Inc.

368 'Tis So Sweet to Trust in Jesus

I will put my trust in Him.
Hebrews 2:13

1. 'Tis so sweet to trust in Je-sus, Just to take Him
2. O how sweet to trust in Je-sus, Just to trust His
3. Yes, 'tis sweet to trust in Je-sus, Just from sin and
4. I'm so glad I learned to trust Thee, Pre-cious Je-sus,

at His word, Just to rest up-on His prom-ise,
cleans-ing blood, Just in sim-ple faith to plunge me
self to cease, Just from Je-sus sim-ply tak-ing
Sav-ior, Friend; And I know that Thou art with me,

Just to know, "Thus saith the Lord."
'Neath the heal-ing, cleans-ing flood!
Life and rest and joy and peace.
Will be with me to the end.

Je-sus, Je-sus,

how I trust Him! How I've proved Him o'er and o'er!

Je-sus, Je-sus, pre-cious Je-sus! O for grace to trust Him more!

Text: Louisa M. R. Stead, c.1850-1917
Tune: TRUST IN JESUS, 8 7 8 7 with refrain; William J. Kirkpatrick, 1838-1921

ONLY TRUST HIM 369

Trust in the LORD forever, for in the LORD God you have an everlasting rock.
Isaiah 26:4

1. Come, ev - 'ry soul by sin op-pressed— There's mer - cy with the Lord, And He will sure - ly give you rest By trust - ing in His word.
2. For Je - sus shed His pre - cious blood Rich bless-ings to be - stow; Plunge now in - to the crim - son flood That wash - es white as snow.
3. Yes, Je - sus is the Truth, the Way, That leads you in - to rest; Be - lieve in Him with - out de - lay And you are ful - ly blest.

Refrain

On - ly trust Him, He will save you, on - ly trust Him, On - ly trust Him now; He will save you, He will save you now.

Text: John H. Stockton, 1813-1877
Tune: ONLY TRUST HIM, CM with refrain; John H. Stockton, 1813-1877

370 ALL MY HELP COMES FROM THE LORD

My help comes from the LORD, who made heaven and earth.
Psalm 121:2

Verses

1. Fa - ther I stretch, I stretch my hands to Thee.
2. When I am weak, when I'm weak He gives me strength.

I know that You, on-ly You, re-mem-ber me. When
When I am lone - ly He com-forts me.

oth - ers for - get, when oth-ers for - get and leave me a - lone,
When I am tired of the load that I am bear - ing,

I know that Je - sus, Je - sus, Je - sus will hear my groan.
He gives me cour-age, cour-age, cour-age to bear my share.

D.C.

Text: Rev. Cleophus Robinson, © 1964, Lion Publishing Co.
Tune: Rev. Cleophus Robinson, © 1964, Lion Publishing Co.; arr. by Evelyn Simpson-Curenton, b.1953, © 2000, GIA Publications, Inc.

371   LEANING ON THE EVERLASTING ARMS

Upon You I have leaned from my birth; it was You who took me from my mother's womb.
Psalm 71:6

1. What   a   fel - low - ship,   what   a   joy   di - vine,
2. O   how   sweet   to   walk   in   this   pil - grim way,
3. What   have   I   to   dread,   what   have   I   to   fear,

Lean - ing   on   the   ev - er - last - ing   arms;
Lean - ing   on   the   ev - er - last - ing   arms;
Lean - ing   on   the   ev - er - last - ing   arms?

What   a   bless - ed - ness,   what   a   peace   is   mine,
O   how   bright   the   path   grows   from   day   to   day,
I   have   bless - ed   peace   with   my   Lord   so   near,

Lean - ing   on   the   ev - er - last - ing   arms.

Text: Elisha A. Hoffman, 1839-1929
Tune: SHOWALTER, 10 9 10 9 with refrain; Anthony J. Showalter, 1858-1924; arr. by Nolan Williams, Jr., b.1969, © 2000,
   GIA Publications, Inc.

372 SATISFIED WITH JESUS

And my God will fully satisfy every need of yours according to His riches in glory in Christ Jesus.
Philippians 4:19

1. I am sat - is - fied with Je - sus,
2. He is with me in my tri - als,
3. I can hear the voice of Je - sus,
4. When my work on earth is end - ed,

He has done so much for me: He has suf - fered to re -
Best of friends of all is He; I can al - ways count on
Call-ing out so plead-ing - ly, "Go and win the lost and
And I cross the mys - tic sea, Oh, that I could hear Him

deem me, He has died to set me free.
Je - sus, Can He al - ways count on me?
stray - ing"; Is He sat - is - fied with me?
say - ing, "I am sat - is - fied with thee."

I am sat - is - fied, I am sat - is - fied, I am sat - is - fied with

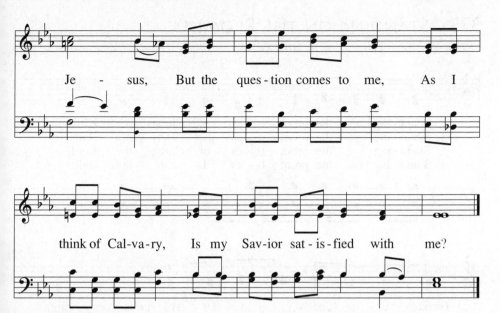

Je - sus, But the ques - tion comes to me, As I think of Cal-va-ry, Is my Sav-ior sat - is - fied with me?

Text: B. B. McKinney, 1886-1952
Tune: ROUTH, 8 7 8 7 with refrain; B. B. McKinney, 1886-1952
© 1926, 1953, Broadman Press

373 STANDING ON THE PROMISES

Not one of all the good promises that the LORD had made to the house of Israel had failed; all came to pass.
Joshua 21:45

1. Stand-ing on the prom-is-es of Christ, my King,
2. Stand-ing on the prom-is-es that can-not fail.
3. Stand-ing on the prom-is-es of Christ, the Lord,
4. Stand-ing on the prom-is-es I can-not fall,

Through e-ter-nal a-ges let His prais-es ring;
When the howl-ing storms of doubt and fear as-sail,
Bound to Him e-ter-nal-ly by love's strong cord,
Lis-t'ning ev-'ry mo-ment to the Spir-it's call,

Glo-ry in the high-est, I will shout and sing,
By the liv-ing word of God I shall pre-vail,
O-ver-com-ing dai-ly with the Spir-it's sword,
Rest-ing in my Sav-ior, as my all in all,

Stand-ing on the prom-is-es of God.

Standing on the promises of God, my Savior;
Standing, standing,
Standing on the promises, Standing on the promises, I'm
standing on the promises of God.

Text: R. Kelso Carter, 1849-1928
Tune: PROMISES, 11 11 11 9 with refrain; R. Kelso Carter, 1849-1928

374 BLESSED QUIETNESS

...and after the earthquake a fire, but the LORD was not in the fire; and after the fire a sound of sheer silence.
1 Kings 19:12

1. Joys are flow-ing like a riv - er, Since the Com - fort - er has come; He a - bides with us for ev - er, Makes the trust - ing heart His home.
2. Bring-ing life and health and glad - ness All a-round this heav'n-ly Guest, Con-quered un - be - lief and sad - ness, Changed our wea - ri - ness to rest.
3. Like the rain that falls from heav - en, Like the sun - light from the sky, So the Ho - ly Spir-it's giv - en, Com - ing on us from on high.
4. See, a fruit - ful field is grow - ing, Bless - ed fruit of right - eous - ness; And the streams of life are flow-ing In the lone - ly wil - der - ness.
5. What a won - der - ful sal - va - tion, When we al - ways see His face, What a per - fect hab - i - ta - tion, What a qui - et rest - ing place.

Bless - ed qui-et-ness, Ho - ly qui-et-ness, What as -

sur - ance   in   my   soul;   On the storm-y sea,   Je - sus

speaks to me,   And the bil - lows cease   to   roll.

Text: Marie P. Ferguson, c.1897
Tune: BLESSED QUIETNESS, 8 7 8 7 with refrain; W. S. Marshall, c.1897; arr. by Nolan Williams, Jr., b.1969, © 2000, GIA Publications, Inc.

375   I Must Tell Jesus

Do not worry about anything, but in everything by prayer... let your requests be made known to God.
Philippians 4:6

1. I must tell Je - sus all of my tri - als,
2. I must tell Je - sus all of my troub - les,
3. Tempt - ed and tried, I need a great Sav - ior,
4. O how the world to e - vil al - lures me!

I can - not bear these bur - dens a - lone;
He is a kind, com - pas - sion - ate Friend;
One who can help my bur - dens to bear;
O how my heart is tempt - ed to sin!

In my dis - tress He kind - ly will help me,
If I but ask Him, He will de - liv - er,
I must tell Je - sus, I must tell Je - sus,
I must tell Je - sus, and He will help me

He ev - er loves and cares for His own.
Make of my troub - les quick - ly an end.
He all my cares and sor - rows will share.
O - ver the world the vic - t'ry to win.

I must tell Je - sus! I must tell Je - sus! I can-not
bear my bur-dens a - lone; I must tell Je - sus! I must tell
Je - sus! Je - sus can help me, Je-sus a - lone.

Text: Elisha A. Hoffman, 1839-1929
Tune: ORWIGSBURG, 10 9 10 9 with refrain; Elisha A. Hoffman, 1839-1929

376 FARTHER ALONG

His disciples did not understand these things at first; but when Jesus was glorified, then they remembered...
John 12:16

1. Tempt - ed and tried we're oft made to won - der,
2. When death has come and tak - en our loved ones,
3. Faith - ful till death said our lov - ing Mas - ter,
4. When we see Je - sus com - ing in glo - ry,

Why it should be thus all the day long;
It leaves our home so lone - ly and drear;
A few more days to la - bor and wait;
When He comes from His home in the sky;

While there are oth - ers liv - ing a - bout us,
Then do we won - der why oth - ers pros - per,
Toils of the road will then seem as noth - ing,
Then we shall meet Him in that bright man - sion,

Nev - er mo - lest - ed though in the wrong.
Liv - ing so wick - ed year af - ter year.
As we sweep through the beau - ti - ful gate.
We'll un - der - stand it all by and by.

Far-ther a - long we'll know all a - bout it, Far-ther a -
long we'll un - der-stand why; Cheer up, don't wor - ry, live in the
sun - shine, We'll un - der - stand it all by and by.

Text: W. B. Stevens, fl.1937
Tune: FARTHER ALONG, 10 9 10 9 with refrain; W. B. Stevens, fl.1937; arr. J. R. Baxter, Jr.
© 1937, Stamps-Baxter Music (BMI)

377 IT IS WELL WITH MY SOUL

"Are you all right? Is your husband all right? Is the child all right?" She answered, "It is all right."
2 Kings 4:26

1. When peace, like a riv - er, at - tend - eth my
2. Though Sa - tan should buf - fet, though tri - als should
3. My sin— oh, the bliss of this glo - ri - ous
4. And Lord, haste the day when my faith shall be

way, When sor - rows, like sea bil - lows, roll; What -
come, Let this blest as - sur - ance con - trol, That
thought: My sin, not in part but the whole, Is
sight, The clouds be rolled back as a scroll, The

ev - er my lot, Thou hast taught me to say,
Christ has re - gard - ed my help - less es - tate,
nailed to the cross, and I bear it no more,
trump shall re - sound, and the Lord shall de - scend,

It is well, it is well with my soul.
And hath shed His own blood for my soul.
Praise the Lord, praise the Lord, O my soul!
"E - ven so," it is well with my soul.

It is well with my soul,

It is well with my soul,

It is well, it is well with my soul.

Text: Horatio G. Spafford, 1828-1888
Tune: VILLE DU HAVRE, 11 8 11 9 with refrain; Philip P. Bliss, 1838-1876

378 JUST A LITTLE TALK WITH JESUS

Beloved, pray for us.
1 Thessalonians 5:25

1. I once was lost in sin But Je-sus took me in,
2. Some-times my path seems drear, With-out a ray of cheer,
3. I may have doubts and fears, My eyes be filled with tears,

And then a lit-tle light from heav-en filled my soul;
And then a cloud of doubt may hide the light of day;
But Je-sus is a friend who watch-es day and night;

It bathed my heart in love And wrote my name a-bove,
The mists of sin may rise And hide the star-ry skies,
I go to Him in prayer, He knows my ev-'ry care,

And just a lit-tle talk with Je-sus made me whole.
But just a lit-tle talk with Je-sus clears the way.
And just a lit-tle talk with Je-sus makes it right.

Have a lit-tle talk with Je-sus, tell Him all a-bout our

Now let us let us

troub-les, Hear our faint-est cry,

He will and He will

an-swer by and by; Feel a lit-tle prayer wheel

Now when you

turn-ing, know a lit-tle fire is burn-ing,

and you you will

right.

Find a lit-tle talk with Je-sus makes it right, makes it right.

Text: Cleavant Derricks, b.1937
Music: JUST A LITTLE TALK, 66 12 66 12 with refrain; Cleavant Derricks, b.1937
© 1937, Stamps-Baxter Music (BMI)

379 Just When I Need Him

And my God will fully satisfy every need of yours according to His riches in glory in Christ Jesus.
Philippians 4:19

1. Just when I need Him, Je - sus is near,
2. Just when I need Him, Je - sus is true,
3. Just when I need Him, Je - sus is strong,
4. Just when I need Him, He is my all,

Just when I fal - ter, just when I fear;
Nev - er for - sak - ing all the way thro';
Bear-ing my bur - dens all the day long;
An - swer-ing when up - on Him I call;

Read - y to help me, read - y to cheer,
Giv - ing for bur - dens pleas - ures a - new,
For all my sor - row giv - ing a song,
Ten - der - ly watch - ing lest I should fall,

Just when I need Him most.

Just when I need Him most, Just when I need Him most; Je-sus is near to com-fort and cheer, Just when I need Him most.

Text: William C. Poole, 1875-1949
Tune: GABRIEL, 999 6 with refrain; Charles H. Gabriel, 1856-1932

380 TRUST AND OBEY

Blessed rather are those who hear the word of God and obey it!
Luke 11:28

1. When we walk with the Lord In the light of His
2. Not a shad-ow can rise, Not a cloud in the
3. Not a bur-den we bear, Not a sor-row we
4. But we nev-er can prove The de-lights of His
5. Then in fel-low-ship sweet We will sit at His

Word, What a glo-ry He sheds on our way! While we
skies, But His smile quick-ly drives it a-way; Not a
share, But our toil He doth rich-ly re-pay; Not a
love Un-til all on the al-tar we lay, For the
feet, Or we'll walk by His side in the way; What He

do His good will He a-bides with us
doubt nor a fear, Not a sigh nor a
grief nor a loss, Not a frown nor a
fa-vor He shows And the joy He be-
says we will do, Where He sends we will

still, And with all who will trust and o-bey.
tear, Can a-bide while we trust and o-bey.
cross, But is blest if we trust and o-bey.
stows Are for those who will trust and o-bey.
go— Nev-er fear, on-ly trust and o-bey.

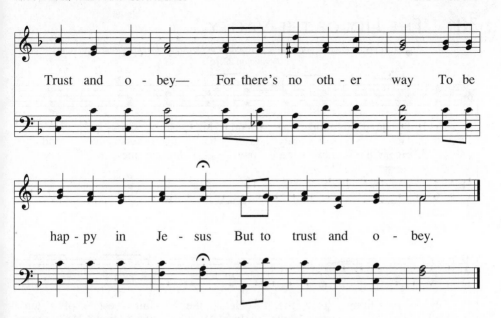

Trust and o - bey— For there's no oth - er way To be

hap - py in Je - sus But to trust and o - bey.

Text: John H. Sammis, 1846-1919
Tune: TRUST AND OBEY, 66 9 D with refrain, Daniel B. Towner, 1850-1919

381 THE LILY OF THE VALLEY

It is I, Jesus... I am the root and the descendant of David, the bright morning star.
Revelation 22:16

1. I have found a friend in Je - sus— He's
2. He all my grief has tak - en and
3. He will nev - er, nev - er leave me nor

ev - 'ry - thing to me, He's the fair - est of ten
all my sor - rows borne, In temp - ta - tion He's my
yet for - sake me here, While I live by faith and

thou - sand to my soul; The Lil - y of the
strong and might - y tow'r; I have all for Him for -
do His bless - ed will; A wall of fire a -

Refrain: Lil - y of the

Val - ley— in Him a - lone I see All I
sak - en and all my i - dols torn From my
bout me, I've noth - ing now to fear— With His

Val - ley, the Bright and Morn - ing Star, He's the

need   to   cleanse and   make   me   ful - ly   whole.
heart, and   now   He   keeps   me   by   His   pow'r.
man - na   He   my   hun - gry   soul   shall   fill.

great - est   of   ten   thou - sand   to   my   soul.

In   sor - row He's my com - fort,   in   trou - ble He's my stay,
Tho'   all   the world for-sake me   and   Sa - tan tempt me sore,
Then sweep-ing   up   to   glo - ry   I'll   see His bless - ed face,

D.S.

He   tells me ev - 'ry care   on Him to   roll;   He's the
Thru   Je - sus   I shall safe - ly reach the   goal;   He's the
Where riv - ers   of   de - light shall ev - er   roll;   He's the

Hal - le - lu - jah!

Text: Charles W. Fry, 1837-1882
Tune: SALVATIONIST, Irregular; William S. Hays, 1837-1907; adapt. by Charles W. Fry, 1837-1882

382 JESUS IS ALL THE WORLD TO ME

For to me, living is Christ and dying is gain.
Philippians 1:21

1. Je - sus is all the world to me, My life, my joy, my
2. Je - sus is all the world to me, My friend in tri - als
3. Je - sus is all the world to me, And true to Him I'll
4. Je - sus is all the world to me, I want no bet - ter

all; He is my strength from day to day, With -
sore; I go to Him for bless - ings, and He
be; Oh, how could I this friend de - ny, When
friend; I trust Him now, I'll trust Him when Life's

out Him I would fall: When I am sad, to
gives them o'er and o'er: He sends the sun - shine
He's so true to me? Fol - low - ing Him I
fleet - ing days shall end: Beau - ti - ful life with

Him I go, No oth - er one can cheer me so;
and the rain, He sends the har - vest's gold - en grain;
know I'm right, He watch - es o'er me day and night;
such a friend, Beau - ti - ful life that has no end;

When I am sad, He makes me glad, He's my friend.
Sun - shine and rain, har - vest of grain, He's my friend.
Fol - low - ing Him by day and night, He's my friend.
E - ter - nal life, e - ter - nal joy, He's my friend.

Text: Will L. Thompson, 1847-1909
Tune: ALL THE WORLD, 8 6 8 6 88 8 3; Will L. Thompson, 1847-1909

383 I Can Do All Things through Christ

I can do all things through Him who strengthens me.
Philippians 4:13

me,   strength - ens   me.

Text: Elbernita "Twinkie" Clark
Tune: Elbernita "Twinkie" Clark

384 Can't Nobody Do Me Like Jesus

But by the grace of God I am what I am, and His grace toward me has not been in vain.
1 Corinthians 15:10

1. Can't no - bod - y
2. Healed my bod - y;
3. Picked me up and

do me like Je - sus.
told me to run on.
turned me a - round. Oh,

Can't no -
Healed my
Picked me

bod - y
bod - y;
up and

do me like the Lord.
told me to run.
turned me a - round.

Can't no-bod - y / do me like Je - sus.
Healed my bod - y; / told me to run on.
Picked me up and / turned me a - round. Oh,

He's my friend!

He's my friend!

Text: Andraé Crouch, b.1945
Tune: HEALING, 9 9 9 3; Andraé Crouch, b.1945; arr. by Nolan Williams, Jr., b.1969
© 1982, Bud John Songs, Inc. (ASCAP)

385 THE SOLID ROCK

...For they drank from the spiritual rock that followed them, and the rock was Christ.
1 Corinthians 10:4

1. My hope is built on noth-ing less Than Je-sus' blood and
2. When dark-ness veils His love-ly face, I rest on His un-
3. His oath, His cov-e-nant, His blood Sup-port me in o'er-
4. When He shall come with trum-pet sound, O may I then in

right-eous-ness; I dare not trust the sweet-est frame, But
chang-ing grace; In ev-'ry high and storm-y gale My
whelm-ing floods; When all a-round my soul gives way, He
Him be found, Dressed in His right-eous-ness a-lone, Fault-

whol-ly lean on Je-sus' name.
an-chor holds with-in the veil.
then is all my hope and stay. On Christ, the sol-id Rock, I stand—
less to stand be-fore the throne.

All oth-er ground is sink-ing sand, All oth-er ground is sink-ing sand.

Text: Edward Mote, 1797-1874
Tune: SOLID ROCK, LM with refrain; William B. Bradbury, 1816-1868

I'VE BEEN 'BUKED 386

My friends scorn me; my eye pours out tears to God.
Job 16:20

1. I've been 'buked an' I've been scorned,
2. Dere is troub-le all o-ver dis worl',
3. Ain' gwine lay my 'li - gion down,

I've been 'buked an' I've been scorned, chil - dren;
Dere is troub-le all o-ver dis worl', chil - dren;
Ain' gwine lay my 'li - gion down, chil - dren;

I've been 'buked an' I've been scorned,
Dere is troub - le all o - ver dis worl',
Ain' gwine lay my 'li - gion down,

I've been talked a - bout sho's you' born.
Dere is troub - le all o - ver dis worl'.
Ain' gwine lay my 'li - gion down.

Text: Traditional
Tune: I'VE BEEN 'BUKED, 7 9 7 8; Negro spiritual; arr. by Carl Haywood, b.1949, from *The Haywood Collection of Negro Spirituals,* © 1992

387 I Am Thine

Know that the LORD is God. It is He that made us... we are His people, and the sheep of His pasture.
Psalm 100:3

1. I am Thine, O Lord, I have heard Thy voice, And it
2. Con - se - crate me now to Thy serv - ice, Lord, By the
3. O, the pure de - light of a sin - gle hour That be -
4. There are depths of love that I can - not know Till I

told Thy love to me; But I long to rise in the
pow'r of grace di - vine; Let my soul look up with a
fore Thy throne I spend, When I kneel in prayer, and with
cross the nar - row sea; There are heights of joy that I

arms of faith, And be clos - er drawn to Thee.
stead - fast hope, And my will be lost in Thine.
Thee, my God, I com - mune as friend with friend!
may not reach Till I rest in peace with Thee.

near - er,

Draw me near - er, near - er, near - er, bless - ed Lord, To the

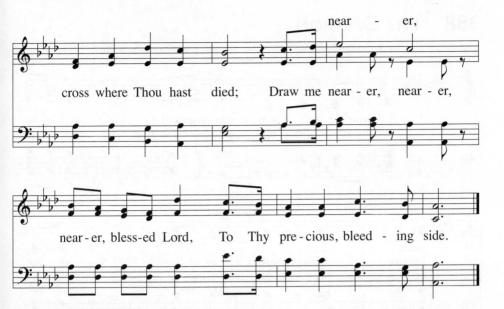

cross where Thou hast died; Draw me near-er, near-er,

near-er, bless-ed Lord, To Thy pre-cious, bleed-ing side.

Text: Fanny J. Crosby, 1820-1915
Tune: I AM THINE, 10 7 10 7 with refrain; William H. Doane, 1832-1915

388 THE DECISION

...I have set before you life and death, blessings and curses. Choose life...
Deuteronomy 30:19

It's your de - ci - sion who you will live for. Will it be
cid - ed who I will live for. I chose

Je - sus or some oth - er god? Since He de -
Je - sus as my Lord and King; Oh, He de -

cid - ed to die just to save you, it's your de -
cid - ed to die just to save me, I have de -

ci - sion, what will you do? Oh, I've de -
cid - ed to live for Him.

It's a priv - i - lege to live for

Je - sus; get-ting to know Him makes my life worth-while.

He fills my emp - ti-ness with peace and

hap - pi-ness. I have de - cid - ed, have you de -

cid - ed? I have de - cid - ed to live for Him.

Text: V. Michael McKay
Tune: V. Michael McKay
© 1992, Schaff Music Publishing Co.

389 WHAT SHALL I RENDER

What shall I return to the LORD for all His bounty to me?
Psalm 116:12

1. What shall I ren-der un-to God for all His
2. All I can ren-der is my bod-y and my

bless-ings? What shall I ren-der, (Tell me)
soul. That's all I can ren-der. That's

What shall I give?
all I can give.

God has ev-'ry-thing; Ev-'ry-thing be-longs to Him.

God has ev-'ry-thing; Ev-'ry-thing be-longs to Him.

What shall I ren - der, Tell me what shall I give?
All I can ren - der, That's all I can give.

Text: Margaret Pleasant Douroux, b.1941, © 1975
Tune: Margaret Pleasant Douroux, b.1941, © 1975; arr. by Stephen Key, © 2000, GIA Publications, Inc.

390 ACCEPTABLE TO YOU

Let the words of my mouth and the meditation of my heart be acceptable to You, O LORD...
Psalm 19:14

Let the words of my mouth and the med-i-ta-tion of my

heart be ac-cept-a-ble in Thy sight. Let the

cept-a-ble Lord, to Thee. Here I am, Lord,

at Your feet, Lord, My soul looks up to

Thee; Make my thoughts, Lord, and my

tongue, Lord, ac - cept - a - ble to Thee.

Text: Eli Wilson, Jr.
Tune: Eli Wilson, Jr.
© 1989, Eli Wilson, Jr.

391 I WILL TRUST IN THE LORD

In God, whose word I praise, in God I trust; I am not afraid; what can flesh do to me?
Psalm 56:4

1. I will trust in the Lord, I will
2. I'm gon - na treat ev - 'ry-bod - y right, I'm gon - na
3. I'm gon - na stay on the bat - tle - field, I'm gon - na
4. I'm gon - na stay on ɣ bend - ed knee, I'm gon - na

trust in the Lord, I will
treat ev - 'ry-bod - y right, I'm gon - na
stay on the bat - tle - field, I'm gon - na
stay on bend - ed knee, I'm gon - na

trust in the Lord till I die.
treat ev - 'ry-bod - y right till I die.
stay on the bat - tle - field till I die.
stay on ɣ bend - ed knee till I die.

I will trust in the Lord, I will
I'm gon-na treat ev-'ry-bod-y right, I'm gon-na
I'm gon-na stay on the bat-tle-field, I'm gon-na
I'm gon-na stay on bend-ed knee, I'm gon-na

trust in the Lord, I will
treat ev-'ry-bod-y right, I'm gon-na
stay on the bat-tle-field, I'm gon-na
stay on bend-ed knee, I'm gon-na

trust in the Lord till I die.
treat ev-'ry-bod-y right till I die.
stay on the bat-tle-field till I die.
stay on bend-ed knee till I die.

Alternate lyrics:
Father, I stretch my hands to Thee;
No other help I know.
If Thou withdraw Thyself from me,
O whither shall I go?

Text: Negro spiritual
Tune: TRUST IN THE LORD, Irregular; Negro spiritual; arr. by Jeffrey Radford and Nolan Williams, Jr., b.1969, © 2000, GIA Publications, Inc.

392 I'd Rather Have Jesus

I regard everything as loss because of the surpassing value of knowing Christ Jesus my Lord.
Philippians 3:8

1. I'd rath - er have Je - sus than sil - ver or gold, I'd
2. I'd rath - er have Je - sus than your ap - plause, I'd
3. He's fair - er than lil - ies of rar - est bloom, He's

rath - er be His than have rich - es un - told; I'd
rath - er be faith - ful to His dear cause; I'd
sweet - er than hon - ey from out the comb; He's

rath - er have Je - sus than hous - es or lands, I'd
rath - er have Je - sus than world - wide fame, I'd
all that my hun - ger - ing spir - it needs, I'd

rath - er be led by His nail - pierced hand.
rath - er be true to His ho - ly name.
rath - er have Je - sus and let Him lead.

Than to be the king of a vast do - main Or be held in
sin's dread sway; I'd rath - er have Je - sus than
an - y - thing This world af - fords to - day.

Text: Rhea Miller, 1894-1966, © 1922, renewed 1950, Word Music, Inc. (ASCAP)
Tune: I'D RATHER HAVE JESUS, 11 11 11 10 with refrain; George Beverly Shea, b.1909, © 1939, renewed 1966, Word Music, Inc. (ASCAP)

393   IS YOUR ALL ON THE ALTAR

...present your bodies as a living sacrifice, holy and acceptable to God, which is your spiritual worship.
Romans 12:1

1. You have longed for sweet peace, And for faith to in-
2. Would you walk with the Lord In the light of His
3. O we nev - er can know What the Lord will be-
4. Who can tell all the love He will send from a-

crease, And have ear - nest - ly, fer - vent - ly prayed.
Word, And have peace and con - tent - ment al - way?
stow Of the bless - ings for which we have prayed,
bove, And how hap - py our hearts will be made,

But you can - not have rest, Or be per - fect - ly
You must do His sweet will To be free from all
Till our bod - y and soul He doth ful - ly con-
Of the fel - low - ship sweet We shall share at His

blest, Un - til all on the al - tar is laid.
ill— On the al - tar your all you must lay.
trol, And our all on the al - tar is laid.
feet When our all on the al - tar is laid!

Is your all on the al-tar of sac - ri-fice laid? Your

heart does the Spir-it con - trol? You can

on - ly be blest, And have peace and sweet rest,

As you yield Him your bod - y and soul.

Text: Elisha A. Hoffman, 1839-1929
Tune: YOUR ALL, 66 9 D with refrain; Elisha A. Hoffman, 1839-1929; arr. by Nolan Williams, Jr., b.1969, © 2000, GIA Publications, Inc.

394 I Love the Lord, He Heard My Cry

Hear my cry, O God; listen to my prayer. From the end of the earth I call to You...
Psalm 61:1-2

Slow, very free (ad lib.)

1. I love the Lord, He heard my cry!

I love the Lord a- He a-heard my cry! And pit-ied ev-'ry groan,

an and pit - ied ev - 'ry groan.

2. As long as I live when troub-le rise,

Long as I

live   a - when   uh-troub   -

le   rise,   *Leader:* I'll has - ten to His   throne,

I   a - has   -

gliss. ten   to   His,   His   throne.

Text: African-American traditional
Tune: Meter hymn, anonymous; lined out by M. Adams and Louis Sykes, © 2000, GIA Publications, Inc.

395 I Love the Lord, He Heard My Cry

Hear my cry, O God; listen to my prayer. From the end of the earth I call to You...
Psalm 61:1-2

I love the Lord, He heard my cry; And pit-ied ev-'ry groan. Long as I

live,   while troub-les rise,   I'll has-ten to

His throne.   I love the

throne. I'll has - ten to His

throne. I'll has - ten to His throne.

Text: Richard Smallwood, © 1990, Century Oak/Richwood Music
Tune: Richard Smallwood, © 1990, Century Oak/Richwood Music; arr. by Nolan Williams, Jr., b.1969, © 2000, GIA Publications, Inc.

I SURRENDER ALL 396

...there is no one who has left house or wife or brothers... who will not get back very much more in this age.
Luke 18:29-30

1. All to Je - sus I sur - ren - der,
   I will ev - er love and trust Him,
2. All to Je - sus I sur - ren - der,
   World - ly pleas - ures all for - sak - en,
3. All to Je - sus I sur - ren - der,
   Fill me with Thy Ho - ly Spir - it—
4. All to Je - sus I sur - ren - der,
   Fill me with Thy love and pow - er,

All to Him I free - ly give;
In His pres - ence dai - ly live.
Hum - bly at His feet I bow;
Take me, Je - sus, take me now.
Make me, Sav - ior, whol - ly Thine;
Tru - ly know that Thou art mine.
Lord, I give my - self to Thee;
Let Thy bless - ings fall on me.

I sur-ren-der all, I sur-ren-der all.
I sur-ren-der all, I sur-ren-der all.

All to Thee, my bless - ed Sav - ior, I sur-ren - der all.

Text: Judson W. Van De Venter, 1855-1939
Tune: SURRENDER, 8 7 8 7 with refrain; Winfield S. Weeden, 1847-1908

397 NOTHING BETWEEN

The grace of God has appeared, bringing salvation to all, training us to renounce impiety and worldly passions...
Titus 2:11-12

1. Noth - ing   be - tween   my   soul   and   the   Sav - ior,
2. Noth - ing   be - tween,   like   world - ly   pleas - ure:
3. Noth - ing   be - tween,   like   pride   or   sta - tion:
4. Noth - ing   be - tween,   e'en   man - y   hard   tri - als,

Naught   of   this   world's   de - lu - sive   dream:
Hab - its   of   life,   though   harm - less   they   seem,
Self   or   friends   shall   not   in - ter - vene;
Though the   whole   world   a - gainst   me   con - vene;

I   have   re - nounced   all   sin - ful   pleas - ure—
Must   not   my   heart   from   Him   ev - er   sev - er—
Though   it   may   cost   me   much   trib - u - la - tion,
Watch-ing   with   prayer   and   much   self - de - ni - al—

Je - sus   is   mine!   There's   noth - ing   be - tween.
He   is   my   all!   There's   noth - ing   be - tween.
I   am   re - solved!   There's   noth - ing   be - tween.
Tri - umph   at   last,   with   noth - ing   be - tween!

Noth-ing be-tween my soul and the Sav-ior, So that His bless-ed face may be seen; Noth-ing pre-vent-ing the least of His fa-vor: Keep the way clear! Let noth-ing be-tween.

Text: Charles A. Tindley, 1851-1933
Tune: NOTHING BETWEEN, 10 9 10 9 with refrain; Charles A. Tindley, 1851-1933; arr. by Don Peterman

398   In Christ There Is No East or West

There is no longer Jew or Greek... male and female; for all of you are one in Christ Jesus.
Galatians 3:28

1. In Christ there is no east or west, In
2. In Him shall true hearts ev-'ry-where Their
3. Join hands then, broth-ers of the faith, What-
4. In Christ now meet both east and west, In

Him no south or north, But one great fel-low-
high com-mun-ion find; His serv-ice is the
e'er your race may be; Who serves my Fa-ther
Him meet south and north; All Christ-ly souls are

ship of love Through-out the whole wide earth.
gold-en cord Close-bind-ing all man-kind.
as a son Is sure-ly kin to me.
one in Him Through-out the whole wide earth.

Text: Galatians 3:28; John Oxenham, 1852-1941
Tune: ST. PETER, CM; Alexander R. Reinagle, 1799-1877

IN CHRIST THERE IS NO EAST OR WEST 399

There is no longer Jew or Greek... male and female; for all of you are one in Christ Jesus.
Galatians 3:28

1. In Christ there is no east or west, In Him no south or north, But one great fellowship of love Throughout the whole wide earth.

2. In Him shall true hearts ev-'ry-where Their high com-mun-ion find; His serv-ice is the gold-en cord Close-bind-ing all man-kind.

3. Join hands then, broth-ers of the faith, What-e'er your race may be! Who serve my Fa-ther as a son Is sure-ly kin to me.

4. In Christ now meet both east and west, In Him meet south and north, All Christ-ly souls are one in Him, Through-out the whole wide earth.

Text: Galatians 3:28; John Oxenham, 1852-1941
Tune: MC KEE, CM; African-American; adapt. by Harry T. Burleigh, 1866-1949

400 I Have Decided to Follow Jesus

A scribe then approached and said, "Teacher, I will follow You wherever You go."
Matthew 8:19

1. I have de-cid-ed to fol-low Je-sus,
2. Though no one join me, still I will fol-low,
3. The world be-hind me, the cross be-fore me,

I have de-cid-ed to fol-low Je-sus,
Though no one join me, still I will fol-low,
The world be-hind me, the cross be-fore me,

I have de-cid-ed to fol-low Je-sus—
Though no one join me, still I will fol-low—
The world be-hind me, the cross be-fore me—

No turn-ing back, no turn-ing back!
no turn-ing back,

Text: Ascribed to an Indian prince; as sung in Garo, Assam
Tune: ASSAM, 10 10 10 8; Indian Folk melody, Paul B. Smith; harm. by Norman Johnson

Jesu Tawa Pano / Jesus, We Are Here 401

Even though I must die with You, I will not deny You.
Mark 14:31

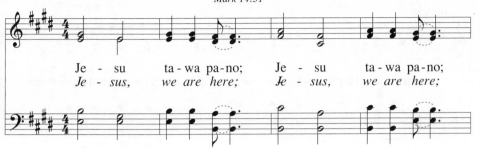

> Je - su ta - wa pa - no; Je - su ta - wa pa - no;
> *Je - sus, we are here; Je - sus, we are here;*

Solo: *Mam-bo Je - su.

> Je - su ta - wa pa - no; ta - wa pa - no, mu zi - ta re - nyu.
> *Je - sus, we are here; we are here for You.*

*Omit last time

African Phonetics:
Yay-zoo tah-wah pah-no
tah-wah pah-no, moo zee-tah ray-noo

Text: Zimbabwean; Patrick Matsikenyiri
Tune: Patrick Matsikenyiri
© 1990, Patrick Matsikenyiri

402 WALKING UP THE KING'S HIGHWAY

Blessed are the pure in heart, for they will see God.
Matthew 5:8

Refrain

It's a high - way to heav - en, none can walk up there but the pure in heart. It's a high - way to heav - en, I am walk - ing up the King's High - way.

Verses

1. My way gets bright - er, my load gets light - er
2. Don't have to wor - ry, don't have to hur - ry
3. If you're not walk - ing, start while I'm talk - ing

Walk-ing up the King's High - way. There's joy in know-ing
Christ walks be - side me,
There'll be a bless-ing

with Him I'm go - ing,
an - gels to guide me, Walk-ing up the King's High - way.
you'll be pos - sess - ing,

D.C.

Text: Mary Gardner and Thomas A. Dorsey
Tune: KING'S HIGHWAY, 55 7 55 7 with refrain; arr. by Mary Gardner and Thomas A. Dorsey
© 1940 (renewed) Warner-Tamerlane Publishing Corp. and Unichappell Music Inc.

403 How Tedious and Tasteless the Hours

...the people wander like sheep; they suffer for lack of a shepherd.
Zechariah 10:2

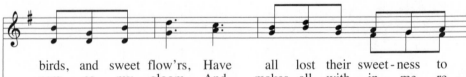

1. How te - dious and taste - less the hours When
2. His name yields the rich - est per - fume, And
3. Con - tent with be - hold - ing His face, My
4. Dear Lord, if in - deed I am Thine, If

Je - sus no long - er I see! Sweet pros - pects, sweet
sweet - er than mu - sic His voice; His pres - ence dis -
all to His pleas - ure re - signed, No chang - es of
Thou art my sun and my song, Say, why do I

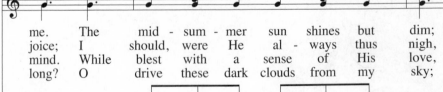

birds, and sweet flow'rs, Have all lost their sweet - ness to
pers - es my gloom, And makes all with - in me re -
sea - son or place Would make an - y change in my
lan - guish and pine? And why are my win - ters so

me. The mid - sum - mer sun shines but dim;
joice; I should, were He al - ways thus nigh,
mind. While blest with a sense of His love,
long? O drive these dark clouds from my sky;

The fields strive in vain to look gay; But
Have noth - ing to wish or to fear; No
A pal - ace a toy would ap - pear; And
Thy soul - cheer - ing pres - ence re - store; Or

when I am hap - py in Him, De -
mor - tal so hap - py as I; My
pris - ons would pal - a - ces prove, If
take me un - to Thee on high, Where

cem - ber's as pleas - ant as May.
sum - mer would last all the year.
Je - sus would dwell with me there.
win - ter and clouds are no more.

Text: John Newton, 1725-1807
Tune: DE FLEURY, LMD; German melody

404 HOLD TO GOD'S UNCHANGING HAND

Jesus Christ is the same yesterday and today and forever.
Hebrews 13:8

1. Time is filled with swift tran - si - tion.
2. Trust in Him who will not leave you.
3. Cov - et not this world's vain rich - es
4. When your jour - ney is com - plet - ed,

Naught of earth un - moved can stand.
What - so - ev - er years may bring.
That so rap - id - ly de - cay.
If to God you have been true,

Build your hopes on things e - ter - nal.
If by earth - ly friends for - sak - en,
Seek to gain the heav'n - ly treas - ures.
Fair and bright the home in Glo - ry

Hold to God's un - chang - ing hand.
Still more close - ly to Him cling.
They will nev - er pass a - way.
Your en - rap - tured soul will view.

Hold to His hand, God's un-chang-ing hand.

Hold to His hand, God's un-chang-ing hand.

Build your hopes on things e - ter - nal.

Hold to God's un - chang - ing hand.

Text: Jennie Wilson
Tune: UNCHANGING HAND, 8 7 8 7 with refrain; F.L. Eiland; arr. by Stephen Key, © 2000, GIA Publications, Inc.

405 KEEP HOPE ALIVE

But if we hope for what we do not see, we wait for it with patience.
Romans 8:25

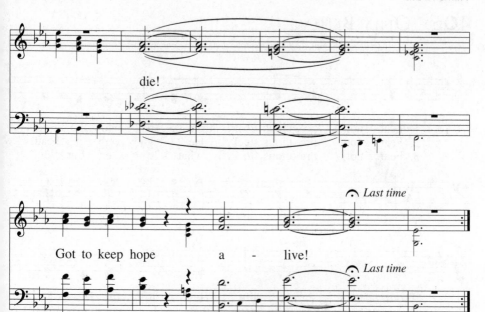

die!

Got to keep hope   a - live!

Last time

Last time

Text: Donald Vails, ©
Tune: Donald Vails, ©; arr. by Nolan Williams, Jr., b.1969, © 2000, GIA Publications, Inc.

406 ONLY BELIEVE

Jesus said to him, "All things can be done for the one who believes."
Mark 9:23

1. Fear not, pre-cious flock, from the cross to the throne,
2. Fear not, pre-cious flock, He go - eth a - head,
3. Fear not, pre-cious flock, what - ev - er your lot;

From death in - to life He went for His own;
Your Shep - herd se - lects the path you must tread;
He en - ters all rooms, "the doors be - ing shut."

All pow - er in earth, all pow - er a - bove,
The wa - ters of Ma - ra He'll sweet - en for thee—
He nev - er for - sakes, He nev - er is gone—

Is giv - en to Him for the flock of His love.
He drank all the bit - ter in Geth - sem - a - ne.
So count on His pres - ence in dark - ness and dawn.

On - ly be - lieve, on - ly be - lieve;

All things are pos - si - ble, on - ly be - lieve;

On - ly be - lieve, on - ly be - lieve;

All things are pos - si - ble, on - ly be - lieve.

Text: Paul Rader, 1879-1938
Tune: ONLY BELIEVE, 10 10 10 11 with refrain; Paul Rader, 1879-1938

407 WE WON'T LEAVE HERE LIKE WE CAME

You who have made me see many troubles and calamities will revive me again...
Psalm 71:20

*We won't leave here like *we came, in Je-sus' name.

Bound, op-pressed, af-flict-ed, sick or lame.

For the Spir-it of the Lord is still the same.

We won't leave here like we came, in Je-sus' name.

*You, I

O HOLY SAVIOR 408

For I am the LORD your God, the Holy One of Israel, your Savior.
Isaiah 43:3

1. O ho - ly Sav - ior! Friend un -
2. What though the world de - ceit - ful
3. Though faith and hope a - while be

seen, Since on Thine arm Thou bid'st me
prove, And earth - ly friends and joys re -
tried, I ask not, need not aught be -

lean, Help me, through - out life's chang - ing
move? With pa - tient, un - com - plain - ing
side: How safe, how calm, how sat - is -

scene, By faith to cling to Thee!
love Still I would cling to Thee.
fied, The souls that cling to Thee.

Text: Charlotte Elliott, 1789-1871
Tune: HOLY SAVIOR, 888 6; Ulysses Elam; arr. by Robert Nathaniel Dett, 1882-1943, © 1936 (renewed), Paul A. Schmitt Music Co., c/o
Belwin-Mills Publishing Corp.

409 FAITH OF OUR FATHERS

...contend for the faith that was once for all entrusted to the saints.
Jude 3

1. Faith of our fa - thers! liv - ing still
2. Our fa - thers, chained in pris - ons dark,
3. Faith of our fa - thers! we will love

In spite of dun - geon, fire and sword:
Were still in heart and con - science free:
Both friend and foe in all our strife:

O how our hearts beat high with joy
How sweet would be their chil - dren's fate,
And preach thee, too, as love knows how,

When - e'er we hear that glo - rious word!
If they, like them, could die for thee!
By kind - ly words and vir - tuous life:

Faith of our fa - thers, ho - ly faith!

We will be true to thee till death!

Text: Frederick William Faber, 1814-1863
Tune: ST. CATHERINE, 8 8 8 8 8 8; Henri Frederick Hemy, 1818-1888

410 FAITH OF OUR MOTHERS

I am reminded of your sincere faith, a faith that lived first in your grandmother Lois and your mother Eunice...
2 Timothy 1:5

1. Faith of our moth - ers, liv - ing yet
2. Faith of our moth - ers, lav - ish faith,
3. Faith of our moth - ers, guid - ing faith,
4. Faith of our moth - ers, Chris - tian faith,

In cra - dle song and bed - time prayer,
The fount of child - hood's trust and grace,
For youth - ful long - ing— youth - ful doubt,
In truth be - yond our man - made creeds,

In nur - s'ry love and fire - side love,
O may thy con - se - cra - tion prove
How blurred our vi - sion, blind our way,
Still serve the home and save the church,

Thy pres - ence still per - vades the air:
The well - spring of a no - bler race:
Thy prov - i - den - tial care with - out:
And breathe thy spir - it through our deeds:

Faith of our moth - ers, liv - ing faith,
Faith of our moth - ers, lav - ish faith,
Faith of our moth - ers, guid - ing faith,
Faith of our moth - ers, Chris - tian faith,

We will be true to thee till death.
We will be true to thee till death.
We will be true to thee till death.
We will be true to thee till death.

Text: A. B. Patten, 20th C.
Tune: ST. CATHERINE, 8 8 8 8 8 8; Henri Frederick Hemy, 1818-1888

411 THERE'S A BRIGHT SIDE SOMEWHERE

The city has no need of sun or moon to shine on it, for the glory of God is its light, and its lamp is the Lamb.
Revelation 21:23

Chorus

There's a bright side some - where, there's a

bright side some - where. Don't you

rest un - til you find it. There's a

bright side some - where.

Special Chorus

When your way seems dark and dreer, don't have to wor-ry cause

God is near. If in your heart there is no song,

just keep the faith and keep hold-ing on.

Turn your plate down, fast and pray. Je-sus will al-ways make a

way. There's a bright side some-where.

Text: Margaret Jenkins, ©
Tune: Margaret Jenkins, ©; arr. by Joseph Joubert, © 2000, GIA Publications, Inc.

412 We've Come This Far by Faith

For we walk by faith, not by sight.
2 Corinthians 5:7

We've come this far by faith, Lean-ing on the Lord; Trust-ing in His ho-ly word, He's nev-er failed me yet. Oh can't turn a-round, We've come this far by faith.

Verse 1

1. Don't be dis-cour-aged when trou-ble's in your life, He'll bear your bur - dens and move all mis - er - y and strife. That's why we've

2. Just the other day I heard someone say
   He didn't believe in God's word;
   But I can truly say that God had made a way,
   And He's never failed me yet.
   That's why we've...

413 HE'LL UNDERSTAND AND SAY "WELL DONE"

I have fought the good fight... I have kept the faith. From now on there is reserved for me the crown of righteousness...
2 Timothy 4:7-8

1. If when you give the best of your serv - ice,
2. Mis - un - der - stood, the Sav - ior of sin - ners,
3. If when this life of la - bor is end - ed,
4. But if you try and fail in your try - ing,

Tell - ing the world that the Sav - ior is come;
Hung on the cross; He was God's on - ly Son;
And the re - ward of the race you have run;
Hands sore and scarred from the work you've be - gun;

Be not dis - mayed when men don't be - lieve you;
Oh! hear Him call - ing His Fa - ther in Heav'n,
Oh! the sweet rest pre - pared for the faith - ful
Take up your cross, run quick - ly to meet Him;

He'll un - der - stand; and say, "Well done."
"Not my will, but Thine be done."
Will be His blest and fi - nal "Well done."
He'll un - der - stand, and say, "Well done."

Oh, when I come to the end of my jour - ney,

Wea - ry of life and the bat - tle is won; Car - ry - ing the staff and the

cross of re - demp - tion, He'll un - der - stand and say, "Well done."

Text: Lucie E. Campbell, 1885-1963
Tune: WELL DONE, 10 10 10 8 with refrain; Lucie E. Campbell, 1885-1963; arr. by Evelyn Simpson-Curenton, b.1953, © 2000, GIA
    Publications, Inc.

414 I Don't Feel No Ways Tired

We are afflicted in every way, but not crushed... persecuted, but not forsaken; struck down, but not destroyed.
2 Corinthians 4:8-9

I don't feel no ways tired

I've come too far from where I've start - ed from.

No-bod-y told me that the road would be eas-y. I

don't be-lieve He brought me this far to leave me.

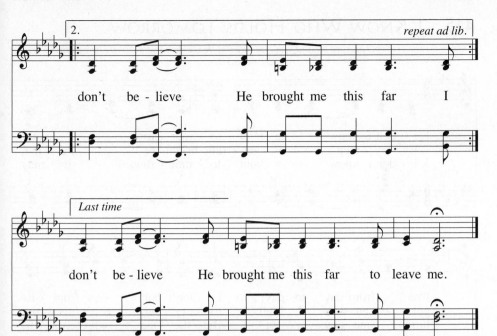

don't be - lieve He brought me this far I

don't be - lieve He brought me this far to leave me.

Text: Curtis Burrell, © 1978, 1984, Savgos Music, Inc.
Tune: Curtis Burrell, © 1978, 1984, Savgos Music, Inc.; arr. by Stephen Key and Nolan Williams Jr., b.1969, © 2000, GIA Publications, Inc.

415 I Know Who Holds Tomorrow

...I know the one in whom I have put my trust, and I am sure that He is able to guard... what I have entrusted to Him.
2 Timothy 1:12

1. I don't know a-bout to-mor-row, I just
2. Ev-'ry step is get-ting bright-er As the
3. I don't know a-bout to-mor-row, It may

live from day to day; I don't bor-row from its
gold-en stairs I climb; Ev-'ry bur-den's get-ting
bring me pov-er-ty; But the One who feeds the

sun-shine, For its skies may turn to gray. I don't
light-er, Ev-'ry cloud is sil-ver lined. There the
spar-row, Is the One who stands by me. And the

wor-ry o'er the fu-ture, For I
sun is al-ways shin-ing, There no
path that is my por-tion, May be

know   what   Je - sus said;   And to - day   I'll   walk   be -
tear   will   dim   the   eye,   At   the   end - ing   of   the
through the   flame   or flood;   But   His   pres - ence goes be -

side   Him,   For   He   knows   what   is   a - head.
rain - bow,   Where   the   moun - tains touch the   sky.
fore   me,   And   I'm   cov   -   ered   with   His blood.

Man - y   things   a - bout   to - mor - row   I   don't

seem   to un - der-stand;   But   I   know   who holds to -

mor - row,   And   I   know   who holds my   hand.

Text: Ira F. Stamphill, b.1914
Tune: TOMORROW, 8 7 8 7 D with refrain; Ira F. Stamphill, b.1914; arr. by Evelyn Simpson-Curenton, b.1953
© 1950, Singspiration Music (ASCAP)

416 It's in My Heart

...be filled with the Spirit, as you sing psalms and hymns... singing and making melody to the Lord in your hearts.
Ephesians 5:18-19

1. Tho' some may sing to pass the wea - ry night a -
2. You ask me why I know His blood can cleanse a -
3. You ask me how I find the time to read and
4. I may not know the skill - ful use of tongue or

long, Tho' some may sing to en - ter - tain a world - ly
lone, You ask me why I know He sits up - on the
pray, You ask me how I smile when things are far from
pen, To prove my Lord's re - turn to un - be - liev - ing

throng, (a world - ly throng,) I sing be - cause I wor - ship
throne, (up - on the throne,) And why I know He chose me
gay, (are far from gay,) And how I sing His prais - es,
men, (un - b'liev - ing men,) But this I know, He's com - ing

God in song,
for His own,
come what may,   It's in my heart, It's in my heart.
back a - gain,

Text: Arthur Slater, b.1941
Tune: IT'S IN MY HEART, 12 12 10 8 with refrain; Arthur Slater, b.1941; arr. by J. G. Boersma

417 It's Real

Have you believed because you have seen me? Blessed are those who have not seen and yet have come to believe.
John 20:29

1. O how well do I re-mem-ber how I doubt-ed day by day, For I did not know for cer-tain that my sins were washed a-way; When the Spir-it tried to tell me, I would

2. When the truth came close and search-ing, all my joy would dis-ap-pear. For I did not have the wit-ness of the Spir-it bright and clear; If at times the com-ing judg-ment would ap-

3. But at last I tired of liv-ing such a life of fear and doubt. For I want-ed God to give me some-thing I would know a-bout; So the truth would make me hap-py, and the

4. So I prayed to God in ear-nest, and not car-ing what folks said. I was hun-gry for the bless-ing; my poor soul it must be fed; When at last by faith I touched Him, and, like

not the truth re - ceive. I en - deav - ored to be
pear be - fore my mind, O it made me so un -
light would clear - ly shine, And the Spir - it gave as -
sparks from smit - ten steel, Just so quick sal - va - tion

hap - py, and to make my - self be - lieve.
eas - y, for God's smile I could not find.
sur - ance that I'm His and He is mine.
reached me; O bless God, I know it's real!

But it's real, it's real, O I know it's real; Praise
it's real, I know

God, the doubts are set - tled, For I know, I know it's real.

Text: H. L. Cox, b.1907
Tune: IT'S REAL, 15 15 15 15 with refrain; H. L. Cox, b.1907

418 WE'LL UNDERSTAND IT BETTER BY AND BY

For now we see in a mirror, dimly, but then we will see face to face. Now I know only in part; then I will know fully...
1 Corinthians 13:12

1. We are of-ten tossed and driv'n On the rest-less
2. We are of-ten des-ti-tute Of the things that
3. Tri-als dark on ev-'ry hand, And we can-not
4. Temp-ta-tions, hid-den snares Of-ten take us

sea of time. Som-ber skies and howl-ing tem-pests oft suc-
life de-mands. Want of food and want of shel-ter, thirst-y
un-der-stand, All the ways that God would lead us to that
un-a-wares. And our hearts are made to bleed for some

ceed a bright sun-shine. In that land of per-fect day, When the
hills and bar-ren lands. We are trust-ing in the Lord, And ac-
bless-ed Prom-ised Land. But He guides us with His eye And we'll
thought-less word or deed. And we won-der why the test When we

mists have rolled a-way, We will un-der-stand it bet-ter by and
cord-ing to His Word, We will un-der-stand it bet-ter by and
fol-low till we die. For we'll un-der-stand it bet-ter by and
try to do our best, But we'll un-der-stand it bet-ter by and

by. By and by when the morn-ing comes,

When the saints of God are gath-ered home, We will

tell the sto-ry how we've o-ver-come; For we'll

un-der-stand it bet-ter by and by.

Text: Charles A. Tindley, 1851-1933
Tune: BY AND BY, 7 7 15 7 7 11 with refrain; Charles A. Tindley, 1851-1933; arr. by Nolan Williams, Jr., b.1969, © 2000,
    GIA Publications, Inc.

419 HIGHER GROUND

I press on toward the goal for the prize of the heavenly call of God in Christ Jesus.
Philippians 3:14

1. I'm press-ing on the up-ward way, New heights I'm
2. My heart has no de-sire to stay Where doubts a -
3. I want to live a-bove the world, Though Sa - tan's
4. I want to scale the ut-most height, And catch a

gain - ing ev - 'ry day; Still pray-ing as I'm on - ward
rise and fears dis - may; Though some may dwell where these a -
darts at me are hurled; For faith has caught a joy - ful
gleam of glo - ry bright; But still I'll pray till heav'n I've

bound, "Lord, plant my feet on high - er ground."
bound, My prayer, my aim, is high - er ground.
sound, The song of saints on high - er ground.
found, "Lord, lead me on to high - er ground."

Lord, lift me up, and let me stand By faith, on

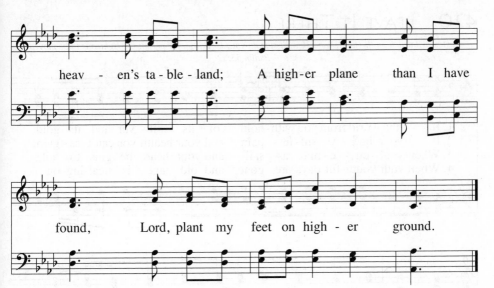

heav - en's ta - ble - land; A high-er plane than I have found, Lord, plant my feet on high - er ground.

Text: Johnson Oatman, Jr., 1860-1948
Tune: HIGHER GROUND, LM with refrain; Charles H. Gabriel, 1856-1932

420 LEAVE IT THERE

Cast your burden on the LORD and He will sustain you; He will never permit the righteous to be moved.
Psalm 55:22

1. If the world from you with-hold of its sil - ver and its gold,
2. If your bod - y suf-fers pain and your health you can't re - gain,
3. When your en - e - mies as - sail and your heart be - gins to fail,
4. When your youth-ful days are gone and old age is steal-ing on,

And you have to get a long with mea - ger fare,
And your soul is al - most sink - ing in de - spair,
Don't for - get that God in heav - en an - swers prayer;
And your bod - y bends be - neath the weight of care,

Just re - mem-ber, in His Word, how He feeds the lit - tle bird—
Je - sus knows the pain you feel, He can save and He can heal—
He will make a way for you and will lead you safe - ly through—
He will nev - er leave you then, He'll go with you to the end—

Take your bur - den to the Lord and leave it there.

Text: Charles A. Tindley, 1851-1933
Tune: LEAVE IT THERE, 14 11 14 11 with refrain; Charles A. Tindley, 1851-1933; arr. by Nolan Williams, Jr., b.1969, © 2000, GIA
  Publications, Inc.

421 COME, YE DISCONSOLATE

Do not fear, for I am with you, do not be afraid, for I am your God; I will strengthen you, I will help you...
Isaiah 41:10

1. Come, ye dis - con - so-late, wher - e'er ye lan - guish—
2. Joy of the des - o-late, light of the stray - ing,
3. Here see the Bread of Life, see wa-ters flow - ing

Come to the mer - cy-seat, fer - vent-ly kneel;
Hope of the pen - i - tent, fade - less and pure!
Forth from the throne of God, pure from a - bove;

Here bring your wound - ed hearts, here tell your an - guish:
Here speaks the Com - fort - er, ten - der - ly say - ing,
Come to the feast of love— come ev - er know - ing

Earth has no sor - row that heav'n can - not heal.
"Earth has no sor - row that heav'n can - not cure."
Earth has no sor - row but heav'n can re - move.

Text: St. 1-2, Thomas Moore, 1779-1852; st. 3, Thomas Hastings, 1784-1872
Tune: CONSOLATOR, 11 10 11 10; Samuel Webbe, 1740-1816

O Thou, in Whose Presence 422

Even though I walk through the darkest valley, I fear no evil; for You are with me...
Psalm 23:4

1. O Thou, in whose pres - ence my soul takes de-
2. Where dost Thou, dear Shep - herd, re - sort with Thy
3. O why should I wan - der, an a - lien from
4. Re - store, my dear Sav - ior, the light of Thy
5. He looks! and ten thou - sands of an - gels re-

light, On whom in af - flic - tion I call, My
sheep, To feed them in pas - tures of love? Say,
Thee, Or cry in the des - ert for bread? Thy
face, Thy soul - cheer - ing com - fort im - part; And
joice, And myr - i - ads wait for His word. He

com - fort by day and my song in the
why in the val - ley of death should I
foes will re - joice when my sor - rows they
let the sweet to - kens of par - don - ing
speaks! and e - ter - ni - ty, filled with His

night, My hope, my sal - va - tion, my all!
weep, Or a - lone in this wil - der - ness rove?
see, And smile at the tears I have shed.
grace Bring joy to my des - o - late heart.
voice, Re - ech - oes the praise of the Lord.

Text: Joseph Swain, 1761-1796
Tune: DAVIS, 11 8 11 8; Wyeth's *Repository of Sacred Music, Part Second,* 1813; harm. by Austin C. Lovelace, b.1919, © 1964, Abingdon Press

423 OH, TO BE KEPT BY JESUS

O LORD, You brought up my soul from Sheol, restored me to life from among those gone down to the Pit.
Psalm 30:3

1. Oh, to be kept by Je - sus,
2. Oh, to be kept by Je - sus,
3. Kept by His Ho - ly Spir - it,

Kept by the pow - er of God.
Kept by His pow - er di - vine.
To me this is best of all.

Kept from the world un - spot - ted,
Kept through toil and tri - als,
I'm safe in His ho - ly keep - ing,

Tread - ing where Je - sus trod.
Kept by His hand in mine.
He'll ev - er hear my call.

Oh, to be kept by Je - sus;
Lord, at Thy feet I fall;
I would be noth-ing, noth-ing, noth-ing,
Thou shalt be all and all.

Text: Thurston Frazier
Tune: 7 7 7 6 with refrain; Thurston Frazier; arr. by Kenneth Morris
© 1966, Frazier-Cleveland Co.

424 SAVIOR, LIKE A SHEPHERD LEAD US

If a shepherd has a hundred sheep... does he not leave the ninety-nine... and go in search of the one that went astray?
Matthew 18:12

1. Sav - ior, like a shep-herd lead us,
2. We are Thine; do Thou be - friend us,
3. Thou hast prom-ised to re - ceive us,
4. Ear - ly let us seek Thy fa - vor;

Much we need Thy ten - der care;
Be the Guard - ian of our way;
Poor and sin - ful though we be;
Ear - ly let us do Thy will;

In Thy pleas - ant pas - tures feed us,
Keep Thy flock, from sin de - fend us,
Thou hast mer - cy to re - lieve us,
Bless - ed Lord and on - ly Sav - ior,

For our use Thy folds pre - pare.
Seek us when we go a - stray.
Grace to cleanse, and pow'r to free.
With Thy love our bos - oms fill.

Blessed Jesus, Blessed Jesus, Thou hast
bought us, Thine we are; Blessed Jesus, Blessed
Jesus, Thou has bought us, Thine we are.

Blessed Jesus, Blessed Jesus, Hear Thy
children when they pray; Blessed Jesus, Blessed
Jesus, Hear Thy children when they pray.

Blessed Jesus, Blessed Jesus, Early
let us turn to Thee; Blessed Jesus, Blessed
Jesus, Early let us turn to Thee.

Blessed Jesus, Blessed Jesus, Thou hast
lov'd us, love us still; Blessed Jesus, Blessed
Jesus, Thou hast lov'd us, love us still.

Text: Dorothy A. Thrupp, 1779-1847
Tune: BRADBURY, 8 7 8 7 D; William B. Bradbury, 1816-1868

425 THE BEAUTIFUL GARDEN OF PRAYER

He said to His disciples, "Sit here while I go over there and pray."
Matthew 26:36

1. There's a gar - den where Je - sus is wait - ing,
2. There's a gar - den where Je - sus is wait - ing,
3. There's a gar - den where Je - sus is wait - ing,

There's a place that is won - drous - ly fair,
And I go, with my bur - den and care,
And He bids you to come meet Him there,

For it glows with the light of His pres - ence—
Just to learn from His lips words of com - fort—
Just to bow and re - ceive a new bless - ing—

'Tis the beau - ti - ful gar - den of prayer.
In the beau - ti - ful gar - den of prayer.
In the beau - ti - ful gar - den of prayer.

O the beau-ti-ful gar-den, the gar-den of prayer, O the
beau-ti-ful gar-den of prayer! There my Sav-ior a-waits, and He
o-pens the gates To the beau-ti-ful gar-den of prayer.

Text: Eleanor Allen Schroll, fl.1920
Tune: BEAUTIFUL GARDEN, 10 9 10 9 with refrain; James H. Fillmore, 1849-1936

426 THE LORD IS MY SHEPHERD

The LORD is my shepherd, I shall not want.
Psalm 23:1

1. The Lord is my Shep-herd, no want shall I
2. Through the val - ley and shad - ow of death though I
3. In the midst of af - flic - tion my ta - ble is
4. Let good - ness and mer - cy, my boun - ti - ful

know; I feed in green pas - tures, safe - fold - ed I
stray, Since Thou art my Guard - ian, no e - vil I
spread; With bless - ings un - meas - ured my cup run - neth
God, Still fol - low my steps till I meet Thee a -

rest; He lead - eth my soul where the still wa - ters
fear; Thy rod shall de - fend me, Thy staff be my
o'er; With per - fume and oil Thou a - noint - est my
bove: I seek by the path which my an - ces - tors

flow, Re - stores me when wan - d'ring, re -
stay; No harm can be - fall, with my
head; O what shall I ask of Thy
trod, Through the land of their so - journ, Thy

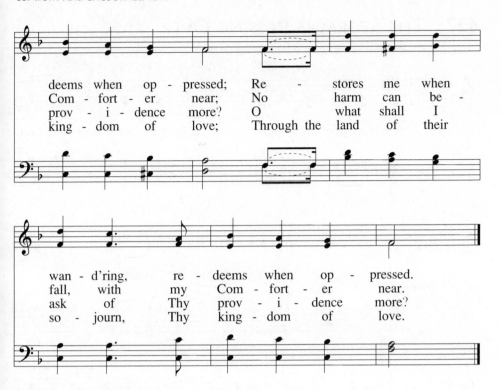

deems when op - pressed; Re - stores me when
Com - fort - er near; No harm can be -
prov - i - dence more? O what shall I
king - dom of love; Through the land of their

wan - d'ring, re - deems when op - pressed.
fall, with my Com - fort - er near.
ask of Thy prov - i - dence more?
so - journ, Thy king - dom of love.

Text: James Montgomery, 1771-1854
Tune: POLAND, 11 11 11 11 11; Thomas Koschat, 1845-1914

427 THE STORM IS PASSING OVER

...and the sea ceased from its raging. Then the men feared the LORD even more.
Jonah 1:15-16

Take cour-age my soul and let us jour-ney on,

tho' the night is dark and

I am far from home. Thanks be to God,

the morn - ing light ap - pears. The

storm is pass-ing o - ver, the storm is pass-ing o -

ver. The storm is pass-ing o - ver. Hal - le - lu.

Hal - le - lu - jah. Hal - le - lu - jah. Hal - le - lu - jah.

The storm is pass-ing o - ver. The storm is pass-ing o -

ver. The storm is pass-ing o - ver. Hal - le - lu.

Text: Charles A. Tindley, 1851-1933, and Donald Vails, ©
Tune: Donald Vails, ©; arr. by Evelyn Simpson-Curenton, b.1953, © 2000, GIA Publications, Inc.

428 Does Jesus Care?

Cast all your anxiety on Him, because He cares for you.
1 Peter 5:7

1. Does Je - sus care when my heart is pained Too
2. Does Je - sus care when my way is dark With a
3. Does Je - sus care when I've tried and failed To re -
4. Does Je - sus care when I've said good - bye To the

deep - ly for mirth and song; As the
name - less dread and fear? As the
sist some temp - ta - tion strong; When for
dear - est on earth to me, And my

bur - dens press, and the cares dis - tress, And the
day - light fades in - to deep night shades, Does He
my deep grief I find no re - lief, Though my
sad heart aches till it near - ly breaks— Is it

way grows wea - ry and long?
care e - nough to be near?
tears flow all the night long?   O yes, He cares— I
aught to Him? does He see?

know   He cares!   His heart   is touched with   my   grief;

When the   days   are wea - ry,   the   long   nights drear - y,   I

cares.

know   my   Sav - ior   cares,   He   cares.

cares.

Text: Frank E. Graeff, 1860-1919
Tune: MY SAVIOR CARES, 9 8 10 8 with refrain; J. Lincoln Hall, 1866-1930

429 YIELD NOT TO TEMPTATION

No testing has overtaken you that is not common to everyone... with the testing He will also provide the way out.
1 Corinthians 10:13

1. Yield not to temp - ta - tion, For yield - ing is sin;
2. Shun e - vil com - pan - ions, Bad lan - guage dis - dain;
3. To him that o'er - com - eth, God giv - eth a crown;

Each vic - t'ry will help you, Some oth - er to win;
God's name hold in rev - 'rence, Nor take it in vain;
Through faith we will con - quer, Though of - ten cast down;

Fight val - iant - ly on - ward, E - vil pas - sions sub - due;
Be thought-ful and ear - nest, Kind - heart - ed and true;
He who is our Sav - ior, Our strength will re - new;

Look ev - er to Je - sus, He will car - ry you through.

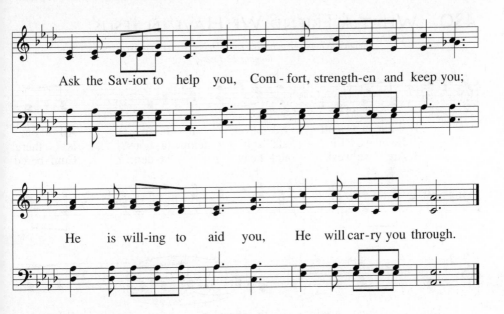

Ask the Sav-ior to help you, Com - fort, strength-en and keep you;

He is will-ing to aid you, He will car-ry you through.

Text: Horatio R. Palmer, 1834-1907
Tune: YIELD NOT, 6 5 6 5 6 6 6 6 with refrain; Horatio R. Palmer, 1834-1907; harm. by Carl Haywood, b.1949, from *Songs of Praise*, © 1992

430 What a Friend We Have in Jesus

Rejoice in hope, be patient in suffering, persevere in prayer.
Romans 12:12

1. What a Friend we have in Je-sus, All our sins and griefs to bear! What a priv - i - lege to car - ry Ev - 'ry-thing to God in prayer! Oh what

2. Have we tri - als and temp - ta - tions? Is there trou - ble an - y - where? We should nev - er be dis - cour-aged— Take it to the Lord in prayer! Can we

3. Are we weak and heav - y - la - den, Cum - bered with a load of care? Pre - cious Sav - ior, still our ref - uge— Take it to the Lord in prayer! Do thy

peace   we of - ten for - feit,   Oh what
find   a friend   so faith-ful,   Who will
friends   de-spise, for-sake thee?   Take it

need - less pain   we bear,   All be -
all   our sor - rows share?   Je - sus
to   the Lord in prayer!   In His

cause   we do   not car - ry   Ev - 'ry-
knows   our ev - 'ry weak-ness— Take it
arms   He'll take and shield thee— Thou wilt

thing   to God   in prayer!
to   the Lord in prayer!
find   a sol - ace there.

Text: Joseph M. Scriven, 1819-1866
Tune: ANNIE LOWERY, 8 7 8 7 D, Traditional Celtic; arr. Valeria A. Foster, © 2000, GIA Publications, Inc.

431 WHAT A FRIEND WE HAVE IN JESUS

For the eyes of the Lord are on the righteous, and His ears are open to their prayer.
1 Peter 3:12

1. What a Friend we have in Je - sus, All our
2. Have we tri - als and temp - ta - tions? Is there
3. Are we weak and heav - y - la - den, Cum - bered

sins and griefs to bear! What a priv - i - lege to
troub - le an - y - where? We should nev - er be dis -
with a load of care? Pre - cious Sav - ior, still our

car - ry Ev - 'ry-thing to God in prayer! O what
cour - aged— Take it to the Lord in prayer. Can we
ref - uge— Take it to the Lord in prayer. Do thy

peace we of - ten for - feit, O what need-less pain we
find a friend so faith - ful Who will all our sor - rows
friends de - spise, for - sake thee? Take it to the Lord in

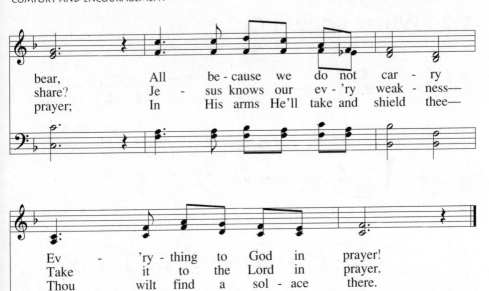

bear,
share?
prayer;

All
Je - sus knows our
In His arms He'll

be - cause we do not car - ry
ev - 'ry weak - ness—
take and shield thee—

Ev - 'ry - thing to God in prayer!
Take it to the Lord in prayer.
Thou wilt find a sol - ace there.

Text: Joseph M. Scriven, 1819-1866
Tune: CONVERSE, 8 7 8 7 D; Charles C. Converse, 1832-1918

May also be sung to I Will Arise

432 WHERE COULD I GO?

All the ends of the earth shall remember and turn to the LORD...
Psalm 22:27

1. Liv - ing be - low in this old sin - ful world,
2. Neigh - bors are kind, I love them ev - 'ry one,
3. Life here is grand with friends I love so dear,

Hard - ly a com - fort can af - ford; Striv - ing a - lone to
We get a - long in sweet ac - cord; But when my soul needs
Com - fort I get from God's own word; Yet when I face the

face temp - ta - tion sore,
man - na from a - bove, where could I go but to the Lord?
chill - ing hand of death,

Where could I go? Oh, where could I go

Seek - ing a ref-uge for my soul? Need - ing a friend to

save me in the end, Where could I go but to the Lord?

Text: James B. Coats
Tune: WHERE COULD I GO, 10 8 10 8 with refrain; James B. Coats; arr. by Valeria A. Foster
© 1940, Stamps-Baxter Music (BMI)

433 KEEP ME, EVERY DAY

Keep my steps steady according to Your promise, and never let iniquity have dominion over me.
Psalm 119:133

1. Lord, I want to live for Thee, Ev - 'ry
2. In my weak - ness be my strength; In my
3. Leave me not to walk a - lone, Lest I

day and hour; Let Thy Spir - it be with
tri - als all, Be Thou near me all the
faint and die; Let Thy Spir - it go with

me, In its sav - ing pow'r!
day, Hear my ev - 'ry call!
me, And at - tend my cry!

Keep my heart, and keep my hand,

Keep my soul, I pray! Keep my tongue to

speak Thy praise, Keep me all the way!

Text: F. L. Eiland
Tune: EVERY DAY, 7 5 7 5 with refrain; Emmet S. Dean, 1876

REMEMBER ME 434

Then he said, "Jesus, remember me when You come into Your kingdom."
Luke 23:42

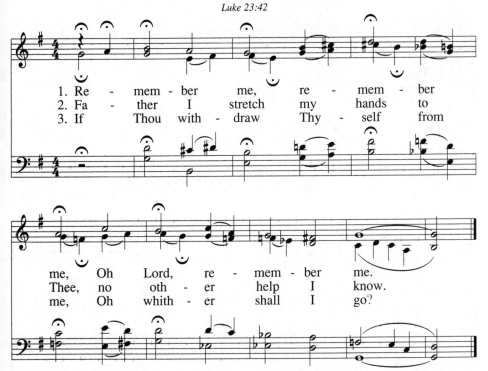

1. Re - mem - ber me, re - mem - ber
2. Fa - ther I stretch my hands to
3. If Thou with - draw Thy - self from

me, Oh Lord, re - mem - ber me.
Thee, no oth - er help I know.
me, Oh whith - er shall I go?

Text: Congregational Praise Song
Tune: Congregational Praise Song; harm. by Leon C. Roberts, from The Mass of St. Augustine, © 1981, GIA Publications, Inc.

435 PASS ME NOT, O GENTLE SAVIOR

See, I am sending My messenger ahead of You, who will prepare Your way before You.
Matthew 11:10

1. Pass me not, O gen - tle Sav - ior, Hear my hum - ble
2. Let me at a throne of mer - cy Find a sweet re -
3. Trust - ing on - ly in Thy mer - it, Would I seek Thy
4. Thou the Spring of all my com - fort, More than life to

cry, While on oth - ers Thou art call - ing,
lief; Kneel - ing there in deep con - tri - tion,
face; Heal my wound - ed, bro - ken spir - it,
me, Whom have I on earth be - side Thee?

I'm call-ing

Solo:

Do not pass me by.
Help my un - be - lief.
Save me by Thy grace.
Whom in heav'n but Thee?

Sav - ior, Sav - ior,

Hear my hum - ble cry; While on oth - ers Thou art

call - ing, Do not pass me by.

Text: Fanny J. Crosby, 1820-1915
Tune: PASS ME NOT, 8 5 8 5 with refrain; William H. Doane, 1832-1915

FIX ME, JESUS   436

If we confess our sins, He who is faithful and just will forgive us our sins and cleanse us from all unrighteousness.

1 John 1:9

Text: Traditional
Tune: FIX ME, 7 6 7 6 with refrain; Negro spiritual; arr. by Nolan Williams, Jr., b.1969, © 2000, GIA Publications, Inc.

437 KUM BA YAH

...hear the plea of Your servant and of Your people Israel... hear and forgive.
2 Chronicles 6:21

1. Kum ba yah, my Lord, kum ba yah.

Kum ba yah, my Lord, kum ba yah.

Kum ba yah, my Lord, kum ba yah.

Oh, Lord, kum ba yah.

2. Someone's prayin', Lord, kum ba yah,...
3. Someone's cryin', Lord, kum ba yah,...
4. Someone needs You, Lord, kum ba yah,...

Text: Marvin V. Frey, © 1957
Tune: DESMOND, 8885; Marvin V. Frey, © 1957; arr. by Dr. Robert J. Fryson, © 2000, GIA Publications, Inc.

COME BY HERE, MY LORD 438

...hear the plea of Your servant and of Your people Israel... hear and forgive.
2 Chronicles 6:21

1. Come by here, my Lord, come by here. Come by here,
2. Some-one needs You, Lord, come by here. Some-one needs
3. Some-one's pray - in', Lord, come by here. Some-one's pray-
4. Kum Ba Yah, my Lord, come by here. Kum Ba Yah,

my Lord, come by here. Come by here, my Lord,
You, Lord, come by here. Some - one needs You, Lord,
in', Lord, come by here. Some-one's pray - in', Lord,
my Lord, come by here. Kum Ba Yah, my Lord,

come by here. Oh Lord, come by here.
come by here. Oh Lord, come by here.
come by here. Oh Lord, come by here.
come by here. Oh Lord, come by here.

Text: Marvin V. Frey, © 1958
Tune: DESMOND, 8885; Marvin V. Frey, © 1958; arr. by Evelyn Simpson-Curenton, b.1953, © 2000, GIA Publications, Inc.

439 COME HERE JESUS, IF YOU PLEASE

Rejoice in hope, be patient in suffering, persevere in prayer.
Romans 12:12

1. No harm have I done You on my knees, on my knees, No harm have I done You on my knees, on my knees, When you see me on my knees, dear Lord, Come here, Je-sus, if You please.

2. O Lord, have mer-cy on po' me, on po' me, O Lord, have mer-cy on po' me, on po'

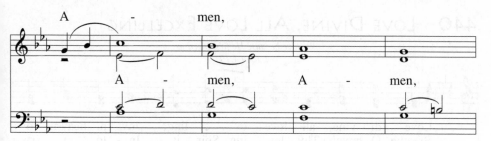

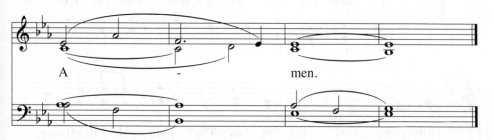

Text: African-American traditional; adapt. by Roland M. Carter, b.1942, © 1978, Mar-Vel
Tune: COME HERE JESUS, 9 9 9 7 with amen; African-American traditional; arr. by Roland M. Carter, b.1942, © 1978, Mar-Vel

440 LOVE DIVINE, ALL LOVE EXCELLING

We love because He first loved us.
1 John 4:19

1. Love di - vine, all love ex - cel - ling, Joy of heav'n, to
2. Breathe, O breathe Thy lov - ing Spir - it In - to ev - 'ry
3. Come, Al - might - y to de - liv - er, Let us all Thy
4. Fin - ish then Thy new cre - a - tion; Pure and spot - less

earth come down! Fix in us Thy hum - ble dwell - ing;
troub - led breast! Let us all in Thee in - her - it,
life re - ceive; Sud - den - ly re - turn, and nev - er,
let us be; Let us see Thy great sal - va - tion,

All Thy faith - ful mer - cies crown. Je - sus, Thou art
Let us find that sec - ond rest. Take a - way our
Nev - er - more Thy tem - ples leave: Thee we would be
Per - fect - ly re - stored in Thee: Changed from glo - ry

all com - pas - sion, Pure, un - bound - ed love Thou art;
bent to sin - ning; Al - pha and O - me - ga be;
al - ways bless - ing, Serve Thee as Thy hosts a - bove,
in - to glo - ry, Till in heav'n we take our place,

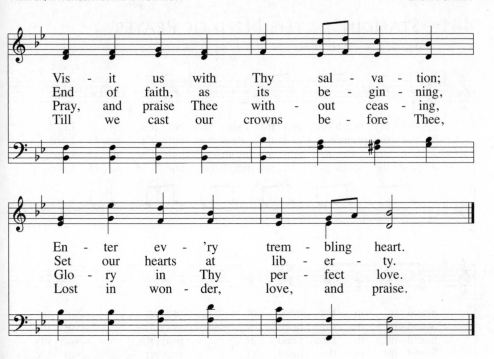

Vis - it   us   with   Thy   sal - va - tion;
End   of   faith,   as   its   be - gin - ning,
Pray,   and   praise   Thee   with - out   ceas - ing,
Till   we   cast   our   crowns   be - fore   Thee,

En - ter   ev - 'ry   trem - bling   heart.
Set   our   hearts   at   lib - er - ty.
Glo - ry   in   Thy   per - fect   love.
Lost   in   won - der,   love,   and   praise.

Text: Charles Wesley, 1707-1788
Tune: BEECHER, 8 7 8 7 D; John Zundel, 1815-1882

441 STANDIN' IN THE NEED OF PRAYER

Hear my prayer, O LORD, and give ear to my cry; do not hold Your peace at my tears.
Psalm 39:12

1. Not my broth-er, not my sis-ter, but it's me, O Lord,
2. Not the preach-er, not the dea-con, but it's me, O Lord,
3. Not my fa-ther, not my moth-er, but it's me, O Lord,
4. Not the stran-ger, not my neigh-bor, but it's me, O Lord,

Stand-in' in the need of prayer; Not my
Stand-in' in the need of prayer; Not the
Stand-in' in the need of prayer; Not my
Stand-in' in the need of prayer; Not the

broth-er, not my sis-ter, but it's me, O Lord,
preach-er, not the dea-con, but it's me, O Lord,
fa-ther, not my moth-er, but it's me, O Lord,
stran-ger, not my neigh-bor, but it's me, O Lord,

Stand-in' in the need of prayer.
Stand-in' in the need of prayer.
Stand-in' in the need of prayer.
Stand-in' in the need of prayer.

It's me,

It's me, it's me, O Lord, Stand-in' in the need of prayer; It's me, It's me, it's me, O Lord, Stand-in' in the need of prayer.

Text: Negro spiritual
Tune: STANDIN' IN THE NEED; 13 7 13 7 with refrain; Negro spiritual

442   SWEET HOUR OF PRAYER

...one of His disciples said to Him, "Lord, teach us to pray, as John taught his disciples."
Luke 11:1

1. Sweet hour of prayer, sweet hour of prayer, That calls me
2. Sweet hour of prayer, sweet hour of prayer, Thy wings shall
3. Sweet hour of prayer, sweet hour of prayer, May I thy

from a world of care And bids me at my
my pe - ti - tion bear To Him whose truth and
con - so - la - tion share, Till from Mount Pis - gah's

Fa - ther's throne Make all my wants and wish - es known!
faith - ful - ness En - gage the wait - ing soul to bless;
loft - y height I view my home and take my flight:

In sea - sons of dis - tress and grief My soul has of - ten
And since He bids me seek His face, Be - lieve His word and
This robe of flesh I'll drop, and rise To seize the ev - er -

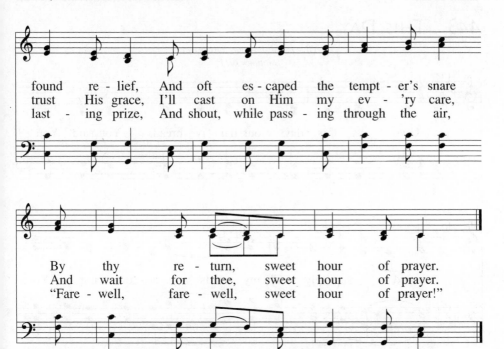

found   re - lief,   And   oft   es - caped   the   tempt - er's   snare
trust   His grace,   I'll   cast   on   Him   my   ev -   'ry   care,
last - ing prize,   And shout,   while pass - ing   through   the   air,

By   thy   re - turn,   sweet   hour   of   prayer.
And   wait   for   thee,   sweet   hour   of   prayer.
"Fare - well,   fare - well,   sweet   hour   of   prayer!"

Text: William W. Walford, 1772-1850
Tune: SWEET HOUR, LMD; William B. Bradbury, 1816-1868

443 THIS DAY

Give us this day our daily bread.
Matthew 6:11

Give us this day our dai-ly bread. You said You would sup-ply all my needs ac-cord-ing to Your rich-es. I have but to ask and I shall re-ceive.

To go from here and share this love You gave to me, to show some-one who's lost and help them find their

way, the way to truth and faith so they can be free like

me, free like me. Lord, we need Your love.

Lord, we need Your peace. Lord, we need Your joy this

day. Thank You for this day. Lord, we thank You for this day.

day.

Text: Edwin Hawkins
Tune: Edwin Hawkins; arr. by Stephen Key, © 2000, GIA Publications, Inc.

444 THY WAY, O LORD

Father, if You are willing, remove this cup from me; yet, not my will but Yours be done.
Luke 22:42

1. Thy way, O Lord, not mine, Thy will be done, not mine; Since Thou for me did bleed, And now do in - ter - cede, Each day I sim - ply plead, Thy will be done.

2. Thy way, O Lord, not mine, Let glo - ry all be Thine; Keep me, lest I may stray, Near Thee from day to day; Teach me to watch and pray, Thy will be done.

3. Hide me from self, O Lord, May I at - tend Thy word; Send pride be - yond re - call, Let each as - sail - er fall, Be Thou my all in all, Thy will be done.

4. Sub - mis - sive - ly I bow; With strength and grace en - dow This wea - ry, sin - ful heart; Shield from each cru - el dart; May I from Thee ne'er part, Thy will be done.

Thy will, Thy will be done, Thy will, Thy will be done;

Thy will be done, Thy will be done;

In - cline my heart each day to say, "Thy will be done."

Text: Nina B. Jackson
Tune: THY WAY, 66 666 4 with refrain; Edward C. Deas

445 Bless This House

The LORD has been mindful of us; He will bless us; He will bless the house of Israel.
Psalm 115:12

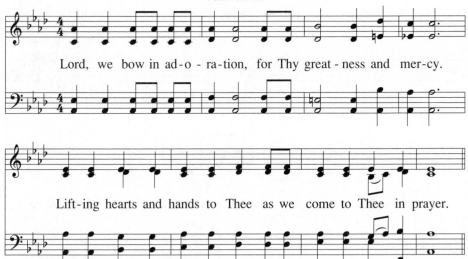

Lord, we bow in ad-o-ra-tion, for Thy great-ness and mer-cy.

Lift-ing hearts and hands to Thee as we come to Thee in prayer.

Optional Chant

1. Melt us and mold us, sanctify and make us holy
2. Send Your presence and Your power for the blessing of this hour
3. Bless this house, oh Lord, we pray,
   and all that is within it bless Your holy name.

oh Lord, we pray. Bless this house, oh

Lord, oh Lord, we pray.

Text: Betty Gadling
Tune: Betty Gadling
© 1994, Betty Gadling. Administered by GIA Publications, Inc.

LORD, HELP ME TO HOLD OUT 446

...those who look into the perfect law, the law of liberty, and persevere... they will be blessed in their doing.

James 1:25

447 FILL MY CUP, LORD

I will lift up the cup of salvation and call on the name of the LORD.
Psalm 116:13

1. Like the wom - an at the well I was seek - ing
2. There are mil - lions in this world who are crav - ing
3. So, my friend now, if the things this world gave you

For things that could not sat - is - fy;
The pleas - ure earth - ly things af - ford;
Leave hun - gers that won't pass a - way,

And then I heard my Sav - ior speak - ing:
But none can match the won - drous treas - ure
My bless - ed Lord will come and save you,

"Draw from My well that nev - er shall run dry."
That I find in Je - sus Christ my Lord.
If you kneel to Him and hum - bly pray:

Fill my cup, Lord, I lift it up, Lord! Come and quench this

thirst-ing of my soul; Bread of heav - en, feed me till I

want no more— Fill my cup, fill it up and make me whole!

448 OH, LORD HAVE MERCY

Be merciful to me, O God, be merciful to me, for in You my soul takes refuge...
Psalm 57:1

1. Oh, Lord have mer - cy. Oh, Lord have
2. While I am pray - ing, While I am
3. While I am wait - ing, While I am
4. When I'm in trou - ble, When I'm in
5. I am Your child, I

mer - cy. Oh, Lord have mer - cy,
pray - ing, While I am pray - ing,
wait - ing, While I am wait - ing, Have
trou - ble, When I'm in trou - ble,
child, I am Your child,

mer - cy on me.

Text: Traditional
Tune: HAVE MERCY ON ME, 5 5 5 5; traditional; arr. by Joseph Joubert, © 2000, GIA Publications, Inc.

HAVE THINE OWN WAY, LORD 449

...yield yourselves to the LORD and come to His sanctuary, which He has sanctified forever...
2 Chronicles 30:8

1. Have Thine own way, Lord! Have Thine own way!
2. Have Thine own way, Lord! Have Thine own way!
3. Have Thine own way, Lord! Have Thine own way!
4. Have Thine own way, Lord! Have Thine own way!

Thou art the pot - ter, I am the clay!
Search me and try me, Mas - ter, to - day!
Wound - ed and wea - ry, Help me, I pray!
Hold o'er my be - ing Ab - so - lute sway!

Mold me and make me Af - ter Thy will,
Bright - er than snow, Lord, Wash me just now,
Pow - er all pow - er Sure - ly is Thine!
Fill with Thy Spir - it 'Til all shall see

While I am wait - ing, Yield - ed and still.
As in Thy pres - ence Hum - bly I bow.
Touch me and heal me, Sav - ior di - vine!
Christ on - ly, al - ways, Liv - ing in me!

Text: Adelaide A. Pollard, 1862-1934
Tune: ADELAIDE, 5 4 5 4 D; George C. Stebbins, 1846-1945

450 Hush! Hush! My Soul

Why are you cast down, O my soul, and why are you disquieted within me? Hope in God...
Psalm 42:5

Hush! Hush! My soul be calm and still. Come, bless-ed Sav-ior, en-ter in. For-give our sins, Heal all our ills, Give strength for tasks, Give peace of mind, And make our spir-its whol-ly Thine. And we shall praise Thee ev-er more. A-men, A-men, A-men.

Text: Rev. S. S. Morris
Tune: Edward C. Deas

I Need Thee Every Hour 451

With my whole heart I seek You; do not let me stray from Your commandments.
Psalm 119:10

1. I need Thee ev-'ry hour, Most gra - cious Lord;
2. I need Thee ev-'ry hour, Stay Thou near - by;
3. I need Thee ev-'ry hour, In joy or pain;
4. I need Thee ev-'ry hour, Teach me Thy will;

No ten - der voice like Thine Can peace af - ford.
Temp - ta - tions lose their pow'r When Thou art nigh.
Come quick - ly and a - bide, Or life is vain.
And Thy rich prom - is - es In me ful - fill.

I need Thee, O I need Thee; Ev - 'ry hour I need Thee;

O bless me now, my Sav - ior, I come to Thee.

Text: Annie S. Hawkes, 1835-1918
Tune: NEED, 6 4 6 4 with refrain; Robert Lowry, 1826-1899

452 IN ME

For I will not venture to speak of anything except what Christ has accomplished through me...
Romans 15:18

1. Thou, O Christ, my Lord and King, Grant in Thine own name my plea. Take the sac - ri - fice I bring, Be Thou "All Thou art" in me. Be Thou "All Thou
2. Thou a won - der work-ing God, Dwell - ing in e - ter - ni - ty, As in flesh our plan - et trod, Work Thy might - y work in me. Work Thy might - y
3. Prince of peace be - yond com-pare, Thou whose pow - er stilled the sea, Chief a - mong ten thou - sand-fair, Speak Thy word of peace in me. Speak Thy word of
4. O Thou might - y God of love, Died Thy - self to set us free. Ho - ly Spir - it, heav'n - ly dove, Mag - ni - fy Thy love in me. Mag - ni - fy Thy
5. Je - sus, Thou the life, the way, In Thine im - age let me be; Keep my heart from day to day, Live Thy ho - ly life in me. Live Thy ho - ly
6. Je - sus, Thou the joy un - told, Like a riv - er flow - ing free. Be Thou ev - er in my soul, Let Thy joy a - bound in me. Let Thy joy a -

art" in me. Be Thou "All Thou art" in me. Take the
work in me. Work Thy might - y work in me. As in
peace in me. Speak Thy word of peace in me. Chief a -
love in me. Mag - ni - fy Thy love in me. Ho - ly
life in me. Live Thy ho - ly life in me. Keep my
bound in me. Let Thy joy a - bound in me. Be Thou

sac - ri - fice I bring, Be Thou "All Thou art" in me.
flesh our plan - et trod, Work Thy might - y work in me.
mong ten thou - sand - fair, Speak Thy word of peace in me.
Spir - it, heav'n - ly dove, Mag - ni - fy Thy love in me.
heart from day to day, Live Thy ho - ly life in me.
ev - er in my soul, Let Thy joy a - bound in me.

Text: Charles A. Tindley, 1851-1933
Tune: IN ME, 7 7 7 7 D; Charles A. Tindley, 1851-1933; arr. by Frederick J. Tindley

453   JESUS, LOVER OF MY SOUL

For You are my refuge, a strong tower against the enemy.
Psalm 61:3

1. Je - sus, Lov - er of my soul,
   While the near - er wa - ters roll,
2. Oth - er ref - uge have I none;
   Leave, ah, leave me not a - lone,
3. Thou, O Christ, art all I want;
   Raise the fall - en, cheer the faint,
4. Plen - teous grace with Thee is found,
   Let the heal - ing streams a - bound;

Let me to Thy bos - om fly,
While the tem - pest still is
Hangs my help - less soul on Thee;
Still sup - port and com - fort
More than all in Thee I find;
Heal the sick, and lead the
Grace to cov - er all my sin;
Make and keep me pure with -

guide,   O   re - ceive   my   soul   at   last!
head   With   the   shad - ow   of   Thy   wing.
am,   Thou   art   full   of   truth   and   grace.
heart,   Rise   to   all   e - ter - ni - ty.

Text: Charles Wesley, 1707-1788
Tune: MARTYN, 7 7 7 7 D; Simeon B. Marsh, 1798-1875; arr. by Nolan Williams, Jr., b.1969, based on original concept by Dr. Pearl Williams-
    Jones, © 2000, GIA Publications, Inc.

454 UNTIL I FOUND THE LORD

Pray in the Spirit at all times in every prayer and supplication.
Ephesians 6:18

1. Lord, I prayed and I prayed,   prayed all night long,

Oh Lord, I

prayed and I prayed, un - til I found the Lord,

Oh Lord, I My Lord

My soul My soul

just could-n't rest con - tent - ed,

My soul

just could-n't rest con - tent - ed,

Lord, I

just could-n't rest con-tent - ed, un - til I found the Lord.

2. Lord, I cried and I cried,...
3. Lord, I moaned and I moaned,...

Text: Clara Ward, 1924-1973
Tune: Clara Ward, 1924-1973
© 1953, 1981, Clara Ward. Assigned to Gertrude Music (JJ)

455 JUST A CLOSER WALK WITH THEE

...but Judah still walks with God, and is faithful to the Holy One.
Hosea 11:12

1. I am weak but Thou art strong;
2. Through this world of toil and snares,
3. When my fee-ble life is o'er,

Refrain: Just a clos-er walk with Thee,

Je - sus, keep me from all wrong;
If I fal - ter, Lord, who cares?
Time for me will be no more;

Grant it, Je - sus, if You please?

I'll be sat - is - fied as long
Who with me my bur - den shares?
Guide me gent - ly, safe - ly o'er

Dai - ly walk-ing close to Thee,

As I walk, let me walk close to Thee.
None but Thee, dear Lord, none but Thee.
To Thy king - dom shore, to Thy shore.

Let it be, dear Lord, let it be.

Text: Anonymous
Tune: CLOSER WALK, 777 8; Anonymous

MY FAITH LOOKS UP TO THEE 456

Turn to me and be saved, all the ends of the earth! For I am God, and there is no other.
Isaiah 45:22

1. My faith looks up to Thee, Thou Lamb of
2. May Thy rich grace im - part Strength to my
3. While life's dark maze I tread, And griefs a -
4. When ends life's tran - sient dream, When death's cold,

Cal - va - ry, Sav - ior di - vine! Now hear me
faint - ing heart, My zeal in - spire; As Thou hast
round me spread, Be Thou my guide; Bid dark - ness
sul - len stream Shall o'er me roll; Blest Sav - ior,

while I pray, Take all my guilt a - way,
died for me, O may my love to Thee
turn to day, Wipe sor - row's tears a - way,
then, in love, Fear and dis - trust re - move;

O let me from this day Be whol - ly Thine!
Pure, warm and change - less be, A liv - ing fire!
Nor let me ev - er stray From Thee a - side.
O bear me save a - bove, A ran - somed soul!

Text: Ray Palmer, 1808-1887
Tune: OLIVET, 66 4 666 4; Lowell Mason, 1792-1872

457 EVEN ME

I will send down the showers in their season; they shall be showers of blessing.
Ezekiel 34:26

1. Lord, I hear of show'rs of bless-ings, Thou art scat - t'ring full and free;
2. Pass me not, O gen - tle Sav - ior, Sin - ful though my heart may be;
3. Bread of heav - en, bread of heav - en, Ev - er let me feed on Thee;

Show'rs the thirst - y souls re - fresh-ing, Let some
I am long - ing for Thy fa - vor, Whilst Thou art
Vine of heav - en, Vine of heav - en, Let Thy

drops now fall on me!
bless - ing, O bless me! E - ven me, Lord,
blood a - tone for me!

e - ven me. E - ven me, Lord, e - ven

Let some drops now fall on me!
Whilst Thou art bless - ing, Lord, bless me!
me. Let Thy blood a - tone for me!

Text: Elizabeth H. Codner, 1824–1919
Tune: EVEN ME, 8 7 8 7 777; William B. Bradbury, 1816–1868; arr. by Nolan Williams, Jr., b.1969, © 2000, GIA Publications, Inc.

458 A PRAYING SPIRIT

Pray in the Spirit at all times in every prayer and supplication.
Ephesians 6:18

Lord, give me a pray - ing spir - it, a
pray - ing spir - it. Lord, help me to say yes,

yes, yes, Lord; yes,

yes, Lord. Lord, when I'm pray - ing tell me

1.
what to say!
2.
what to say! Yes! Yes!

Yes! Yes, Lord! Yes, yes, Lord!

Text: Elbernita "Twinkie" Clark, © 1980, Bridgeport Music, Inc.
Tune: Elbernita "Twinkie" Clark, © 1980, Bridgeport Music, Inc.; arr. by Nolan Williams, Jr., b.1969, © 2000, GIA Publications, Inc.

459   ABIDE WITH ME

God abides in those who confess that Jesus is the Son of God, and they abide in God.
1 John 4:15

1. A - bide with me; fast falls the e - ven - tide;
2. Swift to its close ebbs out life's lit - tle day;
3. I need Thy pres - ence ev - 'ry pass - ing hour;
4. I fear no foe, with Thee at hand to bless;
5. Hold Thou Thy cross be - fore my clos - ing eyes;

The dark - ness deep - ens; Lord, with me a - bide
Earth's joys grow dim; its glo - ries pass a - way;
What but Thy grace can foil the tempt - er's pow'r?
Ills have no weight, and tears no bit - ter - ness.
Shine through the gloom and point me to the skies;

When oth - er help - ers fail and com - forts flee,
Change and de - cay in all a - round I see;
Who, like Thy - self, my guide and stay can be?
Where is death's sting? Where, grave, your vic - to - ry?
Heav'n's morn - ing breaks, and earth's vain shad - ows flee;

Help of the help - less, O a - bide with me.
O Thou who chang - est not, a - bide with me.
Through cloud and sun - shine, Lord, a - bide with me.
I tri - umph still, if Thou a - bide with me.
In life, in death, O Lord, a - bide with me.

Text: Henry F. Lyte, 1793-1847
Tune: EVENTIDE, 10 10 10 10; William H. Monk, 1823-1889; arr. by Evelyn Simpson-Curenton, b.1953, © 2000, GIA Publications, Inc.

JESUS, SAVIOR, PILOT ME 460

O afflicted one, storm-tossed, and not comforted...no weapon that is fashioned against you shall prosper.
Isaiah 54:11, 17

1. Je - sus, Sav - ior, pi - lot me, O - ver
2. As a moth - er stills her child, Thou canst
3. When at last I near the shore, And the

life's tem - pes - tuous sea: Un - known waves be - fore me
hush the o - cean wild; Bois - t'rous waves o - bey Thy
fear - ful break - ers roar 'Twixt me and the peace - ful

roll, Hid - ing rocks and treach-'rous shoal; Chart and
will When Thou say'st to them, "Be still!" Won-drous
rest— Then, while lean - ing on Thy breast, May I

com - pass come from Thee— Je - sus, Sav - ior, pi - lot me!
Sov - 'reign of the sea, Je - sus, Sav - ior, pi - lot me!
hear Thee say to me, "Fear not— I will pi - lot thee!"

Text: Edward Hopper, 1816-1888
Tune: PILOT, 77 77 77; John E. Gould, 1822-1875

461 GIVE ME A CLEAN HEART

Create in me a clean heart O God, and put a new and right spirit within me.
Psalm 51:10

Give me a clean heart so I may serve Thee. Lord, fix my heart so that I may be used by

Thee. For I'm not wor - thy of all these bless - ings.

Give me a clean heart, and I'll fol-low Thee.

Verses

1. I'm not ask - ing for the rich - es of the land.
2. Some-times I am up and some-times I am down.

I'm not ask - ing for the proud to know my name.
Some-times I am al - most lev - el to the ground.

Please give me, Lord, a clean heart, that

I may fol - low Thee. Give me a clean heart

and I'll fol-low Thee.

Text: Margaret Pleasant Douroux, b.1941, © 1970
Tune: Margaret Pleasant Douroux, b.1941, © 1970; arr. by Albert Dennis Tessier and Nolan Williams, Jr., b.1969, © 2000, GIA Publications, Inc.

SANCTUARY 462

Who shall ascend the hill of the LORD? Those who have clean hands and pure hearts...
Psalm 24:3-4

Lord, pre-pare me to be a sanc-tu-ar-y, pure and

ho-ly, tried and true; with thanks-giv-ing, I'll be a

liv-ing sanc-tu-ar-y for You.

Text: John Thompson, b.1950 and Randy Scruggs
Tune: John Thompson, b.1950 and Randy Scruggs
© 1982, Full Armor Music and Whole Armor Music

463 LORD, I WANT TO BE A CHRISTIAN

For where your treasure is, there your heart will be also.
Matthew 6:21

1. Lord, I want to be a Chris-tian In my heart, in my
2. Lord, I want to be more lov-ing In my heart, in my
3. Lord, I want to be more ho-ly In my heart, in my
4. Lord, I want to be like Je-sus In my heart, in my

heart; Lord, I want to be a Chris-tian In my heart,
heart; Lord, I want to be more lov-ing In my heart,
heart; Lord, I want to be more ho-ly In my heart,
heart; Lord, I want to be like Je-sus In my heart,

In my heart,   In my heart,

Lord, I want to be a Chris-tian In my heart.
Lord, I want to be more lov-ing In my heart.
Lord, I want to be more ho-ly In my heart.
Lord, I want to be like Je-sus In my heart.

Text: Negro spiritual, adapt. by John W. Work, Jr., 1872-1925, and Frederick J. Work, 1879-1942
Tune: I WANT TO BE A CHRISTIAN, 8 6 8 3 6 8 3; Negro spiritual, adapt. by Frederick J. Work, 1879-1942

WE ARE CLIMBING JACOB'S LADDER 464

...he dreamed that there was a ladder... and the angels of God were ascending and descending on it.
Genesis 28:12

1. We   are   climb - ing   Ja - cob's   lad - der,   We   are
2. Ev - 'ry   round goes   high - er,   high - er,   Ev - 'ry
3. Chil - dren,   do   you   love   my   Je - sus?   Chil - dren,
4. If   you   love   Him,   why   not   serve Him?   If   you
5. Rise,   shine,   give   God   glo - ry,   Rise,

climb - ing   Ja - cob's   lad - der,   We   are   climb - ing
round goes   high - er,   high - er,   Ev - 'ry   round goes
do   you   love   my   Je - sus?   Chil - dren,   do   you
love   Him,   why   not   serve Him?   If   you   love   Him,
shine,   give   God   glo - ry,   Rise,   shine,

Ja - cob's   lad - der,   Sol - diers   of   the   cross.
high - er,   high - er,   Sol - diers   of   the   cross.
love   my   Je - sus?   Sol - diers   of   the   cross.
why   not   serve Him?   Sol - diers   of   the   cross.
give   God   glo - ry,   Sol - diers   of   the   cross.

Text: Negro spiritual
Tune: JACOB'S LADDER, 8 8 8 5; Negro spiritual

465 GIVE OF YOUR BEST TO THE MASTER

We love because He first loved us.
1 John 4:19

1. Give of your best to the Mas - ter,
2. Give of your best to the Mas - ter,
3. Give of your best to the Mas - ter,

Refrain: Give of your best to the Mas - ter,

Give of the strength of your youth;
Give Him first place in your heart;
Naught else is wor - thy His love;

Give of the strength of your youth;

Throw your soul's fresh, glow - ing ar - dor
Give Him first place in your serv - ice,
He gave Him - self for your ran - som,

Clad in sal - va - tion's full ar - mor,

In - to the bat - tle for truth.
Con - se - crate ev - 'ry part.
Gave up His glo - ry a - bove;

Join in the bat - tle for truth.

Je - sus has set the ex - am - ple—
Give, and to you shall be giv - en—
Laid down His life with - out mur - mur,

Daunt - less was He, young and brave;
God His be - lov - ed Son gave;
You from sin's ru - in to save;

Give Him your loy - al de - vo - tion,
Grate - ful - ly seek - ing to serve Him,
Give Him your heart's ad - o - ra - tion,

D.C. *Refrain*

Give Him the best that you have.
Give Him the best that you have.
Give Him the best that you have.

Text: Howard B. Grose, 1851-1939
Tune: BARNARD, 8 7 8 7 D with refrain; Charlotte A. Barnard, 1830-1869

466   HERE AM I

Then I heard the voice of the Lord saying, "Whom shall I send...?" And I said, "Here am I; send me!"
Isaiah 6:8

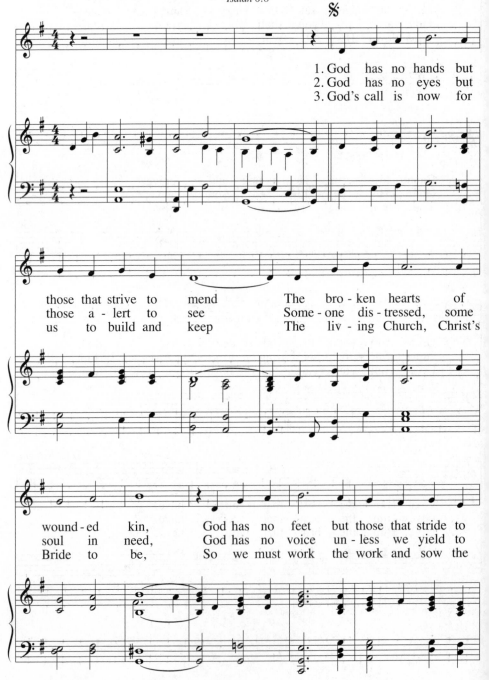

1. God has no hands but those that strive to mend The bro-ken hearts of wound-ed kin, God has no feet but those that stride to
2. God has no eyes but those a-lert to see Some-one dis-tressed, some soul in need, God has no voice un-less we yield to
3. God's call is now for us to build and keep The liv-ing Church, Christ's Bride to be, So we must work the work and sow the

win   An - oth - er   soul   to en - ter   in!
be   A ves - sel willed to bold - ly   sing!
seeds,   And trust God's prom - is - es to   reap!

Here am   I,   Lord, send me. Here am   I,

I'll heed Your voice,   o - bey Your will.

Text: Nolan Williams, Jr., b.1969
Tune: HERE AM I, 10 8 10 8 with refrain; Nolan Williams, Jr., b.1969
© NEW-J Publishing

A Charge to Keep I Have 467

I press on toward the goal for the prize of the heavenly call of God in Christ Jesus.
Philippians 3:14

freely

1. A charge to keep I have, A
2. To serve the pres - ent age, My
Alternate: Come, ye that love the Lord, And

God to glo - ri - fy. A nev - er - dy -
call - ing to ful - fill; O may it all
let your joys be known; Join in a song

ing soul to save, And fit it for the sky.
my pow'rs en-gage To do my Mas - ter's will!
of sweet ac-cord, And thus sur - round the throne.

Text: Charles Wesley, 1707-1788
Tune: Negro spiritual

A Charge to Keep I Have 468

I press on toward the goal for the prize of the heavenly call of God in Christ Jesus.
Philippians 3:14

1. A charge to keep I have, A God to glo - ri - fy,
2. To serve the pres - ent age, My call-ing to ful - fill;
3. Arm me with watch - ful care As in Thy sight to live,
4. Help me to watch and pray, And still on Thee re - ly,

A nev - er - dy - ing soul to save, And fit it for the sky.
O may it all my pow'rs en-gage To do my Mas-ter's will!
And now Thy ser-vant, Lord, pre-pare A strict ac-count to give!
O let me not my trust be-tray, But press to realms on high.

Text: Charles Wesley, 1707-1788
Tune: BOYLSTON, SM; Lowell Mason, 1792-1872

469 ALL THE WAY MY SAVIOR LEADS ME

My foot has held fast to His steps; I have kept His way and have not turned aside.
Job 23:11

1. All the way my Sav-ior leads me— What have I to ask be - side? Can I doubt His ten-der mer - cy, Who through life has been my guide? Heav'n-ly peace, di - vin - est com-fort, Here by faith in Him to dwell! For I know, what-

2. All the way my Sav-ior leads me— Cheers each wind - ing path I tread, Gives me grace for ev-'ry tri - al, Feeds me with the liv-ing bread. Though my wea - ry steps may fal - ter And my soul a - thirst may be, Gush-ing from the

3. All the way my Sav-ior leads me— O the full - ness of His love! Per - fect rest to me is prom-ised In my Fa - ther's house a - bove. When my spir - it, clothed im-mor - tal, Wings its flight to realms of day, This my song through

e'er be - fall me, Je - sus do - eth all things well; well.
rock be - fore me, Lo! a spring of joy I see; see.
end - less a - ges: Je - sus led me all the way; way.

Text: Fanny J. Crosby, 1820-1915
Tune: ALL THE WAY, 8 7 8 7 D; Robert Lowry, 1826-1899

PEOPLE NEED THE LORD 470

Come to me, all you that are weary and are carrying heavy burdens, and I will give you rest.
Matthew 11:28

Chorus

Peo-ple need the Lord, peo-ple need the Lord;

At the end of bro-ken dreams, He's the o - pen door.
When will we

re - al - ize that peo - ple need the Lord?

Text: Greg Nelson, b.1948, and Phill McHugh, b.1951
Tune: Greg Nelson, b.1948, and Phill McHugh, b.1951
© 1983, Shepherd's Fold Music and River Oaks Music Co. (BMI)

471 PRECIOUS LORD, TAKE MY HAND

Lead me, O LORD, in Your righteousness because of my enemies; make Your way straight before me.
Psalm 5:8

Verses 1-3

1. Pre - cious Lord, take my hand, Lead me on, help me stand; I am tired, I am weak, I am worn; Through the storm, through the night, Lead me on to the light, Take my hand, pre - cious Lord, lead me home.

2. When my way grows drear, Pre - cious Lord, lin - ger near; When my life is al - most gone, Hear my cry, hear my call, Hold my hand lest I fall; Take my hand, pre - cious Lord, lead me home.

3. When the dark - ness ap - pears And the night draws near, And the day is past and gone; At the riv - er I stand, Guide my feet, hold my hand; Take my hand, pre - cious Lord, lead me home.

Verse 4

4. Pre - cious Lord, I love Your name, When I look back from whence I came; Some-times stumb-ling, some-times fall - ing, some-times a - lone. Friends and loved ones I love so dear, Man-y are gone, but still I'm here; Take my hand, pre-cious Lord, and lead me on.

472 LIFE'S RAILWAY TO HEAVEN

...let us also lay aside every weight and the sin that clings so closely, and let us run with perseverance the race...
Hebrews 12:1

1. Life is like a moun-tain rail-road, With an en-gi-
2. You will roll up grades of tri-al; You will cross the
3. You will of-ten find ob-struc-tions; Look for storms of
4. As you roll a-cross the tres-tle, Span-ning Jor-dan's

neer that's brave; We must make the run suc-cess-ful, From the
bridge of strife; See that Christ is your con-duc-tor On this
wind and rain; On a fill, or curve, or tres-tle, They will
swel-ling tide, You be-hold the Un-ion De-pot In-to

cra - dle to the grave; Watch the curves, the fills, the
light - ning train of life; Al - ways mind - ful of ob-
al - most ditch your train; Put your trust a - lone in
which your train will glide; There you'll meet the Su - p'rin -

tun - nels; Nev - er fal - ter, nev - er quail; Keep your
struc-tion, Do your du - ty, nev - er fail; Keep your
Je - sus; Nev - er fal - ter, nev - er fail; Keep your
ten - dent, God the Fa - ther, God the Son, With the

hand   up-on the throt-tle,   And your eye   up-on the   rail.
hand   up-on the throt-tle,   And your eye   up-on the   rail.
hand   up-on the throt-tle,   And your eye   up-on the   rail.
heart - y, joy-ous plau-dit,   "Wea-ry pil - grim, wel-come home."

Bless - ed Sav - ior, Thou wilt guide us,   Till we reach   the bliss-ful

shore. Where the an - gels wait to join us   In Thy praise for ev-er-more.

Text: M. E. Abbey
Tune: LIFE'S RAILWAY, 8 7 8 7 D with refrain; Charles D. Tillman, 1861-1943

473 SAVIOR, LEAD ME LEST I STRAY

With my whole heart I seek You; do not let me stray from Your commandments.
Psalm 119:10

1. Sav - ior, lead me lest I lead me lest I stray,
2. Thou the ref - uge of my ref - uge of my soul,
3. Sav - ior, lead me, then at lead me, then at last,

1. Sav - ior, lead me lest I stray,
2. Thou the ref - uge of my soul,
3. Sav - ior, lead me, then at last,

Gen - tly lead me all the lead me all the way;
When life's storm - y bil - lows storm - y bil - lows roll;
When the storm of life is storm of life is past;

Gen - tly lead me all the way;
When life's storm - y bil - lows roll;
When the storm of life is past;

I am safe when by Thy safe when by Thy side,
I am safe when Thou art safe when Thou art nigh,
To the land of end - less land of end - less day,

I am safe when by Thy side,
I am safe when Thou art nigh,
To the land of end - less day,

Text: Frank M. Davis
Tune: LEAD ME, 77 77 with refrain; Frank M. Davis

474 LEAD ME, GUIDE ME

You are indeed my rock and my fortress; for Your name's sake lead me and guide me...
Psalm 31:3

Lead me,   guide me,   a - long   the   way,

For   if You   lead   me,   I   can - not   stray.

Lord,   let me   walk   each   day   with   Thee.

Lead me,   oh   Lord,   lead   me.

Verses

1. I am weak and I need Thy strength and pow'r to help me o-ver my weak-est hour. Help me through the dark-ness Thy face to see, Lead me, oh Lord, lead me.

2. Help me tread in the paths of right-eous-ness, Be my aid when Sa-tan and sin op-press. I am put-ting all my trust in Thee. Lead me, oh Lord, lead me.

3. I am lost if You take your hand from me, I am blind with-out Thy Light to see, Lord, just al-ways let me Thy ser-vant be. Lead me, oh Lord, lead me.

D.C.

Text: Doris M. Akers, b.1922
Tune: Doris M. Akers, b.1922; harm. by Richard Smallwood

475 SAVIOR, MORE THAN LIFE TO ME

For to me, living is Christ and dying is gain.
Philippians 1:21

1. Sav - ior, more than life to me, I am
2. Through this chang - ing world be - low, Lead me
3. Let me love Thee more and more, Till this

cling - ing, cling-ing close to Thee; Let Thy pre - cious blood ap-
gen - tly, gen - tly as I go; Trust-ing Thee, I can-not
fleet - ing, fleet-ing life is o'er; Till my soul is lost in

plied, Keep me ev - er, ev - er near Thy side.
stray, I can nev - er, nev - er lose my way.
love, In a bright-er, bright-er world a - bove.

Ev - 'ry day, ev - 'ry hour Let me

Ev - 'ry day and hour, ev - 'ry day and hour

feel   Thy cleans - ing pow'r;   May Thy ten - der love to

me   Bind me clos - er,   clos - er, Lord,   to   Thee.

Text: Fanny J. Crosby, 1820-1915
Tune: MORE THAN LIFE, 79 79 with refrain; William H. Doane, 1832-1915

476 STAND UP FOR JESUS

...take up the whole armor of God, so that you may be able to withstand on that evil day...
Ephesians 6:13

1. Stand up, stand up for Je - sus, Ye sol-diers of the cross!
2. Stand up, stand up for Je - sus, The trum-pet call o - bey;
3. Stand up, stand up for Je - sus, Stand in His strength a - lone;
4. Stand up, stand up for Je - sus, The strife will not be long;

Lift high His roy - al ban - ner— It must not suf - fer loss.
Forth to the might - y con - flict In this His glo-rious day.
The arm of flesh will fail you— Ye dare not trust your own.
This day the noise of bat - tle— The next, the vic-tor's song.

From vic - t'ry un - to vic - t'ry His ar - my shall He lead,
Ye that are men now serve Him A - gainst un - num-bered foes;
Put on the gos - pel ar - mor, Each piece put on with prayer;
To Him that o - ver - com - eth A crown of life shall be:

Till ev - 'ry foe is van-quished And Christ is Lord in-deed.
Let cour - age rise with dan - ger And strength to strength op-pose.
Where du - ty calls or dan - ger, Be nev - er want - ing there.
He with the King of glo - ry Shall reign e - ter - nal - ly.

Text: George Duffield, Jr., 1818-1888
Tune: WEBB, 7 6 7 6 D; George J. Webb, 1803-1887

LEAD ON, O KING ETERNAL 477

I am the LORD your God, who teaches you for your own good, who leads you in the way you should go.
Isaiah 48:17

1. Lead on, O King E - ter - nal, The day of march has come!
2. Lead on, O King E - ter - nal, Till sin's fierce war shall cease
3. Lead on, O King E - ter - nal, We fol - low— not with fears!

Hence-forth in fields of con - quest Thy tents shall be our home;
And ho - li - ness shall whis - per The sweet A - men of peace;
For glad-ness breaks like morn - ing Wher-e'er Thy face ap - pears;

Thru days of prep - a - ra - tion Thy grace has made us strong,
For not with swords loud clash - ing Nor roll of stir-ring drums—
Thy cross is lift - ed o'er us— We jour-ney in its light:

And now, O King E - ter - nal, We lift our bat - tle song.
With deeds of love and mer - cy The heav'n-ly king-dom comes.
The crown a - waits the con-quest—Lead on, O God of might.

Text: Ernest W. Shurtleff, 1862-1917
Tune: LANCASHIRE, 7 6 7 6 D; Henry T. Smart, 1813-1879; arr. by Jon Drevits, © 1966, Singspiration Music (ASCAP)

478 WHAT A MIGHTY GOD WE SERVE

The mighty one, God the LORD, speaks and summons the earth from the rising of the sun to its setting.
Psalm 50:1

What a might-y God we serve.

What a might-y God we serve.

An-gels bow be-fore Him. Heav-en and earth a-dore Him.

1.
⌒ *Last time*
What a might-y God we serve.

2.
I com-

⌒ *Last time*

mand you, Sa-tan, in the name of the Lord to take

up your weap-ons and flee, for the Lord has giv-en me au-

D.C.

thor - i - ty to walk all o - ver thee.

Text: Traditional
Tune: Traditional; arr. by Stephen Key, © 2000, GIA Publications, Inc.

479 I Shall Not Be Moved

I keep the LORD always before me; because He is at my right hand, I shall not be moved.
Psalm 16:8

1. I shall not, I shall not be moved, I shall not,

Oh,

I shall not be moved. Just like a tree that's plant-ed by the

wa - ter, I shall not be moved.

2. The church of God is march - ing,   The
3. ⁊ Come and join the ar - my,   ⁊
4. King Je - sus is our Cap - tain, I shall not be moved. King
5. ⁊ Sa - tan had me bound,   ⁊
6. ⁊ On my way to heav - en,   ⁊

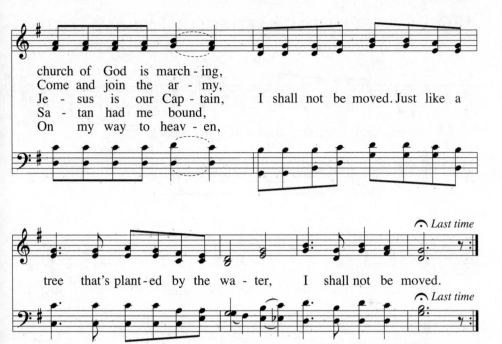

church of God   is march - ing,
Come and join   the   ar - my,
Je - sus   is   our Cap - tain,   I shall not be moved. Just like a
Sa - tan   had me   bound,
On   my   way   to heav - en,

tree   that's plant - ed by the wa - ter,   I   shall not be moved.

Last time

Text: Traditional
Tune: I SHALL NOT BE MOVED, Irregular; Negro spiritual; arr. by Betty Gadling, © 2000, GIA Publications, Inc.

480 I Am On the Battlefield For My Lord

...your servants will cross over, everyone armed for war, to do battle for the LORD...
Numbers 32:27

I am on the bat-tle - field for my Lord, I'm

on the bat-tle - field for my Lord; And I

prom-ised Him that I would serve Him till I die. I am

on the bat-tle - field for my Lord.

Verses

1. I was a - lone and i - dle, I was a sin - ner too, I heard a voice from heav - en Say there is work to do, I took the Mas - ter's hand, And I joined the Chris-tian band, I'm on the bat-tle-field for my Lord.
2. I left my friends and kin - dred Bound for the Prom-ised Land, The grace of God up - on me, Bi - ble in my hand, In dis - tant lands I trod, Cry-ing sin - ner come to God, I'm on the bat-tle-field for my Lord.
3. Now when I met my Sav - ior, I met Him with a smile, He healed my wound - ed spir - it, And owned me as His child, A - round the throne of grace, He ap - points my soul a place, I'm on the bat-tle-field for my Lord.

D.C.

Text: Sylvana Bell and E.V. Banks
Tune: BATTLEFIELD, 7 6 7 6 67 9 with refrain; Gospel Hymn; arr. by Joseph Joubert, © 2000, GIA Publications, Inc.

481 ONWARD, CHRISTIAN SOLDIERS

Share in suffering like a good soldier of Christ Jesus.
2 Timothy 2:3

1. On - ward, Chris - tian sol - diers, March - ing as to war.
2. Like a might - y ar - my Moves the Church of God;
3. Crowns and thrones may per - ish, King - doms rise and wane,
4. On - ward, then, ye peo - ple, Join our hap - py throng;

With the cross of Je - sus Go - ing on be - fore:
Chris - tians, we are tread - ing Where the saints have trod,
But the Church of Je - sus Con - stant will re - main,
Blend with ours your voic - es In the tri - umph song,

Christ, the roy - al Mas - ter, Leads a - gainst the foe;
We are not di - vid - ed, All one bod - y we:
Gates of hell can nev - er 'Gainst that Church pre - vail;
Glo - ry, laud, and hon - or Un - to Christ the King:

For - ward in - to bat - tle, See His ban - ners go.
One in hope and one in faith, One in char - i - ty.
We have Christ's own prom - ise, And that can - not fail.
This through count - less a - ges With the an - gels sing.

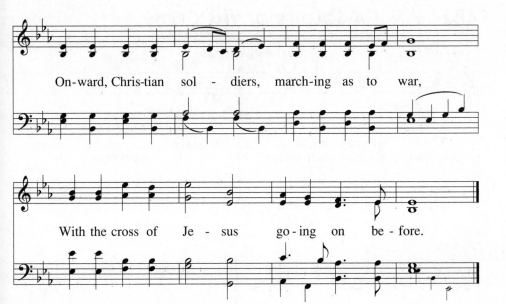

On-ward, Chris-tian sol - diers, march-ing as to war,

With the cross of Je - sus go - ing on be - fore.

Text: Sabine Baring-Gould, 1834-1924
Tune: ST. GERTRUDE, 6 5 6 5 D with refrain; Arthur S. Sullivan, 1842-1900

482 AM I A SOLDIER OF THE CROSS

Keep alert, stand firm in your faith, be courageous, be strong. Let all that you do be done in love.
1 Corinthians 16:13-14

1. Am I a sol - dier of the cross, A
2. Must I be car - ried to the skies On
3. Are there no foes for me to face? Must
4. Sure I must fight if I would reign: In -

fol - l'wer of the Lamb? And shall I fear to
flow - 'ry beds of ease, While oth - ers fought to
I not stem the flood? Is this vile world a
crease my cour - age, Lord; I'll bear the toil, en -

own His cause Or blush to speak His name?
win the prize And sailed through blood - y seas?
friend to grace, To help me on to God?
dure the pain, Sup - port - ed by Thy word.

Text: Isaac Watts, 1674-1748
Tune: ARLINGTON, CM; Thomas A. Arne, 1710-1778

Am I a Soldier of the Cross 483

Keep alert, stand firm in your faith, be courageous, be strong. Let all that you do be done in love.
1 Corinthians 16:13-14

Leader (Spoken): Am I a soldier of the cross, a follower of the Lamb?

Am I a sol - dier of the cross,

a fol - l'wer of the Lamb?

Leader: And shall I fear to own His cause,

And shall I

fear to own His cause,

Leader: Or blush to speak His name?

Or blush to speak His name?

Text: Isaac Watts, 1674-1748
Tune: Meter hymn, lined out by Westerly Robinson; arr. by Evelyn Simpson-Curenton, b.1953, © 2000, GIA Publications, Inc.

484   EZEKIEL SAW DE WHEEL

...when the living creatures rose from the earth, the wheels rose. Wherever the spirit would go, they went...
Ezekiel 1:19

E - ze-k'el saw de wheel   'Way up in de mid-dle o' de air, E-

ze-k'el saw de wheel   'Way in de mid-dle o' de air.   De

big wheel run by faith,   De lit-tle wheel run by de grace o' God,

A   wheel   in a wheel— 'Way   in de mid-dle o' de air.

Verses

1. Bet - ter mind, my sis - ter, how you walk on de cross,
2. Let me tell you, broth - er, what a sin - ner will do,

'Way in de mid - dle o' de air,

Your foot might slip an' your
He'll step on you an' he'll

D.C.

'Way in de mid - dle o' de air.

soul be lost.
step on me.

Text: Traditional
Tune: Negro spiritual; harm. by J. Jefferson Cleveland, 1937-1988, alt., © 1981, Abingdon Press

485 SATAN, WE'RE GONNA TEAR YOUR KINGDOM DOWN

And the devil who had deceived them was thrown into the lake of fire and sulfur...
Revelation 20:10

1. ╕ Sa - tan, we're gon - na tear your king-dom
2. The preach - ers are gon - na preach your king-dom
3. The dea - cons are gon - na pray your king-dom
4. The moth - ers are gon - na moan your king-dom

down. ╕ Sa - tan, we're gon-na tear your king - dom
down. The preach-ers are gon-na preach your king - dom
down. The dea - cons are gon-na pray your king - dom
down. The moth - ers are gon-na moan your king - dom

down. You've been build-ing your king-dom all o - ver this

land. Sa-tan, we're gon-na tear your king-dom down.

Text: Traditional
Tune: KINGDOM DOWN, 10 10 12 10; traditional; arr. by Jimmie Abbington, © 2000, GIA Publications, Inc.

HOLD BACK THE NIGHT 486

Every word of God proves true; He is a shield to those who take refuge in Him.
Proverbs 30:5

Chorus

Hold   back   the night.   Give me strength   to

fight.   I'll   do   Your   will   if You just

say to my soul: peace,   be   still.   O   Lord,   I

love Your name.   Ev - 'ry   day   You're just   the same.

I'll   be   all   right   if You hold back the   night.

487 I Couldn't Hear Nobody Pray

He came to the disciples and found them sleeping; and he said..."So, could you not stay awake with me one hour?"
Matthew 26:40

Text: Traditional
Tune: Negro spiritual; arr. by Carl Haywood, b.1949, from *The Haywood Collection of Negro Spirituals,* © 1992

488 WE ARE SOLDIERS

You then, my child, be strong in the grace that is in Christ Jesus...
2 Timothy 2:1

Chorus

We are sol - diers in the ar - my.

We have to fight al-though we have to cry.

We've got to hold up the blood - stained ban - ner.

We've got to hold it up un - til we die!

Text: Gospel Hymn
Tune: Gospel Hymn; arr. by Nolan Williams, Jr., b.1969, © 2000, GIA Publications, Inc

Victory Is Mine 489

The God of peace will shortly crush Satan under your feet.
Romans 16:20

The melody is in the alto part.

1. Vic - to - ry   is   mine.   Vic - to - ry   is   mine.
2. Joy   is   mine.   Joy   is   mine.
3. Hap - pi - ness   is   mine.   Hap - pi - ness   is   mine.

Vic - to - ry   to-day   is   mine.   I   told   Sa - tan
Joy   to-day   is   mine.   I   told   Sa - tan
Hap - pi - ness   to-day   is   mine.   I   told   Sa - tan

get   thee   be - hind.   Vic - to - ry   to - day   is   mine.
get   thee   be - hind.   Joy   to - day   is   mine.
get   thee   be - hind.   Hap - pi - ness   to - day   is   mine.

Text: Dorothy Norwood and Alvin Darling
Tune: VICTORY, 5 5 7 8 7; Dorothy Norwood and Alvin Darling.; arr. by Stephen Key
© Malaco Music, Inc.

490 BATTLE HYMN OF THE REPUBLIC

In Your majesty ride on victoriously for the cause of truth and to defend the right...
Psalm 45:4

1. Mine eyes have seen the glo - ry of the
2. I have seen Him in the watch - fires of a
3. He has sound - ed forth the trum - pet that shall
4. In the beau - ty of the lil - ies Christ was

com - ing of the Lord; He is tram - pling out the
hun - dred cir - cling camps; They have build - ed Him an
nev - er call re - treat; He is sift - ing out all
born a - cross the sea, With a glo - ry in His

vin - tage where the grapes of wrath are stored; He hath
al - tar in the eve - ning dews and damps; I can
hu - man hearts be - fore His judg - ment seat; O be
bos - om that trans - fig - ures you and me; As He

loosed the fate - ful light - ning of His ter - ri - ble swift
read the right - eous sen - tence by the dim and flar - ing
swift, my soul, to an - swer Him; be ju - bi - lant, my
died to make us ho - ly, let us die that all be

sword; His truth is march - ing on.
lamps; His day is march - ing on.
feet! Our God is march - ing on.
free! While God is march - ing on.

Glo - ry! Glo - ry! Hal - le - lu - jah! Glo - ry!

Glo - ry! Hal - le - lu - jah! Glo - ry! Glo - ry!

Hal - le - lu - jah! His truth is march - ing on.

Text: Julia Ward Howe, 1819-1910
Tune: BATTLE HYMN, 15 15 15 6, with refrain; William Steffe, d.1911

491 CENTER OF MY JOY

...I regard everything as loss because of the surpassing value of knowing Christ Jesus my Lord.
Philippians 3:8

Je-sus, You're the cen-ter of my joy.

All that's good and per - fect comes from You.

play cues 2nd time only

You're the heart of my con-tent-ment, hope for all I do.

1.
Je - sus, You're the cen - ter of my joy.

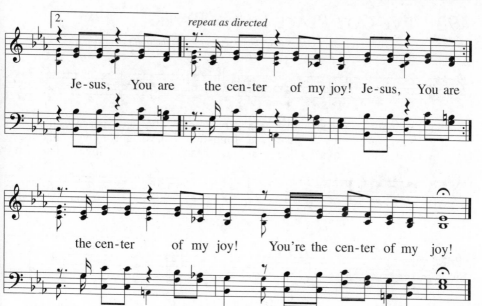

Text: Richard Smallwood, William Gaither, b.1936, Gloria Gaither, b.1942
Tune: Richard Smallwood, William Gaither, b.1936, Gloria Gaither, b.1942; arr. by Nolan Williams, Jr., b.1969
© 1987, Gaither Music Co. and Century Oak/Richwood Music

492 I'VE GOT PEACE LIKE A RIVER

...my peace I give to you. I do not give to you as the world gives.
John 14:27

1. I've got peace like a riv-er, I've got peace like a riv-er, I've got peace like a riv-er in my soul. I've got riv-er in my soul.
2. I've got joy like a foun-tain, I've got joy like a foun-tain, I've got joy like a foun-tain in my soul. I've got foun-tain in my soul.
3. I've got love like an o-cean, I've got love like an o-cean, I've got love like an o-cean in my soul. I've got o-cean in my soul.

Text: Congregational Praise Song
Tune: PEACE LIKE A RIVER, 7 7 10, Congregational Praise Song

SOMETHING WITHIN 493

Now we have received not the spirit of the world, but the Spirit that is from God...
1 Corinthians 2:12

1. Preach-ers and teach-ers would make their ap-peal,
2. Have you that some-thing, that burn-ing de-sire?
3. I met God one morn', my soul feel-ing bad,

Refrain: Some-thing with-in me that hold-eth the reins,

Fight-ing as sol-diers on great bat-tle-fields;
Have you that some-thing, that nev-er doth tire?
Heart heav-y la-den with a bowed down head.

Some-thing with-in me that ban-ish-es pain;

When to their plead-ings my poor heart did yield,
Oh, if you have it— that Heav-en-ly Fire!
He lift-ed my bur-den, made me so glad,

Some-thing with-in me I can-not ex-plain,

All I can say, there is some-thing with-in.
Then let the world know there is some-thing with-in.
All that I know there is some-thing with-in.

All that I know there is some-thing with-in.

Text: Lucie E. Campbell, 1885-1963
Tune: SOMETHING WITHIN, 10 10 10 10; Lucie E. Campbell, 1885-1963; arr. by Jimmie Abbington, © 2000, GIA Publications, Inc.

494 IN THE GARDEN

They heard the sound of the LORD walking in the garden…"
Genesis 3:8

1. I come to the gar - den a - lone, While the
2. He speaks, and the sound of His voice Is so
3. I'd stay in the gar - den with Him Though the

dew is still on the ros - es; And the voice I hear,
sweet the birds hush their sing - ing; And the mel - o - dy
night a - round me be fall - ing; But He bids me go—

fall - ing on my ear, The Son of God dis - clos - es.
that He gave to me With - in my heart is ring - ing.
through the voice of woe, His voice to me is call - ing.

And He walks with me, and He talks with me,

And He tells me I am His own, And the joy we share as we tar - ry there, None oth-er has ev - er known.

Text: C. Austin Miles, 1868-1946
Tune: GARDEN, 8 9 10 7 with refrain; C. Austin Miles, 1868-1946

495 HE WILL KEEP YOU IN PERFECT PEACE

Those of steadfast mind You keep in peace—in peace because they trust in You.
Isaiah 26:3

Refrain

He will keep you in per-fect peace whose mind is stayed on Him, He will strength-en and sus-tain you, tho' all a-round is dim, He'll com-fort you He'll com-fort you— He will keep you in per-fect peace.

Verses

1. When your val - ley is so ver - y deep, And your
2. And with ev - 'ry tri - al that is sore, By His

moun - tain is so high and steep, He will lead so
grace you're a - ble to en - dure. You can sing al -

D.C.

gent - ly by His Hand— For our God does know and un - der - stand.
though it may be night— For you know your morn - ing will be bright.

Text: Betty McCullough
Tune: PERFECT PEACE, 99 99 with refrain; Betty McCullough
© 1980, Josiah Publishing Co.

496 THE REASON WHY WE SING

I will give to the LORD the thanks due to His righteousness, and sing praise to the name of the LORD, the Most High.
Psalm 7:17

Verses

1. Some-one asked the ques-tion: why do we sing?
2. Some-one may be won-d'ring: when we sing our song
3. When the song is o - ver, we all say, "A-men."
4. If some-bod - y asks you: was it just a show?
(5.) when we cross the riv - er, we'll stud - y war no more.

When we lift our hands to Je - sus, ' what
' at times we may be cry - ing ' and
In our heart just keep on sing - ing, and the
Lift your hands and be a wit - ness, ' and
We will sing our song to Je - sus, ' the

1., 3.
2., 4., 5.

do   we real - ly   mean?
noth - ing's e - ven wrong.   *(To refrain)*
song   will nev - er   end.
tell   the whole world, "No."   *(To refrain)*
One   whom we   a - dore.   *(To refrain)*

Refrain

I   sing be-cause I'm hap - py.   I sing be-cause I'm free.

His eye is   on   the spar - row,   that's the

rea - son why I sing.

Glo - ry, hal - le - lu -

jah! You're the rea - son why I sing.

Last time

5. And

Text: Kirk Franklin, © 1996, Lilly Mack Publishing
Tune: Kirk Franklin, © 1996, Lilly Mack Publishing; arr. by Evelyn Simpson-Curenton, b.1953, © 2000, GIA Publications, Inc.

WE SHALL WALK THROUGH THE VALLEY IN PEACE 497

Even though I walk through the darkest valley, I fear no evil; for You are with me...
Psalm 23:4

1. We shall walk through the val - ley in peace;
2. There will be no sor - row there;
3. There will be no dy - ing there;

We shall walk through the val - ley in peace;
There will be no sor - row there.
There will be no dy - ing there.

If Je - sus Him - self shall be our Lead - er,

We shall walk through the val - ley in peace.

Text: A.L. Hatter
Tune: PEACEFUL VALLEY, 99 10 9; A.L. Hatter; arr. by Joseph Joubert, © 2000, GIA Publications, Inc.

498   LET THERE BE PEACE ON EARTH

Pursue peace with everyone, and the holiness without which no one will see the Lord.
Hebrews 12:14

Let there be peace on earth, and let it be-gin with
me.   Let there be peace on earth, the
peace that was meant to be.   With God as our
Fa - ther,   broth - ers all are we.
fam - 'ly
Let me walk with my broth-er   in per - fect har - mo-
us   each oth - er

ny. Let peace be-gin with me; let this be the mo-ment now. With ev-'ry step I take, let this be my sol-emn vow; To take each mo-ment, and live each mo-ment in peace e-ter-nal-ly! Let there be peace on earth, and let it be-gin with me.

Text: Sy Miller, 1908-1941, Jill Jackson, © 1955, 1983, Jan-Lee Music
Tune: Sy Miller, 1908-1941, Jill Jackson, © 1955, 1983, Jan-Lee Music; acc. by Diana Kodner, b.1957, © 1993, GIA Publications, Inc.

499 SINCE JESUS CAME INTO MY HEART

It is no longer I who live, but it is Christ who lives in me.
Galatians 2:20

1. What a won - der - ful change in my life has been wrought
2. I have ceased from my wan - d'ring and go - ing a - stray,
3. I shall go there to dwell in that cit - y, I know,

Since Je - sus came in - to my heart! I have
Since Je - sus came in - to my heart! And my
Since Je - sus came in - to my heart! And I'm

light in my soul for which long I have sought,
sins, which were man - y, are all washed a - way,
hap - py, so hap - py, as on - ward I go,

Since Je - sus came in - to my heart!
Since Je - sus came in - to my heart!
Since Je - sus came in - to my heart!

heart

Since Je-sus came in - to my in - to my heart, Since

in, came

heart,

Je-sus came in-to my in-to my heart, Floods of joy o'er my soul

in, came

like the sea bil-lows roll, Since Je-sus came in-to my heart.

Text: Rufus H. McDaniel, 1850-1940
Tune: McDANIEL, 12 8 12 8 with refrain; Charles H. Gabriel, 1856-1932; adapt. by Louis Sykes, © 2000, GIA Publications, Inc.

500 Glory, Glory, Hallelujah

Cast your burden on the LORD, and He will sustain you; He will never permit the righteous to be moved.
Psalm 55:22

1. Glo - ry, glo - ry, hal - le - lu - jah! Since I laid my bur-dens down.
2. Friends don't treat me like they used to Since I laid my bur-dens down.
3. I'm goin' home to live with Je - sus Since I laid my bur-dens down.

Glo - ry, glo - ry, hal - le - lu - jah!
Friends don't treat me like they used to
I'm goin' home to live with Je - sus

1., 2.
Since I laid my bur-dens down!
Since I laid my bur-dens down!

3.
Since I laid my bur-dens down!

Text: Negro spiritual
Tune: GLORY, 15 15; Negro spiritual; arr. by Nolan Williams, Jr., b.1969, © 2000, GIA Publications, Inc.

JESUS IS REAL TO ME 501

But thanks be to God, who gives us the victory through our Lord Jesus Christ.
1 Corinthians 15:57

Chorus

Real, real, Je-sus is real to me.

Oh yes, He gives me the vic-to - ry.

So man-y peo-ple doubt Him. I can't live with-out Him.

That is why I love Him so, He's so real to me.

Text: Beatrice Brown, © 1963, Beatrice Brown's Music House
Tune: Beatrice Brown, © 1963, Beatrice Brown's Music House; arr. by Stephen Key, © 2000, GIA Publications, Inc.

502 Come, Let Us Sing

Make a joyful noise to God, all the earth; sing the glory of His name; give to Him glorious praise.
Psalm 66:1

Text: African-American traditional
Tune: African-American traditional; arr. by Walter Owens, Jr., © 2000, GIA Publications, Inc.

503 LOOK AND LIVE

Blessed are the eyes that see what you see! Many... desired to see what you see, but did not see it.
Luke 10:23-24

1. I've a mes-sage from the Lord, Hal-le-lu-jah! The mes-sage un-to you I'll give. 'Tis re-cord-ed in His Word. Hal-le-lu-jah! It is on-ly that you "look and live." "Look and live," my broth-er, live.

2. I've a mes-sage full of love, Hal-le-lu-jah! A mes-sage, O my friend, for you. 'Tis a mes-sage from a-bove, Hal-le-lu-jah! Je-sus said it, and I know 'tis true.

3. Life is of-fered un-to you. Hal-le-lu-jah! E-ter-nal life your soul shall have If you'll on-ly look to Him. Hal-le-lu-jah! Look to Je-sus, who a-lone can save.

4. I will tell you how I came, Hal-le-lu-jah! To Je-sus when He made me whole: 'Twas be-liev-ing on His name. Hal-le-lu-jah! I trust-ed and He saved my soul.

"Look and live," my broth-er, live. "Look and live." Look to

Je - sus now and live. 'Tis re - cord - ed in His Word, Hal - le -

lu - jah! It is on - ly that you "look and live."

Text: William A. Ogden, 1841-1897
Tune: LOOK AND LIVE, 11 8 11 9 with refrain; William A. Ogden, 1841-1897

504 LOVE LIFTED ME

...in His love and in His pity He redeemed them; He lifted them up and carried them all the days of old.
Isaiah 63:9

1. I was sink - ing deep in sin, Far from the peace - ful shore, Ver - y deep - ly stained with - in, Sink-ing to rise no more; But the Mas - ter of the sea Heard my de - spair - ing cry,

2. All my heart to Him I give, Ev - er to Him I'll cling, In His bless - ed pres - ence live, Ev - er His prais - es sing. Love so might - y and so true Mer - its my soul's best songs;

3. Souls in dan - ger, look a - bove, Je - sus com - plete - ly saves; He will lift you by His love Out of the an - gry waves. He's the Mas - ter of the sea, Bil - lows His will o - bey;

From the wa - ters lift - ed me— Now safe am I.
Faith - ful, lov - ing serv - ice, too, To Him be - longs.
He your Sav - ior wants to be— Be saved to - day.

me,
Love lift - ed e - ven me, Love lift - ed

me,
e - ven me, When noth - ing else could help,

1.   2.
Love lift - ed me; Love lift - ed me.

Text: James Rowe, 1865-1933
Tune: SAFETY, 7 6 7 6 7 6 7 4 with refrain; Howard E. Smith, 1863-1918

505   Somebody Prayed For Me

I am asking on their behalf; I am not asking on behalf of the world, but on behalf of those whom You gave me...
John 17:9

I'm so glad they prayed for me.

2. The preacher prayed for me...
3. My mother prayed for me...
4. Jesus prayed for me...

Text: Dorothy Norwood and Alvin Darling
Tune: Dorothy Norwood and Alvin Darling; arr. by Nolan Williams, Jr., b.1969, and Stephen Key
© 1994, Malaco Music, Inc.

506 THE LORD IS BLESSING ME RIGHT NOW

Blessed be the God and Father of our Lord Jesus Christ, who has blessed us in Christ with every spiritual blessing...
Ephesians 1:3

The Lord is bless-ing me right now, Oh, right now, now! The Lord is

bless - ing me   right now,   Oh,   right

now,

now!   He woke me up this

morn - ing,   And start - ed me   on   my

way;   The Lord   is

bless - ing me   right now!

The   now!

He Has Done Great Things for Me 507

The LORD has done great things for us, and we rejoiced.
Psalm 126:3

1. He has done great things for me.
2. He has made a way for me.
3. He will give you vic - to - ry.
4. I'm gonna be a wit - ness for Him.
5. I'm gonna let my lit - tle light shine.

Great things, great things.
Made a way, made a way.
Vic - to - ry, vic - to - ry.
Wit - ness, wit - ness.
Shine, shine.

He has done great things for me.
He has made a way for me.
He will give you vic - to - ry.
I'm gonna be a wit - ness for Him.
I'm gonna let my lit - tle light shine.

Text: Shirley M. K. Berkeley, © 1989
Tune: GREAT THINGS, 7 4 7; Shirley M. K. Berkeley, © 1989; arr. by Stephen Key, © 2000, GIA Publications, Inc.

508 Blessed Assurance, Jesus Is Mine

...let us approach (the sanctuary) with a true heart in full assurance of faith, with our hearts sprinkled clean...
Hebrews 10:22

1. Bless-ed as - sur - ance, Je - sus is mine! O what a
2. Per - fect sub - mis - sion, per-fect de - light, Vi-sions of
3. Per - fect sub - mis - sion, all is at rest, I in my

fore - taste of glo - ry di - vine! Heir of sal - va - tion,
rap - ture now burst on my sight; An - gels de - scend - ing
Sav - ior am hap-py and blest; Watch-ing and wait - ing,

pur - chase of God, Born of His Spir - it, washed in His blood.
bring from a - bove Ech - oes of mer - cy, whis-pers of love.
look - ing a - bove, Filled with His good-ness, lost in His love.

This is my sto - ry, this is my song, Prais-ing my

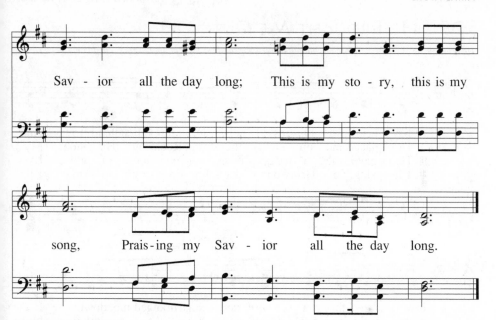

Sav - ior all the day long; This is my sto - ry, this is my

song, Prais - ing my Sav - ior all the day long.

Text: Fanny J. Crosby, 1820-1915
Tune: ASSURANCE, 9 10 9 9 with refrain; Phoebe P. Knapp, 1839-1908

509 He Brought Me Out

He drew me up from the desolate pit, out of the miry bog, and set my feet upon a rock, making my steps secure.
Psalm 40:2

1. My heart was dis-tressed 'neath Je - ho-vah's dread frown, And
2. He placed me up - on the strong Rock by His side, My
3. He gave me a song, 'twas a new song of praise; By
4. I'll sing of His won - der - ful mer - cy to me, I'll

low in the pit where my sins dragged me down; I
steps were es - tab - lished and here I'll a - bide; No
day and by night its sweet notes I will raise; My
praise Him till all men His good - ness shall see; I'll

cried to the Lord from the deep mir - y clay, Who
dan - ger of fall - ing while here I re - main, But
heart's o - ver-flow - ing, I'm hap - py and free, I'll
sing of sal - va - tion at home and a-broad, Till

ten - der - ly brought me out to gold - en day.
stand by His grace un - til the crown I gain.
praise my Re - deem - er, who has res - cued me.
man - y shall hear the truth and trust in God.

He brought me out of the mir-y clay, He set my feet on the
Rock to stay; He put a song in my
soul to-day, And now I can sing, hal-le-lu-jah!

Text: Henry J. Zelley, 1859-1942; refrain, Henry L. Gilmour, 1836-1920, alt.
Tune: HE BROUGHT ME OUT, 11 11 11 11 with refrain; Henry L. Gilmour, 1836-1920

510   He's Sweet I Know

The LORD bless you and keep you; the LORD make His face to shine upon you, and be gracious to you...
Numbers 6:24-25

Refrain: He's sweet, I   know.   He's   sweet, I   know.
   1. I   can't for - get   when   I   was   sad.
   2. I   have my tick-et   here   in   my   hand.

Storm clouds may   rise,   strong winds may blow.
Head   hang - ing   down,   soul   feel - ing   bad.
I'm   go - ing   to   that   beau - ti - ful   land.

I'll tell the world wher - ev - er I go.
All I could say was Lord take my heart.
Some - time I weep and some - time I moan.

That I've found a Sav - ior, and He's sweet, I know.
Je - sus heard and saved me, and gave me a start.
But I'm bound for glo - ry, and I'm go - ing on.

Text: Traditional Gospel hymn
Tune: HE'S SWEET, 88 9 11; Traditional Gospel hymn; arr. by Kenneth Louis and Nolan Williams, Jr., b.1969, © 2000, GIA Publications, Inc.

511   He's Done So Much for Me

He Himself bore our sins in His body on the cross, so that, free from sins, we might live for righteousness...
1 Peter 2:24

1. He's done so much for me, I can-not tell it all,
2. He washed my sins a-way; I can-not tell it all,
3. He walks and talks with me; I can-not tell it all,
4. He gave me vic-to-ry; I can-not tell it all,

I can-not tell it all, I can-not tell it all.
I can-not tell it all, I can-not tell it all.
I can-not tell it all, I can-not tell it all.
I can-not tell it all, I can-not tell it all.

He's done so much for me, I can-not tell it all.
He washed my sins a-way; I can-not tell it all.
He walks and talks with me; I can-not tell it all.
He gave me vic-to-ry; I can-not tell it all.

I can - not tell it all.

Text: Theodore R. Frye and Lillian Bowles, c.1884-1949
Tune: DONE SO MUCH, 12 12 12 6; Theodore R. Frye and Lillian Bowles, c.1884-1949; arr. by Nolan Williams, Jr., b.1969, © 2000, GIA
   Publications, Inc.

I Am Redeemed 512

Christ redeemed us from the curse of the law by becoming a curse for us...
Galatians 3:13

Text: Jessy Dixon, © Dixon Music, Inc.
Tune: Jessy Dixon, © Dixon Music, Inc.; arr. by Nolan Williams, Jr., b.1969, © 2000, GIA Publications, Inc.

513 I Love to Tell the Story

I will sing of Your steadfast love, O LORD, forever; with my mouth I will proclaim Your faithfulness...
Psalm 89:1

1. I love to tell the sto-ry Of un-seen things a-bove, Of Je-sus and His glo-ry, Of Je-sus and His love. I love to tell the sto-ry, Be-cause I know it's true; It sat-is-fies my long-ings As noth-ing else would do.

2. I love to tell the sto-ry, For those who know it best Seem hun-ger-ing and thirst-ing To hear it, like the rest. And when, in scenes of glo-ry, I sing the new, new song, 'Twill be the old, old sto-ry That I have loved so long.

I love to tell the sto-ry; 'Twill be my theme in glo-ry.

To tell the old, old sto-ry Of Je-sus and His love.

Text: A. Katherine Hankey, 1831-1911
Tune: HANKEY, 7 6 7 6 D with refrain; William G. Fischer, 1835-1912

514 I'll Tell It Wherever I Go

The word of God continued to spread; the number of the disciples increased greatly in Jerusalem...
Acts 6:7

Unison

1. I'll tell of the Sav - ior, I tell of His
2. I know Him, a - dore Him, a good life to
3. If Sa - tan op - press me, His grace will ca -

fa - vor, I'll tell it wher - ev - er I go.
show Him, I'll tell it wher - ev - er I go.
ress me, I'll tell it wher - ev - er I go.

I count ev - 'ry bless - ing, I go on con -
He's near - est, He's clear - est, In my life He's
When trou - bles de - press me, He won't fail to

fess - ing, I'll tell it wher - ev - er I go.
dear - est, I'll tell it wher - ev - er I go.
bless me, I'll tell it wher - ev - er I go.

Tho' life is un-cer-tain I can-not un-der-
What He is to you may-be you can't
If I was dy-ing with just one word to

stand, But thank Him, and trust Him, and
see, But this thing I know He's
say, I'd speak it for Je - sus then

praise Him while I can, I'll just tell it, ex-
ev - 'ry-thing to me 'cause He saved me, He
breathe my life a - way 'cause He'll be there, Meet

cell it, let all voic - es swell it,
raised me for - ev - er, I'll praise Him, I'll
me there, then go where He pre - pared,

tell it wher - ev-er I go.

Text: Thomas A. Dorsey, 1899-1993
Tune: I'LL TELL IT, Irregular; Thomas A. Dorsey, 1899-1993

515 WITHOUT HIM I COULD DO NOTHING

For in Him we live and move and have our being.
Acts 17:28

1. With - out Him   I could do   noth - ing,
2. With - out Him   I could be   dy - ing,

With - out Him   I   would   fail;
With - out Him   I'd   be en - slaved;

With - out Him   my   life would be   rug - ged
With - out Him   my   life would be   hope - less,

Like   a   ship   with - out   a   sail.
But with   Je - sus, thank   God,   I'm   saved.

Je - sus, O Je - sus, Do you know Him to - day?

You can't turn Him a - way. O Je - sus, O

Je - sus, With - out Him, how lost I would be.

Text: Mylon R. LeFevre, b.1945
Tune: WITHOUT HIM, 8 6 9 7 with refrain; Mylon R. LeFevre, b.1945; arr. by Nolan Williams, Jr., b.1969
© 1963, Angel Band Music

516 PRECIOUS MEMORIES

I will not leave you orphaned; I am coming to you.
John 14:18

Refrain: Pre - cious mem - 'ries
1. Pre - cious mem - 'ries,
2. As I wan - der
3. In sad hours

how they lin - ger,
how I prize them
o'er life's jour - ney
when I'm lone - ly

How they ev - er flood my
As the wea - ry years un -
Won - d'ring what the years may
The truth of Je - sus' love is

soul.
fold.
hold.
told.

In the still - ness
Je - sus whis - pers,
As I pon - der
In the si - lence

of the mid - night
"I'll be with you."
oh, sweet won - der!
of the mid - night

Sa - cred se - crets He'll un -
What a com - fort to my
Pre - cious mem - 'ries flood my
Pre - cious mem - 'ries flood my

Last time

fold.
soul.
soul.
soul.

Last time

Text: Roberta Martin and Mrs. Georgia Jones, © 1939
Tune: PRECIOUS MEMORIES, 8 7 8 7 with refrain; Roberta Martin and Mrs. Georgia Jones, © 1939; arr. by Joseph Joubert, © 2000, GIA
    Publications, Inc.

517 PRECIOUS MEMORIES

I will not leave you orphaned; I am coming to you.
John 14:18

1. Pre - cious mem-'ries, un - seen an - gels, Sent from some-where
2. Pre - cious fa - ther, lov - ing moth - er, Fly a - cross the
3. As I trav - el on life's path-way, Know not what the

to my soul; How they lin - ger, ev - er near me,
lone - ly years; And old home scenes of my child-hood,
years may hold; As I pon - der, hope grows fond - er,

And the sa - cred past un - fold.
In fond mem - o - ry ap - pear. Pre - cious mem-'ries,
Pre - cious mem - 'ries flood my soul.

how they lin-ger, How they ev - er flood my soul; In the

still-ness of the mid-night, Pre - cious, sa-cred scenes un-fold.

Text: J. B. F. Wright and Lonnie B. Combs
Tune: PRECIOUS MEMORIES, 8 7 8 7 with refrain; J. B. F. Wright

BRIDEGROOM AND BRIDE 518

...they are no longer two, but one flesh.
Matthew 19:6

1. God, in the plan-ning and pur-pose of life,
2. Je - sus was found at a sim - i - lar feast,
3. There-fore we pray that His spir - it pre - side
4. Praise then the Mak - er, the Spir - it, the Son,

Hal - lowed the un - ion of hus - band and wife:
Tak - ing the roles of both wait - er and priest,
O - ver the wed - ding of bride-groom and bride,
Source of the love through which two are made one.

This we em - bod - y where love is dis - played,
Turn - ing the world - ly to - wards the di - vine,
Ful - fill - ing all that they've hoped will come true,
God's is the glo - ry, the good-ness, and grace

Rings are pre - sent - ed and prom - is - es made.
Tears in - to laugh - ter and wa - ter to wine.
Light - ing with love all they dream of and do.
Seen in this mar - riage and known in this place.

Text: John L. Bell, b.1949, © 1989, Iona Community, GIA Publications, Inc., agent
Tune: SLANE, 10 10 10 10; Irish traditional; harm. by Erik Routley, 1917-1982, © 1975, Hope Publishing Co.

519 THE FAMILY OF GOD

...and I will be your Father, and you shall be my sons and daughters, says the Lord Almighty.
2 Corinthians 6:18

Refrain

I'm so glad I'm a part of the fam-'ly of God—

I've been washed in the foun-tain, cleansed by His blood!

Joint heirs with Je-sus as we trav-el this sod, For I'm

part of the fam-'ly, the fam-'ly of God.

Verses

1. You will no-tice we say "broth-er and sis-ter" 'round
2. From the door of an or-ph'nage to the house of the

here— It's be-cause we're a fam-'ly and these
King— No long - er an out-cast, a

folks are so near; When one has a heart-ache we
new song I sing; From rags un-to rich-es, from the

all share the tears, And re-joice in each
weak to the strong, I'm not wor - thy to

D.C.

vic-t'ry In this fam-'ly so dear.
be here, But, praise God, I be - long!

Text: Gloria Gaither, b.1942 and William J. Gaither, b.1936
Tune: FAMILY OF GOD, Irregular; William J. Gaither, b.1936
© 1970, William J. Gaither, Inc.

520 O PERFECT LOVE

...a man leaves his father and his mother and clings to his wife, and they become one flesh.
Genesis 2:24

1. O per-fect Love, all hu - man thought tran - scend - ing,
2. O per-fect Life, be Thou their full as - sur - ance
3. Grant them the joy which bright - ens earth - ly sor - row,

Low - ly we kneel in prayer be - fore Thy throne,
Of ten - der char - i - ty and stead - fast faith,
Grant them the peace which calms all earth - ly strife,

That theirs may be the love which knows no end - ing,
Of pa - tient hope, and qui - et, brave en - dur - ance,
And to life's day the glo - rious un - known mor - row

Whom Thou for ev - er - more dost join in one.
With child-like trust that fears not pain nor death.
That dawns up - on e - ter - nal love and life.

Text: Dorothy F. Gurney, 1858-1932
Tune: O PERFECT LOVE, 11 10 11 10; Joseph Barnby, 1838-1896

THE BOND OF LOVE 521

I give you a new commandment... love one another. Just as I have loved you, you also should love one another.
John 13:34

1. We are one in the bond of love, We are
2. Let us sing now, ev-'ry-one, Let us

one in the bond of love; We have joined our spir-it with the
feel His love be-gun; Let us join our hands that the

Spir-it of God, We are one in the bond of love.
world will know We are one in the bond of love.

Text: Otis Skillings, b.1935
Tune: BOND OF LOVE, 88 12 8; Otis Skillings, b.1935
© 1971, Lillenas Publishing Co.

522 THE GIFT OF LOVE

If I give away all my possessions, and if I hand over my body so that I may boast, but do not have love, I gain nothing.
1 Corinthians 13:3

1. Though I may speak with brav - est fire,
2. Though I may give all I pos - sess,
3. Come, Spir - it, come, our hearts con - trol,

And have the gift to all in - spire,
And striv - ing so my love pro - fess,
Our spir - its long to be made whole.

And have not love, my words are vain,
But not be giv'n by love with - in,
Let in - ward love guide ev - 'ry deed;

As sound-ing brass, and hope - less gain.
The prof - it soon turns strange - ly thin.
By this we wor - ship, and are freed.

Text: Hal H. Hopson, b.1933
Tune: GIFT OF LOVE, LM; Hal H. Hopson, b.1933
© 1972, Hope Publishing Co.

THE LIVING CHURCH 523

Assemble and come, gather from all around to the sacrificial feast that I am preparing for you...
Ezekiel 39:17

1. The King of heav'n His ta - ble spreads, And bless - ings crown the board; Not par - a - dise, with all its joys, Could such de - light af - ford.
2. Par - don and peace to dy - ing men, And end - less life are giv'n, Through the rich blood that Je - sus shed To raise our souls to heav'n.
3. Mil - lions of souls, in glo - ry now, Were fed and feast - ed here; And mil - lions more, still on the way, A - round the board ap - pear.
4. All things are read - y, come a - way, Nor weak ex - cus - es frame; Come to your plac - es at the feast, And bless the Found - er's Name.

Text: Philip Doddridge, 1702-1751
Tune: DUNDEE, CM; *Scottish Psalter*, 1615

524 There Is a Balm in Gilead

Is there no balm in Gilead? Why then has the health of my poor people not been restored?
Jeremiah 8:22

Refrain

There is a balm in Gil-e-ad To make the wound-ed whole;

There is a balm in Gil-e-ad To heal the sin-sick soul.

Verses

1. Some - times I feel dis - cour - aged And
2. Don't ev - er be dis - cour - aged, For
3. If you can - not preach like Pe - ter, If you

think my work's in vain, But then the Ho - ly
Je - sus is your friend; And if you lack for
can - not pray like Paul, You can tell the love of

Spir - it Re - vives my soul a - gain. There is a
knowl-edge, He'll ne'er re - fuse to lend. There is a
Je - sus, And say, "He died for all!" There is a

Text: Negro spiritual
Tune: BALM IN GILEAD, 7 6 7 6 with refrain; Negro spiritual; arr. by Nolan Williams, Jr., b.1969, © 2000, GIA Publications, Inc.

COME ON IN MY ROOM 525

"Stay with us, because it is almost evening and the day is now nearly over." So He went in to stay with them.
Luke 24:29

1. Come on in my room. Come on in my room. Je - sus is my doc - tor, He writes down all of my 'scrip - tions, He gives me all of my med - i-cines in my room.

2. Joy in my room...
3. Peace in my room...
4. Healing in my room...

Text: Negro spiritual
Tune: Meter hymn, lined out by Carolyn Bolger-Payne; arr. by Evelyn Simpson-Curenton, b.1953, © 2000, GIA Publications, Inc.

526 IT'S ALRIGHT

It is Christ Jesus, who died, yes, who was raised, who is at the right hand of God, who indeed intercedes for us.
Romans 8:34

Refrain

It's al - right, it's al - right. My

Je - sus said He'll fix it and it's al - right. It's al - right,

it's al - right. My Je - sus said He'll fix it and it's al - right.

Last time

Verses

1. When it gets dark and I can't see my way,
2. That day when death comes a creep - in' in,
3. Some - times your best friend put you down,

ooh_____

I
I
just

Je - sus said He'll fix it and it's al - right.

know He's gon - na send me a bright - er day.
know you've fought a good fight to the end.
keep your eye on the heav-en - ly crown.

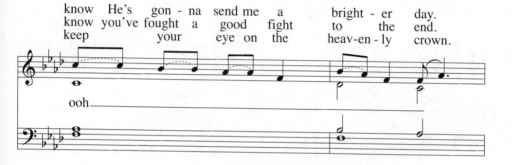

ooh

Je - sus said He'll fix it and it's al - right.

D.C.

Je - sus said He'll fix it and it's al - right.

Text: Negro spiritual
Tune: Negro spiritual; arr. by Bill Cummings, © 2000, GIA Publications, Inc.

527 SHINE ON ME

Let Your face shine upon Your servant; save me in Your steadfast love.
Psalm 31:16

1. I heard the voice of Je - sus
2. With pit - y - ing eyes the Prince of

say, "Come un - to me and rest.
Peace Be - held our help - less grief;

Lay down thou wea - ry one, lay
He saw, and O a - maz - ing

down Thy head up - on my breast."
love! He came to our re - lief.

Shine on me, Shine on me. Let the light from the light-house, Shine on me. Shine on me. Shine on me. Let the light from the light-house Shine on me.

Text: Negro spiritual
Tune: SHINE ON ME, CM with refrain; Negro spiritual; arr. by Jimmie Abbington, © 2000, GIA Publications, Inc.

528 I Am Healed by the Wound

...one of the soldiers pierced His side with a spear, and at once blood and water came out.
John 19:34

I am healed by the wound in His side.

I am healed by the wound in His side, oh

yes. Oh, they pierced Him in His side, Je-sus hung His head and

died. I am healed by the wound in His side.

Text: Virgin Davis
Tune: Virgin Davis, harm. by Bill Cummings, © 2000, GIA Publications, Inc.

WE BRING THE SACRIFICE OF PRAISE 529

...let us continually offer a sacrifice of praise to God, that is, the fruit of lips that confess His name.
Hebrews 13:15

We bring the sac-ri-fice of praise in-to the house of the Lord. We bring the sac-ri-fice of praise in-to the house of the Lord. And we of - fer up to You the sac-ri-fic - es of thanks-giv-ing, and we of - fer up to You the sac-ri-fic - es of praise.

Text: Kirk Dearman
Tune: Kirk Dearman; arr. by Stephen Key
© 1984, John T. Benson Publishing Co. (ASCAP)

530   I Will Bless Thee, O Lord

Every day I will bless You, and praise Your name forever... Great is the LORD, and greatly to be praised...
Psalm 145:2-3

I will bless Thee, O   Lord!   I will bless Thee, O
                      up,   And my mouth filled with

Lord!   With a heart of thanks-giv - ing,   I will bless Thee, O
praise,   With a heart of thanks-giv - ing,   I will bless Thee, O

Lord! With my hands lift-ed

Lord!

Text: Esther Watanabe, © 1970, New Song Music
Tune: Esther Watanabe, © 1970, New Song Music; arr. by Nolan Williams, Jr., b.1969, © 2000, GIA Publications, Inc.

THANK YOU, LORD 531

I will give thanks to You, O LORD, among the peoples, and I will sing praises to You among the nations.
Psalm 108:3

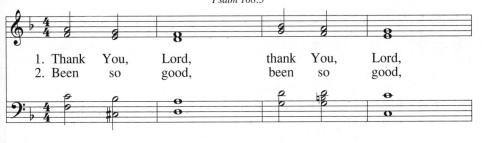

1. Thank You, Lord, thank You, Lord,
2. Been so good, been so good,

thank You, Lord, I just want to thank You, Lord.
been so good,

Text: Traditional
Tune: Negro spiritual; arr. by Stephen Key, © 2000, GIA Publications, Inc.

532 I Thank You, Jesus

He prostrated himself at Jesus' feet and thanked Him. And he was a Samaritan.
Luke 17:16

1. I thank You, Je - sus. I thank You, Je - sus. I thank You, Je - sus. I thank You, Je - sus. Je - sus, I thank You, Lord. Oh, You brought me, yes, You brought me from a might - y, a might - y long way, a might - y long

2. You've been my moth - er, You've been my fa - ther, You've been my fa - ther, sis - ter, my broth - er, too,

533 COUNT YOUR BLESSINGS

Let them thank the LORD for His steadfast love, for His wonderful works to humankind.
Psalm 107:31

1. When up-on life's bil-lows you are tem-pest-tossed,
2. Are you ev-er bur-dened with a load of care?
3. When you look at oth-ers with their lands and gold,
4. So, a-mid the con-flict, wheth-er great or small,

When you are dis-cour-aged think-ing all is lost,
Does the cross seem heav-y you are called to bear?
Think that Christ has prom-ised you His wealth un-told;
Do not be dis-cour-aged, God is o-ver all;

Count your man-y bless-ings, name them one by one,
Count your man-y bless-ings, ev-'ry doubt will fly,
Count your man-y bless-ings, mon-ey can-not buy
Count your man-y bless-ings, an-gels will at-tend,

And it will sur-prise you what the Lord has done.
And you will be sing-ing as the days go by.
Your re-ward in heav-en, nor your home on high.
Help and com-fort give you to your jour-ney's end.

Count your bless-ings, Name them one by one;

Count your bless-ings, See what God has done.

Count your bless-ings, Name them one by one;

Count your man-y bless-ings, See what God has done.

Text: Johnson Oatman, Jr., 1856-1922
Tune: BLESSINGS, 11 11 11 11 with refrain; Edwin O. Excell, 1851-1921; arr. by Evelyn Simpson-Curenton, b.1953, © 2000, GIA
    Publications, Inc.

534 THANK YOU, JESUS

...with gratitude in your hearts sing psalms, hymns, and spiritual songs to God.
Colossians 3:16

Sopranos and Altos unison:

Thank You, Je - sus. Thank You, Je - sus for all You've done for

div.

me; Thank You, Je - sus. Thank You, Je - sus for Cal - va - ry.

All:

The pain You bore to set me free. All this and

more You have done for me. Thank You, Je - sus. Thank You

Je - sus, I thank You, Je-sus, my Lord and King.

Text: Bernadette Blount Salley
Tune: Bernadette Blount Salley
© 1984, Bernadette Blount Salley. Administered by GIA Publications, Inc.

IMELA 535

O give thanks to the LORD, for He is good, for His steadfast love endures forever.
Psalm 118:29

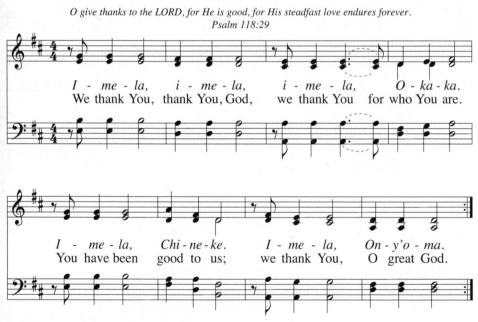

I - me - la,   i - me - la,   i - me - la,   O - ka - ka.
We thank You, thank You, God,   we thank You   for who You are.

I - me - la,   Chi - ne - ke.   I - me - la,   On - y'o - ma.
You have been   good to us;   we thank You,   O great God.

African phonetics:
I-may-lah, I-may-lah, I-may-lah, Oh-kah-kah.
I-may-lah, Chee-nay-kay. I-may-lah, Oh-nyo-mah.

Text: Nigerian traditional; English adapt. by Nolan Williams, Jr., b.1969, © 2000, GIA Publications, Inc.
Tune: Nigerian traditional, © 1990, Christ Church Gospel Band, Uwani-Engu; arr. by John L. Bell, b.1949, © 1990, Iona Community, GIA
   Publications, Inc., agent

536 THANK YOU, LORD

I will render thank offerings to You. For You have delivered my soul from death.
Psalm 56:12-13

Thank You, Lord, for sav - ing my soul,

Thank You, Lord, for mak - ing me whole;

Thank You, Lord, for giv - ing to me

Thy great sal - va - tion so rich and free.

Text: Seth Sykes, b.1905
Tune Seth Sykes, b.1905 and Bessie Sykes, 1892-1950
© 1940, Singspiration Music (ASCAP)

REJOICE, O PURE IN HEART 537

Let us rejoice and exult and give Him the glory...
Revelation 19:7

1. Re - joice, ye pure in heart, Re - joice, give
2. Bright youth and snow - crowned age, All those for
3. Yes, on through life's long path, Still chant - ing
4. Then on, ye pure in heart, Re - joice, give

thanks and sing; Your fes - tal ban - ner
truth do seek; Raise high your free, ex -
as ye go; From youth to age, by
thanks and sing; Your glo - rious ban - ner

wave on high, The cross of Christ your King.
ult - ing song, God's won - drous prais - es speak.
night and day, In glad - ness and in woe.
wave on high, The cross of Christ your King.

Re - joice, re - joice, Re - joice, give thanks and sing.

Re - joice, re - joice,

Text: Edward H. Plumptre, 1821-1891
Tune: MARION, SM with refrain; Arthur H. Messiter, 1834-1916

538 ONE MORE DAY

Rejoice in hope, be patient in suffering, persevere in prayer.
Romans 12:12

1. One more day, one more day, I thank God just for
2. One more chance, one more chance, I thank God just for

one more day. One more day, the Lord has made a
one more chance. One more chance to do the best I

way, I thank God just for one more day.
can, I thank God just for one more chance.

Text: Margaret Pleasant Douroux, b.1941, ©
Tune: ONE MORE DAY, 6 8 9 9; Margaret Pleasant Douroux, b.1941, ©; arr. by Nolan Williams, Jr., b.1969, © 2000, GIA Publications, Inc.

539 SWING LOW, SWEET CHARIOT

...a chariot of fire and horses of fire separated the two of them, and Elijah ascended in a whirlwind into heaven.
2 Kings 2:11

Refrain

Swing low, sweet char - i - ot, Com-ing for to car-ry me home.

Swing low, sweet char - i - ot, Com-ing for to car-ry me home.

Verses

1. I looked o - ver Jor - dan, and what did I see
2. If you get there be - fore I do,
3. The bright - est day that ev - er I saw
4. I'm some - times up and some - times down,

Com-ing for to car-ry me home. A band of an - gels
Com-ing for to car-ry me home. Tell all my friends I'm
Com-ing for to car-ry me home. When Je - sus washed my
Com-ing for to car-ry me home. But still my soul feels

D.C.

com-ing af-ter me, Com-ing for to car-ry me home. O,
com - ing too, Com-ing for to car-ry me home. O,
sins a - way, Com-ing for to car-ry me home. O,
heav'n - ly bound, Com-ing for to car-ry me home. O,

Text: Traditional
Tune: SWING LOW, LM with refrain; Negro spiritual; arr. by Robert Nathaniel Dett, 1882-1943, © 1936 (renewed), Paul A. Schmitt Music Co.,
    c/o Belwin-Mills Publishing Corp.

540 LIFT EVERY VOICE AND SING

Let them praise the name of the LORD, for his name alone is exalted; his glory is above earth and heaven.
Psalm 148:13

1. Lift ev - 'ry voice and sing, Till earth and heav - en
2. Ston - y the road we trod, Bit - ter the chas - t'ning
3. God of our wea - ry years, God of our si - lent

ring, Ring with the har - mo - nies of lib - er -
rod, Felt in the days when hope un - born had
tears, Thou who hast brought us thus far on the

ty; Let our re - joic - ing rise High as the lis - t'ning
died; Yet with a stead - y beat, Have not our wea - ry
way; Thou who hast by Thy might, Led us in - to the

skies, Let it re - sound loud as the roll - ing sea.
feet Come to the place for which our peo - ple sighed?
light, Keep us for ev - er in the path, we pray.

Sing a song full of the faith that the dark past has taught us,
We have come o - ver a way that with tears has been wa - tered;
Lest our feet stray from the plac - es, our God, where we met Thee,

Sing a song full of the hope that the pres - ent has
We have come, tread - ing our path through the blood of the
Lest our hearts, drunk with the wine of the world, we for -

brought us; Fac - ing the ris - ing sun Of our new
slaugh - tered; Out from the gloom - y past, Till now we
get Thee; Shad-owed be - neath Thy hand, May we for

day be - gun, Let us march on till vic - to - ry is won.
stand at last Where the bright gleam of our bright star is cast.
ev - er stand, True to our God, true to our na - tive land.

Text: James W. Johnson, 1871-1938
Tune: ANTHEM, 66 10 66 10 14 14 66 10; J. Rosamund Johnson, 1873-1954
© 1921 (renewed), Edward B. Marks Music Co.

541 WALK TOGETHER CHILDREN

I have no greater joy than this, to hear that my children are walking in the truth.
3 John 4

*Walk to-geth-er chil-dren, don't you get wea-ry,

walk to-geth-er chil-dren, don't you get wea-ry,

walk to-geth-er chil-dren, don't you get wea-ry,

there's a great camp meet-ing in the prom-ised land.

We're gon-na walk and nev-er tire,

* *Sing, Pray, Work*

walk and nev-er tire, walk and nev-er tire, there's a great camp meet-ing in the prom-ised land.

Text: Traditional
Tune: Negro spiritual, arr. Evelyn Simpson-Curenton, b.1953, © 2000, GIA Publications, Inc.

542 WE SHALL OVERCOME

For whatever is born of God conquers the world. And this is the victory that conquers the world, our faith.
1 John 5:4-5

1. We shall o - ver - come. We shall o - ver - come. We shall o - ver - come some - day.
2. We'll walk hand in hand. We'll walk hand in hand. We'll walk hand in hand some - day.
3. We shall live in peace. We shall live in peace. We shall live in peace some - day.
4. We are not a - fraid. We are not a - fraid. We are not a - fraid to - day.
5. God will see us through. God will see us through. God will see us through to - day.

Oh, deep in my heart I do be - lieve. We shall o - ver - come some - day.

GO DOWN, MOSES 543

Then the Lord spoke to Moses, "Go and tell Pharaoh king of Egypt to let the Israelites go out of his land."
Exodus 6:10-11

1. When Is - rael was in E - gypt's land; Let my peo - ple go,
2. Thus saith the Lord, bold Mo - ses said; Let my peo - ple go,
3. No more shall they in bond-age toil; Let my peo - ple go,

Op - pressed so hard they could not stand, Let my peo - ple go.
If not, I'll smite your first - born dead, Let my peo - ple go.
Let them come out with E - gypt's spoil, Let my peo - ple go.

Go down, Mo - ses,
go down, Mo - ses, 'Way down in E - gypt's land.

Go down, go down, Mo - ses,

Tell old Phar - oah, Let my peo - ple go!

Text: Negro spiritual
Tune: GO DOWN MOSES, 8 5 8 5 with refrain; Negro spiritual

544 I'll Overcome Someday

Those who conquer will inherit these things, and I will be their God and they will be my children.
Revelation 21:7

1. This world is one great bat - tle - field, With forc - es
2. Both seen and un - seen pow - ers join To drive my
3. A thou - sand snares are set for me, And moun - tains
4. I fail so of - ten when I try My Sav - ior
5. My mind is not to do the wrong, But walk the
6. Tho' man - y a time no signs ap - pear, Of an - swer

all ar - rayed; If in my heart I do not yield I'll
soul a - stray, But with God's Word a sword of mine, I'll
in my way; If Je - sus will my lead - er be, I'll
to o - bey; It pains my heart and then I cry, Lord,
nar - row way; I'm pray - ing as I jour - ney on, To
when I pray; My Je - sus says I need not fear, He'll

o - ver - come some day. I'll o - ver - come some
o - ver - come some day. I'll o - ver - come some
o - ver - come some day. I'll o - ver - come some
make me strong some day. Lord, make me strong some
o - ver - come some day. To o - ver - come some
make it plain some day. I'll be like Him some

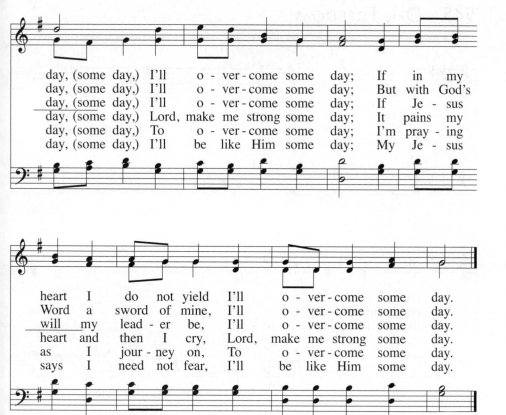

day, (some day,) I'll o - ver - come some day; If in my
day, (some day,) I'll o - ver - come some day; But with God's
day, (some day,) I'll o - ver - come some day; If Je - sus
day, (some day,) Lord, make me strong some day; It pains my
day, (some day,) To o - ver - come some day; I'm pray - ing
day, (some day,) I'll be like Him some day; My Je - sus

heart I do not yield I'll o - ver - come some day.
Word a sword of mine, I'll o - ver - come some day.
will my lead - er be, I'll o - ver - come some day.
heart and then I cry, Lord, make me strong some day.
as I jour - ney on, To o - ver - come some day.
says I need not fear, I'll be like Him some day.

Text: Charles A. Tindley, 1851-1933
Tune: OVERCOME, 8 6 8 6 66 8 6; Charles A. Tindley, 1851-1933

545 OH, FREEDOM

For freedom Christ has set us free. Stand firm, therefore, and do not submit again to a yoke of slavery.
Galatians 5:1

1. Oh, free - dom, Oh, free - dom,
2. No more moan - ing, no more moan - ing,
3. There'll be sing - ing, there'll be sing - ing,

oh, free - dom o - ver me.
no more moan - ing o - ver me.
there'll be sing - ing o - ver me.

And be -

O - ver me.

fore I'd be a slave I'll be bur - ied in my grave,

and go home to my Lord and be free.

Text: Traditional
Tune: OH FREEDOM, Irregular; Negro spiritual; arr. by Valeria A. Foster, © 2000, GIA Publications, Inc.

STEAL AWAY TO JESUS 546

For He will hide me in His shelter in the day of trouble; He will conceal me under the cover of His tent...
Psalm 27:5

Steal a-way, steal a-way, steal a-way to Je - sus!

Steal a-way, steal a-way home, I ain't got long to stay here.

Verses
Unison

1. My Lord, He calls me, He calls me by the thun - der;
2. Green trees are bend-ing, Poor sin - ners stand a trem-bling;
3. My Lord, He calls me, He calls me by the light - ning;

The trum-pet sounds with-in my soul; I ain't got long to stay here.

Text: Negro spiritual
Tune: STEAL AWAY, 5 7 8 7 with refrain; Negro spiritual

547 Lift Him Up

And I, when I am lifted up from the earth, will draw all people to myself.
John 12:32

1. How to reach the mass - es, *men of ev - 'ry birth,
2. Oh! the world is hun - gry for the Liv - ing Bread,
3. Don't ex - alt the preach-er, don't ex - alt the pew,
4. Lift Him up by liv - ing as a Chris - tian ought,

For an an - swer Je - sus gave the key: "And
Lift the Sav - ior up for them to see; Trust
Preach the Gos - pel sim - ple, full and free; Prove
Let the world in you the Sav - ior see; Then

I, if I be lift - ed up from the earth,
Him, and do not doubt the words that He said,
Him and you will find that prom - ise is true,
men will glad - ly fol - low Him who once taught,

Will draw all men un - to Me."
"I'll draw all men un - to Me."
"I'll draw all men un - to Me."
"I'll draw all men un - to Me."

Saints can be substituted for men throughout this text.

Lift Him up, Lift Him up,

Lift the pre-cious Sav-ior up, Lift the pre-cious Sav-ior up,

Still He speaks from e-ter-ni-ty: "And I, if I be lift-ed

up from the earth, Will draw all men un-to Me."

Text: Johnson Oatman, Jr., 1856-1922
Tune: LIFT HIM UP, 11 9 11 7 with refrain; B. B. Beall; adapt. by Nolan Williams, Jr., b.1969, Evelyn Simpson-Curenton, b.1953, and
   Dr. Robert J. Fryson, © 2000, GIA Publications, Inc.

548 ONLY WHAT YOU DO FOR CHRIST WILL LAST

...store up for yourselves treasures in heaven, where neither moth nor rust consumes...
Matthew 6:19-20

1. You may build great ca - the - drals large or small,
2. You may seek earth - ly pow - er and fame,
3. Though your ar - mies may con - trol each hem - i - sphere,
4. Though your songs and prayers are heard and praised by man,

You can build sky - scrap - ers grand and tall,
The world might be im - pressed by your great name,
And your or - bits out in space cause men to cheer,
They've no mean - ing un - less you've been born a - gain,

You may con - quer all the fail - ures of the past,
Soon the glo - ries of this life will all be past,
Your sci - en - tif - ic knowl - edge may be vast,
Sin - ner, heed these words, don't let this har - vest pass,

But on - ly what you do for Christ will last.
But on - ly what you do for Christ will last.
But on - ly what you do for Christ will last.
For on - ly what you do for Christ will last.

Re-mem-ber on-ly what you do for Christ will last.

Re-mem-ber on-ly what you do for Christ will last.

On-ly what you do for Him will be count-ed at the

end; on-ly what you do for Christ will last!

Text: Raymond Rasberry
Tune: LASTING TREASURES, 10 10 10 10 with refrain; Raymond Rasberry; arr. by Valeria A. Foster
© 1963, (renewed) Pronto Music and Simco Music Co., Inc.

549 THIS LITTLE LIGHT OF MINE

Let your light shine before others, so that they may see your good works and give glory to your Father in heaven.
Matthew 5:16

1. This lit - tle light of mine, I'm gon-na let it shine.
2. Ev - 'ry - where I go, I'm gon-na let it shine.
3. Je - sus gave it to me, I'm gon-na let it shine.

oh

This lit - tle light of mine, I'm gon-na let it shine.
Ev - 'ry - where I go, I'm gon-na let it shine.
Je - sus gave it to me, I'm gon-na let it shine.

oh

This lit - tle light of mine, I'm gon-na let it shine.
Ev - 'ry - where I go, I'm gon-na let it shine.
Je - sus gave it to me, I'm gon-na let it shine.

oh   oh

Let it shine, let it shine, let it shine.

4. Shine, shine, shine, I'm gonna let it shine....
5. All in my home, I'm gonna let it shine....

Text: Negro spiritual
Tune: LIGHT OF MINE, 12 12 12 9; Negro spiritual; arr. by Nolan Williams, Jr., b.1969, ©2000, GIA Publications, Inc.

WHERE HE LEADS ME 550

If any want to become my followers, let them deny themselves and take up their cross and follow me.
Matthew 16:24

1. I can hear my Sav - ior call - ing, I can
2. I'll go with Him through the gar - den, I'll go
3. I'll go with Him through the judg - ment, I'll go
4. He will give me grace and glo - ry, He will

Refrain: Where He leads me I will fol - low, Where He

hear my Sav - ior call - ing, I can hear my Sav - ior
with Him through the gar - den, I'll go with Him through the
with Him through the judg - ment, I'll go with Him through the
give me grace and glo - ry, He will give me grace and

leads me I will fol - low, Where He leads me I will

call - ing, "Take thy cross and fol - low, fol - low Me."
gar - den, I'll go with Him, with Him all the way.
judg - ment, I'll go with Him, with Him all the way.
glo - ry, And go with me, with me all the way.

fol - low, I'll go with Him, with Him all the way.

Text: E. W. Blandy, c.1890
Tune: NORRIS, 888 9 with refrain; John S. Norris, 1844-1907

551 COMPLETELY YES

For in Him every one of God's promises is a "Yes." For this reason it is through Him that we say the "Amen..."
2 Corinthians 1:20

Chorus

1. "Yes, Lord!   Yes, Lord!"   From the
(2.) love you!   I   love you!   From the

bot - tom of   my heart   to the depths of   my   soul.   I
bot - tom of   my heart   to the depths of   my   soul.

"Yes, Lord!"   Com - plete - ly   yes!   My   soul   says,
love you!   I   real - ly   do.   My   soul   says,

1.   2.   *rubato*

"yes!"   2. I   "yes!"   3. My soul says, "yes, yes,   yes!

Yes, Lord!" From the bot-tom of my heart,

"Yes, Lord!" To the depths of my soul. "Yes, Lord!"

Text: Sandra Crouch
Tune: Sandra Crouch; arr. by Stephen Key
© Bud John Songs, Inc./Sanabella Music (ASCAP)

552 CLOSE TO THEE

...they began their journey for the sake of Christ.
3 John 7

Thou, my ev - er - last - ing por - tion,

More than friend or life to me.

While I walk this pil - grim jour - ney,

Sav - ior, let me walk with Thee.

Oh, Mas-ter, let me walk with Thee, Oh, Mas-ter, let me walk with Thee. While I walk this pil-grim jour-ney, Sav-ior, let me walk with Thee.

Text: Fanny J. Crosby, 1820-1915
Tune: Wanda Taylor Riddick, b.1939, © 1978, Riddick Taylor Music, Inc.; arr. by Evelyn Simpson-Curenton, b.1953, 2000 GIA Publications, Inc.

553 CLOSE TO THEE

...they began their journey for the sake of Christ.
3 John 7

1. Thou my ev - er - last - ing por - tion, More than
2. Not for ease or world - ly pleas - ure, Nor for
3. Lead me through the vale of shad - ows, Bear me

friend or life to me, All a - long my pil - grim
fame my prayer shall be; Glad - ly will I toil and
o'er life's fit - ful sea; Then the gate of life e -

jour - ney, Sav - ior, let me walk with Thee.
suf - fer, On - ly let me walk with Thee.
ter - nal May I en - ter, Lord, with Thee.

Close to Thee, Close to Thee, Close to Thee, Close to Thee;

All a-long my pil-grim jour-ney, Sav-ior, let me walk with Thee.
Glad-ly will I toil and suf-fer, On-ly let me walk with Thee.
Then the gate of life e-ter-nal May I en-ter, Lord, with Thee.

Text: Fanny J. Crosby, 1820-1915
Tune: CLOSE TO THEE, 8 7 8 7 with refrain; Silas J. Vail, 1818-1884; arr. by Nolan Williams, Jr., b.1969, © 2000, GIA Publications, Inc.

MUST JESUS BEAR THE CROSS ALONE 554

If any want to become my followers, let them deny themselves and take up their cross daily and follow me.
Luke 9:23

1. Must Je - sus bear the cross a - lone And
2. The con - se - crat - ed cross I'll bear Till
3. Up - on the crys - tal pave - ment, down At
4. O pre - cious cross! O glo - rious crown! O

all the world go free? No, there's a cross for
death shall set me free, And then go home my
Je - sus' pierc - ed feet, Joy - ful, I'll cast my
res - ur - rec - tion day! Ye an - gels, from the

ev - 'ry one, And there's a cross for me.
crown to wear, For there's a crown for me.
gold - en crown And His dear name re - peat.
stars come down And bear my soul a - way.

Text: Thomas Shepherd, 1665-1739
Tune: MAITLAND, CM; George N. Allen, 1812-1877

555 If Jesus Goes With Me

Go...and remember, I am with you always, to the end of the age.
Matthew 28:19-20

1. It may be in the val - ley, Where count - less dan - gers hide; It may be in the sun - shine That I, in peace a - bide; But this one thing I know— If it be dark or fair, If Je - sus is with me, I'll go an - y - where!

2. It may be I must car - ry The bless - ed word of life A - cross the burn - ing des - erts To those in sin - ful strife; And though it be my lot To bear my col - ors there, If Je - sus goes with me, I'll go an - y - where!

3. But if it be my por - tion To bear my cross at home, While oth - ers bear their bur - dens Be - yond the bil - low's foam, I'll prove my faith in Him— Con - fess His judg - ments fair, And, if He stays with me, I'll go an - y - where!

4. It is not mine to ques - tion The judg - ments of my Lord, It is but mine to fol - low The lead - ings of His word; But if to go or stay, Or wheth - er here or there, I'll be, with my Sav - ior, Con - tent an - y - where!

If Je-sus goes with me, I'll go. An-y-where! 'Tis
I'll go.

heav-en to me, Where-e'er I may be, If He is
there! I count it a priv-i-lege here. His cross to
His cross, His cross, His

bear; If Je-sus goes with me, I'll go— An-y-where!
cross to bear;

Text: C. Austin Miles, 1868-1946
Tune: IF JESUS GOES, 7 6 7 6 6 6 6 5 with refrain; C. Austin Miles, 1868-1946
© 1962, renewed 1991, Word Music, Inc. (ASCAP)

556 HUSH, HUSH, SOMEBODY'S CALLIN' MY NAME

Do not fear, for I have redeemed you; I have called you by name, you are mine.
Isaiah 43:1

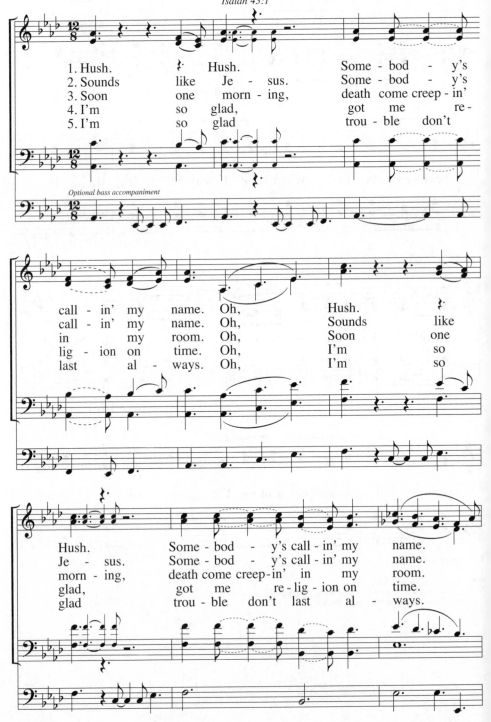

1. Hush.   Hush.   Some-bod - y's call - in' my name. Oh, Hush.   Hush.   Some-bod - y's call - in' my name.
2. Sounds like Je - sus.   Some-bod - y's call - in' my name. Oh, Sounds like Je - sus.   Some-bod - y's call - in' my name.
3. Soon one morn - ing,   death come creep - in' in my room. Oh, Soon one morn - ing,   death come creep-in' in my room.
4. I'm so glad,   got me re - lig - ion on time. Oh, I'm so glad,   got me re - lig - ion on time.
5. I'm so glad   trou - ble don't last al - ways. Oh, I'm so glad   trou - ble don't last al - ways.

Optional bass accompaniment

Hush. Hush. Some - bod - y's call - in' my
Sounds like Je - sus. Some - bod - y's call - in' my
Soon one morn - ing, death come creep-in' in my
I'm so glad, got me re - lig - ion on
I'm so glad trou - ble don't last al -

name.
name.
room. Oh, my Lord, Oh, my Lord, what shall I do?
time.
ways.

what shall I do?

1., 2.

3.

Text: Traditional
Tune: SOMEBODY'S CALLIN', Irregular; Negro spiritual; arr. by Nolan Williams, Jr., b.1969, © 2000, GIA Publications, Inc.

557 WE MUST WORK

...pray for us, so that the word of the Lord may spread rapidly and be glorified everywhere...
2 Thessalonians 3:1

We must work while it is day, Spread-ing the

Word of God as we go a-long the way. We must be

will - ing to do God's will, Spread - ing the

Word of God till it reach-es through-out the hills. We must

wit-ness to ev - 'ry-one we meet in ev - 'ry song we sing.

We must tell them of a soon - com - ing King!

558 JESUS SAVES

...the Father has sent His Son as the Savior of the world.
1 John 4:14

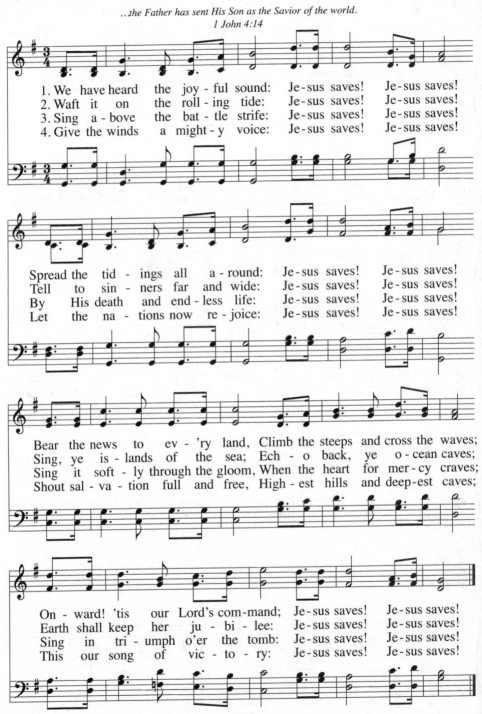

1. We have heard the joy-ful sound: Je-sus saves! Je-sus saves!
2. Waft it on the roll-ing tide: Je-sus saves! Je-sus saves!
3. Sing a-bove the bat-tle strife: Je-sus saves! Je-sus saves!
4. Give the winds a might-y voice: Je-sus saves! Je-sus saves!

Spread the tid-ings all a-round: Je-sus saves! Je-sus saves!
Tell to sin-ners far and wide: Je-sus saves! Je-sus saves!
By His death and end-less life: Je-sus saves! Je-sus saves!
Let the na-tions now re-joice: Je-sus saves! Je-sus saves!

Bear the news to ev-'ry land, Climb the steeps and cross the waves;
Sing, ye is-lands of the sea; Ech-o back, ye o-cean caves;
Sing it soft-ly through the gloom, When the heart for mer-cy craves;
Shout sal-va-tion full and free, High-est hills and deep-est caves;

On-ward! 'tis our Lord's com-mand; Je-sus saves! Je-sus saves!
Earth shall keep her ju-bi-lee: Je-sus saves! Je-sus saves!
Sing in tri-umph o'er the tomb: Je-sus saves! Je-sus saves!
This our song of vic-to-ry: Je-sus saves! Je-sus saves!

Text: Priscilla J. Owens, 1829-1907
Tune: JESUS SAVES, 7 6 7 6 7 7 7 6; William J. Kirkpatrick, 1838-1921

ROCK OF AGES 559

Lead me to the rock that is higher than I; for You are my refuge, a strong tower against the enemy.
Psalm 61:2-3

1. Rock of a - ges, cleft for me, Let me
2. Could my tears for ev - er flow, Could my
3. While I draw this fleet - ing breath, When my

hide my - self in Thee; Let the wa - ter and the
zeal no lan-guish know, These for sin could not a -
eyes shall close in death, When I rise to worlds un -

blood, From Thy wound - ed side which flowed, Be of
tone— Thou must save, and Thou a - lone: In my
known And be - hold Thee on Thy throne, Rock of

sin the dou - ble cure, Save from wrath and make me pure.
hand no price I bring, Sim - ply to Thy cross I cling.
A - ges, cleft for me, Let me hide my - self in Thee.

Text: Augustus M. Toplady, 1740-1778
Tune: TOPLADY, 77 77 77; Thomas Hastings, 1784-1872

560 I'LL BE SOMEWHERE LISTENING FOR MY NAME

Now the LORD came... calling as before, "Samuel!" And Samuel said, "Speak, for Your servant is listening."
1 Samuel 3:10

1. When He calls me I will an - swer, When He
2. With a glad heart I will an - swer, With a
3. When He calls you, will you an - swer? When He

calls me I will an - swer, When He calls me I will
glad heart I will an - swer, With a glad heart I will
calls you, will you an - swer? When He calls you, will you

an - swer; I'll be some-where list-'ning for my name.
an - swer; I'll be some-where list-'ning for my name.
an - swer? Some-where list - 'ning, list-'ning for your name.

1., 2. I'll be some-where list-'ning, I'll be some-where list-'ning,
3. You'll be some-where list-'ning, You'll be some-where list-'ning,

I'll be some-where list-'ning for my name. Oh,
You'll be some-where list-'ning for your name. Oh,

I'll be some - where list - 'ning, I'll be some-where
you'll be some - where list - 'ning, You'll be some-where

list - 'ning, I'll be some-where list - 'ning for my name.
list - 'ning, You'll be some-where list - 'ning for your name.

Text: Eduardo J. Lango
Tune: SOMEWHERE LISTENING, 888 9 66 9 76 9; Eduardo J. Lango; adapt. by Louis Sykes, © 2000, GIA Publications, Inc.

561 GIVE ME JESUS

They came to Philip, who was from Bethsaida in Galilee, and said to him, "Sir, we wish to see Jesus."
John 12:21

1. I heard my moth-er say, I heard my moth-er say, I heard my moth-er say, Give me Je - sus.
2. Dark mid-night was my cry, Dark mid-night was my cry, Dark mid-night was my cry, Give me Je - sus.
3. Oh, when I come to die, Oh, when I come to die, Oh, when I come to die, Give me Je - sus.

Give me Je - sus. Give me Je - sus, You may have all this world, Give me Je - sus.

Text: Negro spiritual
Tune: GIVE ME JESUS, 666 4 with refrain; Negro spiritual, arr. by Nolan Williams, Jr., b.1969, © 2000, GIA Publications, Inc.

LEARNING TO LEAN 562

Trust in the LORD with all your heart, and do not rely on your own insight.
Proverbs 3:5

Learn-ing to lean, learn-ing to lean, I'm
learn-ing to lean on Je - sus.
Find-ing more pow - er than I've ev - er seen. I'm
learn-ing to lean on Je - sus.

Text: John Stallings, b.1938
Tune: John Stallings, b.1938; arr. by Evelyn Simpson-Curenton, b.1953
© 1976, Bridge Building Music, Inc. (BMI)

563 I Want Jesus to Walk with Me

Jesus said to them, "The light is with you for a little longer. Walk while you have the light...
John 12:35

1. I want Je - sus to walk with me,
2. In my tri - als, Lord, walk with me,

I want Je - sus to walk with me,
In my tri - als, Lord, walk with me,

All a - long my pil - grim jour - ney,
When the shades of life are fall - ing,

Lord, I want Je - sus to walk with me.
Lord, I want Je - sus to walk with me.

Text: Negro spiritual
Tune: WALK WITH ME, 88 8 9; Negro spiritual; arr. by Nolan Williams, Jr., b.1969, © 2000, GIA Publications, Inc.

THUMA MINA 564

Lead me in your truth, and teach me, for you are the God of my salvation...
Psalm 25:5

1. Thu - ma mi - na.

1. Thu - ma mi - na, Thu - ma mi - na, Thu - ma
   Je - sus, send me, Je - sus, Send me,
   Je - sus, lead me, Je - sus, Lead me,
   Je - sus, fill me, Je - sus Fill me,

2. Send me, Lord.
3. Lead me, Lord.
4. Fill me, Lord.

mi - na So - man - dla.
Je - sus, send me, Lord.
Je - sus, lead me, Lord.
Je - sus, fill me,

2. Send me,
3. Lead me,
4. Fill me,

Lord.

African phonetics:
Too-mah mee-nah, So-mahn-dlah

Text: South African spiritual, (Zulu)
Tune: THUMA MINA, South African
© 1984, Utryck, Walton Music Corporation, agent

565 MORE ABOUT JESUS

I want to know Christ and the power of His resurrection and the sharing of His sufferings...
Philippians 3:10

1. More a-bout Je - sus would I know, More of His grace to
2. More a-bout Je - sus let me learn, More of His ho - ly
3. More a-bout Je - sus— in His Word Hold - ing com-mun - ion
4. More a-bout Je - sus on His throne, Rich - es in glo - ry

oth - ers show, More of His sav - ing full - ness see,
will dis - cern; Spir - it of God, my Teach - er be,
with my Lord, Hear - ing His voice in ev - 'ry line,
all His own, More of His king - dom's sure in-crease,

More of His love who died for me.
Show - ing the things of Christ to me.
Mak - ing each faith - ful say - ing mine.
More of His com - ing— Prince of Peace.

More, more a-bout Je - sus, More, more a-bout Je - sus; More of His sav - ing full - ness see, More of His love who died for me.

Text: Eliza E. Hewitt, 1851-1920
Tune: SWENEY, LM with refrain; John R. Sweney, 1837-1899

Woke Up This Mornin' 566

Those of steadfast mind You keep in peace— in peace because they trust in You.
Isaiah 26:3

1. Woke up this morn - in' with my mind,
2. No con - dem - na - tion with my mind, stayed on
3. Walk - in' and talk - in' with my mind,

mind, my mind was

Je - sus.
Woke up this morn - in' with my mind,
No con - dem - na - tion with my mind,
Walk - in' and talk - in' with my mind,

mind, my mind was

stayed on Je - sus.
Woke up this morn - in' with my mind,
No con - dem - na - tion with my mind,
Walk - in' and talk - in' with my mind,

mind, my mind was

stayed on Je - sus. Hal - le - lu, hal - le - lu, hal - le - lu - jah.

Text: Congregational Praise Song
Tune: WITH MY MIND, 12 12 12 with hallelujahs; Congregational Praise Song, arr. by Evelyn Simpson-Curenton, b.1953, © 2000, GIA
Publications, Inc.

567 HERE I AM, LORD

I heard the Lord saying, "Whom shall I send, and who will go for us?" And I said, "Here am I; send me!"
Isaiah 6:8

Verses

Descant:

3. Ah_____ Ah_____

Unison

1. I, the Lord   of   sea and sky,   I have heard   my
2. I, the Lord   of   snow and rain,   I have borne   my
3. I, the Lord   of   wind and flame, I will tend   the

Ah_____

peo - ple   cry.   All who dwell in   dark and sin
peo - ple's pain.   I have wept   for love of them.
poor and lame.   I will set   a   feast for them.

My hand will save.   Fin - est bread I

My hand will save.   I who made the
They turn a - way.   I will break their
My hand will save.   Fin - est bread I

will pro - vide   till their hearts be   sat - is - fied.

stars   of   night,   I   will make   their dark - ness bright.
hearts   of   stone,   Give them hearts   for   love   a - lone.
will   pro - vide   Till their hearts   be   sat - is - fied.

I will give my   life to them.   Whom shall I   send?

Who will bear my light to them?   Whom shall I   send?
I   will speak my word to them.   Whom shall I   send?
I   will give my life to them.   Whom shall I   send?

Refrain

Here   I   am,   Lord.   Is   it   I,   Lord?

I have heard You   call - ing in the   night.

I will go, Lord, if You lead me.

I will hold Your peo - ple in my heart.

1., 2.

3.

heart.

Text: Isaiah 6; Dan Schutte, b.1947
Tune: Dan Schutte, b.1947; arr. by Michael Pope, SJ, John Weissrock

I Will Do a New Thing 568

I am about to do a new thing; now it springs forth, do you not perceive it? I will make a way in the wilderness...
Isaiah 43:19

"I will do a new thing in you; I will do a new thing in you;

What -ev - er you ask for, what - ev - er you pray for,

noth-ing shall be de-nied," sa-ith the Lord; sa-ith the Lord! Lord!

Text: Audrey Byrd
Tune: Audrey Byrd; arr. by Nolan Williams, Jr., b.1969, © 2000, GIA Publications, Inc.

569 REVIVE US AGAIN

Will You not revive us again, so that Your people may rejoice in You?
Psalm 85:6

1. We praise Thee, O God, for the Son of Thy love, For
2. We praise Thee, O God, for Thy Spir - it of light, Who has
3. All glo - ry and praise to the Lamb that was slain, Who has
4. Re - vive us a - gain— fill each heart with Thy love; May each

Je - sus who died and is now gone a - bove.
shown us our Sav - ior and scat - tered our night.
borne all our sins and has cleansed ev - 'ry stain.
soul be re - kin - dled with fire from a - bove.

Hal - le - lu - jah, Thine the glo - ry! Hal - le - lu - jah, A -

men! Hal - le - lu - jah, Thine the glo - ry! Re - vive us a - gain.

Text: William P. Mackay, 1837-1885
Tune: REVIVE US AGAIN, 11 11 with refrain; John J. Husband, 1760-1825

Renewal 570

...we are slaves not under the old written code but in the new life of the Spirit.
Romans 7:6

O Lord of re - new - al; re - fresh me, re - store me, re -

new me a - gain. Cleanse the thoughts of my mind, And

fill my heart with love: Guide my hands to share Your bless-ings

from a - bove; Be with me for - ev - er, show me grace to

give. Re - new me for - ev - er; Teach me how to live!

Text: Charlene Moore Cooper, © 2000, GIA Publications, Inc.
Tune: Dr. John W. Robinson, Jr., © 1997; harm. by Charlene Moore Cooper, © 2000, GIA Publications, Inc.

571 SHOWERS OF BLESSING

...I will send down the showers in their season; they shall be showers of blessing.
Ezekiel 34:26

1. "There shall be show-ers of bless - ing"— This is the
2. "There shall be show-ers of bless - ing"— Pre - cious re -
3. "There shall be show-ers of bless - ing"— Send them up -
4. "There shall be show-ers of bless - ing"— O that to -

prom - ise of love; There shall be sea - sons re -
viv - ing a - gain; O - ver the hills and the
on us, O Lord; Grant to us now a re -
day they might fall, Now as to God we're con -

fresh - ing, Sent from the Sav - ior a - bove.
val - leys Sound of a - bun - dance of rain.
fresh - ing, Come and now hon - or Thy Word.
fess - ing, Now as on Je - sus we call!

Show - ers of

Show - ers, show - ers of bless - ing, Show - ers of bless - ing we

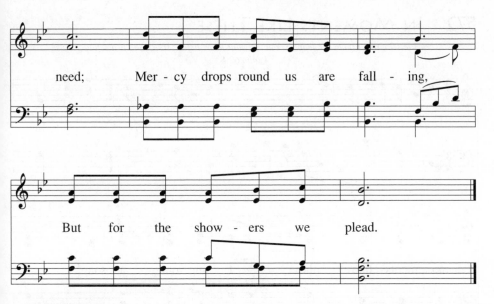

need; Mer - cy drops round us are fall - ing,

But for the show - ers we plead.

Text: Daniel W. Whittle, 1840-1901
Tune: SHOWERS OF BLESSING, 8 7 8 7 with refrain; James McGlanahan, 1840-1907

572 In Moments Like These

Trust in Him at all times, O people; pour out your heart before Him; God is a refuge for us.
Psalm 62:8

In mo - ments like these I sing out a song, I sing out a love song to Je - sus; In mo - ments like these I lift up my hands, I lift up my hands to the Lord. Sing - ing,

"I love You, Lord," sing-ing, "I love You, Lord;" Sing-ing, "I love You, Lord; I love You." Sing-ing, "I love You, Lord, I love You."

Text: David Graham, b.1948
Tune: David Graham, b.1948

573 I Love You, Lord

May all who seek You rejoice... may those who love Your salvation say continually, "Great is the LORD!"
Psalm 40:16

I love You, Lord, and I lift my voice to wor - ship You, O my soul, re - joice! Take

joy, my King, in what You hear: may it be a

sweet, sweet sound in Your ear.

Text: Laurie Klein
Tune: Laurie Klein; arr. by Nolan Williams, Jr., b.1969
© 1978, House of Mercy Music

574 My Jesus, I Love Thee

"...do you love me more than these?" He said to Him, "Yes, Lord; You know that I love You."
John 21:15

1. My Je-sus, I love Thee, I know Thou art mine— For Thee all the fol-lies of sin I re-sign; My gra-cious Re-deem-er, my Sav-ior art Thou: If ev-er I loved Thee, my Je-sus, 'tis now.

2. I love Thee be-cause Thou hast first lov-ed me And pur-chased my par-don on Cal-va-ry's tree; I love Thee for wear-ing the thorns on Thy brow: If ev-er I loved Thee, my Je-sus, 'tis now.

3. I'll love Thee in life, I will love Thee in death, And praise Thee as long as Thou lend-est me breath; I say when the death-dew lies cold on my brow, "If ev-er I loved Thee, my Je-sus, 'tis now."

4. In man-sions of glo-ry and end-less de-light, I'll ev-er a-dore Thee in heav-en so bright; I'll sing with the glit-ter-ing crown on my brow, "If ev-er I loved Thee, my Je-sus, 'tis now."

Text: William R. Featherston, 1846-1873
Tune: GORDON, 11 11 11 11; Adoniram J. Gordon, 1836-1895

More Love to Thee   575

And this is my prayer, that your love may overflow more and more with knowledge and full insight.
Philippians 1:9

1. More love to Thee, O Christ, More love to Thee!
2. Once earth-ly joy I craved, Sought peace and rest;
3. Then shall my lat-est breath Whis-per Thy praise;

Hear Thou the prayer I make On bend-ed knee;
Now Thee a-lone I seek, Give what is best;
This be the part-ing cry My heart shall raise;

This is my ear-nest plea:
This all my prayer shall be; More love, O Christ, to Thee,
This still its prayer shall be;

More love to Thee, More love to Thee!

Text: Elizabeth Prentiss, 1818-1878
Tune: MORE LOVE TO THEE, 6 4 6 4 66 44; William H. Doane, 1832-1915

576 PRECIOUS JESUS

...I regard everything as loss because of the surpassing value of knowing Christ Jesus my Lord.
Philippians 3:8

Pre-cious Je - sus, how I love You. How I lift high my voice with Your praise. Ho-ly Spir-it, I im-plore Thee, drench my heart as my lips part Your grace.

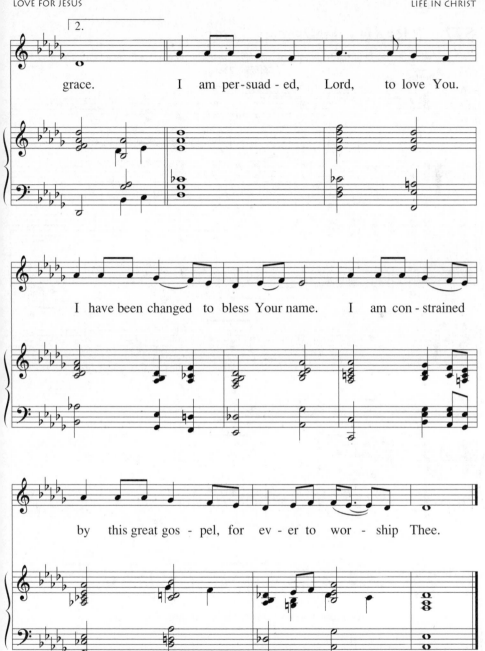

grace. I am per-suad-ed, Lord, to love You.

I have been changed to bless Your name. I am con-strained

by this great gos-pel, for ev-er to wor-ship Thee.

Text: Thomas A. Whitfield
Tune: Thomas A. Whitfield; arr. by Thomas W. Jefferson

577 I REALLY LOVE THE LORD

You shall love the Lord your God with all your heart, and with all your soul, and with all your mind.
Matthew 22:37

*Faith is the vic - to - ry.   I   love   Him,   I   love   Him;

I   real - ly   love   the   Lord!

*Alternate text: Gave me the victory.

Text: Jimmy Dowell, © Sound of Gospel
Tune: Jimmy Dowell, © Sound of Gospel; arr. by Nolan Williams, Jr., b.1969, © 2000, GIA Publications, Inc.

578 IS THERE ANYBODY HERE WHO LOVES MY JESUS

"Simon son of John, do you love me more than these?" "Yes, Lord; You know that I love You." "Feed my lambs."
John 21:15

Refrain

Is there an - y - bod - y here who loves my

Je - sus? An - y - bod - y here who loves the Lord?

I want to know if you love my Je - sus;

I want to know if you love the Lord?

Verses

Unison

1. ⸬ Hap - py day, oh, hap - py day.
2. ⸬ He taught me how to watch and pray.
3. I went to the val - ley but I did-n't go to stay.

I want to know if you love the Lord.

Unison

When Je - sus washed my sins a - way.
And live re - joic - ing ev - 'ry day.
My soul got hap - py and I stayed all day.

I want to know if you love the Lord.

Text: Jubilee Song
Tune: ANYBODY HERE, Irregular with refrain; Jubilee Song; arr. by Jeffrey P. Radford, © 2000, GIA Publications, Inc.

579 KOINONIA

...those who do not love a brother or sister whom they have seen, cannot love God whom they have not seen.
1 John 4:20

How can I say that I love the Lord whom I've
get to say that I love the one whom I

nev - er, ev - - er seen be - fore; and for -
walk be - side each and

ev - 'ry day? How can I look up -

on your face and ig - nore God's love? You I

must em - brace! You're my broth - er; you're my

sis - ter; and I love you with the love of my

Lord. Love of my Lord!

Koinonia, *derived from the original* κοινωνια, *is a Greek word meaning* fellowship.

Text: V. Michael McKay
Tune: V. Michael McKay
© Schaff Music Publishing

580 I Love You, Lord, Today

...Yes, Lord; you know that I love You....
John 21:15

1. I love You. I love You. I love You, Lord, to-day
2. My heart, my mind, my soul be-long to You.

be - cause You care for me in
You paid the price for me way

such a spe - cial way. And yes I praise You. I
back on Cal - va - ry.

lift You up. I mag - ni - fy Your name.

That's why my heart is filled with praise.

Text: William F. Hubbard
Tune: William F. Hubbard
© 1985, Chinwah Songs (SESAC)

581 MY SOUL LOVES JESUS

My soul yearns for You in the night, my spirit within me earnestly seeks You.
Isaiah 26:9

1. My soul loves Je-sus, my soul loves
2. He's a won-der in my soul, He's a won-der in my
3. My soul seeks to please Him, my soul seeks to

Je - sus, my soul loves Je - sus; bless His name.
soul, He's a won-der in my soul; bless His name.
please Him, my soul seeks to please Him; bless His name.

My soul loves Je - sus, my soul loves
He's a won-der in my soul, He's a won-der in my
My soul seeks to please Him, my soul seeks to

Je - sus, my soul loves Je - sus, bless His name.
soul, He's a won-der in my soul, bless His name.
please Him, my soul seeks to please Him, bless His name.

Text: Charles H. Mason
Tune: MY SOUL LOVES JESUS, Irregular; Charles H. Mason; harm. by Iris Stevenson, © 1982, The Church of God in Christ Publishing Board,
    (Benson Music Group)

IF YOU LIVE RIGHT 582

Blessed are the pure in heart, for they will see God.
Matthew 5:8

1. If you live right, heav-en be-longs to you, If you live right,

heav - en be-longs to you, If you live right,

heav-en be-longs to you. O, heav-en be-longs to you.

2. If you walk right...
3. If you talk right...
4. If you pray right...
5. Treat your neighbor right...

Text: Congregational Praise Song
Tune: Congregational Praise Song; arr. by Jimmie Abbington, © 2000, GIA Publications, Inc.

583 WE SHALL BEHOLD HIM

For the LORD is righteous; He loves righteous deeds; the upright shall behold His face.
Psalm 11:7

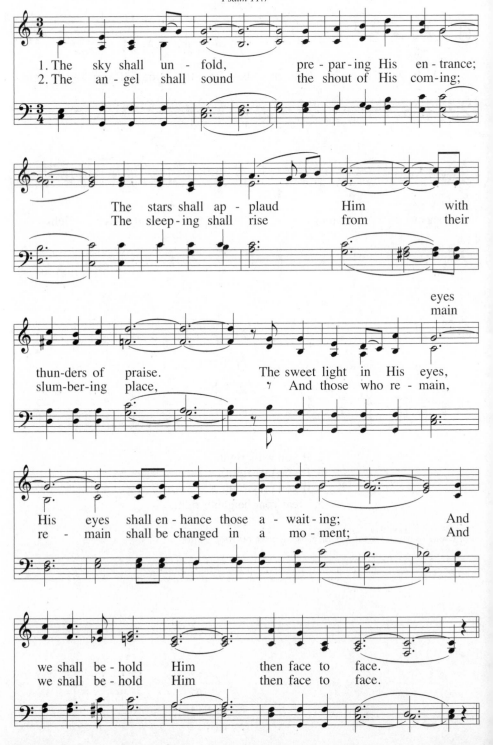

1. The sky shall un-fold, pre-par-ing His en-trance;
2. The an-gel shall sound the shout of His com-ing;

The stars shall ap-plaud Him with
The sleep-ing shall rise from their

thun-ders of praise. The sweet light in His eyes,
slum-ber-ing place, And those who re-main,

His eyes shall en-hance those a-wait-ing; And
re-main shall be changed in a mo-ment; And

we shall be-hold Him then face to face.
we shall be-hold Him then face to face.

And we shall be - hold Him, We shall be - hold Him

Face to face in all of His glo - ry.

glo - ry. O we shall be - hold Him, Him

glo - ry.

Yes, we shall be - hold Him Face to face, our Sav - ior and Lord.

Text: Dottie Rambo
Tune: WE SHALL BEHOLD HIM, 11 11 15 10 wih refrain; Dottie Rambo; arr. by Nolan Williams, Jr., b.1969
© 1980, John T. Benson Publishing Co.

584 Just to Behold His Face

...His servants will worship Him; they will see His face, and His name will be on their foreheads.
Revelation 22:3-4

Solo:

1. Not just to kneel with the an-gels, And
2. Not just to join in the cho-rus, And

not to see loved ones who've gone; And it's not just to
sing with those that are blest; Nor to bathe my

drink at the foun-tain That is un-der the great white
soul that is wea-ry In the sea of heav-en-ly

throne; Not for the crown that He'll give me
rest; But I'll look for the One who has saved me

That I'm try-ing to run this race; I know all that I'll
From a death of sin and dis-grace; I'll have joy when I

Text: Derrick Jackson
Tune: BEHOLD HIS FACE, 8 8 10 8 D with refrain; Derrick Jackson; arr. by Charlene Moore Cooper, © 2000, GIA Publications, Inc.

585 IN THAT GREAT GITTIN' UP MORNIN'

For the Lord Himself... will descend from heaven, and the dead in Christ will rise first.
1 Thessalonians 4:16

Refrain

In that great git-tin' up morn-in', fare ye well, fare ye well, In that

great git-tin' up morn-in', fare ye well, fare ye well. In that

great git-tin' up morn-in', fare ye well, fare ye well. Oh, in a that

great git-tin' up morn-in', fare ye well, fare ye well.

Verses

1. There's a bet - ter day a com-in', fare ye well, fare ye well. There's a
2. There'll be no more dy-in', fare ye well, fare ye well. There'll be
3. Oh, saint's will be a ris-in', fare ye well, fare ye well. Oh,

bet - ter day a com-in', fare ye well, fare ye well. When I
no more dy-in', fare ye well, fare ye well. There'll be
saint's will be a ris-in', fare ye well, fare ye well. There'll be

see king Je-sus, fare ye well, fare ye well. When I
no more cry-in', fare ye well, fare ye well. There'll be
no more striv-in', fare ye well, fare ye well. There'll be

see king Je-sus, fare ye well, fare ye well.
no more cry-in', fare ye well, fare ye well.
no more striv-in', fare ye well, fare ye well.

Text: Negro spiritual
Tune: FARE YE WELL, 14 14 12 12 with refrain; Negro spiritual; arr. by Joseph Joubert, © 2000, GIA Publications, Inc.

586 ON JORDAN'S STORMY BANKS

Now proceed to cross the Jordan, you and all this people, into the land that I am giving to them.
Joshua 1:2

1. On Jor - dan's storm - y banks I stand, And
2. All o'er those wide - ex - tend - ed plains, Shines
3. No chill - ing winds or poi - s'nous breath Can
4. When shall I reach that hap - py place And

cast a wish - ful eye; To Ca - naan's fair and
one e - ter - nal day; There God the Son for -
reach that health-ful shore; Sick - ness and sor - row,
be for - ev - er blest? When shall I see my

hap - py land, Where my pos - ses - sions lie.
ev - er reigns, And scat - ters night a - way.
pain and death, Are felt and feared no more.
Fa - ther's face, And in God's bo - som rest?

I am bound for the prom - ised land, I am

bound for the prom-ised land; Oh, who will come and

go with me? I am bound for the prom-ised land.

Text: Samuel Stennett, 1727-1795
Tune: STORMY BANKS, CM with refrain; American melody; adapt by Rigdon McCoy McIntosh, 1836-1899; arr. by Norman Johnson, © 1968, Singspiration Music (ASCAP)

587 SOON-A WILL BE DONE

When the righteous cry for help, the LORD hears, and rescues them from all their troubles.
Psalm 34:17

Refrain

Soon - a will be done - a with the trou-bles of the world,

Trou - bles of the world, The trou - bles of the world.

Soon - a will be done - a with the trou-bles of the world. Goin'

home to live with God.

Verses

1. No more weep-ing and a - wail - ing, No more
2. I want to meet my moth - er, I want to
3. I want to meet my Je - sus, I want to

weep - ing and a - wail - ing, No more
meet my moth - er, I want to
meet my Je - sus, I want to

weep-ing and a - wail - ing, I'm goin' to live with God.
meet my moth - er, I'm goin' to live with God.
meet my Je - sus, I'm goin' to live with God.

D.C.

Text: Traditional
Tune: SOON-A WILL BE DONE, 888 6 with refrain; traditional

588 THE SWEET BY AND BY

And the city has no need of sun or moon to shine on it, for the glory of God is its light, and its lamp is the Lamb.
Revelation 21:23

1. There's a land that is fair - er than day, And by
2. We shall sing on that beau - ti - ful shore The me -
3. To our boun - ti - ful Fa - ther a - bove We will

faith we can see it a - far, For the Fa - ther waits o - ver the
lo - di - ous songs of the blest; And our spir - its shall sor-row no
of - fer our trib - ute of praise For the glo - ri - ous gift of His

way To pre - pare us a dwell - ing - place there.
more— Not a sigh for the bless - ing of rest.
love And the bless - ings that hal - low our days.

In the sweet by and by, We shall

In the sweet by and by, by and by,

meet on that beau - ti - ful shore; In the

by and by,

sweet by and by, We shall

In the sweet by and by, by and by,

meet on that beau - ti - ful shore.

Text: Sanford F. Bennett, 1836-1889
Tune: SWEET BY AND BY, 9 9 9 9 with refrain; Joseph P. Webster, 1819-1875

589 THE UNCLOUDY DAY

Death will be no more; mourning and crying and pain will be no more, for the first things have passed away.
Revelation 21:4

1. O they tell me of a home far be - yond the skies, O they
2. O they tell me of a home where my friends have gone, O they
3. O they tell me of a King in His beau - ty there, And they
4. O they tell me that He smiles on His chil - dren there, And His

tell me of a home far a - way; O they
tell me of that land far a - way, Where the
tell me that mine eyes shall be - hold Where He
smile drives their sor - rows all a - way; And they

tell me of a home where no storm - clouds rise;
tree of life in e - ter - nal bloom
sits on the throne that is whit - er than snow,
tell me that no tears ev - er come a - gain,

O they tell me of an un - cloud - y day.
Sheds its fra - grance thro' the un - cloud - y day.
In the cit - y that is made of gold.
In that love - ly land of un - cloud - y day.

O the land of a cloud-less day, O the land of an

un-cloud-y day. O they tell me of a home where no

storm-clouds rise, O they tell me of an un-cloud-y day.

Text: Rev. J. K. Alwood
Tune: UNCLOUDY DAY, 12 10 12 10 with refrain, Rev. J. K. Alwood; arr. by Valeria A. Foster, © 2000, GIA Publications, Inc.

590 WE'RE MARCHING TO ZION

The ransomed of the LORD shall return, and come to Zion with singing; everlasting joy shall be upon their heads...
Isaiah 35:10

1. Come, we that love the Lord, And let our joys be
2. Let those re - fuse to sing Who nev - er knew our
3. The hill of Zi - on yields A thou - sand sa - cred
4. Then let our songs a-bound, And ev - 'ry tear be

known, Join in a song with sweet ac - cord, Join
God; But chil - dren of the heav'n - ly King, But
sweets Be - fore we reach the heav'n - ly fields, Be -
dry; We're march - ing through Im - man - uel's ground, We're

in a song with sweet ac - cord, And thus sur -
chil - dren of the heav'n - ly King, May speak their
fore we reach the heav'n - ly fields, Or walk the
march - ing through Im - man - uel's ground, To fair - er

1. And thus sur-round the

round the throne, And thus sur-round the throne.
joys a - broad, May speak their joys a - broad.
gold - en streets, Or walk the gold - en streets.
worlds on high, To fair - er worlds on high.

throne, And thus sur - round the throne.

We're march - ing to Zi - on, Beau - ti - ful,

We're march - ing on to Zi - on,

beau - ti - ful Zi - on; We're march - ing up - ward to

Zi - on, The beau - ti - ful cit - y of God.

Zi - on, Zi - on,

Text: Isaac Watts, 1674-1748
Tune: MARCHING TO ZION, 6 6 88 66 with refrain; Robert Lowry, 1826-1899

591 WHERE WE'LL NEVER GROW OLD

...the world and its desire are passing away, but those who do the will of God live forever.
1 John 2:17

1. I have heard of a land On the far - a - way strand,
2. In that beau - ti - ful home Where we'll nev - er - more roam,
3. When our work here is done And the life crown is won,

'Tis a beau - ti - ful home of the soul;
We shall be in the sweet by and by;
And our trou - bles and tri - als are o'er,

Built by Je - sus on high, There we nev - er shall die,
Hap - py praise to the King Through e - ter - ni - ty sing,
All our sor - rows will end, And our voic - es will blend

'Tis a land where we nev - er grow old.
'Tis a land where we nev - er shall die.
With the loved ones who've gone on be - fore.

old,

Nev-er   grow old, Where we'll   nev-er   grow old,   In a

Where   we'll

land   where we'll   nev - er   grow   old;

old,

Nev-er   grow old, Where we'll   nev-er   grow old,   In a

Where   we'll

land   where we'll   nev - er   grow   old.

Text: James C. Moore
Tune: NEVER GROW OLD, 66 9 D with refrain; James C. Moore

592 AIN'T-A THAT GOOD NEWS

Like cold water to a thirsty soul, so is good news from a far country.
Proverbs 25:25

1. I got a crown up in - a that king-dom,
2. I got a robe up in - a that king-dom, Ain't-a that
3. I got a Sav - ior in - a that king-dom,

good news!
I got a crown up in - a that
I got a robe up in - a that
I got a Sav - ior in - a that

king-dom,
king-dom, Ain't-a that good news! I'm-a gon-na lay down this
king-dom,

world, gon-na shoul - der up - a my cross. Gon-na

take it home-a to my Je-sus, Ain't-a that good news!

Text: Negro spiritual
Tune: GOOD NEWS, 10 5 10 5 16 10 5; Negro spiritual; arr. by Dr. Robert J. Fryson, © 2000, GIA Publications, Inc.

NEW NAME IN GLORY 593

To everyone who conquers... I will give a white stone, and on the white stone is written a new name...
Revelation 2:17

I've got a new *name o-ver in glo-ry, and it's

mine, mine, mine. I've got a new name o-ver in

glo-ry, and it's mine, mine, mine!

Substitute song, shout, etc.

Text: African-American traditional
Tune: African-American traditional; arr. by Dr. Robert J. Fryson, © 1982, Bob Jay Music Co.

594 WHEN WE ALL GET TO HEAVEN

In my Father's house there are many dwelling places...
John 14:2

1. Sing the won-drous love of Je-sus, Sing His
2. While we walk the pil-grim path-way Clouds will
3. Let us then be true and faith-ful, Trust-ing,
4. On-ward to the prize be-fore us! Soon His

mer-cy and His grace; In the man-sions
o-ver-spread the sky; But when trav-'ling
serv-ing ev-'ry day; Just one glimpse of
beau-ty we'll be-hold; Soon the pearl-y

bright and bless-ed He'll pre-pare for us a place.
days are o-ver Not a shad-ow, not a sigh.
Him in glo-ry Will the toils of life re-pay.
gates will o-pen— We shall tread the streets of gold.

When we all   what a

When we all get to heav-en,

day   of   re-joic-ing that will   be!   When we

what   a day   of   re - joic-ing that   will be!

all

When   we all   see   Je   -   sus,   we'll

shout   the vic - to - ry!

sing   and   shout,   and   shout   the   vic - to - ry!

Text: Eliza E. Hewitt, 1851-1920
Tune: HEAVEN, 8 7 8 7 with refrain; Emily D. Wilson, 1865-1942; arr. by Valeria A. Foster, © 2000, GIA Publications, Inc.

595 WHEN THE SAINTS GO MARCHING IN

See, the Lord is coming with ten thousands of His holy ones, to execute judgment on all...
Jude 14-15

1. O when the saints go march-ing in, O when the
2. O when the sun re - fused to shine, O when the
3. O when they crown Him Lord of all, O when they

saints go march - ing in,
sun re - fused to shine, O Lord, I want to be in that
crown Him Lord of all,

num-ber when the saints go march - ing in.
when the sun re - fused to shine.
when they crown Him Lord of all.

Text: Negro spiritual
Tune: WHEN THE SAINTS, 88 10 7; Negro spiritual; arr. by Stephen Key, © 2000, GIA Publications, Inc.

COME AND GO WITH ME 596

For the kingdom of God is not food and drink but righteousness and peace and joy in the Holy Spirit.
Romans 14:17

1. Come and go with me to my Fa-ther's house,
2. Peace and love a - bide in my Fa-ther's house,
3. Peace and hap - pi - ness in my Fa-ther's house,

To my Fa-ther's house, to my Fa-ther's house.
In my Fa-ther's house, in my Fa-ther's house.
In my Fa-ther's house, in my Fa-ther's house,

Come and go with me to my Fa-ther's house;
Peace and love a - bide in my Fa-ther's house;
Peace and hap - pi - ness in my Fa-ther's house;

There is joy, joy, joy!

4. No more dyin' there, in my Father's house...
5. Sweet communion up there, in my Father's house...

Text: Congregational Praise Song
Tune: COME AND GO WITH ME, 10 10 10 5; Congregational Praise Song; arr. by Kenneth Louis, © 2000, GIA Publications, Inc.

597 BEFORE THIS TIME ANOTHER YEAR

If we live, we live to the Lord, and if we die, we die to the Lord...
Romans 14:8

slow and freely

Leader:

Be - fore this time an-oth-er year...

All:

Be - fore this

time an - oth -

Leader:

er year I may be dead and gone!

All:

I may be

dead and gone! I'll

Leader:

All:

let you know be-fore I go... I'll let

you know be - fore I go what will be-come of me!

What will be - come of me!

Text: Anonymous
Tune: Meter hymn; Anonymous, arr. by M. Adams and Louis Sykes, © 2000, GIA Publications, Inc.

598 WILL THE CIRCLE BE UNBROKEN

...you are no longer strangers and aliens, but you are citizens with the saints and members of the household of God.
Ephesians 2:19

1. There are loved ones in the glo - ry
2. In the joy - ous days of child - hood,
3. You re - mem - ber songs of heav - en
4. You can pic - ture hap - py gath - 'rings
5. One by one their seats were emp - ty,

Whose dear forms you of - ten miss,
Oft they told of won - drous love,
Which you sang with child - ish voice,
Round the fire - side long a - go,
One by one they went a - way,

When you close your earth - ly sto - ry
Point - ed to the dy - ing Sav - ior,
Do you love the hymns they taught you,
And you think of tear - ful part - ings,
Now the fam - 'ly is part - ed,

Will you join them in their bliss?
Now they dwell with Him a - bove.
Or are songs of earth your choice?
When they left you here be - low.
Will it be com - plete one day?

Will the cir - cle be un - bro - ken by and

by, yes, by and by? In a bet - ter home a -

wait - ing in the sky, in the sky?

Text: Ada R. Habershon
Tune: UNBROKEN CIRCLE, 8 7 8 7 with refrain; Charles H. Gabriel, 1856-1932; arr. by Evelyn Simpson-Curenton, b.1953, © 2001, GIA
    Publications, Inc.

599 I Bowed on My Knees

...at the name of Jesus every knee should bend... and every tongue should confess that Jesus Christ is Lord...
Philippians 2:10-11

1. I dreamed of a cit-y called glo-ry, so
   en-tered the gates of that cit-y, my

bright and so fair, When I en-tered the
loved ones all knew me well, They took me down the

gates I cried ho-ly, the an-gels all met me
streets of heav-en, on the scenes too man-y to

there. They car-ried me from man-sion to man-sion,
tell. I saw A-bra-ham, Ja-cob and I-saac;

Oh, the sights I saw. Then I
talked with Mark and Tim-o-thy. But I

said I want to see Je - sus, The One who

died for me. I bowed on my knees and cried

ho - ly, ho - ly, ho - ly, I

clapped my hands and sang glo - ry, glo - ry to the

1.
Son of God. 2. Then as I
2.
God.

Text: Nettie Dudley Washington
Tune: CRIED HOLY, Irregular; E. M. Dudley Cantwell; arr. by Louis Sykes
© 1923, 1925 (renewed), Hill and Range Songs, Inc.

600 I Wanna Be Ready

And I saw the holy city, the new Jerusalem, coming down out of heaven from God, prepared as a bride...
Revelation 21:2

Refrain

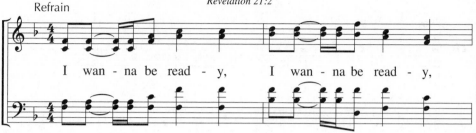

I wan - na be read - y, I wan - na be read - y,

I wan - na be read - y to walk in Je - ru - sa - lem just like John.

Last time

Verses
Solo:

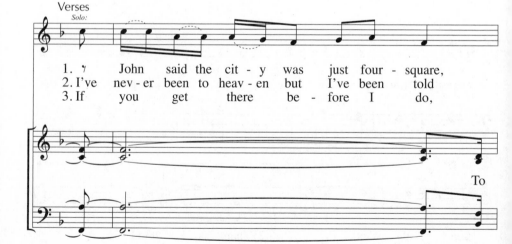

1. John said the cit - y was just four - square,
2. I've nev - er been to heav - en but I've been told
3. If you get there be - fore I do,

To

Text: Negro spiritual
Tune: BE READY, 8 10 8 10 with refrain; Negro spiritual; arr. by Evelyn Simpson-Curenton, b.1953, © 2000, GIA Publications, Inc.

601 I'LL FLY AWAY

O that I had wings like a dove! I would fly away and be at rest.
Psalm 55:6

1. Some glad morn-ing when this life is o'er,
2. When the shad-ows of this life have gone,
3. Just a few more wea-ry days and then,

I'll fly a-way;   To that home on
Like a bird from
To a land where

God's ce-les-tial shore,
pris-on bars has flown,   I'll fly a-way.
joys shall nev-er end,

Well

I'll fly a-way, O glo-ry, I'll fly a-way;

When I die, Hal - le -

lu - jah, by and by, I'll fly a - way.

Text: Albert E. Brumley
Tune: I'LL FLY AWAY, 9 4 9 4 with refrain; Albert E. Brumley; arr. by Evelyn Simpson-Curenton, b.1953
© 1932, Hartford Music Co., renewed 1960, Albert E. Brumley & Sons/SESAC

602 JUST OVER IN THE GLORYLAND

You are no longer strangers... but you are citizens with the saints and also members of the household of God...
Ephesians 2:19

1. I've a home pre - pared where the saints a - bide, Just o - ver in the glo - ry - land; And I long to be by my Sav - ior's side, Just o - ver in the glo - ry - land.

2. I am on my way to those man - sions fair, Just o - ver in the glo - ry - land; There to sing God's praise, and His glo - ry share, Just o - ver in the glo - ry - land.

3. What a joy - ful thought that my Lord I'll see, Just o - ver in the glo - ry - land; And with kin - dred saved, there for - ev - er be, Just o - ver in the glo - ry - land.

4. With the blood-washed throng I will shout and sing, Just o - ver in the glo - ry - land; Glad ho - san - nas to Christ, the Lord and King, Just o - ver in the glo - ry - land.

Just o - ver in the glo - ry - land, I'll
Just o - ver, o - ver in the glo - ry - land, I'll

join the hap - py an - gel band, Just

join, yes, join the hap - py an - gel band, Just

o - ver in the glo - ry - land; Just o - ver in the

o - ver in the glo - ry - land; Just o - ver, o - ver in the

glo - ry - land, There with the might - y

glo - ry - land, There with, yes, with the might - y

host I'll stand, Just o - ver in the glo - ry - land.

Text: James W. Acuff, fl.20th C.
Tune: IN THE GLORYLAND, 10 8 10 8 with refrain; Emmet S. Dean

603 WEAR A CROWN

And when the chief shepherd appears, you will win the crown of glory that never fades away.
1 Peter 5:4

1. Am I a sol - dier of the cross, A fol - l'wer of the Lamb, And shall I fear to own His cause, Or blush to speak His name?
2. Must I be car - ried to the skies On flow - 'ry beds of ease, While oth - ers fought to win the prize, And sailed thro' blood - y seas?
3. Are there no foes for me to face? Must I not stem the flood? Is this vile world a friend to grace, To help me on to God?
4. Sure I must fight if I would reign; In - crease my cour - age, Lord; I'll bear the toil, en - dure the pain, Sup - port - ed by Thy word.

And when the bat - tle's o - ver we shall wear a crown! Yes,

we shall wear a crown! Yes, we shall wear a crown! And when the bat-tle's

o - ver we shall wear a crown In the new Je - ru - sa -

lem. Wear a crown, wear a crown, Wear a

Wear a crown, wear a crown,

bright and shin - ing crown, And when the bat - tle's o - ver

we shall wear a crown In the new Je - ru - sa - lem.

Text: Isaac Watts, 1674-1748
Tune: WEAR A CROWN, CM with refrain; English traditional

604 THE CROWN

Be faithful until death, and I will give you the crown of life.
Revelation 2:10

1. O what love the Sav-ior for my soul has shown, Glad-ly
2. As re-ward for cross-es that I here may bear, There's a
3. I have loved ones wait-ing for my com-ing there, Soon my

I will la-bor for Him; For a-wait-ing
crown with man-y a gem; It through years un-
Lord will call me to them; We shall sing "Ho-

me I know there is a crown,
end-ing I shall sure-ly wear, In the new Je-ru-sa-lem.
san-na," wear-ing crowns all fair,

bright crown

There's a bright crown wait-ing, wait-ing for me, There's a

bright crown

bright crown

bright

crown

bright crown wait - ing, wait - ing for me, There's a bright crown

bright crown

bright

crown

wait - ing, wait-ing for me, In the new Je - ru-sa - lem.

crown

Text: B. B. Edmiaston
Tune: THE CROWN, 11 8 11 7 with refrain; Emmett S. Dean

605 DEEP RIVER

Let me cross over to see the good land beyond the Jordan, that good hill country and the Lebanon.
Deuteronomy 3:25

Deep riv-er, my home is o-ver Jor-dan,

Deep riv-er, Lord, I want to cross o-ver in-to

camp-ground. Oh don't you want to go to that

gos-pel feast, That prom-ised land where

all   is   peace?   Oh,   deep

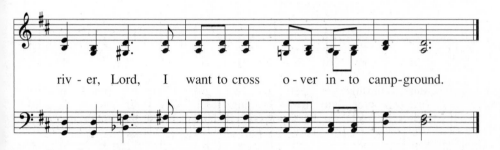

riv - er, Lord,   I   want to cross   o - ver in - to camp-ground.

Text: Traditional
Tune: DEEP RIVER, Irregular; Negro spiritual; arr. Carl Haywood, b.1949, © 1992

THE STAR-SPANGLED BANNER 606

Some take pride in chariots, and some in horses, but our pride is in the name of the LORD our God.
Psalm 20:7

1. O   say   can   you   see   by   the dawn's ear - ly
2. On the shore, dim - ly   seen   thro' the mists   of   the
3. O   thus   be   it   ev -   er when free - men shall

light,   What so   proud - ly   we   hailed   at   the
deep,   Where the foe's haugh - ty   host   in   dead
stand   Be - tween their loved   homes   and the

twi - light's last gleam - ing, Whose broad stripes and bright
si - lence re - pos - es, What is that which the
war's des - o - la - tion! Blest with vic - t'ry and

stars, through the per - il - ous fight, O'er the ram - parts we
breeze, o'er the tow - er - ing steep, As it fit - ful - ly
peace, may the heav'n-res-cued land Praise the Pow'r that hath

watched, were so gal - lant - ly stream - ing? And the
blows half con - ceals, half dis - clos - es? Now it
made and pre - served us a na - tion! Then

rock - ets' red glare, the bombs burst - ing in
catch - es the gleam of the morn - ing's first
con - quer we must, when our cause it is

air,   Gave   proof   through the   night   that our
beam,   In full   glo - ry   re - flect - ed   now
just,   And   this   be   our   mot - to,   "In

flag   was   still   there.   O   say   does   that
shined on   the   stream,   'Tis the   Star - Span - gled
God   is   our   trust."   And the Star - Span - gled

Star - Span - gled   Ban - ner   yet   wave   O'er the
Ban - ner   O   long   may   it   wave   O'er the
Ban - ner   in   tri - umph shall   wave   O'er the

land   of the   free   and the home   of   the   brave?
land   of the   free   and the home   of   the   brave!
land   of the   free   and the home   of   the   brave!

Text: Francis S. Key, 1779-1843
Tune: STAR SPANGLED BANNER, Irregular; John S. Smith, 1750-1836

607 AMERICA THE BEAUTIFUL

...you shall be for me a priestly kingdom and a holy nation.
Exodus 19:6

1. O beau - ti - ful for spa - cious skies, For
2. O beau - ti - ful for pil - grim feet, Whose
3. O beau - ti - ful for he - roes proved In
4. O beau - ti - ful for pa - triot dream That

am - ber waves of grain, For pur - ple moun-tain
stern, im - pas-sioned stress A thor - ough-fare for
lib - er - at - ing strife, Who more than self their
sees be - yond the years Thine al - a - bas - ter

maj - es - ties A - bove the fruit - ed plain!
free - dom beat A - cross the wil - der - ness!
coun - try loved, And mer - cy more than life!
cit - ies gleam, Un - dimmed by hu - man tears!

A - mer - i - ca! A - mer - i - ca! God
A - mer - i - ca! A - mer - i - ca! God
A - mer - i - ca! A - mer - i - ca! May
A - mer - i - ca! A - mer - i - ca! God

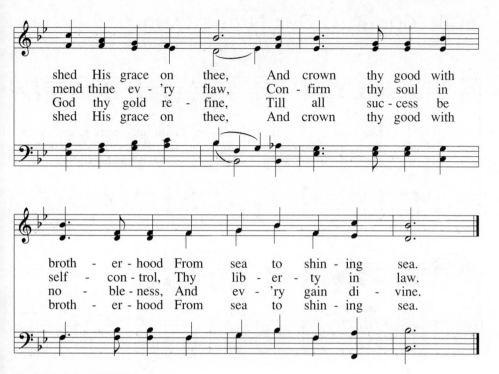

shed His grace on thee, And crown thy good with
mend thine ev - 'ry flaw, Con - firm thy soul in
God thy gold re - fine, Till all suc - cess be
shed His grace on thee, And crown thy good with

broth - er - hood From sea to shin - ing sea.
self - con - trol, Thy lib - er - ty in law.
no - ble - ness, And ev - 'ry gain di - vine.
broth - er - hood From sea to shin - ing sea.

Text: Katherine L. Bates, 1859-1929
Tune: MATERNA, CMD; Samuel A. Ward, 1848-1903

608 GOD BLESS OUR NATIVE LAND

Happy is the nation whose God is the LORD, the people whom He has chosen as His heritage.
Psalm 33:12

1. God bless our na - tive land, With right-eous might we'll
2. God keep us through the year, Thy Prov - i - dence make
3. God bless us through the year, Our homes and friends so

stand; Lift high our ban - ner now un - furled, In
clear, Through all the com - ing storms and rains, Till
dear; Pour out up - on us from a - bove Thy

"Peace" with all the world.
sun - shine comes a - gain.
mer - cy, Lord, Thy love. A - men.

Text: Wellington A. Adams
Tune: NATIONAL ODE, SM; Wellington A. Adams

609 GOD OF OUR FATHERS

May the LORD, the God of your ancestors, increase you a thousand times more and bless you...
Deuteronomy 1:11

Trumpets before each stanza (optional)

1. God of our fa - thers, whose al - might - y
2. Thy love di - vine hath led us in the
3. From war's a - larms, from dead - ly pes - ti -
4. Re - fresh Thy peo - ple on their toil - some

hand   Leads forth in beau - ty all the star - ry
past,   In this free land by Thee our lot is
lence,   Be Thy strong arm our ev - er - sure de -
way,   Lead us from night to nev - er end - ing

band   Of shin - ing worlds in splen - dor thru the
cast;   Be Thou our rul - er, guard - ian, guide, and
fense;   Thy true re - li - gion in our hearts in -
day;   Fill all our lives with love and grace di -

skies,   Our grate - ful songs be - fore Thy throne a - rise.
stay,   Thy word our law, Thy paths our cho - sen way.
crease,   Thy boun - teous good - ness nour - ish us in peace.
vine,   And glo - ry, laud, and praise be ev - er Thine!

Text: Daniel C. Roberts, 1841-1907
Tune: NATIONAL HYMN, 10 10 10 10; George W. Warren, 1828-1902

ETERNAL FATHER, STRONG TO SAVE 610

...He got up and rebuked the winds and the sea; and there was a dead calm.
Matthew 8:26

1. E - ter - nal Fa - ther, strong to save, Whose arm has bound the
2. O Sav - ior, whose al - might - y word The wind and waves sub -
3. O Ho - ly Spir - it, who did brood Up - on the cha - os
4. O Trin - i - ty of love and pow'r, All trav - 'lers guard in

rest - less wave, Who bade the might - y o - cean deep Its
mis - sive heard, Who walked up - on the foam - ing deep, And
wild and rude, And bade its an - gry tu - mult cease, And
dan - ger's hour; From rock and tem - pest, fire and foe, Pro -

own ap - point - ed lim - its keep: O hear us when we
calm a - mid its rage did sleep: O hear us when we
gave, for fierce con - fu - sion, peace: O hear us when we
tect them where - so - e'er they go; Thus ev - er - more shall

cry to Thee For those in per - il on the sea.
cry to Thee For those in per - il on the sea.
cry to Thee For those in per - il on the sea.
rise to Thee Glad praise from air and land and sea.

Text: William Whiting, 1825-1878
Tune: MELITA, 88 88 88; John Bacchus Dykes, 1823-1876

611 THE MASTER'S LOVE

No one has greater love than this, to lay down one's life for one's friends.
John 15:13

1. Car - ing, shar-ing, lov - ing His peo - ple. That's what our
2. Pray - ing, o - bey-ing, lis - t'ning to Je - sus. He is the
3. Bless - ed Sav - ior, we a - dore You. We glo - ri-

Mas - ter does both day and night. Teach - ing, reach - ing,
One who will pro - tect us all. Where He leads us
fy Your ho - ly name from a - bove. Let all things be done de - cent-

Last time to Coda

spread - ing the gos - pel. Help - ing His chil - dren learn to
we will fol - low. With hand in hand we know we'll
ly and in or - der. These are the words that show the

Coda

Mas-ter's love.　　Ah

These　　are　the words that show the　Mas - ter's love!

Text: Geraldine Woods, ©
Tune: Geraldine Woods, ©; adapt. from Pachelbel's *Canon in D* by Nolan Williams, Jr., b.1969, © 2000, GIA Publications, Inc.

612　THE JOY OF THE LORD

Restore to me the joy of Your salvation, and sustain in me a willing spirit.
Psalm 51:12

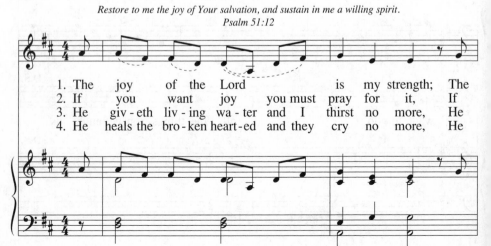

1. The　joy　　of　the　Lord　　　　　　is　my strength;　The
2. If　　you　　want　joy　you must　pray　for　it,　　If
3. He　　giv - eth　liv - ing　wa - ter　and　I　thirst　no　more,　He
4. He　heals the　bro - ken heart - ed　and they　cry　no　more,　He

joy of the Lord is my strength; The
you want joy you must pray for it, If
giv - eth liv - ing wa - ter and I thirst no more, He
heals the bro - ken heart - ed and they cry no more, He

joy of the Lord is my strength; The
you want joy you must pray for it, The
giv - eth liv - ing wa - ter and I thirst no more, The
heals the bro - ken heart - ed and they cry no more, The

joy of the Lord is my strength.
joy of the Lord is my strength.
joy of the Lord is my strength.
joy of the Lord is my strength.

Text: Nehemiah 8:10, Alliene G. Vale, fl.1971
Tune: JOY OF THE LORD, Irregular; Alliene G. Vale, fl.1971
© 1971, Multisongs/His Eye Music/Joy of the Lord Publishing (SESAC)

613 PLEASE, GUIDE ME

You are indeed my rock and my fortress; for Your name's sake lead me and guide me.
Psalm 31:3

1. Guide my
Guide my
2. Guide my
Guide my

feet, Lord, Help me to walk in a Chris-tian way; Guide my
hands, Lord, Let them work for You each day; Guide my
thoughts, Lord, Let me think of You each day; Guide my
words, Lord, Help me to spread Your love each day; Guide my

feet, Lord, Guide them ev-er-y day.
hands, Lord, Guide them ev-er-y   day.
thoughts, Lord, Guide them ev-er-y day.
words, Lord, Guide them ev-er-y   day.

Guide me ev-er-y day, Lord. Guide me ev-er-y day! *(Spoken:)* Guide me!

Text: Leanna Watkins and Nolan Williams, Jr., b.1969
Tune: PLEASE, GUIDE ME, Irregular; Leanna Watkins; arr. by Nolan Williams, Jr., b.1969, © 2000, GIA Publications, Inc.

JESUS WANTS ME FOR A SUNBEAM 614

Depart from evil, and do good; seek peace, and pursue it.
Psalm 34:14

1. Je-sus wants me for a sun - beam, To shine for Him each day;
2. Je-sus wants me to be lov - ing, And kind to all I see;

In ev - 'ry way try to please Him, At home, at school, at play.
Show-ing how pleas-ant and hap - py His lit - tle one can be.

A sun - beam, a sun - beam, Je-sus wants me for a sun - beam: A

sun - beam, a sun - beam, I'll be a sun-beam for Him.

Text: Nellie Talbot
Tune: SUNBEAM, CM with refrain; E. O. Excell, 1851-1921

615 My Help Cometh from the Lord

I lift up my eyes to the hills — from where will my help come? My help comes from the LORD...
Psalm 121:1-2

I will look to the hills   from whence com-eth my help.

My help com-eth from the Lord.   I   will look to the hills

from whence com-eth my help.   My   help   com-eth from the

Coda

help com-eth from the Lord. My help com-eth from the Lord.

Text: Psalm 121; Geraldine Woods, ©
Tune: Geraldine Woods, ©; arr. by Nolan Williams, Jr., b.1969, © 2000, GIA Publications, Inc.

616 JESUS LOVES THE LITTLE CHILDREN

Let the little children come to me; do not stop them; for it is to such as these that the kingdom of God belongs.
Mark 10:14

Je - sus loves the lit - tle chil-dren, All the chil-dren of the

world; Red and yel-low, black and white, They are pre-cious in His

sight, Je - sus loves the lit - tle chil-dren of the world.

Text: C. H. Woolston, 1856-1927
Tune: CHILDREN, 8 7 77 11; George F. Root, 1820-1895

PRAISE HIM, ALL YE LITTLE CHILDREN 617

...have you never read, 'Out of the mouths of infants and nursing babies you have prepared praise for yourself'?
Matthew 21:16

1. Praise Him, praise Him, all ye lit-tle chil-dren,
2. Love Him, love Him, all ye lit-tle chil-dren,
3. Thank Him, thank Him, all ye lit-tle chil-dren,

God is love, God is love;
God is love, God is love;
God is love, God is love;

Praise Him, praise Him, all ye lit-tle chil-dren,
Love Him, love Him, all ye lit-tle chil-dren,
Thank Him, thank Him, all ye lit-tle chil-dren,

God is love, God is love.
God is love, God is love.
God is love, God is love.

Text: Anonymous
Tune: BONNER, 10 6 10 6; Carey Bonner, 1859-1938

618 WE'RE GROWING

...we must grow up in every way into Him who is the head, into Christ.
Ephesians 4:15

grow-ing,   get-ting big and strong, We're grow-ing,
grow-ing,   watch the chan-ges tak-ing place, We're grow-ing,

learn-ing right   from wrong. Lord, keep   us   safe from harm,   As we
Get-ting   a dif-f'rent face.   We don't look quite the same,   As we

go   a - bout our   day,   We're   grow - ing   big and strong, Get-ting
did   when we were born, Help us love who we've be - come,   And

smart - er   ev - 'ry   day.   2. We're   grow-ing.
who we're going to   be.

Scripture recitation after verse 2, recited over the Introduction | Final ending

Optional recitation: 2 Corinthians 5:17
If anyone is in Christ, there is a new creation:
everything old has passed away; see, everything has become new!

Text: Evelyn Reynolds, ©
Tune: Evelyn Reynolds, ©; arr. by Nolan Williams, Jr., b.1969, © 2000, GIA Publications, Inc.

619 THERE'S NO ME, THERE'S NO YOU

For in the one Spirit we were all baptized into one body...
1 Corinthians 12:13

Refrain
2nd time

There's no me, there's no you with-out

Him. There's no me, there's no you with-out

Him. As we go through the day it takes a

Last time to Coda

min-ute to pray. There's no me, there's no you with-out

There's no me, there's no you with-out Him.

you with-out Him. There's no you with-out Him.

rit.

Text: Evelyn Reynolds, ©; adapt. by Nolan Williams, Jr., b.1969
Tune: Evelyn Reynolds ©; arr. by Nolan Williams, Jr., b.1969, © 2000, GIA Publications, Inc.

620 BLESSINGS IN THE LOVE

You bestow on him blessings forever; you make him glad with the joy of Your presence.
Psalm 21:6

I feel those bless-ings in the love of the Fa -

ther; I feel bless-ings in the love of the Son;

bless-ings in the love of the Ho -

ly Spir - it, love to draw ev - 'ry one of God's

chil - dren back home! I feel those

1.

2.

Text: Charlene Moore Cooper
Tune: Charlene Moore Cooper
© 2000, GIA Publications, Inc.

621 Do It All in the Name of the Lord

...whatever you do, in word or deed, do everything in the name of the Lord Jesus...
Colossians 3:17

Unison

What - so - ev - er ye do in word or in deed, do it all in the name of the Lord. Giv - ing thanks,

1. giv - ing thanks to God and the Fa - ther by Him.

2. giv - ing thanks to God and the Fa - ther by Him.

Text: Donna Jones
Tune: Donna Jones
© 1995, Donna Jones

I'VE GOT THE JOY, JOY, JOY 622

...and rejoice with an indescribable and glorious joy.
1 Peter 1:8

1. I've got the joy, joy, joy, joy,
2. I've got the peace that pass - eth un - der - stand - ing,
3. I've got the love of Je - sus, love of Je - sus,
4. For there is there - fore now no con - dem - na - tion,

Down in my heart, Down in my heart, Down in my heart;

I've got the joy, joy, joy, joy,
I've got the peace that pass - eth un - der - stand - ing,
I've got the love of Je - sus, love of Je - sus,
For there is there - fore now no con - dem - na - tion,

Down in my heart, Down in my heart to stay.

Text: George W. Cooke
Tune: I'VE GOT THE JOY, Irregular; George W. Cooke

623 Children, Go Where I Send Thee

All that You have commanded us we will do, and wherever You send us we will go.
Joshua 1:16

Chil-dren, go where I send thee.

How shall I send thee?

I'm gon-na send thee one by one, one is the lit-tle bit-ty

ooh ooh ooh

ba - by was born, born,

ooh born, born,

* Three by three, four by four, etc…
**These two measures get repeated in countdown fashion using the following verses.

Verses

3. three are the He - brew chil - dren,
4. four are the gos - pel writ - ers,

5. five are the five that dressed so fine,

6. six are the six that could - n't get fixed,

7. sev - en are the sev - en came down from heav - en,

8. eight are the eight that stood at the gate,

9. nine are the nine that dressed so fine,

10. ten are the ten com - mand - ments,

11. e - lev - en are the 'lev - en came down from heav - en,

12. twelve are the twelve dis - ci - ples,

Text: African-American traditional
Tune: African-American traditional; arr. by Evelyn Simpson-Curenton, b.1953, © 2000, GIA Publications, Inc.

HIGHER, HIGHER 624

For Your steadfast love is higher than the heavens, and Your faithfulness reaches to the clouds.
Psalm 108:4

1. High-er, high-er,   high-er, high-er, high-er, high-er,
2. Low-er, low-er,   low-er, low-er, low-er, low-er,
3. Su-per, su-per,   su-per, su-per, su-per, su-per,

1., 2.

high-er, high-er.   Lift   Je - sus high-er!
low-er, low-er.   Stomp the dev - il low-er!
su - per, su-per.

3.

Su - per-nat - u - ral pow-er!

Text: Anonymous
Tune: Anonymous; arr. by Nolan Williams, Jr., b.1969, © 2000, GIA Publications, Inc.

625 BLESS THE LORD

Bless the LORD, O my soul, and all that is within me, bless His holy name.
Psalm 103:1

Bless the Lord, oh my soul; Bless God's ho - ly name! Bless the Lord, oh my soul; Bless God's ho - ly name!

Verses

1., 6. And all that is with-in me, And
2. Who for - gives all your in - i - qui-ties, Who for -
3. Who heals all your dis - eas - es, Who
4. Who crowns you with love and hon - or, Who crowns
5. Who nev-er leaves you nor for - sakes you, Who nev-er

all that is with-in me; And all that is with-
gives all your in - i - qui-ties; Who for - gives all your in -
heals all your dis - eas - es; Who heals all your dis -
you with love and hon - or; Who crowns you with love and
leaves you nor for - sakes you; Who nev-er leaves you nor for -

D.S.

in me;
i - qui-ties;
eas - es; Bless God's ho - ly name!
hon - or;
sakes you;

Text: Gene Rice and Charlene Moore Cooper, © 1995
Tune: BLESS THE LORD, Irregular with refrain; © 1995, Gene Rice; harm. by Charlene Moore Cooper, © 2000, GIA Publications, Inc.

626 LORD, YOU ARE WELCOME

...and the temple was filled with smoke from the glory of God and from His power...
Revelation 15:8

Lord, You are wel - come, You're wel - come, You are

wel - come, You're wel-come in this place. You are

place. Lord, our ho - ly hands we raise to

wor-ship and give   You praise.   We in-voke Your ho-ly

pres-ence, Oh Lord, to   come and fill this place.

Text: Warren Jones, ©
Tune: Warren Jones, ©; arr. by Nolan Williams, Jr., b.1969, © 2000, GIA Publications, Inc.

627 THE LORD IS IN HIS HOLY TEMPLE

The LORD is in his holy temple; let all the earth keep silence before Him!
Habakkuk 2:20

The Lord is in His ho-ly tem - ple, The
Lord is in His ho-ly tem - ple: Let all the earth keep
si-lence, Let all the earth keep si - lence be - fore
Him— Keep si-lence, keep si-lence be - fore Him.

Text: Habakkuk 2:20
Tune: George F. Root, 1820-1895

A Glorious Introit 628

Say to God, "How awesome are Your deeds! Because of Your great power, Your enemies cringe before You."
Psalm 66:3

All glo - ry be un - to You, Lord. All
glo - ry we give to You. All hon - or we give un - to
You, Lord. All glo - ry, all hon - or, all praise. We
give them un - to You. A - men.

Text: Michael Kenneth Ross
Tune: Michael Kenneth Ross
© 1995, MKR Music

629 GRACE AND PEACE

May grace and peace be yours in abundance in the knowledge of God and of Jesus our Lord.
2 Peter 1:2

Grace and peace be un-to

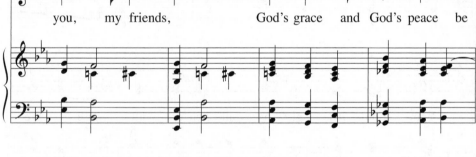

you, my friends, God's grace and God's peace be

in your hearts; And when we join to raise our

voic - es in praise to God,

grace and peace,   fill - ing you
bless - ing you,   grace and peace to

share with God's crea - tures ev - 'ry-where.

630 LET THE HEAVEN LIGHT SHINE ON ME

Now as he was going along and approaching Damascus, suddenly a light from heaven flashed around him.
Acts 9:3

Let the heav'n light shine on me, Let the heav'n light shine on

me, for low is the way to the up-per bright world, Let the

heav'n light shine on me. Shine on me, Shine on

me. Let the light from heav'n shine on

A - men, A - men.

me. A - men, A - men.

Text: African-American traditional; adapt. by Roland M. Carter, b.1942, © 1978, Mar-Vel
Tune: African-American traditional; arr. by Roland M. Carter, b.1942, © 1978, Mar-Vel

THIS IS THE DAY 631

This is the day that the LORD has made; let us rejoice and be glad in it.
Psalm 118:24

This is the day which the Lord hath made.

rit.

Let us re - joice and be glad in it.

Let us re - joice! Let us re - joice! A - men.

Text: Psalm 118:24
Music: Everett Williams, Jr., © 1982, Johnny Jordan Co., Washington, D.C., sole distributors

632 Lord, Make Me More Holy

Pursue peace with everyone, and the holiness without which no one will see the Lord.
Hebrews 12:14

*faithful
**Benediction pronounced here.

men,   un-til   we   meet a-gain.   A   -   men.

Text: African-American traditional; adapt. by Roland M. Carter, b.1942, © Mar-Vel
Tune: African-American traditional; arr. by Roland M. Carter, b.1942, © Mar-Vel

As You Go, Tell the World   633

As you go, proclaim the good news, 'The kingdom of heaven has come near.'
Matthew 10:7

As   you go,   tell the world,   as you go,   tell the world.

Tell   the   world a-bout Je-sus,   tell them a-bout His   love.

Tell   the   world a-bout Je-sus,   tell them a-bout His   love.

Text: Anonymous
Tune: Anonymous; arr. by Valeria Foster, © 2000, GIA Publications, Inc.

634 GOD BE WITH YOU TILL WE MEET AGAIN

You, O LORD, will protect us; You will guard us from this generation forever.
Psalm 12:7

1. God be with you till we meet a - gain; By God's
2. God be with you till we meet a - gain; 'Neath God's
3. God be with you till we meet a - gain; When life's
4. God be with you till we meet a - gain; Keep love's

coun - sels guide, up - hold you, With God's sheep se - cure - ly
wings pro - tect - ing hide you, Dai - ly man - na still pro -
per - ils thick con - found you, Put God's arms un - fail - ing
ban - ner float - ing o'er you, Smite death's threat - 'ning wave be -

fold you: God be with you till we meet a - gain.
vide you: God be with you till we meet a - gain.
round you: God be with you till we meet a - gain.
fore you: God be with you till we meet a - gain.

Till we meet, till we meet, Till we

meet at Je - sus' feet, Till we meet, till we

till we meet,

meet, God be with you till we meet a - gain.

Text: Jeremiah E. Rankin, 1828-1904
Tune: GOD BE WITH YOU, 9 8 8 9 with refrain; William G. Tomer, 1832-1896

BENEDICTION 635

The peace of God, which surpasses all understanding, will guard your hearts and your minds in Christ Jesus.
Philippians 4:7

The peace of God be with you ev - er - y day un - til we

meet a - gain.

Tune: Charlene Moore Cooper, © 2000, GIA Publications, Inc.

636 The Lord Bless You / Sevenfold Amen

The LORD bless you and keep you; the LORD make His face to shine upon you, and be gracious to you...
Numbers 6:24-25

The Lord bless you and keep you; The Lord lift His coun-te-

nance up-on you, and give you peace,

and give you peace, and give you

and give you peace; The Lord make His face to shine up-

peace;

on you, And be gra - cious un-to you, be gra-cious,

And be gra-cious and be gra-cious,

Text: Numbers 6:24-26
Tune: BENEDICTION, Irregular; Peter C. Lutkin, 1858-1931

637 GO YE NOW IN PEACE

The priest replied, "Go in peace. The mission you are on is under the eye of the LORD."
Judges 18:6

Go ye now in peace, and know that the love of

God will guide you. Feel His pres-ence here be - side you.

He will see you through. Go ye now in

peace. Go ye now in peace.

Go in peace.

Text: Joyce Eiler
Tune: Joyce Eiler; arr. by Evelyn Simpson-Curenton
© Unichappell Music, Inc.

TILL WE GATHER AGAIN   638

Peace I leave with you; my peace I give to you.
John 14:27

Till we gath-er a-gain, God be with you. Till we gath-er a-gain, God be with you. May He give you His love, give you His kind-ness, keep you in per-fect peace. God be with you till we meet a-gain.

Text: Stephen F. Key
Tune: Stephen F. Key
© StepKey Music

639 GOD BE WITH YOU

Where can I go from Your spirit? Or where can I flee from Your presence?
Psalm 139:7

God be with you, God be with you,

God be with you, un-til we meet a - gain;

God be with you, God be with you,

God be with you, un-til we meet a - gain.

ALWAYS REMEMBER 640

Remember Jesus Christ, raised from the dead, a descendant of David—that is my gospel...
2 Timothy 2:8

Al - ways re - mem - ber Je - sus, Je - sus.

Al - ways re - mem - ber Je - sus, Je - sus.

Al - ways keep Him on your mind.

Text: Andraé Crouch, b.1945
Tune: Andraé Crouch, b.1945; arr. Evelyn Simpson-Curenton
© Crouch Music (ASCAP)

641 Be With Us All, Lord

...grow in the grace and knowledge of our Lord and Savior Jesus Christ. To Him be the glory...
2 Peter 3:18

May the grace of the Lord Je-sus Christ be

with you, and the love of God, and the

fel - low-ship of the Ho - ly Ghost be with us

all. A - men. Grace,

love, and fel - low - ship be with us all. A - men. A - men! A - men! A - men, a - men!

Text: Uzee Brown, Jr.
Tune: Uzee Brown, Jr.
© 1995, Roger Dean Publishing Co.

642 HALLE, HALLE, HALLE

Hallelujah! Salvation and glory and power to our God...
Revelation 19:1

Hal-le, hal-le, hal-le-lu - jah! Hal-le, hal-le, hal-

Hal-le, hal-le, hal-

lu - jah!

le - lu, Hal-le-lu-jah! Hal-le, hal-le, hal-le-lu -

le - lu - jah!

Music: Traditional Caribbean, arr. by John L. Bell, b.1949, © 1990, Iona Community, GIA Publications, Inc., agent; acc. by Marty Haugen, b.1950, © 1993, GIA Publications, Inc.

ALLELUIA 643

Once more they said, Hallelujah!
Revelation 19:3

Music: George Mxadana; tr. by John L. Bell, b.1949, © 1990, Iona Community, GIA Publications, Inc., agent

644 ALLELUIA

He is your praise; He is your God, who has done for you these great and awesome things...
Deuteronomy 10:21

1. Al-le-lu-ia, al-le-lu-ia, al-le-lu-ia, al-le-lu-ia,

al-le-lu-ia, al-le-lu-ia, al-le-lu-ia, al-le-lu-ia.

2. Thank You, Jesus,... 3. Lord, we praise You,... 4. Lord, we love You...

Text: Jerry Sinclair, 1943-1993
Music: Jerry Sinclair, 1943-1993
© 1972, 2000, Manna Music, Inc.

645 TWOFOLD AMEN

...in Him every one of God's promises is a "Yes." For this reason it is through Him that we say the "Amen,"...
2 Corinthians 1:20

A - men, A - men.

Music: Charlene Moore Cooper, © 2000, GIA Publications, Inc.

646 THREEFOLD AMEN

Continue modulating in half-steps.

A - men, A - men, A - men.

Music: Danish Amen, anonymous; arr. by Nolan Williams, Jr., b.1969, © 2000, GIA Publications, Inc.

SEVENFOLD AMEN 647

Music: John Stainer, 1840-1901

AMEN 648

Music: Fernando G. Allen, © 1990. Administered by GIA Publications, Inc.

649 AMEN

Blessed be the LORD forever. Amen and Amen.
Psalm 89:52

A - men, a - men,

A - men, good Lord - y, a - men, have mer - cy,

Sing it o - ver.

a - men, a - men, a - men.

Verses

1. See the ba - by,
2. See Him in the tem - ple,
3. See Him at the Jor - dan
4. See Him at the sea - side,
5. March-in' in Je - ru - sa-lem,
6. See Him in the gar - den,
7. Led be - fore Pi - late,
8. Hal - le - lu - jah!

men. A -

ly - in' in the man - ger on
talk - in' with the eld - ers who
where John was bap - tiz - in' and
talk - in' to the fish - er - men and
o - ver palm branch - es, in
pray - in' to His Fa - ther, in
then they cru - ci - fied Him, but He
He died to save us and He

men, a -

Christ - mas morn - in'.
mar - velled at His wis - dom.
sav - in' all sin - ners.
mak - in' them dis - ci - ples.
pomp and splen - dor.
deep - est sor - row.
rose on East - er.
lives for ev - er.

men, a -

men, a - men, a - men.

Text: Traditional
Music: Negro spiritual; arr. by Valeria A. Foster, © 2000, GIA Publications, Inc.

650 Praise God from Whom All Blessings Flow

Every generous act of giving, with every perfect gift, is from above, coming down from the Father...
James 1:17

Praise God from whom all bless - ings flow,

Praise Him all crea - tures here be - low.

Praise Him a - bove ye heav - en - ly host,

Praise Fa - ther, Son and Ho - ly Ghost.

Text: Isaac Watts, 1675-1748, and William Keathe, d.1593; adapt. by Thomas Ken, 1637-1711
Music: John Hatton, d.1793; adapt. by George Coles; arr. by Roberta Martin, 1912-1969, © 1968, alt.

651 DOXOLOGY

Blessed be the God and Father of our Lord Jesus Christ...
Ephesians 1:3

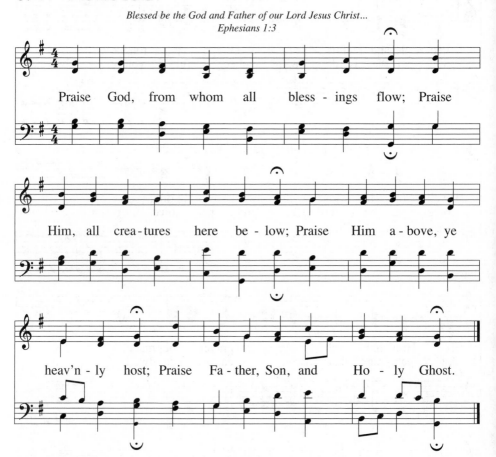

Praise God, from whom all bless - ings flow; Praise Him, all crea - tures here be - low; Praise Him a - bove, ye heav'n - ly host; Praise Fa - ther, Son, and Ho - ly Ghost.

Text: Thomas Ken, 1637-1711
Music: OLD 100TH, LM; *Genevan Psalter*, 1551; attr. to Louis Bourgeois, 1510-1561

652 GLORIA PATRI

To our God and Father be glory forever and ever. Amen.
Philippians 4:20

Glo - ry be to the Fa - ther, and to the

Son, and to the Ho - ly Ghost; As it was in the be -
gin-ning, is now, and ev - er shall be,
world with-out end. A - men, A - men.

Text: 2nd Century
Music: Charles Meineke, 1782-1850

GLORIA PATRI 653

To our God and Father be glory forever and ever. Amen.
Philippians 4:20

Glory be to the Father, and to the Son,
As it was in the beginning, is now, and ev - er shall be,

and to the Ho - ly Ghost;
world with - out end. A - men.

Text: 2nd Century
Music: Old Scottish Chant

654 GLORIA PATRI

"I am the Alpha and the Omega," says the Lord God, who is and who was and who is to come, the Almighty.
Revelation 1:8

Glo - ry be to the Fa - ther, and to the Son, and to the

Ho - ly Ghost; As it was in the be - gin - ning, is now and ev - er

shall be, world with - out end. A - men, A - men.

Text: 2nd Century
Music: Henry W. Greatorex, 1811-1858

655 LORD, HAVE MERCY

Be mindful of Your mercy, O LORD...
Psalm 25:6

1. Lord, have mer - cy, Lord,
2. Christ, have mer - cy, Christ,
3. Lord, have mer - cy, Lord,

simile

have mer - cy, Lord, have
have mer - cy, Christ, have
have mer - cy, Lord, have

mer - cy on us.
mer - cy on us.
mer -

cy, have mer - cy on us.

Music: *Mass of St. Augustine,* Leon C. Roberts, 1950-1999, © 1981, GIA Publications, Inc.

656 LORD, HAVE MERCY

Have mercy on me, O God, according to Your steadfast love...
Psalm 51:1

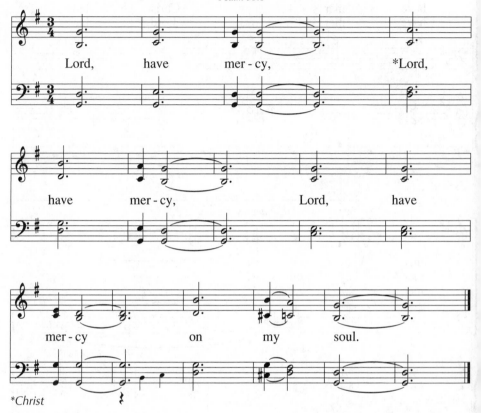

Lord, have mer-cy, *Lord, have mer-cy, Lord, have mer-cy on my soul.

*Christ

Music: Wyatt Tee Walker; harm. by C. Eugene Cooper
© Wyatt Tee Walker and C. Eugene Cooper

657 O LORD, HEAR OUR PRAYER

Hear my prayer, O God; give ear to the words of my mouth.
Psalm 54:2

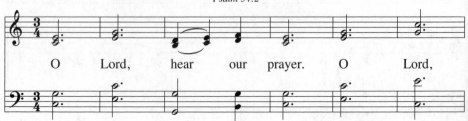

O Lord, hear our prayer. O Lord,

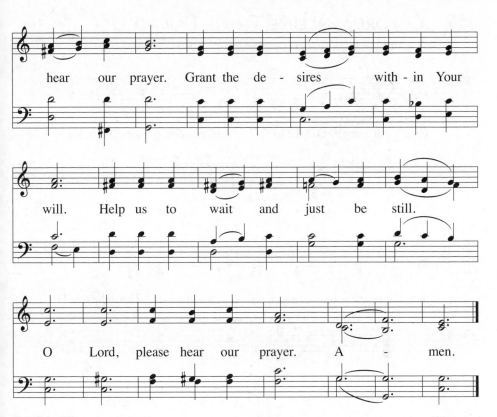

hear our prayer. Grant the de - sires with - in Your will. Help us to wait and just be still. O Lord, please hear our prayer. A - men.

Text: Stephen F. Key
Music: Stephen F. Key

HEAR OUR PRAYER 658

Hear my prayer, O LORD; give ear to my supplications in Your faithfulness; answer me in Your righteousness.
Psalm 143:1

Hear our prayer, O Lord; hear our prayer, O Lord; In - cline Thine ear to us and grant us Thy peace. A - men.

Text: Psalm 143:1
Music: George Whelpton, 1847-1930

659 O Lord, Incline Thine Ear to Us

Hear a just cause, O LORD; attend to my cry; give ear to my prayer from lips free of deceit.
Psalm 17:1

Hear our prayer, O Lord, Hear our prayer, O Lord. In-

cline Thine ear to us And grant us Thy peace. O

2. A - men, A - men, A - men, A -

peace. A - men, A -

men.

men. In-cline Thine ear to us And grant us Thy

peace.* A - men, A - men, A - men, A - men.

peace. A - men, A - men, A - men, A - men.

A separate Amen may begin here.

Text: African-American traditional
Music: African-American traditional; arr. by Bernadette Blount Salley, © 1987. Administered by GIA Publications, Inc.

ISAIAH 6:3 660

One called to another and said: Holy, holy, holy is the LORD of hosts; the whole earth is full of His glory."
Isaiah 6:3

Ho - ly, ho - ly, ho - ly, Lord God of

Hosts! Heav'n and earth are full of Thee!

Heav'n and earth are prais - ing Thee, O Lord most high!

Text: Isaiah 6:3, Mary A. Lathbury, 1841-1913
Music: CHAUTAUQUA, Irregular; William F. Sherwin, 1826-1888

661 SANCTUS

...Holy, holy, holy, the Lord God the Almighty, who was and is and is to come.
Revelation 4:8

Ho - ly, ho - ly, ho - ly Lord, God of pow'r and might. Ho - ly, ho - ly, ho - ly Lord, God of pow'r and might. Heav - en and earth are full, full of Your glo - ry. Ho - san - na in the high - est, ho - san - na in the high - est. Bless - ed is He who

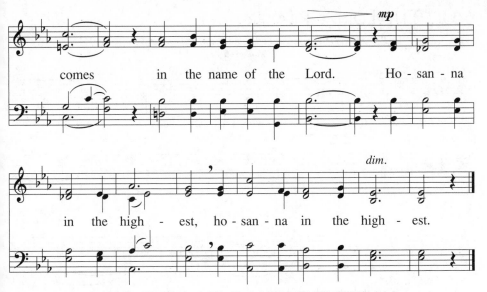

comes in the name of the Lord. Ho - san - na

in the high - est, ho - san - na in the high - est.

Music: *Deutsche Messe*, Franz Schubert, 1797-1828; adapt. by Richard Proulx, b.1937, © 1985, 1989, GIA Publications, Inc.

Santo / Holy 662

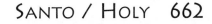

Our heart is glad in Him, because we trust in His holy name.
Psalm 33:21

¡San - to, San - to, San - to, mi cor - a - zón te a - do - ra! Mi
Ho - ly, Ho - ly, Ho - ly, my heart, my heart a - dores You! My

cor - a - zón te sa - be de - cir: San - to e - res Se - ñor.
heart is glad to say the words: You are Ho - ly, Lord.

Music: Unknown; arr. by Nolan Williams, Jr., b.1969, © 2000, GIA Publications, Inc.

663 THE LORD'S PRAYER

Pray then in this way: Our Father in heaven, hallowed be Your name.
Matthew 6:9

Our Fa - ther, which art in heav - en,

hal - low - ed be Thy name.

Thy king - dom come, Thy will be done on

earth as it is in heav - en. Give us this

Oo

Oo

664 THE LORD'S PRAYER

...one of his disciples said to Him, "Lord, teach us to pray..."
Luke 11:1

Verses 1, 2

1. Our Fa - ther, which art in heav-en, Hal-low-ed-a be Thy
2. Done on earth as it is in heav-en, Hal-low-ed-a be Thy

heav - en

name. Thy king - dom come, Thy will be done,
name. Give us this day our dai - ly bread,

1.
Hal - low - ed - a be Thy name.
Hal - low - ed - a be Thy
2.
name.

Verse 3

3. And for - give us all our debts, Hal-low-ed-a be Thy

name. As we for - give our debt - ors,

slower tempo

Hal - low - ed - a   be   Thy   name.

Verse 4

4. Lead us not in - to   temp-ta-tion,   Hal - low-ed - a   be   Thy

name.   But de - liv - er   us   from   e - vil,

rall.

Hal - low - ed - a   be   Thy   name.

rall.

Verses 5, 6
brighter tempo

5. Thine is the king - dom, the pow'r and the glo - ry,
6. A - men, a - men, a - men,

(5.) and the glo - ry,
(6.) a - men,

Hal - low - ed - a be Thy name. For ev - er, and
Hal - low - ed - a be Thy name. A - men, a - men, a -

ev - er, Hal - low - ed - a be Thy name.
men, a - men. Hal - low - ed - a be Thy

1.

2. *rall.*

name. Hal - low - ed - a be Thy name.

rall.

Text: The Lord's Prayer
Music: West Indian traditional; arr. by Nolan Williams, Jr., b.1969, © 2000, GIA Publications, Inc.

LET THE WORDS OF MY MOUTH 665

Let the words of my mouth and the meditation of my heart be acceptable to You, O LORD...
Psalm 19:14

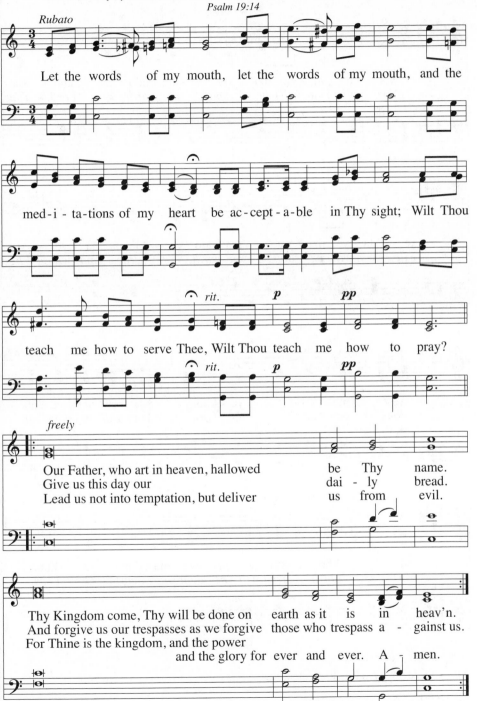

Let the words of my mouth, let the words of my mouth, and the
med-i-ta-tions of my heart be ac-cept-a-ble in Thy sight; Wilt Thou
teach me how to serve Thee, Wilt Thou teach me how to pray?

Our Father, who art in heaven, hallowed be Thy name.
Give us this day our dai - ly bread.
Lead us not into temptation, but deliver us from evil.

Thy Kingdom come, Thy will be done on earth as it is in heav'n.
And forgive us our trespasses as we forgive those who trespass a - gainst us.
For Thine is the kingdom, and the power
and the glory for ever and ever. A - men.

Text: Psalm 19:14 and The Lord's Prayer
Music: C. E. Leslie; adapt. by Nolan Williams, Jr., b.1969, Evelyn Simpson-Curenton, b.1953, and Dr. Robert J. Fryson, © 2000,
   GIA Publications, Inc.

666 MAYENZIWE / YOUR WILL BE DONE

Your will be done, on earth as it is in heaven.
Matthew 6:10

African phonetics:
My-yen-zee-way tahn-doe yah-koe.

Text: from the Lord's Prayer, South African, (Xhosa)
Music: South African traditional, as taught by George Mxadana; transcribed by John L. Bell, b.1949; © 1990, Iona Community,
    GIA Publications, Inc., agent

Yes, Lord 667

For in Him every one of God's promises is a "Yes."
2 Corinthians 1:20

Yes, yes, yes, yes, yes, yes, yes, Lord,

yes, Lord, yes, Lord, yes, Lord, yes, Lord, yes, Lord.

Text: Charles H. Mason
Music: Charles H. Mason

All Things Come of Thee 668

But who am I, and what is my people, that we should be able to make this freewill offering?
1 Chronicles 29:14

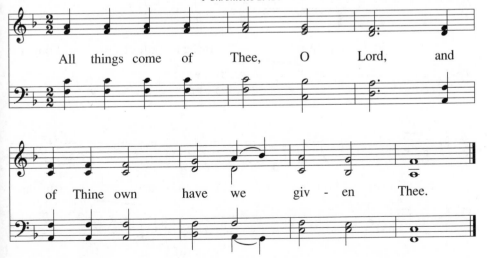

All things come of Thee, O Lord, and

of Thine own have we giv - en Thee.

Text: I Chronicles 29:14
Music: Attr. to Ludwig van Beethoven, 1770-1827

669 BRING A GIFT OF LOVE

...and live in love, as Christ loved us and gave Himself up for us, a fragrant offering and sacrifice to God.
Ephesians 5:2

Bring a gift of love, bring a gift of love, bring a gift of love to-day. Bring an of-fer-ing to our Lord and King, tell the world He is "the Way!" Bring a gift of love, bring a gift of love, bring a gift of love to-day. In this

qui - et hour of wor - ship bring a gift of love.

SITTING AT HIS FEET 670

She had a sister named Mary, who sat at the Lord's feet and listened to what He was saying.
Luke 10:39

Sit-ting at His feet, sit-ting at His feet.

That is where my life is com - plete: sit-ting at His feet.

671 You Can't Beat God Giving

God is able to provide you with every blessing in abundance...
2 Corinthians 9:8

You can't beat God giv-ing, no mat-ter

how you try. And just as

sure as you are liv-ing and the Lord is in

heav-en on high, the more you give, the

more He gives to you. Just keep on giv-ing be-

cause it's real-ly true. That You can't beat God

giv-ing no mat-ter how you try.

Text: Doris Akers, b.1922, © Manna Music
Tune: Doris Akers, b.1922, © Manna Music; arr. by Evelyn Simpson-Curenton, b.1953, © 2000, GIA Publications, Inc.

672 HALLELUJAH, 'TIS DONE

...all the people of Jerusalem were going out to him, and were baptized... in the river Jordan, confessing their sins.
Mark 1:5

1. 'Tis the prom - ise of God full sal - va - tion to
2. Tho' the path - way be lone - ly, and dan - ger - ous
3. There's a part in that cho - rus for you and for

give Un - to Him who on Je - sus, His Son, will be - lieve.
too, Sure - ly Je - sus is a - ble to car - ry me through.
me, And the theme of our prais - es for - ev - er will be:

Hal - le - lu - jah, 'tis done! I be - lieve on the

Son; I am saved by the blood of the

cru - ci - fied One.   cru - ci - fied One.

Text: Philip P. Bliss
Tune: TIS DONE, 12 12 with refrain; Philip P. Bliss
© 1954, First Church of Deliverance

HALLELUJAH, 'TIS DONE   673

...all the people of Jerusalem were going out to him, and were baptized... in the river Jordan, confessing their sins.
Mark 1:5

Hal - le - lu - jah, 'tis done, I be -

lieve on the Son. I am saved by the

blood of the cru - ci - fied One.   One.

Note: This is a baptismal hymn taken from the African-American worship oral tradition.

Text: Traditional
Tune: African-American traditional; arr. by Evelyn Simpson-Curenton, b.1953, © 2000, GIA Publications, Inc.

674 WASH, O GOD, OUR SONS AND DAUGHTERS

Baptism...now saves you—not as a removal of dirt from the body, but as an appeal to God for a good conscience...
1 Peter 3:21

1. Wash, O God, our sons and daugh - ters, Where Your
2. We who bring them long for nur - ture; By Your
3. O how deep Your ho - ly wis - dom! Un - i -

cleans - ing wa - ters flow. Num-ber them a - mong Your
milk may we be fed. Let us join Your feast, par -
mag - ined, all Your ways! To Your name be glo - ry,

peo - ple; Bless as Christ blessed long a - go. Weave them
tak - ing Cup of bless - ing, liv - ing bread. God, re -
hon - or! With our lives we wor - ship, praise! We Your

gar - ments bright and spar - kling; Com - pass
new us, guide our foot - steps; Free from
peo - ple stand be - fore You, Wa - ter -

them   with   love   and   light.   Fill,   a - noint   them;
sin   and   all   its   snares,   One   with Christ in
washed   and   Spir - it -   born.   By   Your grace, our

send Your   Spir - it,   Ho - ly   dove   and   heart's de - light.
liv - ing,   dy - ing,   By Your   Spir - it,   chil - dren, heirs.
lives we   of - fer.   Re - cre - ate   us;   God, trans - form!

Text: Ruth Duck, b.1947, © 1989, The United Methodist Publishing House
Tune: BEACH SPRING, 8 7 8 7 D, attr. to B.F. White; harm. by Ronald A. Nelson, © 1978, *Lutheran Book of Worship*

675 TAKE ME TO THE WATER

"Look, here is water! What is to prevent me from being baptized?"
Acts 8:36

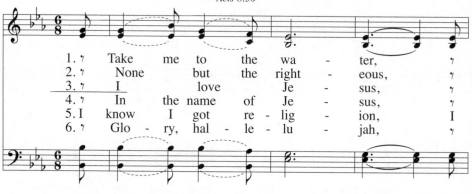

1. Take me to the wa - ter,
2. None but the right - eous,
3. I love Je - sus,
4. In the name of Je - sus,
5. I know I got re - lig - ion, I
6. Glo - ry, hal - le - lu - jah,

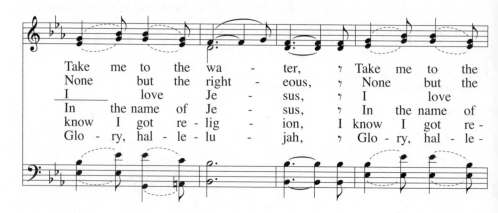

Take me to the wa - ter, Take me to the
None but the right - eous, None but the
I love Je - sus, I love
In the name of Je - sus, In the name of
know I got re - lig - ion, I know I got re -
Glo - ry, hal - le - lu - jah, Glo - ry, hal - le -

wa - ter to be bap - tized.
right - eous shall see God.
Je - sus. Yes, I do.
Je - sus we shall be saved.
lig - ion. Yes, I do.
lu - jah, to be bap - tized.

Text: Negro spiritual
Tune: TO THE WATER, Irregular; Negro spiritual; arr. Valeria A. Foster, © 2000, GIA Publications, Inc.

WADE IN THE WATER 676

So those who welcomed his message were baptized, and that day about three thousand persons were added.
Acts 2:41

Refrain

Wade in the wa-ter, wade in the wa-ter chil-dren,

Wade in the wa-ter, God's gon-na trou-ble the wa-ter.

Verses

1. See that host all dressed in white,
2. See that band all dressed in red, God's gon-na trou-ble the
3. If you don't be-lieve I've been re-deemed,

The lead-er looks like the Is-ra-el-ite,
wa-ter. Looks like the band that Mo-ses led,
Just fol-low me down to Jor-dan's stream,

D.C.

God's gon-na trou-ble the wa-ter.

Text: Negro spiritual
Tune: WADE, 7 8 8 8 with refrain; Negro spiritual; arr. by Jimmie Abbington, © 2000, GIA Publications, Inc.

677 COME, HOLY SPIRIT, DOVE DIVINE

...suddenly the heavens were opened to Him and he saw the Spirit of God descending like a dove...
Matthew 3:16

1. Come, Ho-ly Spir-it, Dove Di-vine,
2. We love Thy name, we love Thy laws,
3. We sink be-neath Thy mys-tic flood;
4. And as we rise, with Thee to live,

On these bap-tis-mal wa-ters shine,
And joy-ful-ly em-brace Thy cause,
O bathe us in Thy cleans-ing blood;
O let the Ho-ly Spir-it give

And teach our hearts, in high-est strain,
We love Thy cross, the shame, the pain,
We die to sin, and seek a grave,
The seal-ing unc-tion from a-bove,

To praise the Lamb, for sin-ners slain.
O Lamb of God, for sin-ners slain.
With Thee, be-neath the yield-ing wave.
The breath of life, the fire of love.

Text: Adoniram Judson, 1788-1850
Tune: ERNAN, LM, Lowell Mason, 1792-1872

CERTAINLY LORD 678

Let the redeemed of the LORD say so, those He redeemed from trouble.
Psalm 107:2

1. Have you got good re - lig - ion, Have you
2. Do you love ev - 'ry-bod - y, Do you
3. Have you been con - vert - ed, Have you
4. Have you been to the wa - ter, Have you
5. Have you been bap - tized, Have you

Cert - 'n-ly Lord!

got good re - lig - ion, Have you got good re - lig - ion?
love ev - 'ry-bod - y, Do you love ev - 'ry-bod - y?
been con - vert - ed, Have you been con - vert - ed?
been to the wa - ter, Have you been to the wa - ter?
been bap - tized, Have you been bap - tized?

Cert-'n-ly Lord!

Cert-'n-ly Lord! Cert-'n-ly, cert-'n-ly, cert-'n-ly Lord!

Last time

Text: Negro spiritual
Tune: CERTAINLY LORD, 7 4 7 4 7 4 10; Negro spiritual; arr. by Evelyn Simpson-Curenton, b.1953, © 2000, GIA Publications, Inc.

679 LORD I HAVE SEEN THY SALVATION

...now You are dismissing Your servant in peace, according to Your word; for my eyes have seen Your salvation...
Luke 2:29-30

1. Lord I have seen Thy sal - va - tion, Lord I have seen
2. Lord I have heard of Thy king - dom, Lord I have heard

Thy sal - va - tion, drank of the blood, held the bod - y,
of Thy prom - ise, looked on Thy birth, cried at Cal-v'ry,

Lord I have seen, seen with my eyes, seen with my heart.
Lord I have heard, Lord I have heard, Lord I have heard.

Fell on my knees, down at the al - tar, bowed down my head, whis-pered a pray-er. Have mer-cy Lord, I'm not wor-thy, I be-lieve, Yes, I be-lieve, now I am sure.

Text: John D. Cooper, b.1925
Tune: THY SALVATION, 8 8 8 12 with refrain; John D. Cooper, b.1925
© 1980, Dangerfield Music Co., 286 Strawberry Hill Rd., Centerville, MA

680 TASTE AND SEE

O taste and see that the LORD is good; happy are those who take refuge in Him.
Psalm 34:8

Taste and see, taste and see the good-ness of the

Lord. O taste and see, taste and

see the good-ness of the Lord, of the

To verses   *Last time*

Lord.   Lord.

To verses   *Last time*

Verses

1. I will bless the Lord at all times.
2. Glo - ri - fy the Lord with me.   To -
3. Wor - ship the Lord, all you peo - ple.

Praise   shall al - ways be on my lips;   my
geth - er   let us all   praise God's name.   I
You'll   want for noth - ing   if you ask.

soul shall glo-ry in the Lord; for
called the Lord who an-swered me; from
Taste and see that the Lord is good; in

God has been so good to me.
all my trou-bles I was set free.
God we need put all our trust.

D.C.

Text: Psalm 34; James E. Moore, Jr., b.1951
Tune: James E. Moore, Jr., b.1951
© 1983, GIA Publications, Inc.

681 LET US TALENTS AND TONGUES EMPLOY

And all of them ate and were filled; and they took up the broken pieces left over, seven baskets full.
Matthew 15:37

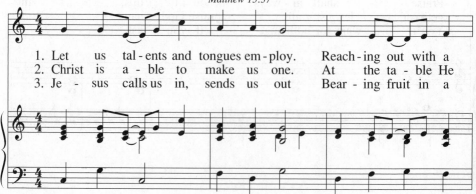

1. Let us tal-ents and tongues em-ploy. Reach-ing out with a
2. Christ is a-ble to make us one. At the ta-ble He
3. Je-sus calls us in, sends us out Bear-ing fruit in a

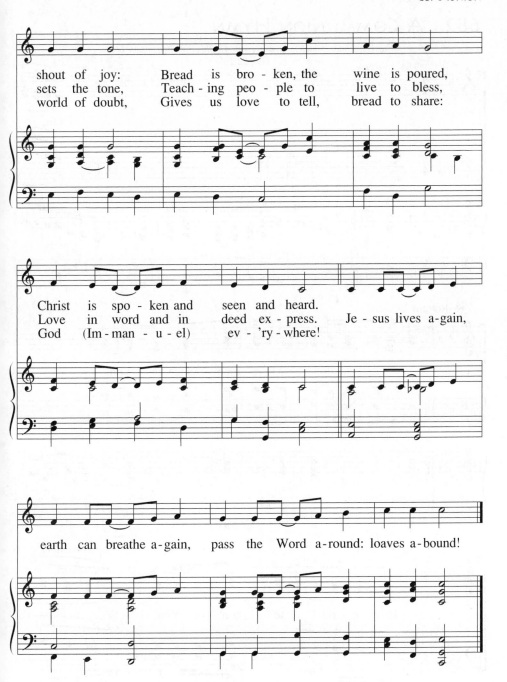

shout of joy: Bread is bro - ken, the wine is poured,
sets the tone, Teach - ing peo - ple to live to bless,
world of doubt, Gives us love to tell, bread to share:

Christ is spo - ken and seen and heard.
Love in word and in deed ex - press. Je - sus lives a - gain,
God (Im - man - u - el) ev - 'ry - where!

earth can breathe a - gain, pass the Word a - round: loaves a - bound!

Text: Fred Kaan, b.1929
Tune: LINSTEAD, LM with refrain; Jamaican folk melody; adapt. by Doreen Potter
© 1975, Hope Publishing Co.

682 A Communion Hymn

This is my body, which is given for you. Do this in remembrance of me.
Luke 22:19

Oh,

Refrain

This we do in re-mem-brance of You,

This we do to hon-or You; Oh,

Last time to Coda

This we do in re-mem-brance of You: Be-

cause You have bid us to. Oh, to.

1. 2.

Verses

1. You said: Take this bread and eat of Me, this
2. You said: Take this cup of sac-ri-fice, it

sym - bol bro - ken rep - re - sents My bod - y;
rep - re - sents My blood which gives you new life; Oh,

In this up-per room, we glad-ly feast with You, com-

mit-ting of our serv - ice back to You. Oh,

D.S.

D.S.

Coda

This we do in re-mem-brance of You: Be-

cause You have bid us to.

683 WE REMEMBER YOU

The cup of blessing that we bless, is it not a sharing in the blood of Christ?
1 Corinthians 10:16

As we drink this cup, we wor-ship You; As we

eat this bread, we hon-or You; And we of - fer You our

lives as You have of - fered Yours for us. We re-

mem - ber   all You've done for us,   We re - mem - ber Your

cov - e - nant with us,   We re - mem - ber,   and

wor - ship You,   O   Lord.

Text: Kirk Dearman, b.1952
Tune: Kirk Dearman, b.1952
© 1988, Maranatha Praise, Inc.

684 Jesus Is Here Right Now

Those who eat my flesh and drink my blood abide in me, and I in them.
John 6:56

Je - sus is here right now. Je - sus is here: With this

685 IN REMEMBRANCE

Take care that you do not forget the LORD your God...
Deuteronomy 8:11

1. In re - mem - brance of
(2. In re -) mem - brance of

Me, eat this bread. In re-mem-brance of Me, drink this
Me, heal the sick. In re-mem-brance of Me, feed the

wine. In re-mem-brance of Me, pray for the
poor. In re-mem-brance of Me, o - pen the

time when God's own will is done. 2. In re -
door and let your broth - er

in, let him in. Take, eat, and be

com - fort - ed; Drink and re - mem - ber, too, that

this is My bod - y and pre - cious blood shed for you,

shed for you. In re - mem - brance of Me,

search for truth. In re - mem - brance of Me, al - ways love.

In re-mem-brance of Me, don't look a-bove, but
in your heart, look in your heart for God.
Do this in re-mem-brance of Me.

Text: Ragan Courtney
Tune: RED, Irregular; Buryl Red
© 1972, Broadman Press, assigned to Van Ness Press, Inc.

LET US BREAK BREAD TOGETHER 686

...we who are many are one body, for we all partake of the one bread.
1 Corinthians 10:17

2. Let us drink wine together...
3. Let us praise God together...

Text: Traditional
Tune: BREAK BREAD TOGETHER, 10 10 14 7; traditional; arr. by Jimmie Abbington, © 2000, GIA Publications, Inc.

687 ACKNOWLEDGMENTS

105 © Bud John Songs, Inc. (ASCAP) Admin. by EMI Christian Music Publishing. International Copyright Secured. All Rights Reserved. Used by Permission

106 Text and tune: © 1992, Joy Publishing Co. (SESAC) Arr.: © 2000, GIA Publications, Inc.

107 © 1993, StepKey Music

108 Tune: © 1967, Scripture in Song (a div. of Integrity Music, Inc.) (ASCAP). All Rights reserved. International Copyright Secured. Used by Permission.

109 Text and tune: © 1981, Sound III. Co-owned by MCA Music Publishing, 2440 Sepulveda Blvd., Suite 100, Los Angeles, CA 90064-1712 and The Lorenz Corporation, P.O. Box 802, Dayton, OH 45401-0802. All Rights Reserved. International Copyright Secured. Arr.: © 2000, GIA Publications, Inc.

110 © 1993, New Spring Publishing, Inc. (ASCAP). A div. of Brentwood-Benson Music Publishing, Inc. All Rights Reserved. Used by Permission.

111 © 1971, Bud John Songs, Inc. (ASCAP) Admin. by EMI Christian Music Publishing. International Copyright Secured. All Rights Reserved. Used by Permission

112 Text: © 1972, Hope Publishing Co., Carol Stream, IL 60188. All rights reserved. Used by permission.

113 © 1996, Zomba Songs, Inc. and T. Autumn Music; admin. by Zomba Songs, Inc. (BMI) All Rights Reserved

114 © 1991, CMI-HP Publishing, admin. by Word Music, Inc. (ASCAP), 65 Music Square West, Nashville, TN 37203./Life Spring Music, (ASCAP), 907 McCall Street, Conroe, TX 77301. All Rights Reserved. International Copyright Secured. Used By Permission.

115 Text and tune: © Margaret Pleasant Douroux, Arr.: © 2000, GIA Publications, Inc.

116 Text and tune: © 1996, Timothy Watson. Arr.: © 2000, GIA Publications, Inc.

118 © 1994, NEW-J Publishing

119 © 1963, 1975, 1993, Fred Bock Music Company

121 Arr.: © 2000, GIA Publications, Inc.

122 Arr.: © 1990, Iona Community, GIA Publications, Inc., agent

125 Arr.: © 2000, GIA Publications, Inc.

126 © 1988, BMG Songs, Inc. (ASCAP). All rights reserved. Used by permission.

127 Arr.: © 2000, GIA Publications, Inc.

128 Arr.: © 2000, GIA Publications, Inc.

129 Text and tune: © 1959, Martin and Morris, Inc. Arr.: © 2000, GIA Publications, Inc.

130 Arr.: © 2000, GIA Publications, Inc.

131 Harm.: © estate of Wendell Whalum

132 Text: © 1989, Robert J. Fryson

133 Arr.: © 2000, GIA Publications, Inc.

134 Text and tune: © 1976, Robert J. Fryson; Arr.: © 2000, GIA Publications, Inc.

139 Arr.: © 2000, GIA Publications, Inc.

141 Text and tune: © 1994, Carlton Burgess. Administered by GIA Publications, Inc. Arr.: © 2000, GIA Publications, Inc.

143 Arr.: © 1992, Horace Clarence Boyer

147 Text: Tr. © 1923 (Renewed), J. Curwen & Sons Ltd. International Copyright Secured. All Rights Reserved. Reprinted by Permission of G. Schirmer, Inc. (ASCAP). Arr.: © 1968, Singspiration Music (ASCAP), a div. of Brentwood-Benson Music Publishing, Inc. All Rights Reserved. Used by Permission.

148 © 1953, S.K. Hine. Assigned to Manna Music, Inc., 35255 Brooten Road, Pacific City, OR 97135. All Rights Reserved. Used by Permission. (ASCAP)

149 Harm.: © 1966, Singspiration, Inc. (ASCAP). A div. of Brentwood-Benson Music Publishing, Inc. All Rights Reserved. Used by Permission.

150 Arr.: © 1990, Hezekiah Brinson, Jr.

151 Text and tune: © Keith Hunter, published by Arrand Publishing Co. Arr.: © 2000, GIA Publications, Inc.

152 Text and tune: © 1973, Davike Music Co. Arr.: © 2000, GIA Publications, Inc.

153 © 1982, Lanny Wolfe Music. All rights controlled by Gaither Copyright Management. Used by permission.

154 Arr.: © 2000, GIA Publications, Inc.

155 © 1948, renewed 1976, John W. Peterson Music Co. All rights reserved.

158 © 1923, renewed 1951, Hope Publishing Co., Carol Stream, IL 60188. All rights reserved. Used by permission.

159 Text and tune: © 1968, Greater Detroit Music and Record Mart. Arr.: © 2000, GIA Publications, Inc.

160 Text and tune: © 1980, Malaco, Inc. d/b/a Savgos Music, Inc., International Copyright Secured. All rights Reserved. Used by Permission. Arr.: © 2000, GIA Publications, Inc.

161 Arr.: © 2000, GIA Publications, Inc.

162 © 1944 (renewed), Martin and Morris Inc. All Rights Administered by Unichappell Music Inc. International Copyright Secured. All Rights Reserved.

164 © 1984, Utryck, All Rights Administered by Walton Music Corporation. International Copyright Secured. All Rights Reserved.

165 © 1988, Gaither Music Co. and Century Oak /Richwood Music. All rights reserved. Used by permission.

166 © 1988 and arr. © 1990, BMG Songs, Inc. (ASCAP), Dick and Mel Music (ASCAP), and Pamela Kay Music (ASCAP). All rights on behalf of Dick and Mel Music administered by BMG Songs, Inc. (ASCAP)

167 Arr.: © 2000, GIA Publications, Inc.

168 © 1983, BMG Songs/Birdwing Music (ASCAP) Admin. by EMI Christian Music Publishing. International Copyright Secured. All Rights Reserved. Used by Permission

169 Arr.: © 2000, GIA Publications, Inc.

171 © 1981, Rocksmith Music c/o Trust Music Management, Inc. P.O. Box 22274, Carmel, CA 93922-0274. Used by Permission. All Rights Reserved.

172 © 1986, Bud John Tunes, Inc. Admin. by EMI Christian Music Publishing. International Copyright Secured. All Rights Reserved. Used by Permission

173 Arr.: © 2000, GIA Publications, Inc.

174 Text and tune: © 1976, Sound III. Co-owned by MCA Music Publishing, 2440 Sepulveda Blvd., Suite 100, Los Angeles, CA 90064-1712 and The Lorenz Corporation, P.O. Box 802, Dayton, OH 45401-0802. All Rights Reserved. International Copyright Secured. Arr.: © 2000, GIA Publications, Inc.

176 Arr.: © 2000, GIA Publications, Inc.

177 © 1991, Leslie Parker Barnes

179 © Schaff Music Publishing

180 © 1984, Utryck, All Rights Administered by Walton Music Corporation. International Copyright Secured. All Rights Reserved.

181 Text and tune: © 1989, Margaret Pleasant Douroux, Arr.: © 2000, GIA Publications, Inc.

182 © 1978, Bob Kilpatrick Music. Assigned 1998 to The Lorenz Corporation.

183 © 1983, Meadowgreen Music Co./Songchannel Music Co. (ASCAP) Admin. by EMI Christian Music Publishing. International Copyright Secured. All Rights Reserved. Used by Permission

185 © 1972, William J. Gaither, Inc. All rights controlled by Gaither Copyright Management. Used by permission.

189 © 1976, C.A. Music (div. of C. A. Records, Inc.) All Rights Reserved. (ASCAP)

190 © 1986, Word Music, Inc. (ASCAP), 65 Music Square West, Nashville, TN 37203. All Rights Reserved. International Copyright Secured. Used By Permission.

192 © 1979, 2000, GIA Publications, Inc.

193 © 1976, Bud John Songs, Inc./Crouch Music (ASCAP) Admin. by EMI Christian Music Publishing. International Copyright Secured. All Rights Reserved. Used by Permission

195 Arr.: © 1990, Melva Costen

198 Text: "A Christmas Hymn" from ADVICE TO A PROPHET AND OTHER POEMS, © 1961, renewed 1989, Richard Wilbur. Reprinted by permission of Harcourt, Inc. Tune: © 1984, GIA Publications, Inc.

Acknowledgments/continued

200 Trans. and arr.: © 1990, Iona Community, GIA Publications, Inc., agent

202 Text adapt.: © Mrs. John W. Work III. Arr.: © 2000, GIA ublications, Inc.

203 © 1996, NEW-J Publishing

209 Arr.: © 2000, GIA Publications, Inc.

210 Arr.: © 2000, GIA Publications, Inc.

212 Arr.: © 2000, GIA Publications, Inc.

213 Arr.: © 2000, GIA Publications, Inc.

216 Arr.: © 2000, GIA Publications, Inc.

217 Arr.: © 2000, GIA Publications, Inc.

221 Arr.: © 2000, GIA Publications, Inc.

222 Arr.: © Wyatt Tee Walker. Administered by GIA Publications, Inc.

223 © 1937, First Church of Deliverance

224 Tune: © Patrick Roaché. Administered by GIA Publications, Inc. Arr.: © 2000, GIA Publications, Inc.

225 Arr.: © 2000, GIA Publications, Inc.

227 © 1981, Glory Alleluia Music, admin. by Tempo Music Publications, Inc. Assigned 1998 to The Lorenz Corporation.

228 © 1975, Word Music, Inc. (ASCAP), 65 Music Square West, Nashville, TN 37203. All Rights Reserved. International Copyright Secured. Used By Permission.

229 Text and tune: © 1994, Schaff Music Publishing. Arr.: © 2000, GIA Publications, Inc.

230 © 1981, Les Presses de Taizé, GIA Publications, Inc., agent

231 © 1986, Kenneth W. Louis

234 Arr.: © 2000, GIA Publications, Inc.

235 Arr.: © 2000, GIA Publications, Inc.

237 Text and tune: © 1975, Bridgeport Music, Inc. Arr.: © 2000, GIA Publications, Inc.

238 Arr.: © 2000, GIA Publications, Inc.

240 © 1976, Albert E. Brumley & Sons/SESAC (admin. by ICG). All rights reserved. Used by permission.

241 © 1924, Stamps-Baxter Music (BMI). A div. of Brentwood-Benson Music Publishing, Inc. All Rights Reserved. Used By Permission.

242 © 1974, Hope Publishing Co., Carol Stream, IL 60188. All rights reserved. Used by permission.

245 © 1946, Singspiration Music (ASCAP). A div. of Brentwood-Benson Music Publishing, Inc. All Rights Reserved. Used by Permission.

246 Arr.: © 2000, GIA Publications, Inc.

248 Arr.: © 2000, GIA Publications, Inc.

249 Text: © 1968, John T. Benson Publishing Co. (ASCAP). A div. of Brentwood-Benson Music Publishing, Inc. All Rights Reserved. Used by Permission.

250 Tune: © 1983, GIA Publications, Inc.

252 Harm.: © 1981, Abingdon Press (Administered By THE COPYRIGHT COMPANY, Nashville, TN) All Rights Reserved. International Copyright Secured. Used By Permission.

255 © 1985, Straightway Music/Mountain Spring Music (ASCAP) Admin. by EMI Christian Music Publishing. International Copyright Secured. All Rights Reserved. Used by Permission.

256 Text and tune: © 1966, renewed 1994, Manna Music, Inc., 35255 Brooten Road, Pacific City, OR 97135. All Rights Reserved. Used by Permission. (ASCAP). Arr.: © 2000, GIA Publications, Inc.

259 © 1987, New Spring Publishing, Inc. (ASCAP). A div. of Brentwood-Benson Music Publishing, Inc. All Rights Reserved. Used by Permission.

260 © Crouch Music. Admin. by EMI Christian Music Publishing. International Copyright Secured. Used by Permission.

261 © 1939, E.M. Bartlett, renewed 1967 by Mrs. E.M. Bartlett. Assigned to Albert E. Brumley and Sons/SESAC (admin. by ICG). All rights reserved. Used by permission.

262 Arr.: © 2000, GIA Publications, Inc.

263 Arr.: © 2000, GIA Publications, Inc.

265 Arr.: © 2000, GIA Publications, Inc.

266 © 1988, Margaret Pleasant Douroux

267 Arr.: © 2000, GIA Publications, Inc.

270 © 1993, Malaco Music, Inc. International Copyright Secured. All Rights Reserved. Used by Permission.

271 Arr.: © 2000, GIA Publications, Inc.

272 Arr.: © 2000, GIA Publications, Inc.

273 © 1963, William J. Gaither, Inc. All rights controlled by Gaither Copyright Management. Used by permission.

274 Arr.: © 2000, GIA Publications, Inc.

275 © 1933, renewed 1962, Word Music, Inc. (ASCAP), 65 Music Square West, Nashville, TN 37203. All Rights Reserved. International Copyright Secured. Used By Permission.

278 Arr.: © 2000, GIA Publications, Inc.

279 Arr.: © 2000, GIA Publications, Inc.

280 Arr.: © 2000, GIA Publications, Inc.

281 © 1971, William J. Gaither, Inc. All rights controlled by Gaither Copyright Management. Used by permission.

282 Descant: © 2000, GIA Publications, Inc.

284 Arr.: © 2000, GIA Publications, Inc.

286 © 1982, Singspiration Music (ASCAP). A div. of Brentwood-Benson Music Publishing, Inc. All Rights Reserved. Used by Permission.

287 © 1972, William J. Gaither, Inc. All rights controlled by Gaither Copyright Management. Used by permission.

290 Arr.: © 2000, GIA Publications, Inc.

292 Arr.: © 2000, GIA Publications, Inc.

295 Arr.: © 2000, GIA Publications, Inc.

296 Text and tune: © 1989, Brenda Joyce Moore. Arr.: © 2000, GIA Publications, Inc.

299 Arr.: © 2000, GIA Publications, Inc.

300 © 1982, Bob Jay Music Co.

301 © 1970, William J. Gaither, Inc. All rights controlled by Gaither Copyright Management. Used by permission.

302 © 1976, Latter Rain Music (ASCAP) Admin. by EMI Christian Music Publishing. International Copyright Secured. All Rights Reserved. Used by Permission.

303 Arr.: © 2000, GIA Publications, Inc.

304 Arr.: © 2000, GIA Publications, Inc.

305 Arr.: © 2000, GIA Publications, Inc.

306 © 1981, Meadowgreen Music Co. (ASCAP) Admin. by EMI Christian Music Publishing. International Copyright Secured. All Rights Reserved. Used by Permission

307 © 1959, renewed 1987, Manna Music, Inc., 35255 Brooten Road, Pacific City, OR 97135. All Rights Reserved. Used by Permission. (ASCAP)

309 © 1944, Singspiration Music (ASCAP). A div. of Brentwood-Benson Music Publishing, Inc. All Rights Reserved. Used by Permission.

310 Arr.: © 2000, GIA Publications, Inc.

311 Text and tune: © 1986, Lehsem Music, LLC. Arr.: © 2000, GIA Publications, Inc.

313 Arr.: © 2000, GIA Publications, Inc.

316 © Benson Music Group. A div. of Brentwood-Benson Music Publishing, Inc. All Rights Reserved. Used by Permission.

318 Text and tune: © Paragon Music Corp. Arr.: © 2000, GIA Publications, Inc.

319 Text and tune: © Century Oak/Richwood Music. Arr.: © 2000, GIA Publications, Inc.

320 © 1935, Birdwing Music (ASCAP) Admin. by EMI Christian Music Publishing. International Copyright Secured. All Rights Reserved. Used by Permission

321 © 1979, Mercy/Vineyard Publishing; admin. by Music Services, 209 Chapelwood Dr., Franklin, TN 37069

322 © 1940, renewed 1969, Word Music, Inc. (ASCAP), 65 Music Square West, Nashville, TN 37203. All Rights Reserved. International Copyright Secured. Used By Permission.

323 Text: © Timothy Wright. Arr.: © 2000, GIA Publications, Inc.

325 Arr.: © 2000, GIA Publications, Inc.

326 © 1962, renewed 1990, Manna Music, Inc., 35255 Brooten Road, Pacific City, OR 97135. All Rights Reserved. Used by Permission. (ASCAP)

Acknowledgments/CONTINUED

328 © 1972, Bud John Songs, Inc. (ASCAP) Admin. by EMI Christian Music Publishing. International Copyright Secured. All Rights Reserved. Used by Permission.

329 Arr.: © 2000, GIA Publications, Inc.

330 © 1972, Maranatha! Music (Administered By THE COPYRIGHT COMPANY, Nashville, TN) All Rights Reserved. International Copyright Secured. Used By Permission.

333 © 1991, Glenn Burleigh (Burleigh Inspirations Music)

337a Alt. text: © 1991, Reverend Pamela June Anderson, D.Min.

338 Text and tune: © 1989, Glorraine Moone. Published by Professionals for Christ Publications (BMI). Adapt.: © 2000, GIA Publications, Inc.

339 Music: From *The English Hymnal,* by permission of Oxford University Press

340 © Schaff Music Publishing

343 Original words by K. L. Cober, © 1960, Kenneth L. Cober, renewed 1985, Judson Press. 1-800-4-JUDSON. www.judsonpress.com.

344 Adapt.: © 2000, GIA Publications, Inc.

346 © 1995, MKR Music, 1421 Rogers Street, Richmond, VA 23223

348 Harm.: © 1986, GIA Publications, Inc.

349 Arr.: © 2000, GIA Publications, Inc.

350 Arr.: © 2000, GIA Publications, Inc.

352 Arr.: © 2000, GIA Publications, Inc.

353 Text and tune: © Wyatt Tee Walker. Administered by GIA Publications, Inc. Arr.: © 2000 GIA Publications, Inc.

354 Arr.: © 2000, GIA Publications, Inc.

355 Text and tune: © 1995, Mo'Berries Music (ASCAP) / Y'Shua Publishing (ASCAP), distributed by the NOAH Company, P.O. Box 11243, Jackson, Mississippi 39283-1243; Arr.: © 2000, GIA Publications, Inc.

356 Text and tune: © 1993, Waymon L. Burwell, Sr. Administered by GIA Publications, Inc. Arr.: © 2000, GIA Publications, Inc.

358 © 1984, Bob Jay Music Co.

360 Arr.: © 2000, GIA Publications, Inc.

362 Tune: Arr. © 1999, Mar-Vel

363 © 1946, (renewed) Unichappell Music, Inc. International Copyright Secured. All Rights Reserved.

364 Arr.: © 1992, Carl Haywood

365 Text and tune: © S. Boddie. Arr.: © 2000, GIA Publications, Inc.

367 Arr.: © 2000, GIA Publications, Inc.

370 Text and tune: © 1964, Lion Publishing Co. Arr.: © 2000, GIA Publications, Inc.

371 Arr.: © 2000, GIA Publications, Inc.

372 © 1926, 1953, Broadman Press

374 Arr.: © 2000, GIA Publications, Inc.

376 © 1937, Stamps-Baxter Music (BMI). A div. of Brentwood-Benson Music Publishing, Inc. All Rights Reserved. Used by Permission.

378 © 1937, Stamps-Baxter Music (BMI). A div. of Brentwood-Benson Music Publishing, Inc. All Rights Reserved. Used by Permission.

383 © 1980, Bridgeport Music, Inc.

384 © 1982, Bud John Songs, Inc. Admin. by EMI Christian Music Publishing. International Copyright Secured. All Rights Reserved. Used by Permission.

386 Arr.: © 1992, Carl Haywood

388 © 1992, Schaff Music Publishing

389 Text and tune: © 1975, Margaret Pleasant Douroux, Arr.: © 2000, GIA Publications, Inc.

390 © 1989, Eli Wilson, Jr.

391 Arr.: © 2000, GIA Publications, Inc.

392 Text: © 1922, ren. 1950, Word Music, Inc.(ASCAP) Tune: © 1939, ren. 1966, Word Music, Inc. (ASCAP), 65 Music Square West, Nashville, TN 37203. All Rights Reserved. International Copyright Secured. Used By Permission.

393 Arr.: © 2000, GIA Publications, Inc.

394 Arr.: © 2000, GIA Publications, Inc.

395 Text and tune: © 1990, Century Oak/Richwood Music. Arr.: © 2000, GIA Publications, Inc.

400 © 1963, Singspiration Music (ASCAP). A div. of Brentwood-Benson Music Publishing, Inc. All Rights Reserved. Used by Permission.

401 © 1990, Patrick Matsikenyiri

402 © 1940 (renewed), Warner-Tamerlane Publishing Corp. and Unichappell Music Inc. International Copyright Secured. All Rights Reserved.

404 Arr.: © 2000, GIA Publications, Inc.

405 Text and tune: © Donald Vails. Arr.: © 2000, GIA Publications, Inc.

407 © Rev. Maceo Woods. Administered by GIA Publications, Inc.

408 Arr.: © 1936 (renewed), Paul A. Schmitt Music Co., c/o Belwin-Mills Publishing Corp. All Rights Controlled and Administered by Warner Bros. Publications U.S. Inc. All Rights Reserved.

411 Text and tune: © Margaret Jenkins. Arr.: © 2000, GIA Publications, Inc.

412 Text and tune: © 1965, renewed 1993, Manna Music, Inc., 35255 Brooten Road, Pacific City, OR 97135. All Rights Reserved. Used by Permission. (ASCAP). Arr.: © 2000, GIA Publications, Inc.

413 Arr.: © 2000, GIA Publications, Inc.

414 Text and tune: © 1978, 1984, by Malaco, Inc. d/b/a Savgos Music, Inc., International Copyright Secured. All rights Reserved. Used by Permission. Arr.: © 2000, GIA Publications, Inc.

415 © 1950, Singspiration Music (ASCAP). A div. of Brentwood-Benson Music Publishing, Inc. All Rights Reserved. Used by Permission.

416 © 1941, renewed 1968, Gospel Publishing House. Assigned 1997 to The Lorenz Corporation.

418 Arr.: © 2000, GIA Publications, Inc.

420 Arr.: © 2000, GIA Publications, Inc.

422 Harm. © 1964, Abingdon Press (Administered By THE COPYRIGHT COMPANY, Nashville, TN) All Rights Reserved. International Copyright Secured. Used By Permission.

423 © 1966, Frazier-Cleveland Co.

427 Text: ©, Charles A. Tindley and Donald Vails. Tune: ©, Donald Vails. Arr.: © 2000, GIA Publications, Inc.

429 Harm.: © 1992, Carl Haywood

430 Arr.: © 2000, GIA Publications, Inc.

432 © 1940, Stamps-Baxter Music (BMI). A div. of Brentwood-Benson Music Publishing, Inc. All Rights Reserved. Used by Permission.

434 Harm.: © 1981, GIA Publications, Inc.

436 Arr.: © 2000, GIA Publications, Inc.

437 Text and tune: © 1957, Marvin V. Frey. Arr.: © 2000, GIA Publications, Inc.

438 Text and tune: © 1958, Marvin V. Frey. Arr.: © 2000, GIA Publications, Inc.

439 Text adapt. and arr: © 1978, Mar-Vel.

443 Arr.: © 2000, GIA Publications, Inc.

445 © 1994, Betty Gadling. Administered by GIA Publications, Inc.

446 Text and tune: © 1974, Planemar Music Co. Arr.: © 2000, GIA Publications, Inc.

447 © 1959, renewed 1988, Word Music, Inc. (ASCAP), 65 Music Square West, Nashville, TN 37203. All Rights Reserved. International Copyright Secured. Used By Permission.

448 Arr.: © 2000, GIA Publications, Inc.

453 Arr.: © 2000, GIA Publications, Inc.

454 © 1953, 1981, Clara Ward. Assigned to Gertrude Music (SESAC). This is a new arrangement.

457 Arr.: © 2000, GIA Publications, Inc.

458 Text and tune: © 1980, Bridgeport Music, Inc. Arr.: © 2000, GIA Publications, Inc.

459 Arr.: © 2000, GIA Publications, Inc.

461 Text and tune: © 1970, Margaret Pleasant Douroux, Arr.: © 2000, GIA Publications, Inc.

Acknowledgments/continued

ACKNOWLEDGMENTS/continued

Augsburg Fortress Publishers
P.O. Box 1209
Minneapolis, MN 55440-1209
(612) 330-3300

BMG Music Publishing, Inc.
400 18th Avenue South
Nashville, TN 37212
(615) 858-1300
(615) 858-1330 fax

Bob Jay Music Co. (Robert J. Fryson)
c/o Rodney L. Adams, CEO
P.O. Box 515, Lincolnton Station
New York, NY 10037-0515
212-283-4980
212) 283-4980 fax
Bobjay7412@aol.com email

Horace Clarence Boyer
c/o Selah Press, LTD
92 Grantwood Dr.
Amherst, MA 01002

Melva W. Costen, PhD
c/o Interdenominational Theological Center
700 Martin Luther King Dr. S.W.
Atlanta, GA 30314-4143

Cotillion Music, Inc.
d/b/a Pronto Music
10585 Santa Monica Blvd.
Los Angeles, CA 90025-4950
310) 441-8600

Dangerfield Music Co.
286 Strawberry Hill Rd.
Centerville, MA 02632

Jessy Dixon
c/o Dixon Music, Inc.
P.O. Box 336
Crete, IL 60417
(708) 672-8682

Edward B. Marks Music Co.
c/o Carlin America, Inc.
126 E. 38th Street
New York, NY 10016
(212) 779-7977
(212) 779-7920 fax

EMI Christian Music Group
P.O. Box 5085
101 Winners Circle
Brentwood, TN 37024-5085
(615) 371-4400
(615) 371-6897 fax

First Church of Deliverance
4315 S. Wabash Avenue
Chicago, IL 60653
(773) 373-7700

Fred Bock Music Company
P.O. Box 570567
Tarzana, CA 91357
(818) 996-6181
(818) 996-2043 fax

Full Armor Publishing Co.
4501 Connecticut Ave. NW, Suite 711
Washinton, DC 20008

Gaither Copyright Management
P.O. Box 737
Alexandria, IN 46001
(765) 724-8233

Genevox Music Group (Broadman Press)
127 Ninth Ave.
Nashville, TN 37234
(615) 251-3770
(615) 251-3727 fax

Gertrude Music
c/o Executive Publishing Administration
10220 Glade Avenue
Chatsworth, CA 91311
(818) 341-2264
(818) 341-1008 fax

Greater Detroit Music and Record Mart
1681 Fleetwood Dr.
Troy, MI 48098

Hal Leonard Corp.
P.O. Box 13819
7777 W. Bluemound Road
Milwaukee, WI 53213
(414) 774-3630
(414) 774-3259 fax
hlcopyright@halleonard.com email

Harcourt Inc.
Permissions Department
62777 Sea Harbor Drive, 6th floor
Orlando, FL 32887-6777

Dr. Carl Haywood
c/o Grace Episcopal Church
1400 E. Brambleton Ave.
P.O. Box 1003
Norfolk, VA 23504

Hope Publishing Co.
380 S. Main Place
Carol Stream, IL 60188
(800) 323-1049
(630) 665-3200
(630) 665-2552 fax
hope@hopepublishing.com email

Integrated Copyright Group
P.O. Box 24149
Nashville, TN 37202
(615) 329-3999

Jan-Lee Music
P.O. Box 4
West Charleston, VT 05872
(802) 895-5357

John W. Peterson Music Co.
13610 N. Scottsdale Rd. Ste. 10-221
Scottsdale, AR 85254-4037
(480) 483-3306 phone & fax
tcatzere@johnwpetersonmusic.com email

Joy Publishing Co.
P.O. Box 26854
Indianapolis, IN 46226-0854
(317) 335-5640

Addresses of Copyright Holders/continued

Life Spring Music
907 McCall St.
Conroe, TX 77301

Kenneth W. Louis
c/o Holy Comforter/St. Cyprian Church
1357 E. Capitol Street SW
Washington, DC 20003
(202) 546-1885 x815
(202) 544-1385 fax

Malaco, Inc.
d/b/a Savgos Music, Inc.
1012 18th Ave., South
Nashville, TN 37212

Manna Music, Inc.
P.O. Box 218
35255 Brooten Road
Pacific City, OR 97135
(503) 965-6112

Martin and Morris Music
7400 S. Euclid
Chicago, IL 60649

Mar-Vel Music Co.
Chattanooga, TN 37401
(423) 267-4505 fax

MCA Music Publishing Co.
2440 Sepulveda Blvd., Suite 100
Los Angeles, CA 90064-1712
(310) 235-4768
(310) 235-4905 fax

MKR Music
c/o Michael K. Ross
1421 Rogers St.
Richmond, VA 23223

Music & Media International, Inc.
o/b/o Lehsem Music, LLC
8756 Holloway Dr.
Los Angeles, CA 90069
(310) 360-7777

Music Services, Inc.
209 Chapelwood Dr.
Franklin, TN 37069
(615) 794-9015

New Dawn Music (OCP Publications)
P.O. Box 13248
Portland, OR 07213-0248
(800) 548-8749
(503) 281-1191

NEW-J Publishing
P.O. Box 75201
Washington, DC 20013

NOAH Company
P.O. Box 11243
Jackson, MS 39283-1243

Oxford University Press
Great Clarendon Street
Oxford OX2 6DP
United Kingdom
(44 0) 1865-556767
(44 0) 1865-267749 fax
wrights@oup.co.uk email

Professionals for Christ Publications
P.O. Box 39090
Birmingham, AL 35208-1958

Rocksmith Music
c/o Trust Music Management, Inc.
P.O. Box 22274
Carmel, CA 93922-0274
(831) 626-1030
(831) 626-1026 fax
ROCKSMITH2@aol.com email

Bernadette Blount Salley
c/o Salley Music Co.
3632 Franklin Road
Stow, OH 44224

Schaff Music Publishing
3919 Regency Street
Houston, TX 77045
(713) 728-1300

Scripture in Song
c/o Integrity Music, Inc.
1000 Cody Rd.
Mobile, AL 36695
(334) 633-9000
(334) 633-5202 fax

Selah Press, Ltd.
92 Grantwood Drive
Amherst, MA 01002

The Copyright Company
40 Music Square East
Nashville, TN 37203
(615) 244-5588
(615) 244-5591 fax

The Lorenz Corporation
501 East Third Street
P.O. Box 802
Dayton, OH 45401-0802
(937) 228-6118

Dr. Wyatt Tee Walker
c/o Canaan Baptist Church
132 W. 116th Street
New York, NY 10026
(212) 866-0301

Warner Bros. Publications
15800 N.W. 48th Ave.
P.O. Box 4340
Miami, FL 33014
(305) 620-1500
(305) 621-1094 fax

Warner/Chappell Music
10585 Santa Monica Blvd.
Los Angeles, CA 90025
(310) 470-6399 fax

Word Music, Inc.
c/o Acuff-Rose Music Publishing, Inc.
P.O. Box 128469
65 Music Square West
Nashville, TN 37212-8469
(615) 321-5000
(615) 327-0560 fax

SCRIPTURE PASSAGES RELATED TO HYMNS 689

SCRIPTURE PASSAGES RELATED TO HYMNS/CONTINUED

SCRIPTURE PASSAGES RELATED TO HYMNS/CONTINUED

Scripture Passages related to Hymns/continued

SCRIPTURE PASSAGES RELATED TO HYMNS/CONTINUED

690 Responsive Reading Index

RESPONSIVE READING INDEX/CONTINUED

RESPONSIVE READING INDEX/CONTINUED

692   BLACK HISTORY INDEX

BLACK HISTORY INDEX/CONTINUED

693 TOPICAL INDEX

TOPICAL INDEX/CONTINUED

TOPICAL INDEX/CONTINUED

TOPICAL INDEX/CONTINUED

317 Breathe on Me, Breath of God
553 Close to Thee
596 Come and Go with Me
327 Come, Thou Almighty King
605 Deep River
356 Follow Jesus
339 For All the Saints
153 For God So Loved the World
500 Glory, Glory, Hallelujah
136 God Leads Us Along
609 God of Our Fathers
142 He Leadeth Me
273 He Touched Me
510 He's Sweet I Know
404 Hold to God's Unchanging Hand
148 How Great Thou Art
556 Hush, Hush, Somebody's Callin' My Name
480 I Am On the Battlefield For My Lord
350 I Am Praying For You
599 I Bowed on My Knees
268 I See a Crimson Stream
600 I Wanna Be Ready
601 I'll Fly Away
514 I'll Tell It Wherever I Go
582 If You Live Right
585 In That Great Gittin' Up Mornin'
155 It Took a Miracle
382 Jesus Is All the World to Me
335 Jesus Loves Me
455 Just a Closer Walk with Thee
602 Just Over in the Gloryland
584 Just to Behold His Face
630 Let the Heaven Light Shine on Me
472 Life's Railway to Heaven
242 Lift High the Cross
503 Look and Live
129 Lord, Keep Me Day by Day
554 Must Jesus Bear the Cross Alone
574 My Jesus, I Love Thee
593 New Name in Glory
170 O God, Our Help in Ages Past
520 O Perfect Love
545 Oh, Freedom
586 On Jordan's Stormy Banks
178 Praise Him! Praise Him!
559 Rock of Ages
473 Savior, Lead Me Lest I Stray
475 Savior, More than Life to Me
193 Soon and Very Soon
587 Soon-a Will Be Done
373 Standing on the Promises
546 Steal Away to Jesus
442 Sweet Hour of Prayer
539 Swing Low, Sweet Chariot
337 The Church's One Foundation
604 The Crown
523 The Living Church
588 The Sweet By and By
589 The Uncloudy Day
261 Victory in Jesus
541 Walk Together Children
583 We Shall Behold Him
497 We Shall Walk Through the Valley in Peace
418 We'll Understand It Better By and By
590 We're Marching to Zion
603 Wear a Crown
186 When Morning Gilds the Skies
191 When the Roll Is Called Up Yonder
595 When the Saints Go Marching In
594 When We All Get to Heaven
196 Where Shall I Be?
591 Where We'll Never Grow Old
598 Will the Circle Be Unbroken

FAITH
459 Abide With Me
469 All the Way My Savior Leads Me
271 Amazing Grace
272 Amazing Grace (meter hymn)
264 At the Cross
135 Be Still, My Soul
625 Bless the Lord
484 Ezekiel Saw de Wheel
409 Faith of Our Fathers
410 Faith of Our Mothers
376 Farther Along
127 Father, I Stretch My Hands to Thee
339 For All the Saints
153 For God So Loved the World
346 Give Your Life to Christ
134 God Is
159 God Never Fails
158 Great Is Thy Faithfulness
672 Hallelujah, 'Tis Done
673 Hallelujah, 'Tis Done
180 Halleluya! Pelo Tsa Rona
142 He Leadeth Me
413 He'll Understand and Say "Well Done"
205 Heaven's Christmas Tree
567 Here I Am, Lord
419 Higher Ground
486 Hold Back the Night
404 Hold to God's Unchanging Hand
146 How Firm a Foundation
403 How Tedious and Tasteless the Hours
414 I Don't Feel No Ways Tired
415 I Know Who Holds Tomorrow
375 I Must Tell Jesus
577 I Really Love the Lord
361 I Will Arise
568 I Will Do a New Thing
391 I Will Trust in the Lord
392 I'd Rather Have Jesus
555 If Jesus Goes With Me
535 Imela
377 It Is Well with My Soul
526 It's Alright
417 It's Real
382 Jesus Is All the World to Me
351 Jesus Is Calling
379 Just When I Need Him
405 Keep Hope Alive
433 Keep Me, Every Day
420 Leave It There
540 Lift Every Voice and Sing
503 Look and Live
446 Lord, Help Me to Hold Out
679 Lord I Have Seen Thy Salvation
632 Lord, Make Me More Holy
440 Love Divine, All Love Excelling
504 Love Lifted Me
456 My Faith Looks Up to Thee
397 Nothing Between
408 O Holy Savior
520 O Perfect Love
423 Oh, to Be Kept by Jesus
161 Old Time Religion
406 Only Believe
369 Only Trust Him
481 Onward, Christian Soldiers
434 Remember Me
570 Renewal
372 Satisfied With Jesus
373 Standing on the Promises
442 Sweet Hour of Prayer
680 Taste and See
531 Thank You, Lord
337 The Church's One Foundation
381 The Lily of the Valley

160 The Lord Is My Light
385 The Solid Rock
588 The Sweet By and By
257 There Is a Fountain
411 There's a Bright Side Somewhere
443 This Day
368 'Tis So Sweet to Trust in Jesus
542 We Shall Overcome
407 We Won't Leave Here Like We Came
418 We'll Understand It Better By and By
412 We've Come This Far by Faith
430 What a Friend We Have in Jesus
431 What a Friend We Have in Jesus
112 When, in Our Music, God Is Glorified
594 When We All Get to Heaven
332 Wonderful Words of Life
429 Yield Not to Temptation
671 You Can't Beat God Giving

FAITHFULNESS of God (See GOD—HIS FAITHFULNESS)

FAITHFULNESS of the Believer (See also COURAGE; SERVICE)
409 Faith of Our Fathers
410 Faith of Our Mothers
339 For All the Saints
142 He Leadeth Me
413 He'll Understand and Say "Well Done"
404 Hold to God's Unchanging Hand
403 How Tedious and Tasteless the Hours
391 I Will Trust in the Lord
392 I'd Rather Have Jesus
382 Jesus Is All the World to Me
405 Keep Hope Alive
446 Lord, Help Me to Hold Out
632 Lord, Make Me More Holy
397 Nothing Between
418 We'll Understand It Better By and By
594 When We All Get to Heaven

FAMILY AND HOME
518 Bridegroom and Bride
409 Faith of Our Fathers
410 Faith of Our Mothers
599 I Bowed on My Knees
584 Just to Behold His Face
516 Precious Memories
517 Precious Memories
587 Soon-a Will Be Done
519 The Family of God
598 Will the Circle Be Unbroken

FELLOWSHIP with God
641 Be With Us All, Lord
553 Close to Thee
552 Close to Thee
152 God Has Smiled on Me
131 Guide My Feet
275 He Lives
511 He's Done So Much for Me
415 I Know Who Holds Tomorrow
563 I Want Jesus to Walk with Me
392 I'd Rather Have Jesus
555 If Jesus Goes With Me
398 In Christ There Is No East or West
399 In Christ There Is No East or West
494 In the Garden
353 Is There Any Room in Your Heart for Jesus?

TOPICAL INDEX/CONTINUED

TOPICAL INDEX/CONTINUED

TOPICAL INDEX/CONTINUED

TOPICAL INDEX/CONTINUED

TOPICAL INDEX/CONTINUED

TOPICAL INDEX/CONTINUED

Topical Index/continued

TOPICAL INDEX/CONTINUED

489 Victory Is Mine
541 Walk Together Children
674 Wash, O God, Our Sons and
    Daughters
407 We Won't Leave Here Like We
    Came
340 Welcome to My Father's House

**REPENTANCE (See CONFESSION
AND REPENTANCE)**

RESURRECTION (See also EASTER)
361 I Will Arise
585 In That Great Gittin' Up Mornin'
554 Must Jesus Bear the Cross Alone
195 My Lord! What a Morning
192 Sign Me Up
191 When the Roll Is Called Up
    Yonder
196 Where Shall I Be?

**REVIVAL, PRAYER FOR
(See RENEWAL AND REVIVAL)**

**SALVATION (See also ATONEMENT;
GRACE, MERCY AND
FORGIVENESS)**
468 A Charge to Keep I Have
467 A Charge to Keep I Have
292 All Hail the Power of Jesus'
    Name
293 All Hail the Power of Jesus'
    Name
294 All Hail the Power of Jesus'
    Name
246 At Calvary
299 Blessed Be the Name
374 Blessed Quietness
282 Christ the Lord Is Risen Today
354 Come to Jesus
248 Down at the Cross
153 For God So Loved the World
465 Give of Your Best to the Master
346 Give Your Life to Christ
202 Go Tell It on the Mountain
132 God Is a Wonder to My Soul
156 God Is So Good
673 Hallelujah, 'Tis Done
672 Hallelujah, 'Tis Done
214 Hark! The Herald Angels Sing
509 He Brought Me Out
275 He Lives
249 He Looked beyond My Fault
205 Heaven's Christmas Tree
567 Here I Am, Lord
528 I Am Healed by the Wound
512 I Am Redeemed
233 I Gave My Life for Thee
236 I Love Him
268 I See a Crimson Stream
109 I Will Call Upon the Lord
514 I'll Tell It Wherever I Go
155 It Took a Miracle
417 It's Real
558 Jesus Saves
602 Just Over in the Gloryland
364 King Jesus Is a-Listenin'
503 Look and Live
679 Lord I Have Seen Thy Salvation
440 Love Divine, All Love Excelling
504 Love Lifted Me
203 Messiah Now Has Come
111 My Tribute
163 Nearer, My God, to Thee
204 O Little Town of Bethlehem
250 O Sacred Head, Sore Wounded
251 O Sacred Head Surrounded
422 O Thou, in Whose Presence
369 Only Trust Him

172 Praise Him
343 Renew Thy Church, Her Min-
    istries Restore
559 Rock of Ages
372 Satisfied With Jesus
536 Thank You, Lord
337 The Church's One Foundation
160 The Lord Is My Light
257 There Is a Fountain
245 There's Room at the Cross for
    You
157 To God Be the Glory
220 What Child Is This
191 When the Roll Is Called Up
    Yonder
432 Where Could I Go?

**SANCTIFICATION (See also
HOLINESS AND PURITY;
CLEANSING)**
445 Bless This House
132 God Is a Wonder to My Soul
146 How Firm a Foundation
396 I Surrender All
359 O Happy Day
244 The Old Rugged Cross
332 Wonderful Words of Life

SATAN
356 Follow Jesus
419 Higher Ground
624 Higher, Higher
479 I Shall Not Be Moved
514 I'll Tell It Wherever I Go
238 I'm So Glad
303 In the Name of Jesus
377 It Is Well with My Soul
364 King Jesus Is a-Listenin'
474 Lead Me, Guide Me
333 Order My Steps
485 Satan, We're Gonna Tear Your
    Kingdom Down
381 The Lily of the Valley
489 Victory Is Mine
478 What a Mighty God We Serve

**SCRIPTURES (See BIBLE—WORD
OF GOD)**

**SECOND COMING (See ADVENT,
Second)**

SECURITY (See also ASSURANCE)
271 Amazing Grace
363 Christ Is All
175 Come, Thou Fount of Every
    Blessing
637 Go Ye Now in Peace
634 God Be With You Till We Meet
    Again
609 God of Our Fathers
563 I Want Jesus to Walk with Me
568 I Will Do a New Thing
555 If Jesus Goes With Me
585 In That Great Gittin' Up Mornin'
501 Jesus Is Real to Me
145 Lead Me, Lord
371 Leaning on the Everlasting Arms
420 Leave It There
504 Love Lifted Me
615 My Help Cometh from the Lord
170 O God, Our Help in Ages Past
164 Siyahamba
373 Standing on the Promises
636 The Lord Bless You / Sevenfold
    Amen
426 The Lord Is My Shepherd
619 There's No Me, There's No You
638 Till We Gather Again
618 We're Growing

**SERENITY (See also CONFIDENCE;
CONTENTMENT)**
135 Be Still, My Soul
491 Center of My Joy
447 Fill My Cup, Lord
495 He Will Keep You in Perfect
    Peace
492 I've Got Peace Like a River
359 O Happy Day
527 Shine On Me
454 Until I Found the Lord

SERVICE
468 A Charge to Keep I Have
467 A Charge to Keep I Have
    (meter)
682 A Communion Hymn
668 All Things Come of Thee
643 Alleluia
644 Alleluia
649 Amen
648 Amen
669 Bring a Gift of Love
651 Doxology
410 Faith of Our Mothers
465 Give of Your Best to the Master
652 Gloria Patri
653 Gloria Patri
654 Gloria Patri
642 Halle, Halle, Halle
180 Halleluya! Pelo Tsa Rona
413 He'll Understand and Say "Well
    Done"
658 Hear Our Prayer
466 Here Am I
480 I Am On the Battlefield For My
    Lord
387 I Am Thine
660 Isaiah 6:3
665 Let the Words of My Mouth
655 Lord, Have Mercy
656 Lord, Have Mercy
666 Mayenziwe / Your Will Be Done
657 O Lord, Hear Our Prayer
659 O Lord, Incline Thine Ear to Us
520 O Perfect Love
481 Onward, Christian Soldiers
650 Praise God from Whom All
    Blessings Flow
343 Renew Thy Church, Her Min-
    istries Restore
661 Sanctus
662 Santo / Holy
647 Sevenfold Amen
670 Sitting at His Feet
476 Stand Up for Jesus
519 The Family of God
663 The Lord's Prayer
664 The Lord's Prayer
258 There Is Power in the Blood
646 Threefold Amen
645 Twofold Amen
464 We Are Climbing Jacob's Lad-
    der
478 What a Mighty God We Serve
594 When We All Get to Heaven
667 Yes, Lord
671 You Can't Beat God Giving

SERVICE MUSIC
668 All Things Come of Thee
643 Alleluia
644 Alleluia
649 Amen
648 Amen
669 Bring a Gift of Love
651 Doxology
652 Gloria Patri
653 Gloria Patri

TOPICAL INDEX/CONTINUED

TOPICAL INDEX/CONTINUED

TOPICAL INDEX/CONTINUED

Index of Composers, Authors and Sources 694

INDEX OF COMPOSERS, AUTHORS AND SOURCES/CONTINUED

INDEX OF COMPOSERS, AUTHORS AND SOURCES/continued

INDEX OF COMPOSERS, AUTHORS AND SOURCES/CONTINUED

INDEX OF COMPOSERS, AUTHORS AND SOURCES/CONTINUED

Index of Composers, Authors and Sources/continued

SM (SHORT METER - 6 6 8 6)
468 BOYLSTON
341 DENNIS
608 NATIONAL ODE
317 TRENTHAM
190 WAITING

SMD (SHORT METER DOUBLED)
288 DIADEMATA
149 TERRA BEATA

CM (COMMON METER - 8 6 8 6)
197 ANTIOCH
482 ARLINGTON
184 AZMON
523 DUNDEE
399 MCKEE
554 MAITLAND
127 263 MARTYRDOM
271 NEW BRITAIN
170 ST. ANNE
314 ST. MARTIN'S
398 ST. PETER

CM WITH REFRAIN
293 DIADEM
253 DUNCANNON
137 GOD CARES
291 HOW I LOVE JESUS
264 HUDSON
155 IT TOOK A MIRACLE
369 ONLY TRUST HIM
527 SHINE ON ME
586 STORMY BANKS
614 SUNBEAM
603 WEAR A CROWN

CMD (COMMON METER DOUBLE)
215 CAROL
607 MATERNA

LM (LONG METER - 8 8 8 8)
276 289 DUKE STREET
677 ERNAN
522 GIFT OF LOVE
243 HAMBURG
651 OLD 100TH
345 WOODWORTH

LM WITH REFRAIN
216 BEHOLD THE STAR
299 BLESSED NAME
239 CALVARY
359 HAPPY DAY
142 HE LEADETH ME
419 HIGHER GROUND
255 LAMB OF GOD
681 LINSTEAD
123 NAZREY
385 SOLID ROCK
565 SWENEY
539 SWING LOW
188 VENI EMMANUEL

LMD
403 DE FLEURY
442 SWEET HOUR

66 4 666 4
327 ITALIAN HYMN
456 OLIVET

66 9 D WITH REFRAIN
591 NEVER GROW OLD
380 TRUST AND OBEY
393 YOUR ALL

7 6 7 6 D
337 AURELIA

477 LANCASHIRE
251 PASSION CHORALE
250 REDDING
187 SHEFFIELD
226 ST. THEODULPH
476 WEBB

7 6 7 6 WITH REFRAIN
524 BALM IN GILEAD
268 CRIMSON STREAM
436 FIX ME
202 GO TELL IT ON THE MOUNTAIN
252 NEAR THE CROSS

7 7 7 7
315 MERCY
259 THROUGH THE BLOOD

7 7 7 7 D
452 IN ME
453 MARTYN
194 ST. GEORGE'S WINDSOR

7 7 7 7 WITH REFRAIN
335 CHINA
322 FILL ME
206 GLORIA
473 LEAD ME
217 WE'LL WALK IN THE LIGHT

77 77 77
460 PILOT
559 TOPLADY

8 5 8 5 WITH REFRAIN
543 GO DOWN MOSES
435 PASS ME NOT

8 7 8 7 D
469 ALL THE WAY
430 ANNIE LOWERY
674 BEACH SPRING
440 BEECHER
424 BRADBURY
431 CONVERSE
120 HYMN TO JOY
175 NETTLETON

8 7 8 7 D WITH REFRAIN
465 BARNARD
472 LIFE'S RAILWAY
415 TOMORROW

8 7 8 7 WITH REFRAIN
374 BLESSED QUIETNESS
553 CLOSE TO THEE
356 FOLLOW JESUS
220 GREENSLEEVES
594 HEAVEN
516 517 PRECIOUS MEMORIES
297 PRECIOUS NAME
361 RESTORATION
372 ROUTH
571 SHOWERS OF BLESSING
324 SPIRIT HOLY
396 SURRENDER
368 TRUST IN JESUS
598 UNBROKEN CIRCLE
404 UNCHANGING HAND

8 8 8 5
437 438 DESMOND
464 JACOB'S LADDER

888 6 WITH REFRAIN
232 HE LIFTED ME
344 JUST AS I AM
587 SOON-A WILL BE DONE

Metrical Index of Tunes/continued

METRICAL INDEX OF TUNES/CONTINUED

METRICAL INDEX OF TUNES/CONTINUED

METRICAL INDEX OF TUNES/CONTINUED

696 TUNE INDEX

697 INDEX OF FIRST LINES AND COMMON TITLES

Index of First Lines and Common Titles/continued

INDEX OF FIRST LINES AND COMMON TITLES/CONTINUED

INDEX OF FIRST LINES AND COMMON TITLES/CONTINUED

INDEX OF FIRST LINES AND COMMON TITLES/CONTINUED

INDEX OF FIRST LINES AND COMMON TITLES/CONTINUED